MANITOBA STUDIES IN NATIVE HISTORY

Manitoba Studies in Native History publishes new scholarly interpretations of the historical experience of native peoples in the western interior of North America. The series is under the editorial direction of a board representative of the scholarly and native communites of Manitoba.

I *The New Peoples: Being and Becoming Métis in North America*, edited by Jacqueline Peterson and Jennifer S.H. Brown.

II *Indian-European Trade Relations in the Lower Saskatchewan River Region to 1840*, by Paul C. Thistle.

III *"The Orders of the Dreamed" : George Nelson on Cree and Northern Ojibwa Religion and Myth, 1823*, by Jennifer S.H. Brown and Robert Brightman.

IV *The Plains Cree: Warriors, Traders and Diplomats, 1790 to 1870*, by John S. Milloy.

V *The Dakota of the Canadian Northwest: Lessons for Survival*, by Peter Douglas Elias.

MANITOBA STUDIES IN NATIVE HISTORY V

The Dakota of the Canadian Northwest: Lessons for Survival

PETER DOUGLAS ELIAS

THE UNIVERSITY OF MANITOBA PRESS

Design by Norman Schmidt
Maps by Caroline Trottier

Cataloguing in Publication Data

Elias, Peter Douglas
The Dakota of the Canadian northwest
(Manitoba studies in native history, ISSN
0826-9416 ; 5)
Includes index.
ISBN 0-88755-142-4

1. Dakota Indians - History. 2. Dakota Indians -
Reservations - History. 3. Indians of North
America - Prairie Provinces - History. 4. Indians
of North America - Prairie Provinces - Reservations -
History. I. Title. II. Series.
E99.D1E44 1988   971.2'00497   C87-098139-0

59,030

This series is published with the financial support of the people of Manitoba, the Honourable Bonnie
Mitchelson, Minister of Culture, Heritage and Recreation. The publication of this volume was also assisted by a grant from the Canada Council.

In memory of my father.

Contents

Maps

Glossary of Dakota Names

Many Dakota people are named in the historic documents. Often, these names appear as English translations, or as an English-speaking person's attempt to render the sound of a Dakota name, or in both forms. Confusion is possible. The Dakota prefer their names in their proper form, and if the names are to be used in an English-language publication, they should be rendered in a form consistent with Dakota usage. In this book, I have used the spellings for names that are used by Dakota people themselves. In general, Canada's Dakota-speaking people write works in English using the orthography developed by Stephen R. Riggs in his English-Dakota/Dakota-English dictionary, first printed in 1855 at St. Paul, Minnesota. This brief glossary includes only the names that appear in English translation in the source documents. The contemporary spelling of the name is given along with the "translations" that appear in the historic sources. All other names that do not appear as translations or interpretations from the Dakota are rendered in this book according to the Riggs orthography, with no attempt at an English translation.

Choate – The Crow
Dowaneya – The Singer
Inkpaduta – Red Point
Istak'pa – Sleepy Eye
Mahpiyahdinape – Enoch
Shak'pay – The Six
Tatankanaje – Standing Buffalo
Taninyahdinazin – Young Chief
Wakanozhan – Medicine Bottle
Wambdiska – White Eagle
Wapahaska – White Cap

Preface

In late 1978, Robert Goodvoice of the Wahpeton Band at Prince Albert, Saskatchewan, led me into a simple discussion of the history of the Sioux in western Canada. He would ask me what I knew of this or that and I would reply, drawing upon what I had learned in two decades of university study and subsequent research. He would listen, nod his head, contemplate my words, and then move on to another topic. By the end of the afternoon, he would suggest that my understanding had serious flaws and that perhaps I would be interested in what he knew to be the correct story of his people. Indeed, I would. In that case, Goodvoice insisted, we would set aside the word *Sioux,* and instead use the correct name of his people – the *Dakota.* Understanding would be tainted if I persisted in using a word that had distinctly offensive overtones in Dakota ears. The word *Sioux* had been coined by French traders from a contraction of an Algonquian phrase meaning *snakes* or *enemy.* More recently, the name *Sioux* is viewed as too embracing of a people who see themselves as being distinctive sharers of a common tradition. There are three primary dialects spoken by all Dakota people. Nakota and Lakota are traditionally viewed as branches from the Dakota trunk. Nakota, the *n-dialect,* is spoken by the Assiniboine or Stonies, the Yankton and the Yanktonai. Lakota, the *l-dialect,* is spoken by several western populations, including the Teton, some of whom remained in Canada after fleeing the Little Big Horn with Tatankaiyotake in 1876. The eastern Dakota include the Wahpeton, Mdewakonton, Wahpekute and Sisseton divisions of the nation, who speak the *d-dialect.* The Dakota are the most numerous of their nation in Canada, and are the subject of this book. Collectively, all the divisions of the three dialects are called *Dakota*, as are the *d-speakers.* Tribal elders say that preserving the name *Dakota* as the name of the nation recognizes the common roots of all the divisions.

My subsequent discussions with Robert Goodvoice lasted four years, but started off with a review of what others had written. Goodvoice had in his possession the few works that deal with the Dakota in Canada, and he was prepared to talk about their contents. His perception of the scholarly literature was uncomplimentary: the ethnographers had a poor grasp of the history of the Dakota, and the historians had an equally poor grasp of the culture of the Dakota. Both, he said, made the mistake of trying to round out their imperfect knowledge by referring to what was known of the Dakota in the United States. Certainly, when in the previous century the Dakota were a unified population, it was proper and necessary to discuss them in terms of a whole, but since his people became established in Canada, the two segments had experienced quite different histories and consequently expressed quite different cultures.

There is no doubt that the study of the Dakota in Canada has been inadequate. The reasons for this inadequacy are many. First, the Dakota are few in number. It has only been in recent years that the total population of Dakota in Canada rose over three thousand. They are, evidently, a distinct minority amongst the tens of thousands of Cree and Ojibwa in the northern prairie. Second, historians and anthropologists have not perceived the Dakota as prime players in Canadian history. Their role in the opening of the West, or as obstacles to the process, is not as obvious as is that of the nations with whom the Crown was obliged to seek treaties. In addition, since the Dakota are not treaty Indians, they do not figure largely in contemporary discussions of aboriginal, native and treaty rights generated by land claims and the Canadian Constitution. As well, the Dakota were amongst the most independent Indians on the prairies and the government was hard put to collect information about Indians they did not control. Finally, the Dakota have been secretive about their history, and for good reason. When they first came to Canada, and for several decades thereafter, the Dakota attempted to assert certain rights on the basis of their own history, but their views were rejected by all authorities. The Dakota simply stopped discussing their background, and indeed did all they could to limit the amount of information available to non-Dakota people.

Goodvoice agreed that these were obstacles to scholarship, but he could not believe that what he had read represented the best that white scholars could do. I agreed. Dakota historians, in particular Archie Eagle of White Cap's Band, Max Goodwill of Standing Buffalo's Band, James Kiyewakan, Emma Pratt and Eli Taylor of Sioux Valley, and George Chaske of Dakota Tipi, were able in the course of narrating their history to name many of the whites who were central in their past – Robert Dickson, Sir George Prevost, James McKay and Pascal Breland, Alexander Morris, David Laird, Lawrence Vankoughnet, Tommy Douglas and John Diefenbaker. Surely, they said, these people had left some record of their dealings with the Dakota. The hunt for the complete Dakota Archive was on.

The Dakota historians did not want a specific point to be made through this research, or some axe ground on their behalf. They simply had an intellectual curiosity to know all there was to know. By no means will this book meet such a "simple" demand, but it is expected that the Dakota will get some satisfaction in seeing documentation in support of what, as they told me, they already knew.

This book is based upon documentary sources, augmented with tribal history and cultural commentary where necessary. This form seems appropriate in a situation where even an accurate outline of history is lacking; it would be inappropriate to undertake extensive theoretical work and to offer broad generalization without first establishing the substance of Dakota history. Furthermore, this volume will greatly simplify for Dakota historians the task of relating and synchronizing the documentary record with what is known from tribal knowledge. This is just the first step in a long and promising journey, and I hope that the Dakota themselves will find that their trip is made easier by the existence of this study.

This volume should appeal to those interested in a relatively new field of scholarship that addresses matters of aboriginal and native rights. Since 1973, when the well-known Calder case went before the Supreme Court of Canada, and it was found that there was merit in the principle of aboriginal and native rights, considerable intellectual effort has been applied to defining those rights. More recently the Canada Act of 1982 enshrined aboriginal rights in sections of the Canadian Constitution. The debate has expanded to include not just the fact of aboriginal rights and an inventory of rights, but also the history of the actual exercise of rights. It is increasingly important to know the circumstances under which rights were exercised, the form that they took, and the manner in which they were changed, enhanced, suppressed, or even extinguished. Historical continuity of rights and the way they are expressed in the institutions of a society are of great interest in these considerations, simply because rights must be defined and demonstrated before they can be defended in the political or legal arena of contemporary Canada.

As will be shown, the Dakota have failed to convince the larger Canadian society that their claims to aboriginal and diplomatic rights in Canada are legitimate. Chapter 1 includes the archaeological and documentary support of their claims. The archaeological record supports the conclusion that there were Dakota antecedents in Canada at least eight hundred years ago. A detailed examination of their role in the War of 1812 shows that the British Crown agreed with Dakota claims and pledged to defend their cultural rights in the British realm. This ancient and early history has been the crux of the Dakota justification of their presence in Canada. It also makes the case for the Dakota having appropriated resources for the base of their own culture. Finally, the continuity and content of Dakota rights in Canada are expressed in terms which support their claim to aboriginal and native rights, as these are now understood to have effect in the Canadian national context.

Recent Dakota history in Canada begins in 1862, when at least three bands, fleeing annihilation in the United States, arrived at Fort Garry and the Red River settlements. Chapters 2 and 3 show how the Dakota adapted to circumstances in the North West, and how the North West adapted to them. The Dakota quickly moved to apply what they had learned in Minnesota and the Dakota Territory. They lacked all of the necessary economic fundamentals – land, acknowledged title, technology and capital. The only assets they brought with them were their labour and their skill – skills learned both in customary pursuits and some from white people who had entered their lands on the American frontier. Each of the bands that came to Canada had somewhat different skills, and so adapted in different ways to the diversity of conditions that existed in Canada's North West.

Chapters 4 through 7 detail the economic history of the bands in Manitoba that elaborated a lifestyle based on agriculture. These were the people who were most learned in farming skills. Particular attention is paid to the ways in which the Dakota at Birdtail, Oak River and Oak Lake reserves structured their resources, labour and capital to establish themselves as commercial agriculturalists on the western frontier of Canada.

Chapter 8 deals with the one band of Dakota in Canada that maintained an economy based upon a hunting, trapping and gathering mode of production. The limitations on the Turtle Mountain Band were such that the entire band and reserve were obliterated. The history of this people is the most dramatic instance in Dakota history of violation of aboriginal and native rights.

Chapters 9 and 10 deal with Standing Buffalo's and White Cap's bands in Saskatchewan. These people adopted a strategy based on livestock production and sale of labour. Having different skills and different resources to work with, the history of their economies is considerably different from that of either the farmers or the hunters. Finally, chapters 11 and 12 describe the Dakota at Portage la Prairie in Manitoba and at Prince Albert in Saskatchewan. These people were almost exclusively urban and rural wage labourers, and were only marginally involved in agriculture.

Each of the bands represented different ways of utilizing resources, technology and labour. Because they were located within and therefore part of the national political and economic context, each was constrained by similar external forces. On the one hand, these forces tended to encourage and promote Dakota institutions that could be reconciled with the institutions of larger Canada and, on the other, they suppressed Dakota expression that did not conform to Canadian conventions.

The concluding chapter is a summary of common structures and processes that can be observed to have been crucial in the economic history of the Dakota in Canada.

I owe a great debt to Robert Goodvoice, who was so generous with his knowledge and understanding. Late one evening, during a break in a wacipe at Sioux Valley in Manitoba, Goodvoice asked what I thought of all that he had told me. I replied that I found it very interesting. He said, "You find our history interesting. That is good. For us Dakota, though, our history is our lesson book, that gives us lessons in survival." It appears that the Dakota have learned their lessons well from people such as Robert Goodvoice.

There are other debts. Jennie Abell, Douglas Leonard and Wallis Smith read and discussed the first draft of the text and recommended changes that were later made. Gerald Friesen dedicated many hours to a full and learned criticism of the text, and I have been profoundly impressed with the results of his diligence. Finally, I thank the many Dakota people in Canada and the United States who did their best to see that I understood things correctly, and refrained from laughing at my ignorance.

Little Crow's village (Chapter 1). Photo courtesy of the Minnesota Historical Society. Artist: Henry Lewis.

Dakota band near the Assiniboine River (Chapter 3). Photo courtesy of National Archives of Canada, NA 550-8.

Dakota man at Whitehorse Plains, 1840 (Chapter 1). Photo courtesy of the Glenbow Archives, Calgary, AW-55.17.2

Fort Ellice, 1879 (Chapter 3). Photo courtesy of National Archives of Canada, PA-551146.

Dakota camp on the Red River (Chapter 3). Photo courtesy of Manitoba Museum of Man and Nature, #6200, P-8-42.

The North American Boundary Commission Depot at Turtle Mountain, 1872 (Chapter 3). Photo courtesy of National Archives of Canada, PA-74659.

House at Oak Lake Reserve (Chapter 7). Photo courtesy of Provincial Archives of Manitoba, N-3327.

Alexander Morris, 1871 (Chapter 3). Photo courtesy of National Archives of Canada, C-7104.

Mission House and YMCA tent at Oak River Reserve, 1906 (Chapter 7). Photo courtesy of Provincial Archives of Manitoba, N-1053.

Dakota singers at the Brandon Exhibition, 1916 (Chapter 7). Photo courtesy of Manitoba Museum of Man and Nature, #3576, P-8-29.

Charles Dowan, Oak River Band (Chapter 7). Photo courtesy of Manitoba Museum of Man and Nature, #3689, P-8-23.

Kiyewakan, Oak River Band, 1916 (Chapter 7). Photo courtesy of Manitoba Museum of Man and Nature, #3567, P-8-39.

Dakota camp west of the Turtle Mountains, 1872 (Chapter 8). Photo courtesy of Provincial Archives of Manitoba, Boundary Commission 205.

Wapahaska and his family, 1885 (Chapter 10). Photo courtesy of the Glenbow Archives, NA-2294-20.

Tatankanaje the Younger, about 1875 (Chapter 9). Photo courtesy of the Glenbow Archives, NA-2791-6.

Masawahoh, a man of Iyanki's band at Prince Albert, 1885 (Chapter 12). Photo courtesy of the Glenbow Archives, NA-1407-2.

Dakota farm labourers clearing land at Portage la Prairie, 1916 (Chapter 11). Photo courtesy of Manitoba Museum of Man and Nature, #6194, P-8-65.

The Dakota of the Canadian Northwest

The old traditions:
Archaeology to 1862

1

Historical records of the late seventeenth century place the Dakota in the Milles Lacs region of Minnesota, yet archaeological data indicate that they had once ranged across western Wisconsin through Minnesota, northwestern Ontario and eastern Manitoba. Although it is often difficult to match archaeological data with historical evidence, the link can be shown for the Dakota.

Archaeologists and historians have found it a trying task to identify the ancient roots of Indian nations in the central regions of North America. The problem lies in finding a tangible link between a living population of Indians and a segment of history as represented by archaeological findings. Thus, archaeologists are able to detail the aboriginal history of a given territory from several hundreds and even thousands of years past until the time of contact with Europeans. Historians, on the other hand, are able to provide detail from the time of contact until the present. Often neither, however, are able to say with conviction which living population is a continuation of the population identified by archaeological remains. This occurs both because Indians were highly mobile and because European trade goods, spreading to the interior more rapidly than did Europeans themselves, quickly rendered a quality of anonymity to the material culture of quite different peoples. This moment of passage from a distinctive aboriginal technology to a "mass-produced" technology most often took place before there were any reliable witnesses to Indian life who could make a record of which peoples were living where at a particular time. The crucial link in the chain of records available to both archaeologists and historians – that is, technology – is broken.

In the ideal situation, a witness would have observed a people just before the events of material displacement, when they were still involved with tools and technology that can be traced back in time. Further, this witness should then have left

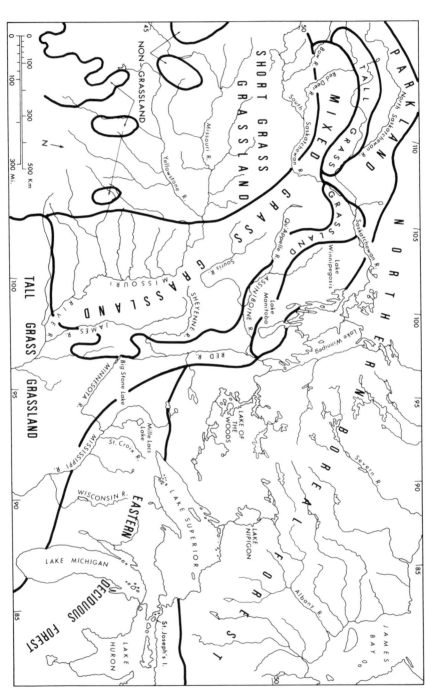

Map 1. The northwest plains

a record of precisely who these people were and exactly where they were. For the Dakota, there is just such an ideal.

In 1680, Father Louis Hennepin was captured by the M'dewakontonwon Dakota when he was serving as spiritual guide on a voyage of discovery down the Mississippi River. He was taken by the Dakota to their village near the mouth of the Rum River on Mille Lacs Lake in present-day Minnesota. His description of the Dakota clearly identifies who his captors were, the location of their village, and the nature of their non-European technology.[1]

In 1972, G.A. Lothson, then a graduate student at the University of Minnesota, excavated the Rum River site. The most distinctive feature of the site is its ceramics, which are also mentioned by Hennepin. Lothson concluded that this pottery, named Sandy Lake ware by archaeologists, was a manufacture of the Isantee Dakota and that the area over which the pottery is to be found identifies at least a part of the territory occupied by the Dakota at the time when that ware had been made. Subsequent research has identified thirty-four sites containing Sandy Lake ware in Wisconsin, Minnesota, western Ontario and eastern Manitoba.[2] The few dates that have been obtained for these sites span the years from 1150 A.D. until slightly after the time of contact with Europeans, when aboriginal technology, notably pottery, was displaced by trade goods.[3] As might be expected, there are archaeological sites that contain both Sandy Lake ware and trade goods of European manufacture.

The earliest travellers in the western regions of the Great Lakes placed the Dakota in the territory that Sandy Lake ware was found. Maps dating from 1650 to 1750 – including a map prepared by Cree Indians in 1728 – described the Dakota as occupying the area from Heron Bay on Lake Superior in the east, to the west of Lake Winnipeg and the Red River and south to the Minnesota River, taking in all of the lands west of the St. Croix River, a tributary of the Mississippi, and east of Rainy Lake.[4]

More often than not these earlier commentators and geographers based their descriptions on second-hand information rather than on their own observations. The records of the fur trade, however, provide some corroboration. Arthur Ray, historian of the trade, notes that even as late as 1717, the Dakota had completely taken over the lands around the Lake of the Woods and Rainy Lake and were reported to be raiding as far north as Kaministikwia. A few years later, in 1722, he says, the French considered establishing a trade post among the Dakota at Rainy Lake. An entry in a Hudson's Bay Company Journal, also cited by Ray, states that the Dakota were warring with the Cree and Assiniboine as far north as the head of the Churchill River.[5]

The Cree who today live along the Churchill River in Saskatchewan confirm this history of long war expeditions to the north. One route used by the Dakota to reach the Cree camps took them through Deschambeault Lake in northern Saskatchewan by way of the Ballantyne River, which is known by the Cree of that region as Puatsipi or Dakota River. Further to the east, and connected by water with Puatsipi is Pelican Narrows, named in Cree *Opowekustikunik* (or Narrows of Fear) following a battle at that place between themselves and the Dakota.[6] On returning from one such engagement, a party of Dakota wintered on the shores of Deschambeault Lake, at the very place where the Cree band's sawmill is located today. Both that particular site and the modern Cree village of Deschambeault Lake are called *Kimosopuatinak* (or Home of the Ancient Dakota.)[7] According to Cree history, these raids took place at a time when the Cree of the middle Churchill River were still making the long trading voyage to York Factory, that is, some time prior to 1774, when Samuel Hearne established Cumberland House, the first inland trade post of the Hudson's Bay Company.

By the early nineteenth century, the Dakota had withdrawn from these northern territories, and much of the country had been taken up by the Cree and Ojibwa moving in from the east. Peter Grant recorded in 1804 that, according to the Ojibwa, the Dakota had occupied the whole region around Rainy Lake, but had moved further west and into a less populated area where game was more plentiful. Grant was also told that the Ojibwa had themselves moved west in order to find lands with more game and fewer people.[8]

If these shifts in population occurred even as early as the mid-eighteenth century, the Ojibwa would have had a distinct advantage over the Dakota. By that time, the Ojibwa and their neighbours, the Cree, had possessed firearms for considerably more than a generation, while the Dakota were just being introduced to guns. The Dakota were slower to establish permanent trading relationships with European suppliers of guns. Generally speaking, the Indian nations that were first supplied with European trade goods radiating out of the St. Lawrence and Great Lakes sought fresh supplies of marketable resources further inland within the territory occupied by their neighbours. These neighbours, unable to withstand armed pressure, immigrated further inland, often armed with a few guns they had received from the very groups who were pressing upon them. Such was the situation for the Ojibwa who had been dislodged from their hunting lands and, in consequence, forced the westward movement of the Dakota. By the end of the eighteenth century, the Dakota had all but abandoned the lands east of the Mississippi and between Lake Winnipeg and Lake Superior. At that same time, French traders from Canada began to establish trading positions along the Blue Earth and Minnesota rivers, and the Dakota were drawn in a southerly direction, rather than to the north.

The Dakota maintained trade and diplomatic relations with the French on the St. Lawrence until 1763, when war in Europe established British possession of

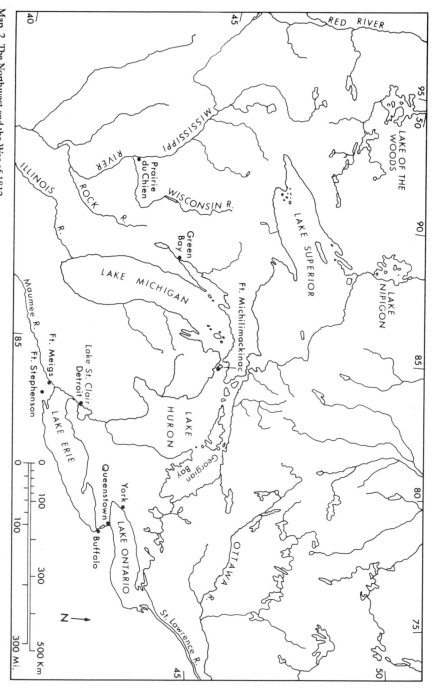

Map 2. The Northwest and the War of 1812

RED RIVER

LAKE OF THE WOODS

MISSISSIPPI RIVER

Prairie du Chien

WISCONSIN R.

ROCK R.

ILLINOIS R.

LAKE SUPERIOR

LAKE NIPIGON

Green Bay

LAKE MICHIGAN

Ft. Michilimackinac

LAKE HURON

Georgian Bay

Maumee R.

Ft. Meigs

Ft. Stephenson

Lake St. Clair

Detroit

LAKE ERIE

Queenstown

York

Buffalo

LAKE ONTARIO

OTTAWA R.

St. Lawrence R.

N →

0   100   300   500 Km
0   100   300   300 Mi.

40

45

50

95

90

85

80

75

50

45

North America. With the signing of the Treaty of Paris, France gave up all claim to her colonies.

One of the first English travellers into Dakota territory after the signing of the Treaty of Paris was Jonathan Carver, who dwelt amongst the Isantee in 1766 and again in 1768.[9] He was present when the Dakota assembled representatives of eight branches of the nation, including Tetonwon members from the far west. On behalf of all, the principal chief affirmed his nation's alliance with the British, and extended an invitation that traders be sent amongst them. The Dakota pledged that they would have nothing to do with the Americans, and that they would stand ready to defend the English King in the far west, a pledge that was honoured through the following decades.

In 1776, the American Revolution began. Both the Americans and British sought military alliances with Indian nations, but the Dakota had already chosen to support the Crown. Wapasha, chief of the M'dewakontonwon, went to Mackinac in 1779 to offer his warriors to the British cause, for which he was given a commission in the British army. When he learned of the defeat of the British in 1783, Wapasha accepted the fact, but refused to transfer his allegiance to the Americans.[10]

In the early nineteenth century, the British were fully occupied in Europe with the Napoleonic wars. In an attempt to stop the flow of goods from the Americas to France, the British enforced a naval blockade on American shipping. The British were well aware that their preoccupations in Europe limited the attention they could give to their colonies and had no desire to enter into a war in another hemisphere. These circumstances encouraged a long-held American dream of acquiring Canada. Sensing that the time was right, the United States declared war upon Great Britain on June 18, 1812.

The Dakota were immediately engaged in the struggle against the Americans. When war was declared, Robert Dickson, a trader who had headquartered at Michilimackinac, addressed the principal chiefs of the Dakota, who were assembled near Wapasha's village. He asked for a re-affirmation of the ties between the Dakota and the British. The Dakota call the War of 1812 *Pahinshashawacikiya*. Wahpetonwon Tribal Historian Robert Goodvoice of Prince Albert, Saskatchewan, translates this to mean "When the Redhead Begged for Our Help," referring to Dickson's reddish hair.

Wapasha of the M'dewakontonwon, spokesman for all the branches of the Dakota nation, replied to Dickson's appeal. He first stated that there was no reason for his people to disavow the British, since all British promises made to the Dakota had been kept. The matter of the present conflict had been discussed by the general assembly of the Dakota, and, "from the last band of our nation to the west, we hold each others hands . . . we rejoice again in hearing the voice of our English Father who has never deceived us, and we are certain never will."[11]

The first battles of the war were a success for the British largely because of the support given by the Indians, especially by the forces with Dickson, who siezed and held Michilimackinac, and by Tecumseh in pushing General Hull and his American army back across the Detroit River.[12] The British had been very reluctant to take up the offer of military assistance from the Indians. They viewed the use of Indian warriors, who fought with a fierce style unappreciated by British soldiers, as an inappropriate tactic. General Hull had issued a manifesto from Sandwich, while still on the Canadian side of the Detroit River, warning that if the British used the Indians in their military, there would be no mercy shown by the American forces for Indians or whites. Sir George Prevost, newly appointed governor of Canada, did all he could to disavow the use of Indian warriors in his campaigns. Prevost kept Tecumseh (who had come to Canada with the specific intention of making war on the Americans) under close supervision and went to considerable diplomatic lengths to explain to the Americans that they intended to fight a "gentleman's war."[13]

The British were coming to realize the value of their Indian allies, a realization that was reinforced by a directive from Lord Bathurst of the Colonial Office in London. Bathurst suggested that if the Indians were not included as Britain's allies in the conflict, they would certainly become her enemies, and that being the case, "upon every principle of self defence, therefore, [they could] not but be justified in conciliating them."[14] As a footnote, Bathurst revealed a major reason that this change of policy had come about: the war in Europe made it impossible for Britain to lend the colonial conflict anything but the slightest assistance in the way of armed men and money.[15]

With this authority in hand, Prevost designed what he thought was a suitably limited role for the Indians. In their position to the south of the Great Lakes, Britain's Indian allies would serve as a buffer zone through which the Americans would have to fight before they were within shooting range of the British regulars and Canadian militiamen. As well, they would serve as an offensive reserve which could be brought up on the flank and rear of any advancing American force. In order to maintain even this small objective, however, the trust of the Indians had to be assured and the line of supply and communications secured from Canada to the Mississippi River. In effect, Prevost proposed using the Indians as a force of mercenaries who would be given provisions and "Indian presents" in exchange for their support when and if needed.[16]

Further letters from London made it clear that there were to be no additions to the war chest or to the corps of regulars, and so Prevost could not afford the expenses of a mercenary force. In the autumn of 1812, Prevost, with the enlightened encouragement of Isaac Brock, moved toward a real alliance with the Indians, one that respected them as having political objectives as valid as those of Britain and Canada. The governor of Canada advised London to have the commission of armistice then in Washington attempting to end the hostilities, speak for Indian interests as well as those of the British.[17]

Bathurst was receptive to Prevost's policy, stating that he had recommended to the secretary of state for foreign affairs "that whenever negotiations for peace may be entered into, the security of the Indian possessions may not be either compromised or forgotten." Until he actually received official approval for his revised policy, Prevost had done little to broadcast his plans. After Prevost read Bathurst's letter, word was spread to all the allied Indian nations notifying them of British concurrence with their terms of alliance.[18]

Before their arrival at Michilimackinac, Dickson and the Indians of the west were acting very much upon their own initiative. In January 1813 a board of enquiry was convened in Quebec to consider the role played by this force, and it was recommended that Dickson be "Agent for the Indians to the Westward of the East side of Lake Huron," and that he be compensated for all expenses incurred. His commission was antedated one year in order to make legitimate the services so far rendered. The board of enquiry also recommended that the Indians be presented with a large belt of wampum, six silk flags and five large medals "intended to be given to the Principal Chief of each nation for the purpose of descending from him to his successor for ever in testimony of the happy Alliance and friendship subsisting between their respective nations and their Great Father the King of England."[19] Prevost endorsed the Board's recommendations and sent along his own official report for Bathurst's ratification. With this, Prevost was confident that the British and Indian Alliance would hold, as he reported to Bathurst: "The assurance that your Lordship has enabled me to make to the Indian tribes that, whenever negotiations for peace may be entered into, the security of the Indian possessions shall not be compromised or forgotten, will no doubt have the effect of securing the cordial cooperation of those Nations which upon so many occasions have proved of the utmost importance to His Majesty's Government."[20]

Through the spring and summer of 1813, the Dakota repulsed an invasion of Americans at Prairie du Chien, and fought beside the British and other Indian nations at Fort Meigs, Sandusky and at Fort Stephenson, where Little Crow and Waneta distinguished themselves for bravery.[21] On the Mississippi, Wapasha convinced all of the settlers in the region to support the British and to refuse any aid to the American army.[22]

Prevost had planned to reinforce the garrison at Michilimackinac over the summer of 1813, but control of the Lakes had fallen to the Americans, and as the winter ice set in, he abandoned the fort to its own resources.[23] The Committees of Trade in Montreal and Quebec saw this as a grave tactical error and directed their agent in London, Nathan Acheson, to impress upon the ministers of the Crown that "the preservation of the command of the Lakes and the friendship of the Indians as indispensable to the security of the Canadas." They advised that a new boundary establishing an inviolate territory for the Indians be regarded as "a sine qua non in any treaty" of peace between Britain and the United States. They even wanted Great Britain to guarantee Indian rights within their own tribal territory, ready to prevent encroachment and avenge violations.[24]

These representations had their effect, and in accordance with Bathurst's instructions, Prevost ordered a reinforcement troop under the command of Lieutenant Colonel McDouall to proceed to Michilimackinac as soon as possible when the ice went out in the spring. After a journey of severe hardship, McDouall and his men arrived at the British-held outpost on May 18, 1814. He immediately started improving the fortifications, and convened an assembly of the Indians who had remained at their posts throughout the winter.[25]

Wapasha reported that the efforts of the Indians had faltered in late winter through a lack of ammunition and food. Indeed, it was said that over half of the Dakota along the Mississippi had died from starvation, having been reduced to eating their moccasins. The late summer campaigns, which extended into winter, had kept the Indians from securing an adequate store of food, and the Americans were pressing on the Mississippi. Nevertheless, the Dakota stood ready to defend their lands and those of the British as was agreed. Little Crow told of his experiences at Fort Meigs, Sandusky and Fort Stephenson and said that to fight such wars, the heavy guns and soldiers of the British would be needed. His people, too, were ready to move immediately into the field.[26]

In response, McDouall delivered a speech embodying all of the pledges made by the British to protect Indian rights and lands. He said: "My Children. Should the King and your Great Father deign to listen to the proposal which the enemy have made for peace, it will be on the express condition that your interests shall be first considered, your just claims admitted, and no infringement of your rights permitted in future. My Children, doubt not that will be the case. The King your Great Father has assured you that he will never abandon his Red Children whom he has so long fostered and adopted."[27]

McDouall was considerably heartened by what he saw and heard at Michilimackinac, especially in light of the privations and hardships experienced by Indians and British soldiers alike. His confident report to Prevost was amplified in the governor's own dispatch to London, in which Prevost praised the faith of the Indians, and again pointed out "the necessity . . . of attending to their interests in any negotiation for a peace with America."[28]

The summer of 1814 offered only a steady grind of hardship and uncertainty. No provisions made their way from Canada, the war in Europe ended with Napoleon's defeat, and rumours of peace negotiations between the United States and Britain were widespread.[29] As well, the Americans had succeeded in driving up the Mississippi from St. Louis and establishing a fortification at Prairie du Chien, directly within the territories of the Sauk and on the border of Dakota lands.

As soon as the Indians could make their way from Prairie du Chien to Michilimackinac, they requested that McDouall aid them in pushing the Americans back. McDouall agreed and set about organizing an offensive force which he armed and supplied to the point that Michilimackinac was bare to the walls.[30] This major battle was fought and won on July 17, 1814, and by the end of summer, two more attacks by the Americans were turned back, one on Michilimackinac in early August and another on Prairie du Chien in September.[31] In his reports, McDouall had nothing but praise for his Indian allies, and reported them to be more strongly unified than they had been in recent generations.[32] Even the Ihanktonwon, Ihanktonwona and Tetonwon entered the alliance, remaining far out on the prairies and insulating the Mississippi from attack by Indians of the south and west who were sympathetic to the Americans. This left the entire area from the Rock River in the south to the Great Lakes in the secure control of the alliance.

By the late summer of 1814, Prevost had learned that Britain and the United States had begun to negotiate peace in Ghent, Belgium, and he speedily sent assurances that the Crown would remain faithful to the terms of the alliance with the Indians of the west.[33] To give this confidence real support, McDouall was ordered to send the troops of the Royal Newfoundland Fencibles under Captain Andrew Bulger to reinforce Prairie du Chien. When he arrived at the outpost in November, Bulger wrote describing the appalling conditions. In the coming winter, no fewer than 20,000 Indians would be entirely dependent upon hunting, having no trader amongst them from whom they could purchase supplies, and having had no opportunity over the summer to plant their corn. He reported, "Many of them had been from home all the summer fighting for us, and now, on the approach of winter to see them suffering all the horrors of want without the power to relieve them was distressing in the extreme."[34]

Conditions at Prairie du Chien became much worse. The garrison was virtually cut off from all outside information, and neither supplies nor instructions made their way from the Canadian provinces to the fort. A winter assault by the Americans was expected from St. Louis, reports trickled through that some Indian nations in the east had signed treaties with the Americans, supplies of all kinds were short, and the winter was severe. The militia plotted to turn coat when the Americans appeared on the Mississippi, and many Indians were refusing to leave their families for another season of starvation.[35]

The garrisons and Indians at Michilimackinac and Prairie du Chien did not know that peace had been concluded with the signing of the Treaty of Ghent on December 24, 1814. Two months later, some seemingly important but actually faulty information reached the frontier. McDouall wrote Bulger that he had received word from Sir Gordon Drummond, commander-in-chief of the forces, that the peace discussions had broken off. The British ambassadors, it was said, had insisted that the Indians be included in the treaty of peace, with full respect being paid to their territorial rights. In his communication to McDouall, Drummond had considered this matter to be of prime significance to the Indians, affording "strong evidence of the religious observance of those promises which I was commanded to make to them and on behalf of H.R.H., the Prince Regent."[36]

In turn, McDouall instructed Bulger to spread the news widely as proof of the British commitment to the alliance. He found it to be a natural course that a treaty of peace would include the Indian Nations "after having so repeatedly recognized them as intimately allied with us in one common cause." McDouall had composed a speech which he was to read to the Indians assembled in Grand Council. Bulger did this early in April 1815, standing before the Great Wampum Belt, coloured red for war, and before an assembly of twelve hundred Indians. In the speech he stated the agreed terms of the alliance between the Indians and the British, and reported to them that the war would not cease until all Americans, following the example of the British, had agreed to withdraw from Indian lands "and the country thus restored to you, to be entirely independent, as well as all the Indian Nations, whose rights were in the future to be held sacred."[37]

These assurances had the desired – and expected – result. McDouall reported from Michilimackinac, "The Indians are here, all staunch."[38] Immediately after forwarding this encouragement to Bulger, McDouall learned even more of the peace treaty, and what he learned filled him with horror and disgust: the Treaty of Ghent had been signed and the Indians had been utterly abandoned.[39]

The information that McDouall possessed in April was little better than rumour, but by late May, the truth arrived from distant Quebec. Prevost ordered that the soldiers be evacuated from Prairie du Chien and all ties with the Indians be severed.[40] Mere days before he received this directive, Bulger had sent his interpreter, Lieutenant Renville, into the Dakota camps to "say everything likely to confirm their attachment to us and increase their exertions in the common cause."[41] Black Hawk, chief of the Sauk, and spokesman for all the nations, had visited Bulger and reminded him of the promises made by Sir George Prevost when he, Wapasha, Little Crow and other chiefs were at Quebec.[42] Bulger was now forced to repudiate all that had been said in the previous few days. McDouall tried to relieve Bulger's conscience.

He said, "I am in great hopes that we shall succeed in gilding the bitter, bitter pill which the Indians of this neighbourhood must swallow."[43]

The bitter pill was rejected, since the treaty "contained no provision in regard to the fulfillment of the promises by which the tribes of the west on taking up arms on the British side at the beginning of the war had been led to expect. The Indian Chiefs who believed that they had been purposely deceived were in a state of great excitement. Their indignation at what they considered a breach of faith on the part of the British in not fulfilling the promises which were made to them was intense."[44] Only by training his loaded cannon upon his "allies" as he read his orders to abandon the fort and the Indians was Bulger able to flee unharmed to Michilimackinac.

That act completed the betrayal of the Indians and all that had been agreed when the British colony was in grave danger. In later years, the British permitted a small delegation of officers to go to Drummond's Island in Lake Huron to deliver goods to Indians who had fought with their army. In 1816, Wapasha and Little Crow of the Dakota made the journey of more than a thousand miles to attend the meeting, where they were presented with a small pile of cheap goods. Wapasha spoke:

My Father, what is this I see before me? A few knives and blankets! Is this all you promised at the beginning of the year? Where are those promises you made at Michilimackinac and sent to our villages on the Mississippi? You told us you would never let fall the hatchet until the Americans were driven beyond the mountains; that our British Father would never make peace without consulting his red children. Has that come to pass? We never knew of this peace. We are told it was made by our Great Father beyond the water, without the knowledge of his war chiefs, that it is your duty to obey his orders. What is this to us? Will these paltry presents pay for the men we have lost in battle and in the war? Will they soothe the feelings of our friends? Will they make good your promises to us? For myself, I am an old man. I have lived long and always found the means of subsistence, and I can do so still!

When Wapasha finished speaking, Little Crow rose.

After we have fought for you, endured many hardships, lost some of our people and awakened the vengeance of our powerful neighbours, you make a peace for yourself and leave us to obtain such terms as we can! You no longer need our services, and offer us these goods to pay for having deserted us. But no! We will not take them; we hold them and yourselves in equal contempt![45]

Following the War of 1812, treaties of "peace and friendship" were forced upon the Dakota by the Americans. In late 1815, the M'dewakontonwon were signators to such a treaty, as were the Wahpetonwon and Wahpekute the following year. The treaties, of course, provided for the admission of whites to the Dakota lands, and in 1820, Major Lawrence Taliaferro was assigned as Indian agent in the upper Mississippi River region.

Taliaferro's objectives were to gain Dakota recognition of American sovereignty, to protect them from the traders who were flooding into the area, to stop intertribal warfare, and to move the Dakota towards what passed for civilization amongst the Americans of the frontier. Taliaferro believed that he could realize his objectives by turning the Dakota from hunting and subsistence gardening toward large-scale agriculture. In the winter of 1828–29, he had assistance from the forces of nature. There were no game animals and thirty lodges of Dakota starved to death. The following summer, Mahpiyawichasta and Kiyeheie joined the farmer at Fort Snelling behind a plow. From this cautious beginning, the Dakota developed their abilities as agriculturalists.

Another treaty between the Americans and Dakota, drawn up in 1830, made a small amount of money available to pay for programs initiated by the Indian Bureau, including the establishment of an experimental farm on Dakota lands. Six years after the farm was begun, there were forty-six families engaged in farming at some level. In 1833, Taliaferro had requested permission from his superiors to hire farming instructors, as was provided in the Indian Bureau's terms of reference. To this end, the agent hired the Pond brothers, Gideon and Samuel. The Ponds were freelance missionaries, not attached to any particular institution, who held to the belief that civilization and Christianization of the Indians must attend each other, and they set about to teach the Indians the cultivation of both the soil and the Gospels. These appointments opened the door, and between 1834 and 1837 the Dakota villages were all but inundated by missionaries. In these early years, almost all of the missionaries joined the Indian agency staff of farmer instructors in the various Dakota villages, even though, as they admitted, they were quite incompetent as farmers.

In 1837, the United States government went again to the Dakota to treat, this time for a cession of all the nation's lands to the east of the Mississippi. One immediate effect of the treaty was that the traders raised their prices so as to absorb the annuity cash that the treaty had introduced into a cashless society. By this time, game resources near the Mississippi and Minnesota Rivers were very scarce, but the annuities instilled a false sense of security in the Dakota villages. Indeed, though the distribution of goods and gold was often delayed until the autumn hunting season, the Dakota had no choice but to await their arrival, thereby missing a supply of winter meat in favour of annuities.

The Treaty of 1837 increased the amount of money available for agriculture, but it was not an increase in keeping with real requirements. Even at that time, it cost between $300 and $500 to establish an operating farm in remote Minnesota Territory, and so the $10,000 set aside for the purchase of farming requirements would supply only twenty or thirty farms with the basics. There were, however, about seventeen hundred M'dewakontonwon, or about 340 families. It is clear that the government, through the treaty, was not committing itself to anything but an expansion of the subsistence level of farming then practised by the Dakota.

Again Taliaferro conserved the small resource of money by employing the missionaries as farm instructors. Agricultural expansion was definite but slow, and missionaries took the opportunity to address other aspects of their calling. By this time, most of them could speak at least passable Dakota and by 1836, the first religious tracts and books were being printed in that language. A translation dictionary was completed later, in 1851, but even before then there were a few Dakota men who could read and write English; by 1862, the number who could function in English had grown considerably.

The trigger for the crisis that all but shattered the Dakota in 1862 were the Treaties of Traverse des Sioux and Mendota. In these treaties, entered into in 1851, the Dakota were forced by the guns of the army and the words of the missionaries to cede all remaining lands in Minnesota and a small part of South Dakota. They were compelled to uproot their villages and move well up the Minnesota River to a narrow strip of land that was supposed to be, but was not until years later, confirmed as a reserve. The Sissetonwon and Wahpetonwon were already living on lands included within the reserve tract, but the M'dewakontonwon and Wahpekute had to move. Thus, those villages that had progressed the furthest in agriculture abandoned all the improvements they had made to that time.

Even though the Dakota had to start over again on new soil, within a few years many were living in frame or brick houses and had acquired enough experience as farmers that they had displaced the missionaries and were on the government payroll as instructors for their own villages. A great many more were farming on their own.[46] These farmers had access to agricultural technology – oxen power, breaking and walking plows, wagons, scythes and grain cradles – comparable to that used by the white settlers who were pouring into the lands ceded in the 1851 treaty. On Dakota farms, there were cattle, milk cows, draught and riding horses, sheep, poultry and hogs. By the spring of 1862, the M'dewakontonwon at the Lower Agency had over fourteen hundred acres planted to corn, potatoes, turnips, spring wheat and a great variety of garden vegetables. In that same year, there were fifteen hundred acres planted at the Upper Agency, and the two districts were expected to harvest over 150,000 bushels of various produce.[47]

Settlers did not and could not expand intensive agriculture in Minnesota until after 1851 and the signing of the treaties which opened up much of the territory's rich farm lands. One of the primary factors influencing the expansion of farming after that time was the availability of transportation, which in those days was conducted almost exclusively along the waterways. The treaties had not even been ratified by the Congress of the United States when settlers began to pour along the rivers into the ceded region. After the Dakota retired to their reserve the flood of settlement swelled, so that in some localities the number of farms was increasing by many hundreds of percent each year. By 1852, wheat was being shipped to markets outside the state, and in 1859 the volume of exports of crops of all kinds went over 700,000 bushels, most of which moved along the waterways. The first custom gristmill was built in St. Anthony in 1851, and the first fully commercial mill was built in 1854. In 1858, Minnesota farmers were able to supply all of the domestic market for wheat, and some flour was being exported to other states. By 1860, commercial agriculture was well-established and growing in Minnesota.

The Dakota, however, enjoyed no more than marginal benefits from these developments. They continued to practise small-scale agriculture, they had access to education in the English language (primarily Christian literature), and they owned houses and received haircuts, but they had no real control over the legal and political institutions of their communities. Instead, they were stripped of their extensive lands and forced within the confines of the reserves. The Dakota were coerced into obedience by the annuities that replaced the game they had once been free to hunt. Their national unity was shaken by religious division and the inequalities that attended the different treaties signed by the various bands and villages.

By the summer of 1862, the Dakota would surrender no more of their culture to the wasicu [white men], and no longer grovel at the doors of the Indian agent's warehouse. They rose with their guns, bows, arrows and axes to reclaim their own lives and land. By September of that same year, a few short months later, the Isantee Dakota were crushed, and the survivors had begun the long trek to the north, seeking the protection of Canada.

In 1862, when the Dakota appealed to the authorities in the Red River settlement at Fort Garry for sanctuary and protection, they claimed a right to be on British soil. In support of this right, they cited their tribal history, which described how the Dakota people had, in generations past, constructed an entire lifestyle on soil since claimed by the British Crown. Further, they said, King George III, the ancestor of the reigning "great mother," Queen Victoria, had made a mighty oath to the Dakota assuring them that for their part in allying themselves with the British in the War of 1812, their culture and freedom would always be respected and honoured wherever British rule prevailed.

These claims drew the minimal amount of attention that could be expected of the very few representatives of law, order and the Union Jack then in the Red River, especially when suddenly and unexpectedly confronted by over a thousand people who had, as could be plainly seen, the blood of war still upon their hands. The

Dakota did in the long run re-establish their all-but-ruined lives in the British West, but not as a result of any acknowledgement of their rights. To the contrary, the representatives of government, both in Ottawa and in Fort Garry, pronounced the Dakota to be "alien Indians" who would be tolerated in Canada as a matter of grace, not to mention as a matter of expediency, since there was no force then in the West sufficiently powerful to expel them.

Since that time in the last weeks of 1862, the Dakota in Canada have been, in many ways, separated from the course of the history experienced by other nations of Indians occupying the West – they were not invited to participate in the treaties of the 1870s, they received little assistance from government, and lands set aside for them were much smaller in area than were those taken up by immigrant homesteaders of the same era. They were largely permitted to succeed or fail by their own abilities.

Fortunately, the abilities of the Dakota had been honed and tested on a frontier that was much in advance of that just beginning to take form in western Canada. The Dakota were able to survive in this hostile environment by immediately applying the lessons that they had learned. Most important, perhaps, they had learned to anticipate the unfolding of events in a frontier setting, and to prepare themselves for them and then act in an appropriate fashion. They were, in many respects, given the unique opportunity to live their history twice.

Negotiated admission:
Flight to security in Canada,
1862 and 1863

2

While developments along the Mississippi and Minnesota rivers may have been instructive for the Dakota, the lessons were cruel. By summer's end in 1862, many thousands of Dakota had been seized by the military and imprisoned in stockades. Thirty-eight were hanged as war criminals, and many hundreds who failed to endure the prison camps died of starvation, exposure and torment. Only a small part of the surviving Dakota nation returned to live in Minnesota. Most were forced onto small reservations far in the western prairies, lands that had been virtually abandoned by other Indians as worthless. Eventually, a few were allowed to return to the Upper and Lower Agencies on the Minnesota River. Several hundred others, perhaps a thousand, moved north toward the "medicine line" that separated the British and the Americans.

The Dakota had made a last armed attempt to free themselves from government rule and regain their lands from the white settlers. The Sioux Uprising of 1862 began at Acton, Minnesota, on August 17, and had been crushed in the settled areas by September 23. Eight days after the uprising began, it had been decided by the Dakota that they would move north into British territory if the battle went against them. Late in November or early in December of 1862, the first of the bands arrived in Red River Settlement.

The Dakota entered the Canadian Northwest at a time of great political uncertainty. The governments in Ottawa and London, the administrators of the Hudson's Bay Company, and the leaders of the churches all had conflicting interests; as well, there were local groups who disagreed, among which the Métis were the most coherent and powerful. The Indians had virtually abandoned the areas around the settlements and along the Red and Assiniboine rivers, but otherwise conducted their own internal affairs as they saw fit. There was as yet no conclusion about whether the Northwest should become an agricultural frontier or a preserve for trappers and traders, and the issue could not be addressed until a suitable access route from Canada to the new land was established. While these problems introduced no end of contention and confusion into the Northwest, they also indicated to the Dakota that there was no set and rigid social structure in Canada that could inhibit their attempts to settle north of the border. There was still plenty of room in 1862 for adaptation and participation in the development of the character of the Northwest, and the Dakota had learned that adaptation was necessary.

In the last days of the uprising, the bands of Dakota that had been located closest to the mouth of the Minnesota began to work their way back up the river. When they reached Mazaska's village, that chief, backed by Tatankanaje and other leaders of the upper Dakota, refused to let them pass and bring the war trailing after them. Little Crow, Shak'pay, Red Middle Voice, Wakanozhan and other M'dewakontonwon chiefs then left the vicinity of the Minnesota River, moving west toward the Missouri River. There they met with the Ihanktonwon who hunted on the plains around the James and Sheyenne rivers, and swung toward the north.

The upper Sissetonwon and Wahpetonwon fled the Minnesota somewhat later, when it became apparent that Governor Ramsey of Minnesota intended to make real his vow to eliminate every Dakota in the territory. They headed north and west of the river, turning east briefly to attack a small American garrison at Fort Abercrombie, then moving on to join the Ihanktonwon.

What the Dakota needed was a refuge beyond the reach of the pursuing American army where they could rest and regroup. All of the fleeing bands moved west and north to Devil's Lake in present-day North Dakota, an area used extensively by the Ihanktonwon. The Minnesota Dakota were able to use their relatives' "corridor of influence" as a highway away from danger, without exposing themselves to the hostile Ojibwa further east. The lake was an oasis of plenty surrounded by prairies and plains, with sufficient wood, water, food and protection to accommodate a large gathering. As a final advantage, it was near the international boundary. By the winter, there were over six hundred lodges of Dakota from all branches of the nation camped by the lake.

While the majority of the remnant nation remained for the winter at Devil's Lake, at least three bands of Dakota slipped into British territory during the winter of 1862–63, unnoticed by the sparse white community. H'damani, originally from Mazaska's village below Lac qui Parle on the Minnesota River, crossed the international boundary at the Turtle Mountains, where he and his band remained until the first decade of the twentieth century. Wambdiska and his followers from Mazomani's Wahpetonwon village joined Tahampegda and his larger band of Sissetonwon and Wahpetonwon to cross the boundary at the Souris River. Wapahaska, leading a band of Sissetonwon from Istak'pa's village and a smaller number of Wahpetonwon from Mazomani's village, crossed at the north loop of the Souris River and may have passed as far north as the Moose Mountains.

Late in 1862, the fugitives at Devil's Lake sent a party to Fort Garry to discuss their entry into the Northwest. The emissaries arrived in Fort Garry directly from the south along the cart trails bordering the Red River, which were kept open by the Ihanktonwon, who were reported to be active that autumn as far west as Fort Ellice.[1] By late December, there were ninety Dakota at Upper Fort Garry, hoping to gain an audience with the company and civil authorities there. This was not a fruitful visit, and the party withdrew from the settlement in January 1863, returning to Devil's Lake where they remained for the winter.

Early in the spring of 1863, the Dakota again moved into Canada from Devil's Lake and proceeded to Red River Settlement, this time with more concrete political objectives in mind. During the previous hard winter, the Dakota had come to realize that they faced unending peril as long as they were within reach of the United States Army, and that the only place to avoid annihilation was in British territory. At the same time, they learned that they would not be able to move across the line without dealing with the political realities of the Northwest. They required an acknowledgement by the British that the Dakota had a right to be in Canada and that some obligation was owed to them. They also required peace with the Indians and Métis of the region and agreement on rights to land.

In the spring of 1863, Little Crow and sixty men arrived at the fort.[2] Staying only long enough to obtain some provisions and to test the settlement's reaction to the Dakota presence, Little Crow and sixteen men returned to Minnesota to replenish their horse herd. Little Crow was shot by a settler at Hutchinson, Minnesota, on July 3, 1863. The rest of his band remained north of the international boundary.

In May, William Seward, the United States secretary of state, asked permission of the British Embassy in Washington for American troops to cross the international boundary in pursuit of the Dakota. The American Civil War had begun two years earlier. In an effort to avoid involuntary inclusion of the British in the war, Queen Victoria had issued the Proclamation of Neutrality in 1861, in which British subjects were forbidden to enlist in armies of either side or to sell arms to either force, and all foreign armies were prohibited entry into Canada. Accordingly, the American request to pursue the Dakota into Rupert's Land was rejected.[3] The Union did not press the matter at that time, because two large companies of cavalry were then travelling into the plains.

One column, under General Sibley, made its way overland toward the headwaters of the Sheyenne River while the other, led by General Sully, moved along the east bank of the Missouri from Fort Pierre to Bismarck. They expected in this fashion to trap the Dakota below the boundary in the jaws of a pincer action. When the two forces lost track of each other in the vast northern plains, the textbook strategy devised by Sully and Sibley was replaced by ambush and massacre. The hungry and poorly equipped Dakota who remained on the American side of the boundary were no match for an army fresh from its barracks. In late June, running battles at Big Mound, Dead Buffalo Lake and Stony Lake in the Dakota Territory left 150 Dakota dead and much of their food, clothing, horses and shelter destroyed. In August, Sully swept out of the early morning and through a camp of Dakota at Whitestone Hill along the James River and killed two hundred men, women and children. He seized the few survivors as captives and returned to the comfort of his barracks, leaving the winter prairies to the Indians.

By late autumn, the Dakota had again assembled at Devil's Lake and by mid-winter most of the M'dewakontonwon and Wahpetonwon who remained south of the boundary went into the British territory. In early December 1863, sixty lodges, housing 445 Dakota, arrived at Fort Garry. In the following months, some of these Dakota surrendered to the American army and others returned to the Devil's Lake area, but with the passage of the years, the Wahpetonwon and M'dewakontonwon participants in this influx settled at Portage la Prairie in Manitoba.

When the Dakota arrived at Fort Garry during the bitter winter of 1863–64, they needed sanctuary. Governor Dallas of the Hudson's Bay Company reported that the Dakota were "in a state of absolute starvation." The American army had followed them up the Red River and at that very moment, four hundred of the United States Cavalry were at Pembina, within sight of the boundary. The Dakota told Dallas that they were not going back onto the prairie to perish in the snow. The Dakota had no provisions at all, and Dallas reported that they were in such desperation that they were selling their children.[4]

Dallas had hoped that by giving the Dakota sufficient food for ten or fifteen days, along with a little ammunition for hunting, the bands would leave the settlement. He estimated that there were 494 Dakota around the fort, with thirteen other lodges in the neighbourhood, a total of six hundred men, women and children. The Hudson's Bay Company had sent eight sleds of food out to the Dakota – charged to public expense – but still they refused to leave. Dallas wrote that the settlement was in no position to quarrel with the Dakota, and that the Ojibwa were much disturbed by the invasion of their territory. With the settlement itself on the edge of poverty, he concluded that outright war with the Dakota should be avoided at any cost; the expense of keeping the Dakota for ten years would be less than the suffering a war would entail. If war became inevitable, Dallas was prepared to call on the American troops at Pembina, but this would be a last resort. The settlers, however, were already clamouring for the admission of troops, and Dallas begged imperial advice on this course of action.[5]

Tensions in Red River Settlement eased a little the following week, when all but one of the Dakota lodges were struck and the band moved off, it was reported, to the Turtle Mountains. Dallas hoped that this was the last he would see of the Dakota. The surrounding Indian nations were distressed by the presence of the Dakota, and the settlers were crying for American troops. While the settlement itself had no means of driving out the intruders, the Dakota could not have withstood the combined hostility of outraged Ojibwa and vengeful American soldiers. Therefore, the band quietly withdrew from the settlement.[6]

From his headquarters, Major General John Pope, commander of the American army's Department of the Northwest at Milwaukee, asserted the urgent necessity for crossing the boundary with his force. He hoped and even expected that his superiors would give him permission to do so whether the British approved or not.[7] Sibley suggested that the Americans seek the extradition of the Dakota, but Pope saw this as hopeless, "if for no other reason than the criminals to be turned over to us exceed in number and defensive power the population of the settlements whose duty it would be to make the arrest."[8] Secretary of State Seward resisted these appeals, and early in January 1864 he renewed his application to the British Embassy in Washington for permission to pursue the Dakota into Canada. Seward was offered a polite promise of immediate consideration, but nothing more.[9]

In mid-January, Governor Dallas learned that the Dakota had not left Rupert's Land. The settlers were frantic. Some had even gone to Pembina to invite the American cavalry across the line. Sensibly, the commanding officer at Pembina refused to go unless he was given orders to do so by his own superiors or an invitation from the governor. Dallas refused to bend.[10] While the Americans may have been reluctant to attempt any official foray into British territory without the express permission of the authorities there, clandestine invasion was not discounted.

At the very time that Dallas was denying permission to the Americans, the latter were conniving to kidnap the Dakota chiefs Shak'pay and Wakanozhan. This daring raid was completed successfully on January 17 or 18, 1864, by Lieutenant Cochrane of the Pembina garrison. Shak'pay and Wakanozhan had refused to consider returning to the United States, but they were drugged with opium and chloroform, tied to a sled and quickly hauled across the line to Pembina. Shortly thereafter, a number of the followers who had been in the chiefs' camp voluntarily surrendered to the American troops. Eventually, Shak'pay and Wakanozhan were taken to Fort Snelling where they were hanged on November 11, 1865.

It took some months for the news of this event to reach the proper authorities in England and Canada. In the meantime, Seward renewed his plea that the United

States force be allowed to cross the boundary. He argued that either the Dakota should be restrained by the British or the Americans should be allowed to "pursue, subdue and disperse them."[11] Early in February 1865, the recently appointed governor general, Edmund Head, reported to the British government that Red River was facing an uncomfortable situation, but that he deplored the decision of the Rupert's Land residents to turn to the Americans for protection. Moreover, he said that the Hudson's Bay Company, a mere commercial enterprise, should not be permitted to undertake the discussion of such important international matters, much less to enter into negotiations with the commander of an alien force. The British again rejected Seward's request.[12]

Later in February 1865, Governor Dallas received a message from Tatankanaje, Mahtowakan, Red Dog, Blackmoon and Waanata, the Sissetonwon chiefs then camped on the Missouri River, asking whether or not they should surrender to the Americans. None of these chiefs had actively participated in the uprising of 1862, and all were still hoping that a negotiated settlement might leave them in peace. Dallas assured the chiefs that the Americans would not harm any innocent Dakota, but he added that the army intended to mount a great force in the spring to capture any who were still on the prairie at that time. Dallas immediately sent out two reports on this exchange – one to Canada and one to Pembina. Dallas also reported to Pembina that large numbers of Dakota remained around the Red River settlements, but that the mild weather had enabled them to move onto Lake Manitoba where they were taking great numbers of fish through the ice. He expected that all would leave soon to join the other Dakota on the Missouri.

In his report to Canada and in contradiction of his earlier dispatches, Dallas denied having given the Dakota ammunition and claimed to have so restricted their access to supplies that starvation was common in their camps. He wrote that while the Dakota had not molested any person along the Red or Assiniboine rivers, their very presence was generating hysteria in the communities. He also noted that Major Hatch, in command at Pembina, stood ready to ride north should an emergency erupt. Dallas concluded that it was wise to do nothing that would arouse the Dakota.[13] Soon after Dallas sent his report, London sent him instructions to maintain his position, as "nothing short of actual and imminent peril to the lives of yourself and the settlers would justify the intervention of a foreign force on British Territory."[14] Unfortunately, a message sent from London at the end of February would not reach the Red River before spring, and matters were moving very rapidly.

By early March, the newspapers in eastern Canada had heard of the capture of Shak'pay and Wakanozhan and were describing the episode as a violation of British sovereignty. *The Canadian News* wrote first of the inhuman treatment of the Indians at the hands of the Americans and concluded that the uprising was more or less what could be expected of a national policy of annihilation. Dallas's refusal to bring in the American troops was lauded, since the Dakota, "savages though they are, had sought refuge under the British flag, and protection was therefore extended to them."[15]

Dallas had not communicated to Canada anything of the kidnapping in the belief that to do so would bring a final refusal to admit the Americans, an option which he wished to keep available. When in April 1865 Major Hatch again asked permission to enter Canada, Dallas responded: "[I have] no hesitation in complying with your request, stipulating only that, in the event of active operations taking place within the settlements, you will communicate with the authorities, and take such measures as will prevent bloodshed or violence in the houses or inclosures of the settlers, should any of the Sioux Indians take refuge there."[16]

Both Dallas and Hatch were aware that the Dakota were then camped near the Métis community at Poplar Point, placing any "active operations" beyond the governor's view and limited range of authority, but the governor was not comfortable in having taken such an important decision upon himself. He ordered the convening of the local Council of Assiniboia where he expected and obtained their endorsement.[17] In explaining his decision to London, Dallas stated that the Dakota might otherwise remain in British territory permanently. When they had arrived at Red River, he said the Dakota chiefs had narrated their ancient history of northern origins and had displayed the medals their fathers received from King George in 1812. They had recalled the pledges of protection that successive generations of Dakota had cherished. Dallas was ignorant of this history and could neither comment upon it nor use it to guide his actions. While he would have liked to expel the Dakota, he was unable to do so, and while he would have liked to call in the Americans, he foresaw unpleasant repercussions. Finally, he begged for guidance in this very difficult situation.[18] While awaiting a response, which Dallas knew would take many weeks and even months, the tension at Red River dissipated. The Dakota were reported to have left the vicinity of the settlement and gone to join the Ihanktonwon on the Missouri. Dallas was hoping that the American troops would trap the Dakota far to the south, and find no reason to enter Red River at all.[19]

Eventually, London learned of the illegal capture of Shak'pay and Wakanozhan, and of Dallas's permission for the American army to enter Canada. The resulting publicity, both in the press of eastern Canada and on the floor of the Commons in London, ended any fleeting ideas of loosing the American army on British soil. The government in London notified the governor general of Canada that the only appropriate action in the Northwest was to deny entry to the Americans.[20] By mid-April, Major Hatch and his soldiers were ordered to withdraw from Pembina to

Fort Abercrombie. The United States command finally understood that the troops would never be given permission to cross the boundary.

The vast majority of Dakota who had been in Canada remained there, and did not go to the Missouri as Dallas had supposed. The M'dewakontonwon and Wahpetonwon who had been in Shak'pay and Wakanozhan's camp had been reviled by the other bands as the ones who had got them into their present difficulties. They prudently moved west along the Assiniboine River and encamped – twenty-two lodges in all – at Portage la Prairie. Others moved even further west to the vicinity of the Turtle Mountains, Fort Ellice and the Moose Mountains.

In the summer of 1864, General Sully caught up with the last large band of Dakota south of the boundary. By the last light of July 28, he and twenty-two hundred soldiers attacked sixteen hundred lodges of Dakota at Kildeer Mountain and massacred 150 men, women and children and destroyed all the lodging, food, clothing and horses the fugitives left behind. Shortly after this, the last battle of the Dakota, Tatankanaje quietly crossed the international boundary and headed for Fort Qu'Appelle. Mahpiyahdinape moved into the Northwest through the Turtle Mountains or along the Souris River and went toward Fort Ellice. Other survivors moved into what is now western Manitoba, and with a few exceptions the dispersion of the Dakota into Canada was complete. The United States Army made further expeditions into the plains to find the Dakota, but the last tour in 1865 failed to come across a single one; the Dakota were either in Canada, in prison or dead. Very few were in Minnesota as free people.[21]

By the winter of 1864–65, the various Dakota bands had distributed themselves across the Northwest in a pattern that has remained without substantial alteration to this day. The first to cross the border into British North America had been the band of M'dewakontonwon under Little Crow in late 1862. After Little Crow left for his death in Minnesota, his people who remained in Canada went the following summer to fish in Lake Manitoba and returned to camp for the winter at Sturgeon Creek, where it flowed into the Assiniboine, and at Upper Fort Garry. In late 1863, they were joined by the M'dewakontonwon and Wahpetonwon under Shak'pay and Wakanozhan. The remnants of these three bands had by the spring of 1864 distributed themselves along the Assiniboine from Sturgeon Creek to the White Horse Plain and had moved even further west to Poplar Point and Portage la Prairie by 1865.

In late 1862, H'damani had moved directly from Mazaska's village in Minnesota, where he had been a sub-chief, to the Turtle Mountains, and remained there for the rest of his life. Further west, Tahampegda and Wambdiska, a sub-chief of Mazomani's Wahpetonwon village, remained along the Souris River and Oak Lake for a number of years, finally moving onto the Assiniboine in 1865 or 1866. Wapahaska also moved into British territory in late 1862, and for a number of years he camped in the Moose Mountains, amicably, it would seem, with the resident Assiniboine. Toward the end of the 1860s, he had shifted his territory west and north as far as the North Saskatchewan River.

Mahpiyahdinape, originally a chief in Iyangmani's Wahpetonwon village, went directly from the battle at Kildeer Mountain to the vicinity of Fort Ellice on the Assiniboine. There he remained.

Tatankanaje also went north from Kildeer Mountain, crossing the boundary along the west arm of the Souris River and travelling from there along the river system to Fort Qu'Appelle. His was the last band to make regular expeditions into the United States, since the American troops were far away from the Qu'Appelle, and the Missouri, the Ihanktonwon and the buffalo were so close. In 1866, most of Tatankanaje's family died in a smallpox epidemic. Stricken with grief, he pledged himself to a war party against the Crow and died in battle that summer.

A small party of Wahpetonwon and M'dewakontonwon under Hupa Yakta remained south of the boundary, where they took sanctuary in the deep woods of northeastern Minnesota. They did not cross the line until 1876.

When the Dakota entered the Northwest, they fully understood that they were approaching the periphery of their territory, an area already occupied by the Cree, Assiniboine, Ojibwa and Métis. These nations had no reason to welcome the newcomers, even though they recognized that the arriving Dakota groups were not the same as the Ihanktonwon, with whom they had been in conflict for at least the preceding century. There were, however, pressures in Rupert's Land which caused the inhabitants to resist the Dakota influx.

In the early 1860s, the Métis were threatened by shifting government and Hudson's Bay Company policy which would make the Northwest an administrative colony of eastern Canada. The change in policy was occurring without reference to Métis interests, and might abrogate their aboriginal rights to the land. The Métis simply did not want to see another claimant to lands and political consideration in the Northwest. Like the tribes of Indians, the Métis also saw the Dakota as strong competitors for the declining food and commercial resources.

In the first four years after their arrival in the Northwest, the Dakota were harassed and attacked by the resident nations. In the summer of 1866, Tatankanaje and forty of his men went into Fort Garry, where they met with a camp of Ojibwa from the Red Lake district. The Dakota entered into what they thought was a peace discussion and, after the appropriate ceremony, took their leave for the West. They were followed and fired upon by the Ojibwa, who killed six of the Dakota.[22] That

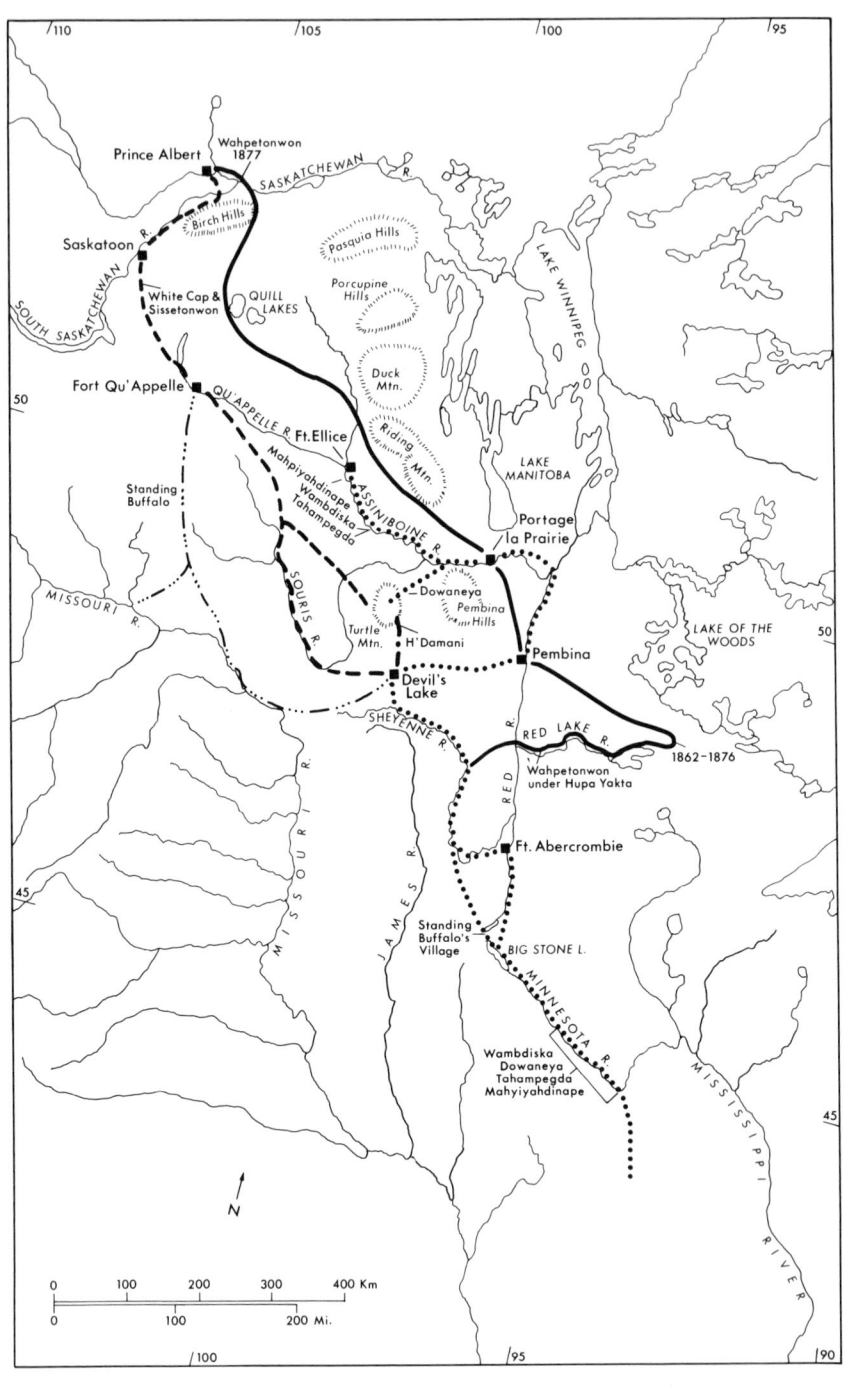

110 / 105 / 100 / 95

Prince Albert Wahpetonwon
1877
SASKATCHEWAN R.
Birch Hills
Saskatoon
SOUTH SASKATCHEWAN R.
Pasquia Hills
Porcupine Hills
White Cap & Sissetonwon
QUILL LAKES
Duck Mtn.
Fort Qu'Appelle
50
QU'APPELLE R. Ft.Ellice
Mahpiyahdinape
Riding Mtn.
LAKE MANITOBA
Standing Buffalo
Wambdiska Tahampegda
ASSINIBOINE R.
Portage la Prairie
MISSOURI R.
SOURIS R.
Dowaneya
Pembina Hills
LAKE OF THE WOODS
Turtle Mtn.
H'Damani
Pembina
50
Devil's Lake
SHEYENNE R.
RED LAKE R.
1862-1876
MISSOURI R.
RED R.
Wahpetonwon under Hupa Yakta
Ft. Abercrombie
45
JAMES R.
Standing Buffalo's Village
BIG STONE L.
MINNESOTA R.
Wambdiska
Dowaneya
Tahampegda
Mahyiyahdinape
45
MISSISSIPPI RIVER
N

0   100   200   300   400 Km
0   100   200 Mi.

100 / 95 / 90

Map 3. Routes to Canada

same summer, the Ojibwa attacked Tahampegda in the vicinity of Portage la Prairie, killing the chief and his eldest son. These were the last recorded accounts of violence between the Dakota, the Indian nations and the Métis of the Northwest.

In the summer of 1874, Tatankanaje the Younger and Wapahaska told Lieutenant Governor Alexander Morris that the elder Tatankanaje had made an enduring peace with the Cree of the prairie. This peace must have been struck before 1866, since the elder chief died that year leading his last war party. In 1874, too, H'damani told Morris that the Dakota had acquired from the Ojibwa the right to live in and use the Turtle Mountains; the Ojibwa were often resident there. H'damani gave the chief warrior of the Ojibwa four horses and five sacred pipes in return for the lands. H'damani must have been able to make his arrangements soon after he arrived in the Northwest, as in 1874 he told Morris that he had been living in peace for twelve years, that is, since 1862.[23]

Once free of the immediate and deadly threat of annihilation from their neighbouring nations, the Dakota scattered themselves across the region in a manner highly reminiscent of their existence in the United States. In Minnesota, the Dakota were centred in the transitional environment between plains and forests, with the easternmost villages just inside the broadleaf forest and the westernmost on the edge of the grassland. In their new homes in the Northwest, where the lower part of the Assiniboine flows through wooded parkland and the northern edge of the tallgrass prairie, the M'dewakontonwon occupied the lands furthest downstream, closest to the wooded environment. The Sissetonwon were furthest upstream and closest to the grasslands. The Wahpetonwon lived in the transitional zone between the two districts. The differences in the environments occupied by the various bands of the Dakota nation were reflected in their human ecology. In Minnesota, the M'dewakontonwon had been most occupied with horticulture from the time of earliest written records until 1862, while the Sissetonwon were primarily known as buffalo hunters on the prairie. In the years before the Minnesota uprising of 1862, it was the population of M'dewakontonwon who first and most intensely experienced the effects of intrusive change – missionaries, commercial agriculture, annuities, land cessions, government agents, reduction of game animals – while the Sissetonwon remained relatively untouched.

By the mid-1860s, the Dakota had completed their relocation into the Northwest and had established themselves in environments they perceived to be suitable for their new lives. They had come to terms with the Métis and Indian nations and were no longer targets of the United States Army. The Dakota had attempted to assert their right to be in Canada and had laid claims to the protection of the Crown, but these claims were scarcely heard, much less heeded. This was not so much a problem for the Dakota as the failure of negotiations with the Indians and Métis would have been. The small number of fearful and disorganized settlers were no threat, but any of the Indian nations would have been able to eliminate the Dakota had they been so inclined. Once the bands moved away from the Upper Fort, and the crisis of immediate emergency passed, the settlers and authorities along the Red River simply ignored the Dakota. This was just as well, because the Dakota were able to begin the reconstruction of their lives free from interference.

Rupert's Land was in political turmoil in the 1860s. Early in this decade, it became clear that the Hudson's Bay Company was losing its position as the pre-eminent political and legal body in the Northwest. Each of the many interests that made up the population of the settlement began to push for the supremacy of its views. The Americans at Red River mocked both the juvenile government provided by the Hudson's Bay Company and the form of direct rule from Ottawa that was probably planned by the Dominion government. They supported annexation of the Northwest to the United States. The Canadians, while dismissing the American call for annexation, also deplored the form of government proposed by the Dominion in its North-West Territories Act of 1868. They argued for a fully representative government, rather than an appointed lieutenant governor and council. Both the Indians and Métis came to realize that there were no Dominion guarantees of land titles because they were viewed as nothing more than squatters by many recently arrived Canadians. The uncertainty lay behind the Red River Resistance of 1869 and 1870.

Colonel Garnet Wolseley's troops suppressed Riel and the Métis in the late summer of 1870 and cleared the way for the inclusion of the Northwest in Canada. Manitoba, defined as a small rectangle of land embracing some eleven thousand square miles of the vast Northwest, became a province. All lands outside this tract formed the North-West Territories, completely under the control of the federal government. While control of natural resources in both jurisdictions remained firmly in the hands of the Dominion, 1,400,000 acres of land in the North-West Territories was set aside for the French Métis and English Halfbreeds, and a commitment was made to conclude treaties with the Indians. With the installation in late August of the newly appointed lieutenant governor, Adams G. Archibald, the inclusion of Manitoba as a province of Canada and of the Northwest as a territory of the Dominion were complete.

Much of this political action took place far from where the Dakota had settled. The Dakota were too much involved in their own efforts at reconstruction and diplomacy to take an active part in the politics of the white and Métis settlements.

When the M'dewakontonwon and Wahpetonwon moved west, they formed four separate camps – at High Bluff, Poplar Point, Portage la Prairie and Beaver or Rat Creek, which enters the Whitemud River near Lake Manitoba. The Dakota at High

Bluff and Poplar Point laboured for the farming settlers in the area, cut construction timber and firewood, and fished and trapped to the northeast around the Shoal Lakes and the southeast end of Lake Manitoba. Surplus fish were sold or bartered in the settlements. Members of the camp at Portage la Prairie worked in the village or on the farms, and also cut wood and sold fish. Most of their fishing was done from the south shore of Lake Manitoba. The Dakota at Rat Creek laboured for the traffic passing over the Prairie Portage to Lake Manitoba and trapped in the marshes to the southwest of the lake. All of these camps, numbering perhaps a hundred lodges, recognized Weeokeah or Waoke as their leader, since Little Crow, Shak'pay and Wakanozhan all were dead. This would suggest that the division into separate camps was the result of economic strategy rather than of political division. During these early years, most of the Dakota left the vicinity of Portage la Prairie during the winter to hunt and trap in the Turtle Mountains, where they maintained their close ties with the bands under H'damani, Wambdiska and Taninyahdinazin, and renewed their acquaintance with Wapahaska, Tatankanaje and Mahpiyahdinape.

H'damani, Wambdiska and Taninyahdinazin all remained in what is now southwestern Manitoba, between Oak Lake and the eastern slopes of the Turtle Mountains, making excursions south to Devil's Lake, where they joined the Ihanktonwon. They rarely went north of the Assiniboine River, but often followed that water east to Portage la Prairie and the other settlements. In the main, they hunted and fished for subsistence, but also traded furs, meat, pemmican, robes and manufactured items such as carts to the Hudson's Bay Company post at Fort Ellice. Some time before 1870, however, people from these bands started small gardens at Oak Lake and on the Assiniboine.

Mahpiyahdinape and his band stayed in the vicinity of Fort Ellice, camping mostly along the Birdtail River. From there, they hunted north into the Riding Mountains and Duck Mountains and south in the Moose Mountains.

Tatankanaje's band stayed west of Fort Ellice but frequently went to that post to trade and to work. The territory used by this band until the early 1870s extended from Fort Ellice in the east to the Qu'Appelle Lakes in the west and south to the Missouri, where they could join the camps of the Ihanktonwon. Tatankanaje's territory overlapped in the north with that of Wapahaska, and until the two bands selected separate reserves in the 1880s, may have spent a good part of each year together. When the elder Tatankanaje died, the band looked to Wapahaska for leadership, because their own rightful chief, named Tatankanaje after his father, was but a young man and as he said of himself, not yet the equal of his father. The bands, however, remained distinct and Wapahaska routinely occupied the territory from the Moose Mountains in the east and to the Saskatchewan River in the Northwest. Both bands joined the Métis of the Qu'Appelle Lakes for the buffalo hunt along the Missouri and on the plains to the south and west.

The few extant records from Fort Ellice give some idea of how the Dakota bands survived. During the early and mid-summers of 1868 and 1869, the Dakota were reported to be on the high plains hunting buffalo, although some remained within travelling range of the fort. During the months of June and July, small groups of Dakota travelling in parties of three to eight families would come in to trade a few furs, mostly muskrat, that they still had from their spring trapping. In August 1869, Tatankanaje came in to trade and remained near the post for more than a week. Earlier that spring, he had been at the post for eleven days with thirty-one lodges, trading buffalo hides that had been taken over the winter.

In the summer months, there were Dakota at Moose Mountain and Oak Lake. The manager at Fort Ellice sent a man to trade at their camps and from time to time an individual Dakota might appear at the post. In September, large parties of Dakota would arrive at Fort Ellice to make ready for the winter. In October and November, a Cree and a Métis were sent out to trade at the Dakota's autumn trapping camps, taking in muskrat, red fox, fisher, a few mink and bags of pemmican. In November 1868, one band traded four oxen at the post. In late autumn, many of the Dakota moved onto the plains to intercept the movements of the buffalo, and other small camps were scattered in the Moose Mountain and Oak Lake districts. Occasionally, one man would come into the post to seek a trader; he would accompany a man back to the camp and then return with a load of bear, mink, lynx, fisher, muskrat, skunk, badger and deer hides.

At the harshest time of the winter, when game and fur were scarce, a few families would move up to the post and plead starvation, where they would be hired. In January 1868, five men cut firewood for six days, picket logs for three days, and river ice for two days. Other small groups came into the fort in February and March and then later in April when the spring thaw made hunting and trapping difficult and food shortages were most likely to be felt. In April 1869, six Dakota worked at the fort cutting firewood and boat-building lumber. They also sold a cart which they had made over the winter. By late spring, animals were more plentiful and easier to take, and the Dakota were back to trapping and trading.[24]

The Fort Ellice Journals for 1868 and 1869 paint a grim image of the Dakota existence. Seasonal starvation was common, and the Hudson's Bay Company men insisted on immediate payment for goods, in either fur or labour. Fortunately, their labour was in some demand, as were a few Dakota-manufactured items. Through the combination of furs, labour, handcrafts and oxen, as well as the production of their own food, shelter, clothing and other basics, the Dakota were able to subsist.

By 1871–72, the Dakota were doing much more work around the post, especially cutting wood, making and hauling hay, and working the crops of barley and garden stuff. Most of this work was concentrated in the times around breakup and freezeup. During the prime hunting weeks in summer and winter the Dakota were away from the post. In 1871–72 alone, the Dakota did 230 person-days of work at Fort Ellice.

In June 1871, a few Dakota, including Bookpa from H'damani's camp, travelled from the Turtle Mountains to trade five oxen. The men arrived in advance of the main camp, and were followed one or two days later by the women and children. The practice of travelling separately was not done in the earlier years, and suggests that the Dakota had become more comfortable in their environment. In July, some of Mahpiyahdinape's band came to trade, and a number were put to work hoeing potatoes in the fort's garden. Later that month, there were over thirty lodges at the post, and many of the men were hired to cut hay on the prairie and then haul and stack it at the fort. On July 24 and 25, the assembled Dakota held a dance, after which most of them took provisions for the summer hunt and departed for the plains. A few remained into August and were put to work harvesting and threshing barley, cutting hay, and labouring at various construction tasks around the fort.

In September, some construction work was available, but most bands were off hunting and the demand for labour slowed. When the garden was ripe, Dakota members were taken on to harvest the crop. By the end of the month, large parties were coming in from the plains to trade and celebrate with a dance. Through October, furs from the summer and autumn hunt were brought in, along with fresh meat, and a few men and women were set to cutting firewood, working on the cattle buildings, and butchering fresh meat. Work of this sort continued through November, but most of the Dakota were at their campsites, and only a few went up from Turtle Mountain and Mahpiyahdinape's camp to trade. Late in November a Dakota and a Métis were sent to escort the cart train of goods sent to Fort Ellice from the Red River.

The winter of 1871–72 was again hard. A number of Dakota were said to be starving, but most of the bands had enough furs to purchase supplies. In early December, it was necessary for the manager at Fort Ellice to send a sled loaded with pemmican to a small band of Dakota who had no food, but who were heading to the post with furs. For the rest of the winter, a tripper was sent regularly to the Riding Mountains where many camps had gone to hunt. During January, a camp of Dakota remained at Fort Ellice, where they were put to work on a variety of tasks, and then moved to Oak Lake when the fishing was good. In February, those who had been in the Riding Mountains headed south, and as they passed the fort, they traded and did a little work in exchange for supplies.

By late February, families were going to Fort Ellice from the Moose Mountain district. A few went back after a brief bit of trading, while others remained near the

post until March when they were joined by many more Dakota leaving their hunting and trapping camps. Again, some of these had exhausted all their food supplies
and were quickly put to work cutting wood; by mid-March, they had cut 162 cords
of fuel. In that month, the fort began to send cart trains to Fort Qu'Appelle and
often these were driven exclusively by Dakota. In April and May, game became
more plentiful, as did work around the post, especially in the garden, and the Dakota
celebrated with another dance.[25]

There were some considerable changes over the years from 1868–69 to 1871–
72. In the later years, the Dakota were admitted to the old practice of credit at the
post and permitted to pay their debts out of future earnings, whether labour or trade.
The post records indicate that the Dakota were cautious in the amounts and kinds
of debt they assumed, prompt in paying them off and unlikely to resort to outright
begging. Many of the jobs that they were given around the post were done without
supervision of any kind. They even undertook trips to outlying camps and to Fort
Qu'Appelle on their own, taking as many as five carts of the Hudson's Bay
Company's goods for up to ten days. They frequented Fort Ellice in later years, but
as they acquired reserve lands in the early 1870s, and as trade at the old post wound
down, the Dakota were less inclined to linger around the post. Nevertheless, Fort
Ellice had been an important and even crucial institution during their transition to
life in Canada.

Between late 1862 and 1870, the Dakota who fled to Canada from the United States
were pressed to use all of the skill they commanded simply to keep alive. Their
traditional skills at diplomacy, polished through at least a century of dealing with
representatives of the French, British and Americans, as well as with other Indian
nations, secured the rights to land and resources without which survival would have
been impossible. They then turned to establishing the basics of an economy by
hunting, fishing, trapping, selling commodities, and by seeking work when it was
available. This precarious political and economic balance protected the Dakota
from starvation and attack from hostile neighbours for the better part of a decade.

By the early 1870s, however, rapid social and political change was occurring in
Manitoba and the North-West Territories. Responsibility for government and the
administration of laws had been transferred from the Hudson's Bay Company to
federal and local authorities, lands were being surveyed and opened for settlement,
treaties were extinguishing some Indian rights on the prairies, the North West
Mounted Police force was established, plans were laid for railroad and telegraph
connections with the east, mail services were improved, and emigration from the
old provinces was being actively promoted. As well, animal resources were
diminishing throughout the prairie region and expansion of the settler-military fron-

tier in the United States promised that even less game would move north of the Missouri. The survey of the international boundary would soon place even greater restrictions on the north-south movement of hunters.

The Dakota had witnessed similar events in Minnesota during the previous decade. The signs were clear, and within weeks of Archibald's installation as lieutenant governor of the new province in September 1870, a delegation of Dakota arrived at Fort Garry to seek lands of their own.

Surviving the early years, 1863 to 1875

3

By the mid-1870s, there were about 1,780 Dakota in western Canada. Some two hundred lived in the five camps near Portage la Prairie. Further west there were two hundred people on the Assiniboine, five hundred at Oak Lake, and 155 near Fort Ellice. H'damani had 125 Dakota with him at Turtle Mountain, and there were about 340 in the vicinity of Fort Qu'Appelle, and 260 on the North Saskatchewan. It took two generations for all of the Dakota in Canada to secure reserve lands. For most of the 1870s, H'damani's band, and the bands further to the west, maintained a lifestyle that was essentially unchanged since the 1860s – hunting, fishing, trapping and gathering, supplemented by trade and occasional wage employment. The bands near the central Assiniboine River, however, intended to farm. For that, they needed a secure and productive land base.

The early 1870s was none too soon for the Dakota to acquire lands. Progress in all its many shapes and forms was opening the West. As the treaties were signed, settlers, land speculators and merchants followed. The network of cart trails out of the Red River district proliferated, and heavy wagons, suitable for transporting settlers and their gear, began to replace the two-wheeled oxcart. As the International Boundary Commission worked its way across the plains, settlers followed, using the good trails established by the surveyors. Riverboats had made it as far up the Missouri as Fort Benton during the previous decade, and by the mid-1870s, boats were travelling the Assiniboine as far as Fort Ellice, and later, Fort Pelly. Smallpox swept through the West in 1871, killing many Blackfoot and Cree, who were already weakened by war. American traders carried whiskey into British territory, massacring Indians who tried to keep them out of their lands.

These threats to the West limited Dakota expansion in that direction, and may have contributed to their decision to stay in Manitoba and the eastern part of the

Northwest Territories. About this time, shortly after Lieutenant Governor Archibald took office in 1870, the Dakota began to frequent the Hudson's Bay Company store at Fort Garry to see him. The lieutenant governor was empowered to deal with Indian concerns, including land matters.

By the early 1870s, the Assiniboine River from Winnipeg to Portage la Prairie was fringed with river lots. The Whitemud and Rat rivers, favoured lands of the Dakota, were settled by 1871, and farmers were even moving away from the river banks and onto the prairie itself. All of this looked familiar to the Dakota, who were able to see the consequences of large-scale immigration as clearly as were the officials and entrepreneurs in the rapidly growing city of Winnipeg. The sites best suited for farming and close to transportation would be taken up first. Considering the fact that the Dakota approached Archibald within weeks of his arrival at Red River, they must have been among the first to request agricultural lands of the government, but it was not until five years later that some of the Dakota were actually settled on a reserve. They were able to escape the full effects of this extraordinary delay only because of the great depression of 1874 and 1875; and the locusts of 1875 and 1876, had at least temporarily flattened pioneer enthusiasm.

In early 1872, the Dakota appeal for land, which had been addressed to the government through the lieutenant governor of Manitoba, was finally placed before the governor general.[1] The Dominion government had considerable difficulty with the Dakota request because in its view the Dakota were American Indians who had no rights in the Northwest, much less to have land there. The practical problem of getting the Dakota out of the province and territory, however, made both local and distant authorities quite receptive to any positive evaluations of them. William Spragge, the Indian commissioner for the North-West Territories, penned a most convincing argument about why the Dakota should be allowed lands in Canada: "To the foreign immigrant of white blood who applies for land, no objection is made, providing he be an orderly law abiding man. And the question, should these expatriate red people have granted to them a few hundred acres of land wheron to establish their homes, is to be met."[2]

Spragge reported that six hundred Dakota had claimed consideration from the Crown, saying that their ancestors had been faithful allies, and producing four or five King George III medals as proof. While supporting the idea of a reserve, Spragge dismissed their claim of rights, and wrote that the Dakota, "having no territorial rights appertaining to the territory, it is to the goodwill of the Government towards them that they must look for such appropriations of land as may be set apart for their benefit."[3] However, he did feel that more recent history gave some limited support for the Dakota claim and suggested that "in considering the present claim it will be proper to keep in view that this Band, although a foreign one, had localized itself previously to the North West being brought within the Dominion, and that from the Hudson's Bay Company they had received occasional presents."[4]

By January 1872, Spragge had had considerable contact with the Dakota, and reported them to be "a well disposed class of Indians" and recommended that a reserve be set aside. Governor Archibald wrote the secretary of state for the provinces, Joseph Howe, to endorse this proposal. The government required a mere six months to make their final policy decision, when the Dakota reserve was approved in principle.[5] Many months passed, however, before the reserve was a reality.

Spragge had estimated that there were eighty families in the band and suggested that a hundred acres be given to each. He finally recommended giving twelve thousand acres so that there would be sufficient agricultural land after allowing for indifferent farm lands. He defended the generosity of his plan by pointing out that the Indians who had signed Treaties One and Two received 160 acres per family, as well as other benefits that were not offered to the Dakota.[6]

In June 1872, Spragge reported that an Order in Council had been passed authorizing a hundred acres for each family of Dakota residing near the English communities of the Assiniboine. Word spread quickly to the other Dakota bands. In the summer of 1872, the Dakota at Fort Ellice, then outside of Manitoba, made known their interest in acquiring lands and intended to travel to Fort Garry to speak to the lieutenant governor.[7]

Locating and populating the reserve was delayed over the summer of 1872. Wemys Simpson, the Indian commissioner for Manitoba, had been alerted that he would be responsible for settling the Dakota and he visited their camps at Portage la Prairie several times over the summer and autumn. The Dakota were confused about their future and unsure about what to do while awaiting action. Their confusion and apparent aimlessness was frightening the settlers and making the neighbouring Ojibwa wary. Simpson urged that steps be taken quickly to select the lands for the reserve and move the Dakota upon it.[8]

Alexander Morris, who succeeded Archibald as lieutenant governor in 1872, seems not to have known that a reserve had been approved. When he entered office, he resumed the campaign for a Dakota reserve, and in so doing introduced more confusion. In mid-December of 1872, Morris had cited a figure of nine hundred as the population of Dakota wintering at Portage la Prairie, a number considerably higher than Spragge's estimate. He had also recommended that the reserve be located on the Souris River so as to "remove a serious annoyance from the western portion of the province," and proposed that, once on the reserve, the Dakota be given "certain presents," again contradicting Spragge's earlier advice that the Dakota be given nothing whatever except the reserve land.[9]

While officials in Ottawa mulled over these discrepancies, Morris met with a party of eighteen Dakota men, including Wambdiska and Tatankanaje, who had travelled to Fort Garry to visit the lieutenant governor. Morris wrote that they "came to testify, White Eagle said, to their friendship with the English. They had clasped hands with them and could never let them go." They asked that they be given lands to take up in the spring, and Morris promised to ask for a reserve on their behalf. He was apparently unaware that Tatankanaje had no intention of moving from the Qu'Appelle district where he had settled with his father a decade earlier. What the Dakota chief sought was a separate reserve that could be used as a home when he and his people were not hunting buffalo with the Cree and Métis on the northern prairie.[10]

Even though introducing some confusion, Morris's and Simpson's letters had the desired effect, that of prompting action from Ottawa. Spragge was directed to prepare a briefing paper for his Minister and to spell out what he recommended for the Dakota. This he did on the last day of 1872. He reduced his proposal from a hundred to eighty acres for each family, but "with the understanding that an additional quantity will be reserved should their actual numbers require it."[11] He rejected the idea that the reserve be located on the Souris River, because there the Dakota would be too close to their old enemies across the boundary. He recommended that the precise location of the reserve be "left open for future arrangement."[12]

Joseph Howe submitted the whole of Spragge's report to the Privy Council, and on January 4, 1873, it was approved by the governor general. This order in council incorporated three points that would later form the basis of policy for dealing with Dakota land matters: eighty acres of land would be allowed for each family, the reserve was subject to increase if warranted, and Dakota reserves would be located well away from the international boundary.[13]

Morris was notified by telegram of the Order in Council, and Molyneaux St. John, Indian agent for the Province of Manitoba, was directed to prepare for land selection as early as possible in the spring. St. John made himself ready and asked that he be assigned a guide familiar with the country so as "to ensure the selection of a place which while adapted to the wants of the Indians would not withdraw from settlement land suitable for incoming agriculturists."[14]

A further Order in Council, dated April 24, 1873, recognized that the Dakota would be "remaining under the British Flag," and proposed that the band should be placed "in a proper locality in the vicinity of Lake Manitoba."[15] (This act was later interpreted to define the Dakota as "Status Indians," even if not "Treaty Indians.") The order was wired to Morris, and on June 6, he met with the Dakota chiefs to prepare them for selecting and taking up the reserve. He advised the Dakota that their American relatives could not join them on the reserve and that it was set aside solely for those who had been in Canada for the previous twelve years. He "impressed upon them the necessity for their being orderly and quiet; told them that they must on no account trouble the settlers or the other Indians, and must go at once on to their reserve lands – all of which they promised." After they had settled on their reserve in the autumn, they would receive axes, fish hooks, muskrat darts, twine and ammunition. Morris also promised to request seed, hoes, oxen and ploughs for the spring, and concluded that he thought there was "reason to believe that the band would settle down and become useful."[16]

Morris had asked that a surveyor be assigned to lay out the boundaries of the reserve, a process which took considerably longer than the fourteen days Morris promised the chiefs. But, in August, when the Dakota chiefs arrived in Fort Garry to assess the delay, Morris was able to send them back with surveyor Russell and Indian Commissioner J.A.N. Provencher to select their lands.[17] When the train of surveyors and Indians was within twenty miles of the site selected by the government, however, the Dakota realized that they were being taken onto Ojibwa land.[18] They had established peace with the Saulteaux some years earlier, and it was with Saulteaux agreement that they occupied the lands they did. The Dakota, by refusing to take up what were clearly Ojibwa lands, were conforming to the terms of the peace agreement. Their own history had taught the Dakota that there was no honour in violating such agreements, and no value in being surrounded by hostile neighbours. Provencher placed little credence in such agreements and had ordered the surveyor to proceed. He totally misread the situation.

In 1872, the International Boundary Commission had begun to survey the border between Canada and the United States, and by 1873 had started to work across the prairies. In September, Captain D.R. Cameron of the Boundary Commission reported that the Dakota residing in the Turtle Mountains had pressed him to ask the authorities on their behalf for a reserve at Oak Lake.[19]

In late December 1873, Morris was contemplating this recent and new request for a reserve when some chiefs of the Dakota who had been promised land but not yet settled on a site arrived at his office to find out what was going on. Morris "enquired what was about the number of Sioux Indians, now in the Province, and was informed that there were between 400 and 500 men, probably representing about 1,500 persons in all." This was considerably more than there were reported to be in 1872. The lieutenant governor could not tell them much new about their lands, but assured them that "as the spring opened, [he] would send some person to meet them and show them the reserve selected for them on the west shore of Lake Manitoba."[20]

Within a few days, Morris was again visited by representatives of the Dakota. This time, Taninyahdinazin made the journey to speak for himself. At the meeting in late December 1873, Wambdiska had allowed the discussion to centre on a reserve on Lake Manitoba, a reserve which the Dakota had already rejected. Taninyahdinazin, however, speaking as the hereditary chief of the band, set the matter straight, as was recorded by Morris: "I learn that the Sioux desire to be placed, not on the west of the Lake Manitoba, but at the junction of the Little Saskatchewan and the Assiniboine Rivers." As will be seen, even this understanding was flawed, since the Dakota had intended to identify the junction of the Berry River (now called the Oak River) with the Assiniboine, not the Little Saskatchewan as Morris believed. At least, a site within the area approved for the Dakota by the Ojibwa was now being contemplated. No immediate action was planned until Morris and the Dakota had decided upon a location acceptable to all.[21]

Later, in January 1874, another request for land was submitted to the Crown through the officers of the International Boundary Commission. Arthur Hill, storekeeper at the Commission's Turtle Mountain depot, wrote two letters for H'damani. The first contains H'damani's petition for lands.

I Aahdamane – a Dakota of the Mocktow Band – desire to have the grant of land from the Queen which is to be given to each of us, in the Turtle Mountain, in a part where you think the land is good. I speak for myself and my three sons. We have been in this place for twelve years.

I saw the Ojibwa here and gave him four horses and five sacred pipes.

The Chief Warrior of the Ojibwa give the Turtle Mountains to me and my people.

I want some land from the Queen for myself and my three sons – and at present know not where they intend to send us.

If you will let what I say be known and tell me what they say, I would be very grateful. My God hears what I say.[22]

This brief note contains much of interest. H'damani identified himself as a member of the Mocktow Band, a misrepresentation of the Dakota phrase *ma-k' a'to* (or blue earth). In Minnesota, H'damani and his family were a part of Mazaska's village and part of the Wahpetonwon branch of the Dakota nation. The chiefs who had up to then been promised reserve lands in Canada were of different political realms at the band and village levels. Since H'damani was not identified as a part of Taninyahdinazin's or Wambdiska's followers, he asked for lands in his own right, and more specifically, for himself and his three sons. This latter point was to be the cause of considerable bitterness in coming years.

Another issue raised by this letter was the agreement between H'damani and the "Chief Warrior of the Ojibwa." Again, this would be a transaction quite in keeping with Dakota diplomacy, as the transfer of land use rights was a key feature of international agreements to which the Dakota were a party. Certainly, the Ojibwa rarely entered the territory after the Dakota took up occupancy, and the Dakota lived there many years free from any threat directed at them by the Ojibwa.

H'damani's second note was a plea for supplies to help get through a particularly trying winter. Hill found H'damani to be "a very good Indian and firmly attached to the British. He seems to be afraid of being left out by his absence from the settlement during the disposal of the rest of the Sioux by the government."[23]

In the spring of 1874, a rumour was being spread throughout the Dakota bands that the Boundary Commission's store was nothing more than a ruse to attract them close enough to the border that American troops could sweep upon them and carry the Dakota back to sure punishment in the United States. Arthur Hill wrote his superior, Captain Cameron, that the Ihanktonwon were warring with the Americans on the Missouri and that the battle could interfere with the Commission's work, especially since the Canadian and American surveyors were travelling together. With his own letter, Hill also enclosed a note from Bogaga, one of H'damani's people, who asked for garden seeds and a few small agricultural tools. Considering the circumstances, Cameron wished to show the good faith of the Commission and the government. When he forwarded Hill's correspondence, he implored Morris "to cause Bogagah's petition for seeds to be complied with in such an official manner as may clearly indicate to him and his companions the friendly disposition of the British authorities towards the Sioux."[24] Morris immediately cautioned Cameron not to do anything that would give the Dakota reason to believe that they enjoyed the favour and recognition of the Crown, and this included the giving of seeds to Bogaga. Cameron hastily corrected himself. "The possibility of the Sioux construing a gift from the government as an invitation to them to stay at Turtle Mountain or at least as a recognition of their title to remain there is one which had not occurred to me – but when mentioned is self evident. . . . I have avoided punctiliously raising any definite expectations in their minds. I assured them of British friendliness and left them in doubt as to whether they would ever be acknowledged as British themselves."[25] Instead, Cameron suggested that the controversial seeds be given simply as a gift from the commission and not from the government. This was acceptable to Morris, but he had no comment to make on the request for another reserve.

The season for planting crops was fast approaching and in mid-May, H'damani, representing his band of twenty-five tents, and Weeokeah, at the head of a hundred tents of M'dewakontonwon and Wahpetonwon, again approached Hill about lands. In response, Morris wrote that "it is the policy of the Government that all the Sioux should be upon the reserve allotted to them and not at Turtle Mountain or any other place, the contiguity of which to the U.S. frontier might result in difficulty."[26]

In April, David Laird, minister of the interior, had approved a reserve site on the Assiniboine, but it was also thought that eight thousand acres would be sufficient and that all the Dakota at Portage la Prairie, Turtle Mountain, Fort Ellice and Oak

Lake should be sent there. The option of the Lake Manitoba site for the reserve was kept open. The appropriate Order in Council was passed on April 27, 1874, and two days later, Morris was advised by telegram.[27] Shortly after, Morris was visited by Wambdiska and Antoine, a member of his band. They asked that their band be located on the Assiniboine River. "This we ask as a matter of favour and good will from the Queen. In asking this we agree to settle on the reserve and pledge ourselves that we will live at peace with Her Majesty's white subjects and other Indian tribes, and will obey all the commands and laws of Her Majesty."[28]

Morris agreed with this request and, accepting the Dakota pledge, telegraphed Minister of the Interior Laird, indicating that a final selection of the reserve site had been made.[29] By early July, however, the site had still not been approved. Again the chiefs came in to Fort Garry to speak with Morris.

On this occasion, Morris was visited by a party of 150 Dakota led by Mahtomani and Taninyahdinazin. They asked Morris to allocate a separate reserve for their people, but Morris reminded them that they, along with all other chiefs in Canada, had signed an agreement to accept the lands approved for all the Dakota in Canada.[30] The chiefs conceded that they had made this commitment, and Morris was able to report that he thought it to be "a very fortunate circumstance that I have been enabled to induce these people to agree to settle down at a point far removed from the frontier and our own white settlements."[31] Two days later, David Laird instructed W. Wagner of the Dominion Lands Survey to lay off the approved reserve. He requested that Morris provide Wagner with the number of Indians who were to be located there.[32]

About this time, news came into Red River of an attack upon the Métis of St. Joseph (now Valhalla), Minnesota. The Dakota, more particularly the Dakota in Canada, were suspected, and, under pressure from both sides of the border, Morris ordered Molyneaux St. John to investigate. Morris sent along a prepared text to be delivered to the assembled Dakota at Portage la Prairie, warning them that if they persisted in visiting the United States, they would lose both their promised reserve lands and the protection of the Crown. St. John was told by the Dakota that, "since the time, twelve years ago, when they first came into English territory, they had remained at peace with everyone, putting aside the remembrance of all former acts and keeping steadily to the words that had been spoken to them by the Chief of the Whites."[33]

As to the matter of taking up the reserve, St. John was told that the Dakota had been assured by Morris that they would be able to remain in their old camps where they could continue to work for settlers until the autumn. A few men were prepared to go to the reserve immediately in order to prepare land for seeding the next spring. St. John explained the delay: "The Sioux resident in Manitoba are divided into five camps, the first of which is a little westward of Poplar Point and the last or westernmost one at Rat Creek some few miles beyond Portage la Prairie. They are thus scattered for the better convenience of working on the farms in that district, and I mention this because it indirectly aids to bear out their assertion that they have no thought of war with anyone, Americans or Indians, and that their only desire is to live at peace and cultivate the land."[34]

Matters were then left until after the harvest season. In late summer, Lieutenant Governor Morris and David Laird travelled into the North-West Territories to visit the Indians on the plains in preparation for the making of Treaty Four. On September 16, 1874, they met with the Dakota at the Qu'Appelle Lakes. Morris wrote that he talked with "a party of Sioux from the Woody Mountains, headed by the Chiefs 'White Cap,' 'Little Standing Buffalo' and 'The Crow' – representing in all some six hundred souls, as nearly as I could estimate them." He went on to record that he found that "this tribe are generally in Manitoba and at Fort Ellice displaying a disposition to work for the settlers and others in harvesting the crops, making hay, cutting fence rails and doing farm labour – a fact which gives great encouragement as to their future, if arrangements can be effected for settling them, which I anticipate can be done."[35]

Here Morris makes a significant, but not particularly harmful error in identifying these bands. Very few of the Indians attached to these chiefs were at that time engaged in agricultural labour, and few had been to Manitoba after the early 1860s, when they had established themselves farther to the west. This mistaken history worked to the advantage of these bands, in that a plea for lands from hard-working, farm-oriented Indians was viewed with much more favour than would one coming from buffalo-hunting nomads.

In discussions with Morris, Wapahaska told the lieutenant governor that he had 140 lodges with him, and that all wished to remain under the protection of the British, a position which they had enjoyed during the previous twelve years. Morris told the Dakota to keep well away from the international boundary and the Americans. He explained that the Queen had allowed a reserve on the Assiniboine River for the Dakota. In speaking for his people, Tatankanaje told Morris that he, like his father and grandfather, was loyal to the British, and had great faith that the Crown would treat him honourably. However, both Tatankanaje and Wapahaska stated that the reserve on the Assiniboine would not be adequate for the western Dakota, as there was no room for horses and no herds of buffalo to hunt. Morris replied that the day was coming when there would be no buffalo anywhere, and that the bands should look to settling down with their relatives. He encouraged them to go and examine the proposed reserve and tell him what they thought. This the chiefs promised to do, and as a pledge, Kangiunginca gave Morris his sacred pipe, "the pipe of peace that makes the peace strong."[36]

Morris could not have received a greater token of sincerity than the pipe given to him by Kangiunginca.[37] Morris must have understood the Dakota's concerns, for he did not insist that they go to the reserve set aside for the bands in Manitoba. Rather, he merely asked that they look at the lands and then let him know if they found them to be acceptable or not.

On their return journey from Fort Qu'Appelle, Morris and Laird met with the Dakota at Fort Ellice. Mahpiyahdinape told Morris that he had gone to look at the location where the reserve had been set aside, but found it wanting a good supply of wood. He and his thirty-one lodges, each housing five people, wished to remain on the Birdtail River, where they had been camped for the previous twelve years. Morris could promise nothing and instead asked that they go again to the place selected; perhaps the chiefs would change their minds now that the survey of the reserve had been completed and they could see exactly what lands were included within its limits. Mahpiyahdinape agreed and reaffirmed their good faith by once more reciting their history of alliance with the British Crown and by displaying the medals given to the band's grandfathers, since passed to their fathers and finally kept by the current generation. As with the Dakota at Fort Qu'Appelle, Morris could make no promises, but his letters make it clear that he had no quarrel with the Dakota at Fort Ellice. In due course, Mahpiyahdinape's wish for a reserve on the Birdtail was granted.[38]

Soon after his return to Fort Garry, Morris was notified by William Wagner that the survey of the reserve on the Little Saskatchewan and Assiniboine rivers had been completed. Wagner had been accompanied by Wambdiska, who had observed that there was little wood within the limits of the reserve: "There is timber enough there itself for a settlement of agriculturists but should the Chief of this Band of Indians not be satisfied with the quantity of wood and wish to ascend more up the Assiniboine more into the wooded part it may be perhaps quite judicious to let them, and retain this portion of the country for a more profitable settlement, since when once the Pacific Railway crosses these prairies, the settlement will rapidly extend to these regions and will eventually prove to the Exchequer of the Dominion more remunerative than a few hundred families of Sioux Indians."[39]

Wagner anticipated what was later to become the primary reason for the Dakota rejection of the reserve – insufficient wood. The time had come for the bands to move, however, and Molyneaux St. John was delegated to take the Dakota to the reserve as soon as the harvest season ended. When he arrived at Portage la Prairie, St. John found that all but one band had left as soon as their harvesting jobs ended. They had gone to fish in Lake Manitoba, and had let it be known through the Dakota who remained near the settlements that they were not going to move onto the reserve. St. John had taken with him the oxen, wagons, seed and implements that had been promised the bands, and he could wait no longer, as the season was quite advanced. When he arrived at the reserve site, he found forty men, women and children in seven lodges awaiting his arrival. St. John was pleased that the people had arrived as families with all of their possessions; had only the men come and the women remained at the settlements, he felt it would be a matter of only a short time before the men drifted back to their families.

St. John immediately distributed the implements he had brought and the men and women set to work erecting stables for the oxen, cutting hay and breaking the prairie soil. St. John reported that "the women in an Indian camp are generally as good workers as the men." St. John made a tour of the reserve and, like the Dakota, saw that it was "not sufficiently wooded for Indian occupation." While he was considering this problem, Mahpiyahdinape came into his camp with a letter from Surveyor Wagner. The chief from Fort Ellice had been instructed to go and look at the reserve and decide if it might be a good place for him to settle. Mahpiyahdinape, however, "had already twice examined the place and was emphatic in his opinion that it would not support the Indians for whom it was intended. This man spoke very good English and from the experiments in raising crops which he said he made in various localities which he named, appeared to be a man of intelligence. I mentioned to him . . . that such a reservation would be gladly accepted by the Mennonites and his reply was that the land was good and that for careful whitemen the wood might be sufficient but that for Indians there was none."[40]

Mahpiyahdinape argued that the lieutenant governor had told him that if the reserve was not adequate, then he might allow a reserve to be selected on the Birdtail River. Wambdiska and Taninyahdinazin objected to this, saying that even though the reserve was not all that they wanted, they would rather stay there than move onto a reserve with Mahpiyahdinape. St. John found that there were three hundred lodges of Dakota west of Manitoba, and he was "quite sure that if any such array of lodges were to settle on the Reservation it would very shortly be completely stript of what wood there is on it. " Even his interpreter told him that he himself would not settle on the reserve for fear of freezing.

St. John concluded that the Dakota would, if compelled, take up the reserve that had been surveyed, "for the Indians had selected it themselves," but he did not expect them to remain there. He wrote that if the government was indifferent to where the Dakota roamed, and only intended the reserve to be a home base, then the place was as good as any. If it was intended that the Dakota settle permanently, then the reserve was inadequate. Again, Wambdiska told St. John that the Dakota had not selected the location of the reserve. They had intended to indicate the joining of the Berry Creek and the Assiniboine, some twelve miles further west, where there was plenty of wood and good farm soil. At this, St. John determined to return to Winnipeg with Wambdiska to discuss the problem with Lieutenant Governor Morris.

Before St. John left, the Dakota set to work preparing for winter and the next spring's planting. The oxen were left in care of Wambdiska, and St. John directed that two large meadows were to be available as haylands for all the Dakota; they were not to be kept by one or two individuals to the exclusion of the rest. One or two families intended to winter in the Turtle Mountains hunting, and St. John arranged for a supply of food for those who were to remain on the reserve. When he passed through the Portage la Prairie district, he met a party of the Dakota who had refused to move to the reserve. He lectured this party on the error of their ways.

Most of these men know that their lives depend upon the forbearance and protection of the British authorities and have therefore a very proper fear of displeasing the government. I learnt while with them at various times that they are not altogether free from danger even amongst their own nation. The Sioux of the Missouri are much harassed by American troops and are regarded with deadly enmity by all American settlers and frontiersmen. They attribute this to the misdeeds of the Sioux who are now in the Province of Manitoba and the gulf between them has been somewhat widened by the refusal of the Manitoba Sioux to join their brethren on the plains against the Americans. They are not therefore in a position to disobey the instructions they may receive from the Dominion Government, even were they disposed to do so.[41]

At the time they first discussed the reserve with Lieutenant Governor Morris, the Dakota believed that the lands they had identified as most acceptable were located upon the Oak River, not the Little Saskatchewan. The error could have been discovered mere days before their departure for the reserve and what could they do? As St. John's report illustrates, the Dakota had every reason not to raise the ire of the government, especially a government represented by people who were only too quick at bringing up the spectre of deportation to the United States. The manner in which the Dakota attempted to deal with this problem may be criticized, but their very reaction, which threatened the reserve they had so long sought, indicates the extent of confusion in the Dakota community at that time.

The Dakota were not as unified as St. John seems to have expected. There were at least ten separate Dakota bands in Canada, each with its own internal political structures and distinctive lifestyles. It seems likely that the bands in the vicinity of Portage la Prairie, having been told that they would get only one reserve for all of them, decided that they would move to the lands on the Assiniboine. This was a compromise because the band preferred a separate reserve. When this decision seemed to be leading them to the Little Saskatchewan, rather than to the Oak River as they thought, some of the lodges simply refused to go. This rupture was permanent and the Dakota who remained at Portage la Prairie were never induced to leave the area, and they remain there to this day.

St. John certainly did the right thing in returning to Fort Garry with Wambdiska in order to have these conflicts discussed with the appropriate decision makers. Wambdiska told Morris that four lodges were willing to winter at the reserve, even if there was not enough wood for fires. Morris invited Wambdiska to speak freely on whatever concerned him. Wambdiska replied," I will accept your goodness, even if I starve with cold and hunger. I do not want to find fault with the Reserve, but there is not wood enough for the Sioux to live there. I would like to go beyond Berry Creek (Oak River), that there might be wood for the winter."[42]

When he later discussed the problem with St. John, Morris concluded that there was very likely not enough wood on the reserve. Furthermore, if three hundred lodges of Dakota were seeking a reserve, perhaps it would be best to consider separate lands for Wambdiska, Mahpiyahdinape and Wapahaska. Morris wrote to Ottawa to justify his advice in favour of separate reserves. "First, I now doubt if it would be good policy to collect so large a body of Sioux in our locality and, Secondly, the tribe affords much aid to the settlers, by working as farm labourers, that in view of the high price of labour here, I am disposed to think that the settlement of the Sioux in localities whence they could work in the settlements, would then have a tendency to induce white Settlers to select localities, in the Territories, for settlement, convenient to this source of labour."[43]

This was a most favourable report as far as Dakota interests were concerned. After late 1874, the government abandoned the idea of placing all of the Dakota upon one reserve. Band requirements were accepted as differing in major aspects, and considerable effort was made to comply with the requests for separate ~reserves. The Dakota, however, would have been amused to learn that they were now being seen not as the "Scourge of the Plains," but as a positive part of prairie life whose experienced labour would attract rather than repel settlers. In this, however, ~Morris was correct, and almost from the day the Dakota settled upon their reserves, their neighbours were eager to hire them.

Morris's suggestions were approved by Surveyor General Wagner, who appended a note that "Mr. St. John should at the same time obtain a surrender, if necessary, of any and all claim on the part of the Sioux to the land contained within the previous reservation."[44] On November 10, 1874, the ministry of the interior submitted a recommendation to the Privy Council that incorporated all of the suggestions made by St. John, Morris and Wagner. On November 12, the separate reserves were approved by Order in Council.[45]

The first of these reserves was surveyed at Oak River, where the Dakota wanted it, in the spring of 1875.[46] Shortly after the reserve was selected and surveyed, Morris paid a visit to the Dakota still at Portage la Prairie, intending to persuade them to leave for the reserve. During his stay in the settler community, Morris found that

> . . . a portion of the settlers were averse to their removal, as the men are useful to them, in farm labour, and the women in household work. Efforts had been made by certain parties to impress the Sioux with the belief, that it was not to their interest to remove to the reserve, as they would be confined on it and would not be able to hunt. They now live by their labour, and by hunting and fishing at Lake Manitoba.
>
> I succeeded in removing the erroneous impression, and caused them to be assured, that while the reserve was to be their home, they would be at liberty to hunt and fish, and their men could in the ploughing and harvest seasons, hire out their labour, taking care to plant and harvest their own crops.[47]

Even while giving his assurances, however, Morris hesitated to oblige the Dakota to move to the reserve. Early in the spring of 1875, it was clear that the prairies would be overrun with grasshoppers, and if the Dakota lost their crops on the reserve, Morris "did not see how they could find the means of living on the reserve next winter, as they could not there get fish, as they can at the lake."[48] Morris was prepared to "await the course of events," but he soon learned that many of the lodges had left the Whitemud River camp and gone to the reserve, anxious to get their crops planted. While at Portage la Prairie, Morris learned that H'damani's band wished to remain at Turtle Mountain, but this he refused, insisting that they move to Oak River. Morris was "very confident that the Sioux can be induced to combine growing crops, with the pursuit of game, fur-bearing animals and fishing, and eventually, to adopt the habits of civilization."[49]

When Morris returned to Fort Garry from Portage la Prairie, Indian Commissioner Provencher went on to Fort Ellice to select the reserve for Mahpiyahdinape's people. By early June, Provencher had completed his task and presented to Morris what he described as a surrender of the reserve already approved at the Little Saskatchewan. It was later found that the document did not constitute a surrender and that, in any event, he had taken the "surrender" from the wrong band of Dakota. This error has never been corrected, but the main purpose of Provencher's expedition was accomplished – the band of Dakota at Fort Ellice had the reserve they wanted and exactly where they wanted it.[50]

By mid-July, William Wagner had laid out the Oak River and Birdtail reserves and the Dakota were making all efforts to get their gardens in and houses started. Thus the first two Dakota reserves in Canada were allotted and occupied.

On September 10, 1875, Indian Commissioner W.I. Christie met with Wapahaska at Fort Qu'Appelle, where Christie was meeting with the Cree and Saulteaux bands about to enter treaty. Wapahaska told Christie that he did not wish to move to the reserve on the Assiniboine. He and his fifty-two lodges preferred to remain on the western prairie, hunting with the Métis. When Morris received Christie's report, he sent a letter to Wapahaska and Tatankanaje encouraging them to find lands that they would take for their reserve, and then to notify him of their decision.[51] A year later, Tatankanaje did make his selection, but when his application was received in Ottawa, David Laird could not believe that Morris had promised the chief that he could select his own reserve lands. The establishment of the more westerly reserves would await another year until this disagreement was settled.[52]

At this point, when all of the Dakota in the North West had identified themselves and their land needs to the government, the land and economic concerns of each band began to diverge more sharply. From this time on, the bands became firmly connected to particular lands, and it is best to consider their histories separately. The Dakota selected their lands with careful planning, and since the bands did not all share a single vision of the future, they needed various environments in which to continue and develop their differing lifestyles. By this time, however, policy for the establishment of Dakota reserves in Canada had been established with the allocation of the Oak River and Birdtail reserves. The future setting aside of land was guided by the experiences of 1874 and 1875 – the Dakota would be allowed to select their own reserve sites; they would receive lands on the basis of eighty acres per family of five; all land allotments would be as a benefit from the Crown, not as a matter of right; and the reserves could later be increased in size, as requirements demanded.

Over the years during which the Dakota negotiated their first land agreement with the Crown, they attempted as best they could to support themselves in the environment and economy of the far West. As early as 1866, a part of the population that had settled at Portage la Prairie moved west to the vicinity of Oak Lake. This reduction of people at Portage la Prairie eased the competition for jobs and resources available in that area, and the remaining Dakota quickly moved to take advantage of the demand for farm labour. They were so successful at using the skills they had acquired while still in Minnesota, that even before Archibald was approached for reserve land in 1871, they had made clear their reluctance to move away from the economic opportunities they had created for themselves. Indeed, when it was first learned that a reserve outside the boundaries of Manitoba was being contemplated, a petition was circulated around Portage la Prairie asking that the Dakota not be forced away. This petition, which was signed by three members of the provincial legislature and a Presbyterian clergyman, is one of the few documents that even acknowledges a Dakota claim of rights on Canadian soil:

We the undersigned do hereby petition in behalf of the tribe of Aborigines who have ever been faithful to the British Crown for many generations. The same are now among us in a destitute condition in consequence of a misunderstanding between the Americans and them and ever since they have been among us they have behaved more like Christians than heathens. For proof of their loyalty they have now in their possession a British Flag and several medals which they have retained through four Monarch's reigns. A Flag which neither savage nor civilized men could wrest from them. We humbly ask that you will grant them a home in perpetuity. And your petitioners will ever pray.[53]

Of primary concern to the petitioners, of course, was the willingness and ability of the Dakota to perform farm labour in the countryside and domestic labour in the communities. One settler's anecdote outlined how some of the Dakota were making a living just before they moved onto the Oak River Reserve. In 1875, William Taylor, a local settler, wrote of a fishing trip that he undertook to Lake Manitoba from the settlement of Woodlands.

The Sue Indians had caught 100 [fish], so they bought and traded with the Red Man, bread, flour, shots, tea, tobacco, etc. for fish and by that means they brought a few home. The Sue Indians work a little making baskets, etc., but the squaws chop wood, scrub and do lots of dirty work in their [the settlers'] shanties; the men can be hired for a trifle to go and fish all day at the lake. One of the party just mentioned hired a young Indian to go along with them to fish, but they could not induce him to ride, and all the way, though the distance was 20 miles, he ran along with them, and when they returned, he was the last to start, but he got the lead and kept it, and they whipped their ponies up and run them fast for a long way to try to beat him, yet he kept his ground, taking the lead all the way home. It is wonderful how wiry and smart they all are, though they live so poor and are very thinly clad, anxiously waiting all winter for the spring; they can cure hides, make nice robes of a ox hide, and they are not worth much here – about $1. each, and they cure them for $2.50, so we get a nice robe for $3-$4, and they are better than a buffalo robe for wear.[54]

This was obviously not an easy life, but it was a sustaining one nonetheless. The movement of some of the M'dewakontonwon to Oak Lake eased pressures on local income sources, but at the same time added to those further west, where the Turtle Mountain and Souris River regions were already occupied by H'damani and Wambdiska and Taninyahdinazin. This acted as an additional incentive for the latter two chiefs to make an early application for lands. When they and their two hundred followers moved into the vicinity of Portage la Prairie in order to establish themselves for land negotiations, they were much resented by those Dakota already established there.

Wambdiska and Taninyahdinazin had never suggested that they wished to remain at Portage la Prairie, or have their reserve located there. They were thoroughly familiar with that area and were sensitive to the resentment of their relatives who had located there. Like the settlers, the Dakota wanted lands that offered the most for agriculturalists such as themselves – access to water and transportation, good soil, and open prairie for tilling and cutting wild hay. There were few such locales left around Portage la Prairie, but suitable sites had been identified farther west along the Assiniboine. While the Dakota at Turtle Mountain with H'damani, and the M'dewakontonwon at Oak Lake were interested mainly in carrying on with hunting, fishing and trapping, and viewed land as a site for winter housing and for cooking-pot gardens, Wambdiska and Taninyahdinazin wanted especially to farm and therefore required the best lands available.

Mahpiyahdinape and his band also wished to farm and had made crop experiments in an effort to find the best lands around Fort Ellice. For some years, the members of this band had been working as farm labourers for the Hudson's Bay Company post at Fort Ellice, and had owned a number of cattle. By 1875, it had become the practice at the post to turn their cattle over to Mahpiyahdinape's people for winter keeping, and Wahokaza, with his wife and daughter, were full-time employees of A.L. Russell, an early settler in the area.[55]

In spite of official rejection of their historic relationship with the Crown, the diplomatic efforts of the Dakota secured for the bands very much what they wanted – an acknowledged right to occupy Canadian territory, and reserves in locations most suited to their needs. It seems clear that Morris and most other officials in Manitoba recognized the aspirations of the Dakota and appreciated the fact that simply because they were all of the same ethnic and language stock and had a shared history, they did not all have the same view of the future, and lands were set aside in recognition of these differences. The differences became more marked as the years passed and the Dakota communities began to realize their economic strategies and to develop lifestyles focussed upon an identifiable plot of land.

Those Dakota with ambitions for farming moved onto the first two reserves set aside at Oak River and Birdtail Creek, and immediately set about developing the land for fields, gardens and pastures, and to build permanent houses. At the same time, they supported themselves through increased wage employment and trade, as well as hunting, fishing and gathering. They would need this versatile economy for some years to come; progress was slow on the western frontier and agriculture did not expand as rapidly as had been anticipated. By the mid-1870s, though, the Dakota were much more prepared to deal with the vagaries of progress than they had been five years earlier.

Settlement of the farmers:
Oak River, Birdtail and Oak Lake bands,
1871 to 1878

A secure land base did not immediately improve life for the Dakota. It was assumed by the provincial and federal governments, by the Department of Indian Affairs and by the Dakota themselves that the bands would very soon become settled agriculturalists. This was not to happen so quickly. The Dakota had moved onto the reserves with very little preparation. Molyneaux St. John reported to David Laird that, in September 1874, he had travelled with the first group of Dakota to settle the reserve at Oak River. He spent two days with them, imparting more "good advice" than agricultural knowledge, and then left them to their own devices. At the time, it was widely felt that the western economy was on the brink of a complete transformation. All the amenities of a fully developed economy were expected to be in place and functioning by the time the Dakota got their bearings. In fact, Canada, like most of the world, was just then moving into a long period of stagnation and depression, which did not end until the late 1870s.

The frontier of Canadian settlement reached the area slightly to the west of Portage la Prairie by the mid-1870s, but there it stopped. The first of the reserves at Oak River and Birdtail Creek were well beyond the limited area of economic integration. Stagnation and the lack of transportation affected all persons in the province and the North-West Territories, but the settlers and entrepreneurs closest to the Red River were most seriously damaged. It was impossible for them either to ship out their products or to ship in needed technology and consumer goods. In this situation, all farmers were obliged to practise what was, at best, an enhanced form of subsistence farming that had for its limited market those few "urban" people who were not themselves directly engaged in agriculture. Once that market was satisfied, there was little incentive to increase production.

The Dakota, of course, excelled at operating subsistence economies, and during

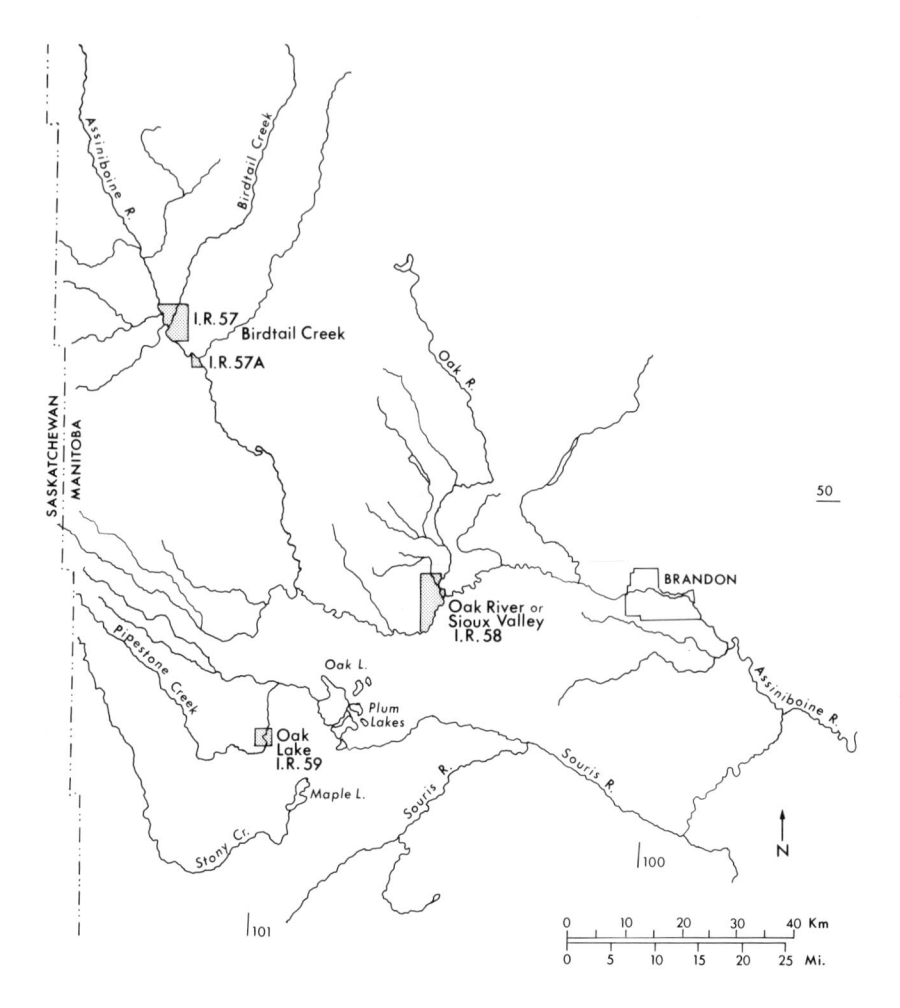

Map 4. The Oak River, Birdtail and Oak Lake reserves

the decade from the early 1870s until the 1880s, they probably did as well on the frontier as many of their distant white neighbours did. The last mention of extreme deprivation experienced by the Dakota was in the early 1870s, and from the time the reserves were allocated, the Dakota left those days forever in the past.

Not only did the hiatus in white settlement relieve the Dakota of competition for subsistence resources, such as was felt in the more densely populated Province of Manitoba, but it also spared them direct intervention by the Indian Branch. The government wanted the Dakota to have reserves not only as a site for their future economic development, but also as a home where they would be beyond white settlement. When expansion of settlement halted in the early 1870s, the government promptly forgot the Dakota. They were not Treaty Indians, had not been enumerated, and received no annuities or much else from the government, except a gift of a few farming tools. They were allowed to design their own economic strategies with a freedom not enjoyed by other Indians of the prairies, or even by the Dakota themselves since the 1840s in Minnesota.

This is not to say that the Dakota had an easy time of it; to the contrary, the first years were very hard, and reflected the combined adversity of a lack of their own economic resources, a large reserve population competing for scarce subsistence, and environmental conditions unfavourable to farming and gardening. There was not much the Dakota could do about the lack of development capital. Since they were unable to generate their own, they appealed to the government for assistance in making initial purchases of seed, cattle and implements. They were, however, able to do something about the population pressures on the subsistence resources of an unfavourable environment. By spreading the population out quite considerably, especially the larger population in the Oak River district, the Dakota commenced their economic adaptation to the Canadian West.

By the spring of 1875, a number of families had moved onto the Oak River and Birdtail reserves. They felt their future was assured. The people at Oak River immediately put their small stock of oxen to work preparing garden sites, even though it was late in the season. As well, they were able to sustain themselves with fish taken from the Assiniboine. Mahpiyahdinape and his band at the Birdtail had an advantage in that their reserve was where they had been living for over a decade, and the chief had already conducted experiments with a variety of seed there. As well, they had the long-established tradition of working for the Hudson's Bay Company at Fort Ellice, and they continued this. Finally, they too fished. As an example of the value of the fish resource, Surveyor Wagner reported that in four nights in July, the Dakota took from Birdtail Creek over twenty-five hundred fish, including three sturgeon.[1] Most of Mahpiyahdinape's people were already with him at the Birdtail Reserve, but those at the Oak River Reserve formed only a small advance party making preparations for the main emigration. Morris reported that there were still 160 lodges of Dakota around Portage la Prairie during the early summer of 1875.[2]

In July 1875, Morris had asked Kenneth McKenzie to visit the Dakota at Oak River, and report on their welfare. McKenzie was a member of Manitoba's legislature and a major farmer in the province. He had over the years employed many Dakota on his own farm, and was trusted and liked by them, a sentiment he returned. McKenzie visited the Dakota twice a year from 1875 until 1878, when the bands were assigned an Indian agent. He gave the Dakota much good practical advice with very little moralizing, and his own economic and political prestige carried a great deal of weight when he spoke on behalf of the Dakota.[3]

In his first report, McKenzie attempted to design a plan for the Oak River Band's immediate future. He recommended several short-term objectives and suggested that over the summer each family plough two acres and cut enough fencing materials to enclose the ploughed land. He wanted them to receive small seeds in the spring, especially peas, as the Dakota had no gristmill for grinding grain, and they liked the peas. If land was ready, a little seed wheat could also be planted. He recommended cows for milk and breeding. The Dakota requested pigs, which McKenzie promised to give them himself if they put up enough feed for wintering. He expected that the band would be able to plough forty to sixty acres of land for the next season, and after seeding they could open a considerable amount more, especially if they had more oxen and ploughs. He concluded that "by a little encouragement and liberal government aid, I think in a few years they would be self-sustaining or nearly so."[4]

Less than a month later, however, it was clear that this vision was a little premature. In August 1875, Morris met with Taninyahdinazin and Mahpiyahdinape at Portage la Prairie. The chiefs reported that there were thirty tents at Oak River and twenty at Birdtail Creek. All the gardens had been destroyed by grasshoppers, except for the potatoes, which were in fine condition. Morris asked when they intended moving to the reserve permanently. Taninyahdinazin replied that as they had no farm produce and no work by which they could earn their keep, they were planning to return to the Portage settlements until the following spring. Morris noted that there were only fifty tents still remaining around Portage la Prairie and High Bluff. He found their plans to be "reasonable and could not in the circumstances urge them to go to the reserve this autumn."[5]

Later, in the fall of 1875, Wambdiska went to pay a call on the lieutenant governor. He told Morris that he and Taninyahdinazin planned to stay on the reserve and take care of their oxen. He had already built a large stable and had enough feed on hand for the winter. Ten lodges of his band were to be with him, but as the grasshoppers had consumed all of their crops and gardens, he was obliged to ask for winter supplies. Morris, who described Wambdiska as a man who "displays an excellent spirit," gave each of the two camps three oxen and a plough so that they would be ready to seed crops and gardens early in 1876.

Indian Commissioner Laird later approved Morris's gift with the admonition that "it would be well that the Sioux should be given to understand that in future they must not depend on Government for aid in the matter of provisions." To that point, it might be noted, the Dakota had received food and small tools to a value of about $600. Morris had also forwarded a request from Choate and Dowaneya leaders of the Wahpetonwon who had settled near Oak Lake asking for assistance over the winter. This, too, Laird approved, on the understanding that they would both, with all of their people, go to the reserve in the spring.[6]

So, for the winter, Wambdiska, Taninyahdinazin and eighteen lodges stayed at the reserve. Most of the others and all of the people with Choate and Dowaneya went back to Portage la Prairie to work for the farmers, cut and haul wood, and fish in Lake Manitoba. Mahpiyahdinape and his people remained at the Birdtail, but even a few of this band went to look for work at Fort Ellice and Portage la Prairie.

Early in the spring of 1876, Laird was prompting Morris to have the Dakota return to the reserve. He wanted them back in time to get the most of the coming crop season, and not be forced near the settlements another winter. To this end, he sent along $800 to defray any costs. In spite of the minister's expressions of urgency, it took well over a month for the funds to be transferred to Morris's account in Winnipeg.[7] At last, by the end of June, Morris was able to arrange for the bands to go back to the Oak River Reserve.[8] The delay was most unfortunate for the Dakota. As it turned out, 1876 was a bumper-crop year, but since the Dakota did not arrive back at the reserve until early July, the growing season was too advanced for them to do much. They missed out on the last good year of the decade.

Kenneth McKenzie visited the Dakota camps toward the end of July 1876, and reported in detail:

The Portage Indians was camped at the Little Sasquatchewan at their fishing ground having left the reserve for want of provisions and very little game. There was eighteen tents of them and getting considerable fish here. They had a basket across the river here to catch them. The squaws were digging Indian turnips and drying them which seemed plentiful over the prairies. I visited the reserve next day about eighteen miles off and saw their plowing. They have it broke very irregular here and there over two or three sections of land, not more than seventeen or eighteen acres in all in eight or nine small parcels of land, some not more than half an acre, the largest not more than four acres in one place, generally about two acres in each plot ploughed. I saw two plots with seven or eight furrows not finished. When I enquired the reason for not finishing, they said their flour and provisions went down and Indians not strong to work without meat. They sowed a few turnips on some of the breakings which was too thick to mature. I pointed out the necessity to thin them to get a good crop. In one parcel of over an acre which they had cultivated well, they had about three quarters of it in potatoes, well hoed and earthed up. This looked as well as any in Manitoba. About forty hills of corn well cleaned and looking well, three small beds of onions very good and a few carrots, over twenty hills of pumpkin and squashes and a few peas.

I next visited the Poplar Point reserve about ten miles further up the river. There was ten tents of them. The men were mostly all away hunting. They have about four acres broke in two parcels. The land on this reserve is not so good. It is rather too light, sandy and gravelly, although I have seen fair crops on as poor land in Minnesota. They do not seem to be altogether satisfied with their selection.

The following day I went with White Eagle to see the first reserve they had taken up. It is near the junction of the Little Sasquatchewan and Assynaboine. The Chief, his son and an Indian named Tom had three acres ploughed here and under crop – over one acre in potatoes well cleaned and hilled, about one-fourth acre in Indian corn and potatoes were not so luxuriant here as on the other reserve, but still a fair crop, about half an acre of spring wheat. It is very short. They sowed it by far too thick. One fourth an acre of barley rather too thick sown, but still a fair crop will be ready to harvest in ten days. 1/4 acre peas looking very well, a few rows of beans and onions which was too thick. Turnip in drills and broadcast matted thick. I thinned them out to the proper distance and explained to them the necessity to ensure a good crop. They seemed very attentive and the boys and squaws set to work to thin them and was doing them very well. They plough on the whole very well as several of them ploughed for us in the settlement, but they have no idea to set their plough when out of order as we used to set them for them. I set their ploughs and let them see how to do it after they seemed quite ready to learn and plead to be instructed.

The Chief . . . has a cow stable that he built last year. A very fair one 15 feet by 21 inside and well mudded. He has his ploughs and implements carefully stowed in it. He was anxious I would tell the Big Chief to give them a few cows to give them milk. I told them I would and believed they would get two or three if they cut plenty of hay and keep all their stock fat. They said they would cut plenty. I think the Chief will plow and remove to the other reserve next season. Tom ploughed two acres there this season. I think the Poplar Point Indians could get sufficient good land and hay in this reserve also if they are to remain in this section of country, and the other scattered Indians in the settlements that has not gone already. I was advising them that they had better plough all in one large plot together as it would economize fencing as timber is not very plentiful. Still, with care, it might last a long time. They seemed to agree with the suggestion and ho-hoed their approval of the plan as it is, or as they are breaking, it will take a great many fences or have their crops destroyed by the cattle. They have no fence as yet enclosing what crops they have growing, but herding their cattle.[9]

McKenzie speaks very highly of the Dakota and it is clear that he was sad to be leaving them when he returned to his own farm, and the Dakota were sad to see him go. They asked him to tell the "Big Chief" about everything he had seen, and McKenzie agreed that they had every reason to be proud.

As McKenzie reported, in the summer of 1876, Choate and Dowaneya were camped at the Little Saskatchewan, Taninyahdinazin and his people were ten miles above the Oak River, and Wambdiska was at the reserve proper.[10] These divisions do not represent political dissension. Rather, the bands were spread out so as to take best advantage of scarce game and other resources, and all were quite prepared to move to the reserve when possible. Together, the three camps had about twenty-five acres broken and as far as McKenzie could see, were doing quite well, considering that they had few implements or work oxen and even less in the way of provisions necessary for the hard work of breaking virgin, prairie soil. They were unfamiliar with some technological matters, such as setting the ploughs to work efficiently, but by the fall, the Dakota had mastered all of the implements.

Even though they were showing great promise, the Dakota did not do well in the summer of 1876. Their crops were not sufficient for all their needs, and they were obliged to call again on Morris for a supply of winter basics. In 1876, a total of $2,154 was spent for the Dakota along the Assiniboine. In March 1877, Morris requested an additional $1,500 to offset anticipated costs in the coming year.[11]

Matters were much worse at Birdtail than at Oak River. Morris wrote that "owing to some misapprehension, the Sioux at Birdtail Creek were not furnished by the local Indian Department with seed last spring although they had ground broken and it had been promised to them." Mahpiyahdinape and his people did not even have the small gardens planted by their relatives on the Assiniboine. Had it not been for the work available at Fort Ellice, an emergency would have arisen. As it was, a large part of the Birdtail population went west to hunt buffalo, and there they met up with a party of Ihanktonwon and Tetonwon fleeing the Little Big Horn. At this, Morris encouraged Ottawa to give the Dakota what they needed with minimal complaint: "In view of the presence of American Sioux in the Territories, it is desirable to retain the friendship of the Sioux who have resided here for some years and who display a greater aptitude for farming operations than any other of our Indians."[12]

By the early spring of 1877, the Dakota were preparing for another season, and a number of them went to Government House to get scythes and other small tools. They returned immediately to begin work on their crops and gardens, but the season was a disaster for the Dakota, as it was for many other farmers.[13] The rains were relentless and floods were common along all waterways. Morris reported on discussions he had with Mahpiyahdinape, known to the authorities as Enoch, at Fort Garry in late autumn of 1877.

Enoch can read and write and speaks English well. He stated that they had raised some potatoes, he having 40 bushels, but owing to the wheat and potatoes being planted on low ground, they had lost all of the former, and a large quantity of the latter from the heavy rains, and owing to the scarcity of game, would be obliged to consume what potatoes they had for food, and even then would be very badly off. They had this fall broken up new ground, on the side of a hill, to avoid the difficulty in the future. In all they had 37 acres ready for crop, and would get out rails this winter, and enclose the unfenced portion.

He expected 15 more families to settle on the reserve this winter, including some from the Turtle Mountain. They were erecting five houses and wanted a few tools. They had raised three calves from their cows, and had hay cut for the cattle. They had plenty of milk, but the women wanted to make butter, and he therefore desired a churn and milkpans, which I gave him – it being the first application of the kind I had had from any Indians.

During last winter, he had taught the children, but now he said, the Presbyterian Church was sending them a native Sioux Minister to live with them on the reserve.

He applied for barley and wheat to sow in spring 15 acres; potatoes to sow ten acres and garden seeds for 2 acres. He said the barley and potatoes could be got in spring from the Hudson's Bay Company's post at Fort Ellice, and the wheat from some of the settlers at the Beautiful Plain. I told Him I could not promise this, but would recommend it.

It is fortunate that so intelligent an Indian is at the head of this reserve, and the progress they are making in endeavouring to support themselves gives good reason to hope that others of the wandering Sioux will settle around the nucleus which he has formed and that thus it will be developed into a valuable center of civilization.

P.S. I add that Enoch informed me that Sitting Bull had asked him to go see him, but that he had not done so, as he thought that instead of doing so, he ought to remain and look after the breaking up of ground on the reserve, cutting hay and looking after the cattle.[14]

Mahpiyahdinape was coping with his situation in a competent manner and, like any other settler in a bad year, was putting the harsh season behind and preparing for a better next year. The chief reported to Morris that he and his men had found four oxen, five cows, one heifer and two calves running wild on the prairie. Morris authorized Mahpiyahdinape to keep the animals unless they were properly identified by their owner. The cattle were never reclaimed, and they formed the nucleus of the band herd in later years.

In early November 1877, Kenneth McKenzie again reported on a visit to Oak River. The band was still spread out along the Assiniboine, ten miles above and below the reserve proper. Their fishing weir at the Little Saskatchewan had been swept away in the summer floods and they had been compelled to leave their crops and seek work in the Portage la Prairie settlements. They had sown six more acres than in 1876, but their crops and gardens had failed. At the time of McKenzie's visit, many of the men were away hunting. McKenzie had brought six cows, six calves and one bull for the band, but Taninyahdinazin refused to take delivery, as he did not have enough hay for the herd, and was not at all sure when the rest of the people would return to the reserve.[15]

Morris and McKenzie agreed that a man be assigned to supervise the farming at the Oak River and Birdtail reserves and, if possible, to give the Dakota some religious and practical instruction. Morris hoped that an agent would keep the Dakota near Oak River from spreading their camps along the Assiniboine, a division that he attributed to undefined "jealousies." By the end of 1877, provision for the funding of an agent had been approved.

Morris also suggested that the government recognize only one of the four chiefs in the area, and he named Wambdiska as "the most industrious among them, and a man of good disposition." The Dakota, however, wished to have their own form of leadership and this, no doubt, was the basis for the jealousies mentioned by Morris. In recommending Wambdiska to be the overall chief, Morris identified the one of the four men who had the least claim to chieftainship, as his band had been all but exterminated at Kildeer Mountain in 1863.[16]

Mahpiyahdinape spent the end of 1877 tracking down sources of seed grain and potatoes and then he visited McKenzie to itemize the band's needs. Morris retired as lieutenant governor that autumn and Mahpiyahdinape was uneasy as to whether Morris's promises would be kept. In mid-January 1878, he wrote the new lieutenant governor, Joseph E. Cauchon, asking if he could still expect the cattle and seed Morris had offered him the previous November. Cauchon had no interest in the Dakota and little knowledge of their affairs, so he simply passed all enquiries on to Ottawa. In Indian matters, Cauchon was not the equal of Morris, who had been careful to protect Indian interests, and when Morris left Manitoba, the Dakota lost a good friend. Cauchon was indecisive, claiming that he had no jurisdiction to deal with Indian matters. By spring, there had been no response to Mahpiyahdinape's letter.[17]

In May 1878, James Robertson and George Bryce of the Presbyterian missions in Winnipeg telegraphed David Mills, minister of the interior, to notify him that unless the seed and cattle were delivered to the Birdtail Reserve, the band of twenty lodges would break up and join the Tetonwon then in the North-West Territories. Meredith immediately wired back, saying that Mahpiyahdinape had been promised no cattle, but that McKenzie had been authorized to give them seed to a value of $300.[18] This did not satisfy the church officials, so they wrote to Thomas Nixon, the Indian department's procurement officer. Mahpiyahdinape had been in Winnipeg the day before and had told Robertson "that the Government has given them two yoke of oxen already and two ploughs, but that one yoke of oxen were too old. They have, however, kept them, and hunger has never tempted them to take their lives. They have also received cows and are rearing all their calves. Enoch asks of what service seed can be to them if they have no cattle to cultivate the land and anxious that if the Government intended anything by giving them land and seed and provisions during the season of planting, they ought not to withhold what alone can render the rest of value."[19]

Mahpiyahdinape knew that $300 had been allowed for seed and provisions, and by his reckoning the band had not yet received that total benefit. He asked that instead of more provisions, the balance be put against cattle and implements. As it was, he had only one team of oxen to do all of the next season's work. The chief's arguments seemed straightforward, and should have been sufficient for decision-making. He offered to remain at Portage la Prairie until some decision was reached, but it took over a year for the problem to be solved, and progress in farming was again retarded. Even Morris was unable to settle the dispute, as he no longer had access to his files.[20]

The winter of 1877–78 had been difficult for the Dakota not only in terms of food shortages, but in social and political matters as well. The assignment of Wambdiska as chief at Oak River, the retirement of Morris, the approval of Oak Lake Reserve, and the reneging on earlier promises prompted migrations of Dakota. Choate and several of his band left the Assiniboine permanently and joined Wapahaska to hunt in the Wood Mountains, and a small band under Iyanki left Fort Ellice and went to Prince Albert. These, however, were the last major emigrations of the Dakota away from the borders of the province and into the West.

Once again, in 1878, the Dakota commenced a growing season. Many of the supplies that had been budgeted the year before had not been distributed, and so Wambdiska went to see the lieutenant governor in Winnipeg. He asked for grain cradles and for provisions to last over the harvest. Cauchon knew nothing of these matters, and Acting Indian Superintendent James Graham telegraphed Ottawa for a decision. Lawrence Vankoughnet promptly wired back that the Dakota at Oak River and Birdtail Creek were to receive together and in all, $60 toward the purchase of grain cradles and $75 for provisions.[21] That was all that the Dakota received from the government in 1878, but over the summer, Lawrence W. Herchmer arrived as the Dakota's first Indian Agent.

Herchmer, like so many other Indian agents, was a political appointee, his brother being the commissioner of the North West Mounted Police. He does not seem to have possessed any particular skill or ability germane to the task he had assumed. Even though he started off well, the Dakota came to dislike him. In early September, Herchmer submitted his first report. He stated that there were sixteen lodges at Birdtail Creek, and most of the Dakota there were finishing permanent houses. All had gardens, "the vegetables being very fine, and not surpassed in any part of Manitoba." He criticized the Dakota at Birdtail for planting yellow and white Indian corn and those at Oak River for growing a corn of "a very inferior native variety," stating as a fact that it did not ripen in Manitoba. The Dakota had, in actuality, been growing the corn for many years in Manitoba, having brought the seed from Minnesota in 1862.[22]

The fields at Birdtail Creek were well ploughed but irregular in shape. Gardens were planted to potatoes, onions, corn, cabbages, turnips and sunflowers, "growing in great luxuriance." The band had over fifty acres broken, but were unable to work it all with their old and overly fat oxen. As well, they had not received enough seed grain in the spring, and had been able to plant only a small part of their prepared lands. Mahpiyahdinape still had six of the twelve cows he had found the previous summer. He had, no doubt, culled for beef the older stock, which Morris had described as being wild as buffalo. They also had a large herd of small ponies. Herchmer thought the Birdtail Dakota were doing very well, and showing promise of being trend-setters for settlers and other Indians who might farm in the area.

The Oak River Band was not doing as well. Of the eighteen families at that reserve, only Wambdiska had built a house and all the others expected to winter under canvas. A number of families had returned to Portage la Prairie, and others went to the Turtle Mountains to hunt and trap for the winter. When they left the reserve, they took the band's working oxen with them, and those who remained were unable to do their fall ploughing. Although they had eleven head of oxen, in addition to a single cow, most of the cattle were unfit for field work. The Oak River people, too, had about fifty acres broken. Herchmer could see that that there was not enough fire- or lumber-wood on the reserve, and he feared that this would be "a great drawback to the prosperity of this settlement." Herchmer recommended that as soon as possible in the spring all the useless oxen be sold or exchanged for better stock. He suggested two yoke of oxen and ten cows for Oak River, and three yoke and five cows for Birdtail. With proper working stock, he thought that the bands should be able to put in over a hundred acres of crop the next year, for which he also requested sufficient seed. Vankoughnet accepted Herchmer's recommendations and passed them along to Sir John A. Macdonald, then superintendent general of the Indian Affairs Branch, with the note that a lesser number of cattle would suffice.[23]

It took two months for the authorities in Ottawa to respond to Herchmer's requests, and in that time, the agent wrote again, detailing his plans. He wanted four yoke of oxen delivered to Birdtail by January to be used in drawing out logs and fencing posts. In February, Herchmer intended to have the bands haul seed grain and provisions from the nearest sources of supply. He also wanted to buy bred cows and have them calve on the reserve.

Finally, Herchmer asked for a supply of flour. Without it, the Dakota could not remain on the reserve in March, April and May, when they would be obliged to go to the hunting grounds. In all, Herchmer asked to spend about $4,000, most of it in the form of implements, cattle and seed. He thought that this sum would be greatly reduced in 1880, as construction of the railroad would have begun in the district and work would be available.[24]

Vankoughnet wrote that the sum suggested was far in excess of what had been voted for the Dakota, and that Herchmer would have to revise his estimate downward. He later suggested that Herchmer could save money by selecting cattle from a herd being held by the department's purveyor. This came as quite a disappointment to Herchmer, who had already pared his estimates to the minimum, but he further reduced his costs to $1,500. Vankoughnet then approved the agent's plans.[25]

By late January, Herchmer had looked over the cattle being held by Purveyor Nixon, and found them to be "very inferior." However, he completed his cattle purchases and sent the stock and supplies to the reserves, just in time for the coming season, but much too late for drawing out building materials. The entire transaction had taken almost five months.[26]

While the Dakota at Oak River and Birdtail were establishing themselves on their reserves, those at Turtle Mountain and at Oak Lake carried on with their efforts to secure lands. The request for a reserve at Oak Lake had been made in November 1873, and H'damani had made his most recent request for lands in the Turtle Mountains in January 1874. In both instances, these requests were presented to government through the International Boundary Commission. A little more than a month after the Order in Council established the Oak River and Birdtail reserves, H'damani again sent a letter to Morris through Captain Cameron: "In the summer I saw you. I wish the Turtle Mountains to be mine, and plainly marked out for a grant. The Little Saskatchewan is Wahunigle Scah's own (the Waughpatoan). At Beaver Creek the Sisseton – also the Waughpatoans – have ground. The Mocha Low Band want the Turtle Mountain to plant in. The place is good for fur; therefore I am anxious for it. I would like you to tell the Governor to give us this for our grant, with oxen and a plough. I wish harm to no man. God is my witness."[27] There was no response from Ottawa, as it had been decided shortly before this time not to permit the Dakota to settle near the border. H'damani's request was simply ignored.

In early 1877, Morris received yet another request for land in the Turtle Mountains. This request is not preserved in any archive, but it must have mentioned lands at Oak Lake. David Mills, minister of the interior, responded when Morris forwarded the request along with his recommendation of compliance, by assuring him that the matter would be given full consideration.[28] Mills wrote J.A.N. Provencher, a person whom he seemed to feel was more in touch with the day-to-day lives of the Dakota than was the lieutenant governor. In May, Provencher reported, stating that "the reasons that prevented the Government from giving the Sioux a reserve at that locality, or anywhere near the frontier, have now more weight than ever."[29] Provencher reasoned that many of the treaties between the Dakota and the United States were about to expire and when this happened, a reserve populated by Dakota would be a great refuge for those wishing to leave America. Vankoughnet reviewed Provencher's report and agreed with both his reasoning and his conclusions, suggesting instead that they go onto the reserves already set aside.[30] On the bottom of Vankoughnet's note, there is the following comment, written by "D.M.," probably David Mills: "These Indians might perhaps be assigned reserves in the vicinity of the other reserves or upon the northern border of the desert. It is doubtful whether grain, implements or cattle would be any use to them."

It was a foot in the door at least, since the idea of a separate reserve was being contemplated. The site suggested by Mills, however – what are now the Carberry Sand Hills and the site of the Canadian Army's artillery range – would scarcely have interested the Dakota.

Over the summer of 1877, Morris had two further meetings with the Dakota. At the first, Morris could only repeat what the Dakota had already been told – that they could not have lands in the Turtle Mountains or at Oak Lake, and that without land, there would be no point in issuing them agricultural supplies and livestock.[31] At the second meeting, H'damani repeated his request for land, and presented Morris with a list of thirty-four heads of families on whose behalf he was making his appeal. To Morris, H'damani's people were "very intelligent and superior Indians." Even though he had been told that no reserve for the Dakota would be allowed near the international boundary, he again recommended that the land they wanted be given to them.

Morris reported that H'damani agreed he had no claim upon the Queen "unless she chose to help them out of her benevolence."[32] It is difficult to be sure how accurately Morris represents what was said to him through the imperfect interpreting of James McKay. However, Morris was not given to such petty tricks as altering in a report things that were said to him. H'damani knew quite well that he did have a historic claim upon the Crown. It can only be said that as the individual bands were settled upon reserves, the Dakota ceased to speak of their earlier alliance with the Crown and the rights they assumed had been won through that alliance.

Morris met with Mills over the summer and formed the idea that he had been given permission to locate the Dakota where he thought best. This he did by implying to the Dakota that they would be able to take lands at Turtle Mountain and Oak Lake. When he later presented this to the minister, he was told that the authority to do so had, in fact, not been given. Nevertheless, Mills sought the opinion of the surveyor general, who could see no difficulty in allowing the grant of lands at Oak Lake. With that, an Order in Council was drawn up and approved, and the Oak Lake Reserve came into being. After considerable delay, caused by budget constraints, the reserve was surveyed in the summer of 1878.[33]

Waoke and his people immediately took possession of the reserve, but since these were not the lands requested by H'damani, he and his band remained where they were in the Turtle Mountains.

Almost from the day the Dakota began to take up their reserve lands in the mid-1870s, they were dogged by a succession of environmental disasters. Like their few and scattered neighbours, however, they lived for another season and carried on as best they could. Their very isolation, far from the infant province of Manitoba, served them at this time, as they were able to shift readily between small-scale agriculture and horticulture to hunting, fishing and trapping. When pressed by economic necessity, the easterly communities were close enough that the Dakota could seek work in the settlements and on the farms, and even find a market for modest surplus production of fish and handcrafts. This isolation also placed the Dakota beyond the day-to-day attentions of the Indian Department.

Agricultural success eluded the Dakota in the first few years of settlement on the reserves. In those early years, they had virtually nothing of the capital, equipment, seed, tools, information and supplies needed for a farm enterprise. The Birdtail Band had a few cattle and some individuals had small handtools suited for gardening, but none of what was needed for large-scale agriculture. Up to 1875, the government had invested $2,250 in productive technology and cattle for the three reserves. Considering the fact that there were about three hundred people at Oak River, Birdtail and Oak Lake by the end of the decade, this investment amounted to about $37 for each family of five.

It has been estimated that it cost about $1,000 to establish a farm enterprise at that time, including about $550 for expenses related to the farm venture, $250 for establishing the settler household, and the remainder for operating expenses. For this investment, the beginning farmer could bring forty acres into crop, maintain two draft animals and small livestock, construct housing for the family, and fences and shelter for the cattle, hogs and chickens.[34]

In his estimates of expenses for equipping the Dakota in 1879, Agent Herchmer had first requested $2,200, later revising this to $1,500. With the $2,250 already expended, this would have increased total family capital to $62.50, or a bit better than six percent of what was required. It is surprising that the Dakota were able to make any progress at all during these years, but they did, though they had to make severe adjustments.

The Dakota were able to take on new challenges at a gradual rate, and by the end of the decade they had acquired a variety of livestock, including milk cattle, pigs, and chickens. More remarkable, the band at Birdtail also had its own school, where English was taught, and their own church, built and funded by Mahpiyahdinape's people. The strategy of sedentary agriculture adopted by the reserve bands required social innovations on the part of the Dakota, resulting in physical division of the bands, re-organization of labour, and task specialization. In order to significantly increase their levels of agricultural production, however, the Dakota required capital in the form of seed, breeding cattle and technology. Since they had no assets of their own, these came from the Indian department. In return, the government insisted that aspects of their economic strategy be controlled by an appointed Indian agent and limited by departmental budgets. The government took over short-term planning, specified the quality, quantity and sources of livestock, seeds and tools, and instituted the permit system for the sale of agricultural products. This erosion of political autonomy, best represented by the department's appointment of a "head chief" at Oak River, combined with a series of very poor farming years, triggered the migration of families to the far West and even to the United States. By the late 1870s, there were eighty Dakota at Birdtail Creek, ninety at Oak River, and about sixty-five at Oak Lake. Together, these numbers represent about half the Dakota that had been in the same areas at the close of the previous decade. By 1880, the Dakota who remained in Canada had been tested by the disappointments of farming on the harsh northern prairie, and were poised for progress.

A decade of learning the basics, 1879 to 1889

5

The 1880s were the real test for the Dakota farmers, as they were for all the settlers on the prairie. The devastation of drought, frost and wild grassfires countered each advance the Dakota made in this decade. Immigrant settlers had begun to move into the area in the late 1870s, increasing the demand for labour, commodities and handcrafts. At the same time, the settlers increased pressure on the wild game, fuel and building wood, fish and other natural resources still crucial in the Dakota economy. An increasing government presence was felt on the reserves. Trends in reorganization that had been initiated in the 1870s were elaborated in the 1880s. The decade was also a period of tremendous increase in knowledge amongst the Dakota, especially knowledge of the skills, practices and technologies of production.

In 1880, the population at Oak River was once again obliged to spread out for much of the year, and so there were still three centres of gardening and cropping along the Assiniboine during the summer, with many families moving in the winter either to Portage la Prairie to work for the settlers, or to the Turtle Mountains to hunt and trap. Mahpiyahdinape was better off because his band had a smaller population and had been settled in the Fort Ellice area for many years. The Birdtail people had winter and summer jobs available close by at the post and along the Saskatchewan Trail, and in their area there was less pressure on subsistence resources. A small band of Wahpetonwon under Iyankee had spent one season at Birdtail, but then decided to proceed on to Prince Albert, suggesting that the area was already fully occupied by the resident Dakota.

In 1875, Morris had estimated there were 160 lodges of Dakota at Portage la Prairie. By 1879, about twenty lodges were still year-round residents near the settlement. Fifteen lodges had left with Iyanki, another twenty with Choate, and thirty-eight lodges were in the vicinity of the Oak River Reserve. During these early years after the reserves were assigned a large number of Dakota also moved back to the United States, especially to the areas around Fort Totten and Poplar River, Montana. This effectively reduced economic competition.

The Dakota reorganized their remaining labour force and their manner of production. Before taking up the reserves, each lodge, assumed to represent a household, followed an economic round very similar to that of all the other lodges in a band: where one lodge went to labour, hunt, fish, trap or trade, as the season and locality dictated, so did all the rest. The reserves imposed new labour requirements: the livestock and housing had to be tended year-round; the crops required work for four or five consecutive months; and equipment repairs were needed from time to time throughout the year. Many other tasks had to be done as well, tasks that could be done only on the reserve. The acquisition of livestock, even of a single ox, implied full-time residence on the reserve for at least a some of the band population. Thus, for matters that required an expedition off the reserve, fewer people went, and these ones were better equipped and prepared to take care of the problem. Gone were the days when over a hundred men, women and children would travel all the way from the middle Assiniboine to Winnipeg for a few supplies.

Hunting, fishing, trapping and gathering expeditions were smaller and more closely timed so as to coincide with peak seasons of production. As soon as they were able, the Dakota began to invest in driving teams, wagons and buggies, traps, shotguns, fish nets, and other tools that would help them add wild food to their subsistence base. The Oak River Reserve had a population of 190 in 1876 and 1877, and a community that large required considerable food. Wild game was none too plentiful in the late 1870s, as the reports from Morris, McKenzie and Herchmer make plain; they had to resort to skunks, for example, which were considered strictly starvation rations. In order to add wild food resources to their subsistence base, travel and technology were absolutely essential.

Those Dakota who remained regularly on the reserve became noted as the most capable farmers, not only by the Indian agent or other officials, but by the Dakota themselves. This suggests a degree of task specialization, or more likely emphasis, and it is equally likely that those who went hunting, fishing or trapping were specialists in those pursuits. This strategy would be compatible with a community striving to maximize farm production, while minimizing the abandonment of other resources.

As well, there is some suggestion of differences in productivity amongst those who farmed. Fields ranged in size from a fraction of an acre to several acres. Much of this difference can be attributed to the sizes of the households that attended these fields; the presence of a grown boy or girl in a household of five would increase the amount of labour available by a third. Big families could and did work more land and enjoy a potentially higher standard of living. The fact that the Dakota were tilling their lands separately indicates that they were making a change toward individualization of property, whereas previously land was communally held.

Task emphasis made it possible for a community to take advantage of labour alternatives. Farming is notorious for its long periods with no income and its single short season of high cash flow, while hunting and fishing produce relatively low incomes spread throughout the year. The mechanism that tended to level the economic differences in the reserve communities was the giveaway, during which a household would make itself destitute by giving virtually all of its possessions to others in the band. The guiding principle was that those who could gave, and those who couldn't received. No person was obliged to become a public beggar in order to partake of his relatives' good fortune. As well, the giveaway was, and still is, undertaken in good humour, attended by much fun. With the actual dispersion of goods being understated, no person could appear a braggart by giving.

There is no record of giveaways amongst the Dakota from the time that they arrived in Canada in 1862 until they began to prosper on the reserves in 1879. It is most unlikely that anyone had anything to give away in those years. The first good year, however, was marked by the revival of the giveaway, which continued until it was outlawed by the government later in the century.

While the Dakota lacked material assets, they had other potential for economic growth. Of primary importance, they were able and willing to incorporate all manner of new ideas, techniques and technology into what remained essentially a Dakota culture. They were multilingual, many were literate in two languages, and they valued education. The school, which was organized and taught by Mahpiyahdinape in both Dakota and English, was one of the first schools west of Portage la Prairie. They were eager to learn new ways of doing things, either by taking instruction or by experimenting. Mahpiyahdinape planted test plots of crops, and he was one of the earliest farmers in the West to plant Red Fife wheat, a new high-yielding seed. Their cultural flexibility allowed them to operate simultaneously in several distinct economic fields – domestic production for subsistence, production of surpluses for market sale, and sale of wage labour. By putting their abilities to the best possible use, the Dakota were able not only to maintain themselves through the very difficult 1870s, but also to materially improve their economic situation. They entered the 1880s in much better shape that they had the 1870s.

During the late 1870s, settlement began to move west along both sides of the Assiniboine River valley. By 1877, settlers to the north of the Assiniboine had taken up lands as far west as Tanner's Crossing on the Little Saskatchewan River. By 1879, the Blue Hills were taken up, followed by the Turtle Mountains and the area around the newly established town of Deloraine. Farmers were leaving the Sas-katchewan Trail at the Birdtail River by 1879, and in the next two years all of that river's valley was settled. Most of these settlers were of Ontario British stock, some were graduates of the Ontario Agricultural College at Guelph, and most were ex-perienced practical farmers. They had been exposed to advanced farming practices, and brought both their skills and tools with them – seed drills, tempered steel gang and sulkey ploughs, self-binders, steam power and barbed wire. They also brought new concepts of political organization, and in 1878 these settlers formed the first county municipality of Westbourne, just to the east of the Dakota lands on the As-siniboine.

These developments were a mixed blessing for the Dakota. On the one hand, they were immediately able to fill the demand for labour created by the settlers and to gain familiarity with new farming ideas. On the other hand, game dwindled even more rapidly, and smaller rivers were so disrupted as to no longer support a spring run of fish. More important for aspiring agriculturalists, however, was the competi-tion that the settlers represented. Being well-equipped and trained, the settlers quickly expanded the size of their holdings and levels of production. This intense competition opened even further the gap between subsistence and commercial farming.

Until lands were taken up by settlers, the Dakota had unrestricted access to resources, but that came to an end and the Dakota fell into conflict with the recent arrivals. In late 1881, Taninyahdinazin wrote to the authorities in Manitoba com-plaining that their timber was being taken by settlers:

The white settlers around us are robbing us of our timber and represent that they have procured the lands from the agent in Winnipeg. We have more faith in the justice of the government than believe such a statement and are convinced that these men think we are so ignorant that we will believe. But we are now convinced that when we once get a promise from our Great Mother, that promise is not made to be broken.

Therefore, we your humble petitioners pray that an investigation may be made and these men dealt with according to law, otherwise we shall have to expel these intruders ourselves by force and protect our property which may bring about trouble, which we are anxious to avoid. Now, Your Honour, we have notified the head of affairs in this province, if any trouble arises we will be blameless, but we will protect our timber or else we fight to the death.[1]

Herchmer was immediately directed to take firm action with the trespassers. The strong talk, however, arose from a misunderstanding on the part of the Dakota. They still believed that their lands extended from the reserve ten miles up and down the Assiniboine. Herchmer explained the borders of the reserve to Taninyahdinazin, who it seems accepted the agent's words, and that ended this particular matter.[2] Over the next few years, there were other land and resource disputes where the

Dakota were the ones wronged. They quickly brought the matter to the attention of the government and then pressed until the problem was resolved.[3]

By 1881, the Dakota bands had experienced three consecutive good years. The great "Manitoba land boom" had commenced, and the Dakota were quick to take the opportunities that this represented. While admiring the crops and on-reserve developments, Agent Herchmer complained that "very little new ground has been broken this year as the Sioux find it more profitable to hire out, and most of the able bodied men are on surveys or working for settlers at about $25 per month." Herchmer did not expect great improvements in farming operations while such high wages were available, but he conceded that the Dakota were using their gains to improve their houses, much to their own betterment.

The farmers at Birdtail Reserve planted most of their prepared land to corn, from which they got more food than they did from wheat. There was no gristmill near the reserve, and so long as the grain had to be hauled for milling or sold in order to buy flour, wheat culture was not profitable. They even went so far as to expand their gardens onto plots that had been in grain the year before.

The Oak River Dakota worked for the Canadian Pacific Railway, which was then passing through Griswold, only eight miles to the south of the reserve. Here, too, labour was in constant demand, and the men were receiving top wages. They were attempting to improve their housing with the gains from their labour, but as the band did not have access to good building logs or sawlogs, the new houses were still inadequate.

Those families at Oak Lake, having started to plant on the reserve only two years earlier, were still not able to supply all of their own seedstocks, but with their wages and the fish they took for sale and home use, were doing well. None of the bands required government assistance of any kind.[4]

The years of 1881 and 1882 were the last good farming seasons that the Dakota and their settler neighbours saw for some time. The following three years were all very dry with severe frosts in the late spring and early fall that all but wiped out the crops. By harvest time in 1883, the Dakota found that their not yet fully matured potatoes were frozen into the ground, and much of their wheat was frozen and unfit for sale or grinding. Most of the crop was used as cattle feed. They had learned a lesson, however, and in the season of 1884 all bands put more emphasis on the raising of root crops, corn and cattle.

The Oak River Band planted over eight hundred bushels of seed potatoes in 1883, but with the frost the crop barely reached six thousand bushels. Even this much-reduced crop greatly increased band income. The Dakota had mastered the delicate technique of storing potatoes over the winter, and then selling them at Brandon in spring when prices were most favourable. Opportunities for the sale of labour were not as great as in previous years, since by 1884 the great land boom was over and another bout of regional economic stagnation was settling in.

The Oak Lake Band had temporarily given up on grain crops and dedicated most of their prepared land to potatoes and corn for home use. Their gardens were supplemented by hunting, but they lost their fishing resource when a dam was built on Plum Creek to power a gristmill.[5] For the first time in two years, Herchmer was obliged to make supplies of food available for the Dakota.

Because of the flexibility of their subsistence, wage labour and farming economy, the bands managed rather well in the years of drought and frost. Mahpiyahdinape's people were so confident in 1885 that they sent a letter to the *Birtle Observer* in which they described their farms in terms of quiet satisfaction. The letter, written by Joseph Eastman, describes farming as being done by "two companies, one . . . composed of young men and the other of older ones." The young men did the heavy field work, such as breaking, ploughing and harvesting, while the older men attended to seeding, to maintaining the all-important gardens, to raising cattle, and marketing and distributing produce. This method of organizing labour, unique to the Birdtail Reserve, persisted for a number of years. Even though the division of labour was communal, the actual fields and farmsites were considered to be the property of individual households. Eastman described eight farms. Each farmer had between seven and thirty-two acres broken and cultivated, the smaller acreages being held by younger men. All had good houses and at least one stable. Farmers with a variety of livestock – cattle, horses, pigs, chickens – had separate housing for each, an approved agricultural practice. Those with larger acreages under cultivation had granaries and sheds for storing their implements. Many had used the cattle they had found years previously to start their own herds. One man had started with one cow in 1878, and by 1885 he had eighteen head of breeding stock and two trained work oxen, and at the same time had increased one chicken to a laying flock of sixty-seven. The Dakota saw themselves as doing very well. They had one important problem, as Eastman describes: "Our company owns 13 yoke of oxen, but we have not all got ploughs and harrows yet. When the government sees fit to supply us with a full complement, we hope to be just as good farmers as our white neighbours. On our reserve, we have a church, we have collections every Sunday for church expenses for home missions. We have a minister and a school teacher and we hope that our children will all grow up to speak English."[6]

Eastman's letter does not make it clear, but the band members had paid for and built their own church, were supporting their own clergyman, and were making contributions to the Presbyterian Home Mission for the support of churches in less advantaged communities. This report delighted Herchmer, who sent the clipping on to Lawrence Vankoughnet, where it was received with "much pleasure."[7]

This pleasure soon became acrimony when the Dakota decided that they were ready to manage more of their own affairs. In the summer of 1885, Wambdiska, Mahpiyahdinape and Taninyahdinazin sent a petition to Ottawa demanding the removal of agent Herchmer. The chiefs complained that Herchmer was unable to teach the Dakota any improved or progressive ways of doing things and, in an effort to mask his own shortcomings, was "cross and unkind, complaining and scolding." Specifically, Herchmer had arrested two of the leading men at Oak River and had them jailed in Brandon for selling what they believed to be one of their own cattle. In spite of these irritations, the chiefs proclaimed themselves to "still love our Great Mother, and wish to do only those things that will please her, and we feel sure that she would not wish us to be ill-used." However, things had degenerated to the point that the "young men dislike him more and more, and we fear they may do something we would be sorry for if Mr. Herchmer is not removed."[8] The year 1885 was not the best time to hint at threats against an Indian agent, no matter how mild or how much the chiefs may have deplored issuing them. The government was in no mood to yield to threats after the events that spring on the Saskatchewan River.

Herchmer composed a reply to the chiefs' accusations. He admits that in June he had "occasion to severely reprimand Enock, one of the Sioux living on the Birdtail Reserve." He gave no reason for this reprimand, but the occasion was seen as an impertinence by Mahpiyahdinape. Herchmer claimed that the Dakota had no cattle of their own to sell, as all the livestock on the reserves was government issue. Here, the agent was clearly mistaken, as the majority of the animals on the Birdtail Reserve were owned by the Dakota. He claimed that the Dakota understood perfectly well that they could not sell cattle without a permit from him. This may have been the practice in earlier years, but by 1885, the Dakota had progressed to the point that they wanted to take control of these matters themselves, especially when it came to selling their own property. Herchmer also admitted that at times he was cross and angry, but only when the Indians had earned his wrath, and that while he had not taught them very much, the bands had made considerable progress. He concluded that all of the charges were trumped up, without foundation, and sprang from petty slights. As well, he had heard that the petition was not supported by all the rank and file of the bands.[9]

Herchmer and the Indian department were a little slow in answering the charges and before a response could be framed, the conflict was reported in the *Toronto Globe*.

In August last, the Indians petitioned government to take cognizance of their grievances against their agent, a Mr. Herchmer. In October, they were informed that their case had been considered and relegated to Lieutenant Governor Dewdney. In November, Mr. Dewdney informed the petitioners that Mr.

Herchmer had been promoted to the office of Inspector of Indian Agencies and would in a short time visit his old agency, when he would enquire into the cause of the complaints and report upon them. Inspector Herchmer was, therefore, sent to enquire into the cause of complaints as to the conduct of Mr. Agent Herchmer.

The death of Riel is not the only thing the government will have to answer for before Parliament and the people.[10]

Dewdney, Vankoughnet and Herchmer were outraged and claimed that the newspaper article misrepresented the truth, in that the Dakota had been told nothing. Dewdney thought Herchmer was one of the best agents in the Indian department, and discarded the complaints as trivial. Vankoughnet urged Dewdney to discuss the problem with the three chiefs, but nothing more came of the matter. This conflict continued to fester for many years and engendered considerable bad feeling amongst the Dakota, who resented being treated as children.[11]

In spite of their wrangle with Herchmer, the Dakota did well in 1885, and by 1886 were preparing for another good year. The spring weather seemed better than in recent years, and all bands were trying to put in more crop than before. The Oak River people renewed a request for new and improved implements, especially a mechanical thresher, as they were then threshing with a flail, which even in 1886 was outdated.

The Oak Lake Dakota found themselves caught in a bureaucratic web: they were unable to plant as much as they wished, especially potatoes, because they were unable to secure seedstocks anywhere near their reserve. The department's response was that they would get no seed unless they returned from the Portage and took up permanent residence on the reserve. However, the Dakota could not stay full-time on the reserve unless they were assured the capacity to support themselves and working around Portage la Prairie was the only alternative they had.

The season of 1886 did not turn out well for the Dakota or the settlers. As drought deepened, crops were short and stunted, and the meagre yield was struck by autumn frosts. In early February 1887, John Taylor, a neighbour and friend of the people at Oak River who was able to speak a little Dakota, was asked by Dewdney to visit the reserves. Taylor found that the Oak Lake people had been camped over the winter at the mouth of Pipestone Creek, where it empties into Oak Lake. As in years past, they had moved there to take fish from the river, but during the previous summer a dam had been built and no fish were available. As well, the band had lost most of the housing at the Pipestone when a huge prairie fire swept across that drought-stricken territory. The Dakota were considering building permanent structures on the reserve and applying themselves almost exclusively to farming, especially as game became increasingly scarce. The fire and drought also reduced their hay crop and while their cattle were able to survive the winter, they were not thriving.

Hay was in such short supply at the Oak River Reserve, however, that the band had lost five head of cattle, and it was doubtful that the Dakota would have had enough feed to carry their whole herd over the winter. The crops had been so poor that the people were forced to ask for seed and food for the first time in over five years. Many of the band members had been obliged to leave the reserve in early winter to hunt in the Riding Mountains, something they had not done since the previous decade. Taylor noted that there had been fewer dances and giveaways than in past years, which was to be expected in times of hardship.[12]

Even the Birdtail people had reverted to an earlier economic strategy. When Alexander McGibbon, inspector of Indian agencies, visited the reserve in June 1887, he found that the Dakota had put in their crops and, leaving a few families behind as caretakers, had departed to hunt gophers for bounty, or had ranged far away hunting, or had gone to find work with the surrounding settlers. All those who had left took their whole families with them. Those who remained were doing a good job tending the crops and gardens, all of which were free of weeds and looking good in the early summer. At this time, weeds were infesting all the fields in the West, due to improperly cleaned seedstock and the use of cattle and horses for power. McGibbon saw it, rightly, as a credit to the Dakota that they were so well in control of weeds. Hard times or not, the people at Birdtail were reported to be content, and asked only that they be given some fish nets.[13]

Frosts struck in July and weakened crops that had just been reviving with timely rains earlier in the month. Prairie fires of the year earlier had burned out much of the sod, and hay was going to be scarce. Labour was not in high demand, since few settlers could afford to hire in 1887. In August, Indian Agent Markle, who replaced Herchmer, was speaking of the Indians as all being "hopeful of a good living the coming winter," but this was not to be. As soon as the crop was taken off and threshed, many of the families from all reserves departed for the evermore distant hunting lands in an attempt to make do. Fortunately, game was plentiful that winter and the price for fur was high, so the Dakota did not have to ask Agent Markle for supplies.[14]

Just before the beginning of the 1888 planting season, the Dakota went on a last hunting and trapping expedition, and returned with a good catch. They had been short of hay for their cattle, but all the animals made it through the winter, if not in the best working condition. That year, the Dakota put in maximum effort to bring all possible lands into crop. They did almost seventy acres of new breaking at Oak River, and lavished special attention on their gardens. By that time, the Dakota had learned that while the price of grain crops went up and down, the value of garden produce always remained high, in terms of providing a basic food supply. As well, the band had befriended the Reverend A.W. Burman, a man of considerable knowledge and experience in gardening. In 1883 he had founded one of the oldest agricultural societies in the West, the Forestry and Horticultural Association at Griswold, and by so doing gave the Oak River people direct access to a wealth of practical agricultural knowledge.

Inspector McGibbon found the wheat crops at Oak River to be "as fine as any I had seen among white settlers, and I saw some magnificent fields passing along Griswold district." In early July, wheat stocks measured to thirty-three inches, a good stand in any terms. There were no weeds in the fields or gardens. Over the winter, the Dakota had built a round building for their dances and a new corral for the cattle. A number of farmers had invested in wagons, mowers, rakes and even a thresher. They asked the Indian Department for eight breaking ploughs, eight cross plows and a self binder, which by that time was a common farm implement. They did not want or need supplies or food. McGibbon recommended that they receive all that they requested, except for the binder which he felt they could buy out of the proceeds of their crops in the autumn. The Inspector concluded that the Dakota were "a very nice lot of Indians and seem to be industrious and therefore are deserving of encouragement."

The Oak Lake people did not recover as quickly from the previous three or four years of crop failure, and in 1888 had sown only a little more than half the crop they had sown the year before. They still did not have enough seed to properly plant their wheat, and the land they were using was not well prepared. McGibbon attributed this to the old age of their oxen, and recommended that they be exchanged for younger stock. By and large, the band was subsisting on the hunted and gathered foods, which were plentiful that summer. The inspector complained that the band had very little contact with people who might be in a position to give advice, and that they were not progressing as fast as either he or they wished. The Oak Lake Dakota got along well with their neighbours, and not owning a mower or reaper themselves, had arranged to borrow them from their white neighbours, for which they paid with their labour. In a similar manner they obtained their wheat and potato seed from the settlers. McGibbon suggested that they receive new implements, including a mower and reaper, but Indian Commissioner Reed denied this request.

At the Birdtail Reserve, McGibbon found that a considerable amount of new land had been broken, but that the old fields had been abandoned. This is the first ominous indication of the future for this band; the land on the reserve was light and sandy and soon exhausted to the point that a crop would scarcely sprout, much less ripen. The band was still using an age division of labour to do the heavy work, and the inspector found the ploughing to be as well done as that on any settler's farm. The Dakota were continuing to experiment and had put in a test crop by seeding directly onto the broken sod, and by July had learned that this was not a good way to plant. They had saved over $85 to buy a new organ for their church. They needed nothing from the Indian Department, but in a symbolic sort of way asked for a little tea for the harvest season. Indian Commissioner Reed denied them the tea.[15]

All of the hard work paid off that season. Frosts struck heavily and often, just when the wheat was maturing, but the Dakota farms were missed, while their white neighbours were wiped out. Agent Markle reported that the Dakota at Birdtail were "very jubilant over their success and are of the opinion that the whites must be either very wicked or poor farmers."

With the good times came the giveaways and the dancing, into which the Dakota entered with such enthusiasm that the local church officials were compelled to complain to the authorities. Not only were the Indians dancing on the reserve, but they were also moving into the towns, where they were "an annoyance to the respectable inhabitants." When these complaints reached the Commissioner's ears, he responded by sending them a clipping from a local newspaper, in which a committee of the "respectable citizens" announced their plans for Dominion Day celebrations featuring a "war dance" conducted by the Dakota. Reed pointed out the hypocrisy of the matter, and since at that time the Indian Department could not compel the dances to be stopped, refused to do anything more. His refusal came in spite of Agent Markle's more strident criticism deploring the dances and his suggestion that the department use a private detective agency to pursue the dancers. Reed's money sense prohibited anything of that sort.[16]

With a good crop in the bins, the Dakota did little hunting or trapping in late 1888, and those who did were not very successful. As well, a boarding school had opened at Birtle, and the Reverend Burman opened a church school at Oak River where several children were enrolled. Parents were reluctant to travel away from home for long stretches of time, and by the end of the 1880s, plentiful game was to be found only far to the north and west. Hunting was still much better around Oak Lake Reserve, and people there took whatever game they could.[17]

In the spring, the Dakota went to work with a renewed confidence and again managed to increase the total number of acres in crop. One last year of drought, however, crushed their hopes. Markle's reports over the summer of 1889 read like a chronicle of impending doom. Frosts in June and July were followed by drought and a gopher invasion in August. By September, there was no crop to speak of. As soon as the last pathetic straws were gathered from the fields, all the Dakota who were able departed to hunt and trap. Even Markle registered a note of sympathy for the Indians: "Many have turned out to hunt for a short time, but game of much value is not plentiful near the reserves, excepting [Oak Lake] where they yet get a few deer. They apparently are satisfied with game that many treaty Indians would complain loudly about; few treaty Indians within this agency would be content to gain a living hunting if they had to depend upon foxes, muskrats, etc."[18]

In this passage, Markle was describing the Dakota's harvest of food animals, not a quest for hides or pelts. He even went so far as to wish that the Dakota had been originally placed near or in the Riding Mountain so they could have access to game in times of crop failure. That would scarcely have been a solution, as most of the slopes of the Riding Mountain were and are unfit for farming. More important, Markle feared that the Dakota had not seen the last of the bad years; their land was light and unable to hold a reserve of moisture for the spring seeding. He was thinking of trying to plough the seed into the ground the next season, so as to place the seed close to the subsurface moisture. (This rarely works, it might be noted, unless the farmer is satisfied with a fractional crop rather than none at all.)

The Dakota were able to secure enough income from hunting to purchase flour, the first they were forced to buy in over ten years. This was possible only because local towns had constructed gristmills in the past summer and the price of flour was down to $1.50 a sack, compared to over $4 as it had been in earlier years. But the Dakota were still not asking for rations, unlike many white settlers. As Markle commented, "an Indian can gain a livelihood where a white man would starve."[19]

The Dakota, of course, were not the only ones to suffer from a merciless environment; so did all their neighbours, white or Indian. This assurance, however, has never served to make a farmer feel good about his own crop of bad luck, and the Dakota were no exception. All things considered, and when compared to their neighbours, the Dakota had not done too badly for themselves. They had managed a slight cash surplus which they spent on public works such as a school, a church and church furnishings, bridges and trail improvements, a dance house; and they even supported missionaries. They had increased the amount of land under cultivation, made modest investments in farm implements and transportation equipment and had tried experiments in crop practices. They improved their housing and living conditions. None starved or went bankrupt and they received public assistance only in those most grim years when virtually everyone on the prairies received assistance in one form or another, or left the land. So the Dakota struggled through the 1880s and into the 1890s.

Regulated success:
Commerce, competition and the Crown,
1890 to 1899

6

The decade of the 1890s was one of momentous change for the Dakota farmers in western Canada. Until the winter of 1888–89, the Dakota still had control of the major aspects of their economic, political and cultural institutions. But this was not to last. During this decade, the Indian department finally displaced the traditional leadership of the bands; it wrested management of most aspects of the Dakota economies from Indian decision makers and entrusted them to agency representatives; and it imposed political guidance upon them. The Dakota were compelled to have agents dwelling full time in their midst, to acquiesce to the agents' decisions on land use and possession, and to accept the division of labour imposed upon them by the new decision makers.

These changes did not come about because of failures on the part of the Dakota. Following the Riel Rebellion of 1885, the Government of Canada sought to exercise all possible control in Indian matters. In the course of time, new bodies of regulation were imposed upon the Dakota, backed by the coercive power of the law.

The poor crops of 1889 had left the Dakota in a weakened position. In January 1890, Agent Markle reported that many families from the reserves had gone to hunt and fish and were, for the most part, making do "by not living so extravagantly as they would in time of plenty." A few of the Dakota from Birdtail had been bringing firewood to sell in the town of Birtle. While all the bands were suffering from a raging influenza epidemic, they were still making their own way.[1]

In March, Markle saw that most of the Dakota were very short of hay for their cattle, which was a problem for other settlers as well.[2] Markle, however, branded as "indolent" those Dakota whose cattle were suffering feed shortages. On his own authority, he expropriated cattle from those Dakota whom he thought would not have enough hay to last the few remaining weeks of winter, and sent them to those who would. He also expropriated surplus hay where it existed and gave it to Indians in need. In this way, the Dakota at Oak River lost seven head of breeding stock to the Oak Lake Band, and a number of farmers on all reserves lost a source of cash income. This was the first in a series of moves that separated the Dakota from the management of their own affairs.

There was nothing to justify Markle's acts; the Dakota had seen other years when hay was short, but there were rarely reports of starving or neglected animals among them. When asked by Indian Commissioner Hayter Reed to explain his actions in transferring cattle without departmental authority, Markle responded by stating that because the spring had been mild the expected catastrophe had not occurred. Rather, he wrote, the Dakota had stables which were poorly built and cold, and these conditions caused him to act the way he did.[3] This ingenuous response was the sign of a man caught exceeding his authority; Markle knew perfectly well that the reason there were no good stables on the Oak River and Birdtail reserves was that building and saw logs were unavailable at either place. Following the trying winter of 1889–1890, and his own bout of influenza, Markle became increasingly rigorous in the application of departmental regulations that gave him control over the conduct of the Dakota.

There is no doubt, however, that the work oxen on the reserves were not in good shape when the time for spring field work came around; this was also true for the white settlers. The weather was wet and cold for seeding, but the Dakota got a fair crop into the soil, and those who could went out to work for the settlers. By this time, well into a series of less than favourable crop years and the growing stagnation of national and local economies, labour was not in great demand, and wage levels had fallen. The Dakota were unable to find as much work as they wished, and many again tried hunting and fishing, but with poor results, since the sere prairie and dried-out lakes and rivers had little to offer.[4]

Frost struck in late August, autumn was wet and cold, and a considerable amount of hay and grain were lost. On the Dakota reserves, the wetness created a great deal of work: people were obliged to simultaneously cut and store their hay, harvest and thresh their grain crops, and take in their gardens. Since their turn with the travelling threshers came too early in the season, yields of all kinds were light and downgraded.[5]

In this season, the Dakota and their white neighbours learned the same hard lessons: inclement weather at the beginning and end of each crop season left too short a growing and harvesting time. There were only a limited number of ways in which to deal with this immutable problem. First, the Dakota could reduce their scale of operations so as to ensure that they had enough time to plant and harvest a smaller, but perhaps higher quality, crop. No matter how much higher the crop quality, though, this strategy implied a reduction in gross income, since any reduction in crop size would have to be substantial. In the long run, this plan would leave many farmers frustrated in good years for not having larger crops. The Dakota rejected this alternative.

Second, they could increase the labour supply at the times of peak demand, in spring seeding and fall harvest. By 1890, though, the Birdtail people had lost control of the deployment of labour. The season before, the Department of Indian Affairs had subdivided the reserve into eighty-acre farmsites, and assigned one to each of the farmers. Old patterns of communal labour organization gave way to the household organization of labour. For the Birdtail Dakota, this did away with the organization of labour by age groups, and many families who did not have children of appropriate ages were suddenly without the energies of vigorous and strong youth. The authority and decision-making capacities of the elders was diminished since each farmer was on his own land and responsible for his own success or failure. Now, families did their own planning and decision making, or they sought out the advice of experienced farmers on their own initiative. Taninyahdinazin had died that winter and after the subdivision of the Oak River Reserve the following year, the band did not recognize a chief for several years, as they no longer had any need for one.

Manipulation of a large and integrated labour force was no longer a possibility, so the Dakota turned to a third alternative, more efficient technology. In 1890, the Dakota had experimented with custom threshers, but found them unsatisfactory. Thus the two largest bands – Oak River and Birdtail – sold their crops of 1890, and immediately invested in superior technology. Using what Inspector of Indian Agencies G.P. Wadsworth referred to as "their private means," farmers at Birdtail purchased two binders, one fanning mill, one mower, one plough and one wagon. The Oak River farmers bought three binders, six mowers, six rakes, a thresher, six wagons and a number of ploughs and harrows. With the exception of the thresher, all the additional gear consisted of relatively small-scale implements – essentially farm tools typically used at that time.

Indian Commissioner Hayter Reed was outraged. He strongly opposed the use of "labour-saving mechanisms" by the Indians, and preferred to have them toiling with grain cradles and scythes instead of mowers, reapers and binders, hand rakes and forks rather than drawn rakes, flails instead of fanning mills and threshers. Reed's insistence was ignored by both the Indians and the agents. The Indians simply refused to work with tools that, by the 1890s, had no place on the agricultural frontier of Canada. The Dakota tried to ignore the commissioner's directives, but Reed had a powerful ally in Agent Markle, who was firm in the application of departmental policy.

These recent developments – appropriation of agricultural produce, forced reorganization of labour, the division of land, and the suppression of technology – all but ruined a developing economic strategy that had been effective up to that time. Until 1890, as reported often by Wadsworth and even Markle, the Dakota had not uttered any complaint about their lot in life. With each year, they were better able to satisfy their modestly defined needs and even produce a surplus. After these imposed structural changes, however, Dakota agriculture was on the verge of collapse. Indeed, in the early 1890s there occurred another migration of Dakota people from Canada to reservations in the United States.

Wadsworth had made some practical suggestions in his report for 1890. He saw that all of the bands were planting too much wheat, and had urged the farmers to diversify and increase the production of garden stuff and livestock. The problem was that the policy of subdivision and individual use of land would compel each of the farmers to provide their own pastures, byres and barns. Wadsworth admitted that "how each Indian is to acquire all of the above, I am unable to suggest, for although a good deal can be done by labour, certain parts will require cash."[6]

The same suggestions were being made by agricultural advisers to all farmers in the West, white and Indian, as it became frighteningly clear that one week of adverse weather could ruin a wheat-based economy. The other side of the coin, however, showed that wheat was the crop that promised sufficient return in those years of stagnation to make pioneer farming worth the risk, and it was some time before any settler made a significant expansion into diversified cropping and mixed farming. Indeed, because the Dakota had acquired significant herds of cattle early in their farming history, they were in advance of most of their neighbours in this respect.

Over the winter, the Dakota put considerable effort into improving cattle housing as Wadsworth had recommended. The Oak River people cut all the hay they had and sold it to surrounding farmers. As well, they hunted and fished, and since the winter was mild, they had great success. By spring, the three bands were well-prepared to go into another season.[7]

All of the Dakota bands brought more land into production in 1891, especially the Birdtail and Oak River bands, where acreage in crop was doubled. Much of the increase can be attributed to investment in technology, and the confidence the Dakota felt in their ability to make good use of their new tools. Wadsworth described the effect in his report of 1891: "Upon reaching my destination [Birdtail

Reserve] I could not help making comparisons between the Indians' crops on the Reserve, and those so lately passed through [the settlers'], the verdict was strongly in favour of the Indians."[8]

Most gardens included many vegetables that the Dakota had not grown before – cucumbers, radishes, melons, citrons and rhubarb – and a few even had large flower beds, all in prime bloom when the inspector visited the reserves. Until that time, most of the garden work had been done by the men, and Wadsworth "pointed out to them that this gardening work is for their women to do, and they must be made to do it." As he had suggested the year before, the Dakota had built a home pasture, and their cattle were better tended on a daily basis. The pasture, being communal, was less than the departmental ideal, but Wadsworth noted it as an improved farm practice. In 1890, eighteen men had engaged in farming, but in 1891, twenty-five were putting in field crops.

At the same time, the number of farmers at Oak River had increased from thirty-nine to forty-two, and more than double the acreage was broken and in crop. Wadsworth observed that "the extensive operations places this band in the van of the army of Indian Farmers in this country." In order to keep up with the expansion of their fields, the Dakota had further invested in technology by adding five new binders, two more mowers and rakes, three lumber wagons and six ploughs, all out of their own private funds. Wadsworth agreed that the implements were necessary, but he cautioned the Dakota to save their earnings and purchase lumber to make their homesteads more comfortable, rather than purchase any additional implements. Wadsworth noted that the cattle "were much thought of by their owners," but recommended that the band receive a blooded bull, as the one they were using was of inferior form. The Oak River people had learned that it was risky to plant their crops on the river bottom, as the earliest frost always struck hardest there, and then moved up to the top of the valley. The reserve was being subdivided that year and, as a result, the prime highlands would be at a premium. Dissension was on the horizon.

That summer, the first resident farm instructor was appointed to the Oak River Reserve. It was Wadsworth's opinion that this move was "an experiment of doubtful utility, any success they have attained up to the present must be attributed to the Agent and to the Indians themselves; having gained such a full measure of success I think it would be better to stick to the old lines."[9]

But instructing farming was not the real purpose of the man the department sent to Oak River. Markle had long suspected that one or two of the men at the reserve were using alcohol, and he wanted someone there to suppress the traffic and gather evidence for prosecution. Commissioner Reed managed to find money for this, but did not provide a cent for schools, grain storage facilities or any other amenities.

With the appointment of a resident farmer and subdivision of the land, control over farm production passed out of the hands of the Dakota community.

Even the small band at Oak Lake had increased their cultivated acreage, and made a modest investment in technology by purchasing a used binder for $50, three mowers and two farm wagons, all of which Wadsworth approved. The inspector reported that "these Indians are workers, for as they receive no assistance from the Department, must – while resting from their own work – work for the settlers, this being the only means of subsistence until they can realize from their own crops."[10]

Like the people of the Oak River Band, those at Oak Lake had fenced a loop in the river for their cattle, but they needed a bull. Wadsworth suggested they be sent the inferior one from Oak River when that band received their new bull. He concluded: "They certainly deserve great praise for their farming operations this year, and diversity of crops sown, when it is realized that they provided their own seed, and the variety was entirely of their own planning."[11]

One would imagine from reading Inspector Wadsworth's reports that the Dakota were doing well, and as he himself had suggested, did not require interference from the Indian department any more than they still required rations and assistance. As was usual in good times, the giveaway sprang into prominence, and Agent Markle complained that "several of the best workers of this band [Birdtail] yet cling to the heathen custom of giving away too much of their earnings at dances, and it seems no easy task to get them to discontinue this foolish practice."[12] Over the next few years, the agent tried to suppress the giveaway with a vengeance. He also stepped up his crusade to ferret out those involved with liquor, and was planning surprise visits to the Oak River Reserve. He complained that as the Indian Act was then worded, it was necessary for him to actually apprehend an Indian while under the influence. He asked that the act be changed so that he could arrest an Indian for drinking as long as two months after the fact. The appropriate change was made in the spring of 1891, placing a powerful coercive tool in the hands of the agent.

In 1891, all the Dakota bands were compelled to obtain permits to sell any product of the reserves, including firewood, hay, cattle, grain and garden produce. On the surface, this regulation was intended to protect the Indians from themselves; the regulation made it illegal for them to commit their produce to the purchase of goods and services that were unnecessary in the opinion of the department. To Hayter Reed, it meant any and all kinds of "labour-saving mechanisms," and to Markle, it meant suppression of traffic in liquor, and of the wacipi and giveaway. For the Indians, the regulation meant that they no longer had any control in the market aspect of their economic strategies. The regulation was universally condemned by Indians and even by the settlers, who were incapable of imagining themselves having to operate under such strictures. The settlers sympathized with the

Dakota in their long and wearisome battle to gain exemption from these provisions of the Indian Act.[13] The agent, however, had the law on his side, and the permit regulations combined with the Indian liquor laws and the agent's right to assign lands out of the subdivisions gave him authority over all aspects of Dakota economic and social life. Markle was quick to brand those who objected to the permits as drunkards, incompetents who were undeserving of additional lands, and moral degenerates to whom he would refuse permits if he even suspected them of intending to participate in a giveaway.[14]

In the spring of 1892, Markle made his first arrests on Oak River Reserve and sent two men to jail on liquor charges. To put this matter in perspective, during the ten years Markle pursued his sacred objective, he managed to secure fewer than five convictions from a population in excess of five hundred. As he reported in April, however, this aspect of his work took up so much of his time that he was unable to visit the reserves in the spring, having been fully occupied putting two Dakota in Brandon Gaol for a month.[15]

The Indian department had not been able to fund the "farm instructor" over the winter of 1891–1892, and Markle had been busy chasing down those involved with liquor, so that by the time a resident farmer returned to Oak River, seeding was almost complete. As soon as the farmer got there, the agent noticed another offense: the Dakota had retained grain on a communal basis over the winter for milling into flour and for seed. Farmers who had saved enough grain for their own purposes and had some surplus were making their surplus available to those who did not have enough for both domestic use and seedstock. Those Dakota who required more than was available in the community purchased what they needed from off-reserve sources on credit. To Markle's mind, this would not do. Now that the reserve was subdivided, as were all management and production aspects of the farms, each farmer should be compelled to save his own grain for domestic and seed use. To this end, the agent proposed that the Indian department build a large storage facility, where each farmer would be obliged to place a part of his crop. This he could draw upon as he needed it for milling, but only in small lots, so that he would not feel tempted to sell it. He felt that if this plan were adopted for a few years, a number of the "reliable Indians could then be trusted to store their own grain, and I trust in a short time they would all see that it would be to their own interests to do it and require no pressure from departmental officials to get them to do so."[16]

Markle's suggestions on grain reserves was a part of a grander idea to suppress all access that the Dakota might have to credit.

Many of these Indians seem to be able to get any article they fancy on credit and this to my mind is detrimental to their interests as it leads them to purchase articles that they could get along without and articles not at all required. I have informed the Indians that this practice must be stopped and instructed

Mr. Scott to discountenance the receiving of goods by the Indians on credit and to report to me if this order is contravened. No doubt the Indians have been encouraged in this by parties who have goods to sell and it is my intention . . . not to allow the Indians to sell grain this season only under permit of the Instructor. In this way, I hope to assist the Indians to expend their gains from farming to best advantage."[17]

Markle had found that, the year before, even though the department had imposed the permit system, as soon as the farm instructor had departed in the autumn, the Dakota sold their grain. For the winter of 1892–93, however, Farmer Scott was going to be in full-time residence, and so it would be possible to maintain control at all times. The Dakota would not have physical possession of their own produce, nor would they have control over its marketing, or over the revenue thereby gained. No doubt, some individuals were purchasing useless equipment, but the progress the Dakota made in farming, which was reported regularly by the inspector and the agent, would seem to make a lie of Markle's contention that they were generally irresponsible. The Dakota were, however, in violation of two major policies imposed by the Indian department: they were using technology not thought to be suitable for Indians, and they were continuing to maintain certain "primitive" economic institutions, such as pooling resources. The way to eradicate such habits was to eliminate access to technology by making it impossible for the Dakota to pay for their purchases, and to remove their produce from direct access by individual farmers.

Markle was completely out of touch with what was then the established way of doing things in Manitoba. The management strategy assumed by many settlers who wished to maximize their production involved extensive assumption of credit. Farmers would sell all of their crop over the winter in order to meet cash-flow needs for supporting the household and for winter farming operations. By doing so, they postponed the purchase of their spring requirements until the last minute, thus conserving capital and making as short as possible the time that money was borrowed – from seeding to harvest. As well, in the past few years, the price of grain had been falling in step with the stagnation of national economies in general, and the only hope for increasing income was to increase production, which implied an increased investment in technology. It is hard to believe that Markle was unaware of these trends, but he saw as distinct and separate the legitimate business of farming and whatever it was the Indians were doing. Unfortunately, all of his views were accepted by Commissioner Reed and put into immediate effect.[18]

Markle's sparse reports came in over the summer and indicated that drought had again visited Manitoba.[19] Inspector Wadsworth's detailed report came in on schedule near the end of October and confirmed the agent's earlier observations on the crop season. Wadsworth reported that in 1891 there had been twenty-five farmers at the Birdtail Reserve, and in 1892 there were twenty-two. Two had returned to the United States, and one had simply quit farming and turned to other things, mostly farm labour. All three had given up farming in reaction to the recent imposition of regulations on the reserve.

One of those who left was referred to in the documentary literature as "Sioux Ben," and was described as an "agitator" by the inspector. That is, he had spoken out against and organized resistance to the permit system. Both Wadsworth and Markle were pleased to see this bad influence leave. Sioux Ben had been mentioned in the journals of the old Hudson's Bay Company post at Fort Ellice, where he was spoken of as a hard worker. In the 1860s and early 1870s, he had worked as a trapper, herdsman, woodcutter, oxen breeder and freighter. By the late 1880s, Sioux Ben had planted about twelve acres in garden and field crops, all by hand, about the average for the farmers of the Birdtail Reserve. When he left the reserve, he had over twenty-five acres prepared for planting, and was maintaining several head of cattle, horses and other livestock. There is no record of Sioux Ben ever having received assistance of any kind from the Indian department, nor is there recorded a single word of complaint about his behaviour. It is impossible to view this man as a malingerer. He was just a man who was not prepared to be bullied into surrendering control over his own life. Like many of the people who later poured into the Northwest as settlers, Sioux Ben moved beyond the reach of repressive government, never to return. He left behind all his own improvements, his house and his family of two sons, whose descendants form part of the present community at Birdtail. The other man who went to the United States was Daniel Tonococa, who left his standing crops, house, cattle and most of his other possessions. Of him, Wadsworth writes, "he was well spoken of."[20]

Those farmers who remained at Birdtail put in a much larger crop in 1892, but it was stunted from lack of rain. The soil was becoming seriously depleted and could not support a good crop without plentiful rain. As well, the land was becoming weed infested, a condition which generally accompanies depleted soil, and leaving summer fallow was not solving the problem. The Dakota were abiding by the rules of the subdivision of the reserve : "Each man knows his own lines and keeps within them," reported Inspector Wadsworth. Each farmer was entitled to eighty acres of land. Considering the fact that some farmers had all of their plot in crop, and since the reserve lands were not able to stand an increase in the numbers of cattle and other livestock, it is apparent that the Birdtail Dakota had, by 1892, outgrown their lands. The depletion of the soil was probably exacerbated by the imposition of the subdivision system; before that time, as a farmer increased his crops, he ploughed where he could, preferring the best available soils, and often left strips of broken, but uncropped land between the rows of cultivated soil. This practice would have conserved soil fertility and moisture. After the subdivision, however, any farmer wishing to increase acreage in crop was unable to do so beyond the borders of an eighty-acre plot. Instead, he would have been obliged to put most of the land more or less continuously into crop. Depletion was inevitable.

To compensate for the shortage of arable land, the Department of the Interior set aside 28-14-27-W1M for the Birdtail Band in the spring of 1889. This section of land is immediately to the south and east of the main body of the reserve lands. In 1909, this land was lost to the band when the lands agent in Brandon mistakenly assigned it to a settler. Even though the band had been short of land since 1892, alternate lands were never made available.[21]

The Birdtail people secured enough income to pay off all their machinery debts in 1892, and, since Markle had threatened implement dealers who might sell to Indians and grain dealers who might buy from Indians, they added little to their technology that year. The gardens were excellent. Wadsworth described that of Awichan as looking "like a large market garden, vegetables of almost every variety being grown by him in great profusion; it had been well-attended to, and he was well rewarded for his labour, which, by the way, was mostly done by his wife." Clearly, Dakota labour organization was moving toward Wadsworth's concept of civilization. The hay crop was adequate. The corn crop had been very good, and much of it was sold to the townspeople, the income from which was spent on food for the late summer.

The Dakota at Birdtail were, by 1892, largely dependent upon agriculture for their living, with seasonal additions from a variety of other sources that had been exploited over the previous twenty-five years. With an estimated population of 130, total yearly income was about $25.20 per person, or $126 for a family of five. At that time, the average settler farmer might expect to gross about $900 a year from his enterprise, with an average of seventy acres in crop.[22] For the average settler, the gross return per acre farmed was $12.85 and $4.82 for the Birdtail Dakota. This gross return was not realized uniformly by all Dakota farmers. Farms ranged in size from eighty acres in crop down to less than ten acres, and some members of the band were not engaged in agriculture beyond a kitchen garden, having selected other sources of income. All of the twenty-two farmers, however, had cattle, and since communal herding had been stopped, we might infer that those responsible for the animals were more or less continuously at home. The bookkeeping done by the department at that time suggests that only the farmers participated in the agricultural returns, in that only the producing farmer could get a permit to sell farm produce, and only he could draw on funds or produce recognized to be his in order to make purchases. If so, farm incomes ranged from about $50 for a farm of ten acres to as much as $400 for Moses Bunn, who had eighty acres. Of course, the giveaway went far to level these differences, but by this time the Dakota reserves were taking on the traits of a market-production, stratified community.

Arable land was short at Birdtail Reserve after 1892, as it was at the other reserves in later years. Not everybody had access to eighty arable acres, and with the subdivision they would likely never have. It was departmental policy not to grant the eighty-acre divisions to young men who were unmarried and had no family, even on those reserves where some land was available. Since the Dakota tended to marry late, this policy created a surplus of young labour, thereby reducing productivity of operations that were already underproductive. Individuation of land and productive assets, individual access to produce, suppression of communal labour, and the system of land management assured the development of income gradients on the reserves. An additional effect was that disputes began to erupt over matters of land access and use, and boundary arguments were common from this time onward.

The band at Oak River was experiencing more or less the same events as their relatives at Birdtail were. At Oak River, 1,076 acres of land had been planted, but the results were disappointing. Drought had stunted the crop, the wheat yield was less than ten bushels an acre, and the oat yield was even poorer. They had paid off most of their debts from the previous year, a year of heavy investment, but Markle and Wadsworth were applying with vigour the penalties for those caught buying and selling with Indians who had no permits. All of the local implement dealers had been warned. The Indians greatly resented this continuing intrusion. Wadsworth reported: "At present, the Indians are restive over the threatened enforcement of the law, for they think (foolishly) that they can look after their own interests, and I believe they will lose no opportunity of assisting the whitemen to break it, and that they will sell clandestinely, and thereby get lower prices than if they took their produce into the open market; for there are always to be found men who will take a risk where there are a few dollars to be made."[23]

A.E. Forget, assistant commissioner of Indian affairs, noted the official view of their objection, in a marginal note to Wadsworth's report: "Indians often resist at first measures intended for their own protection, but as a rule, they soon come to see the benefit and acquiesce." Inspector Wadsworth did not know at the time he wrote his report that it had been decided in Ottawa that Farmer Scott would not be retained on the reserve for the winter. Forget also expressed concern that the Dakota should not be left to market their own grain, or they would "recklessly squander" the income. Forget pencilled in a note: "The Agent will have to do his best in this matter."[24]

The agent offered Farmer Scott the free use of the school on the reserve as a house for the winter, if he did nothing else but issue permits to the Indians. Markle did not tell the Indian department about this arrangement until he inadvertently made reference to Scott in a letter to Ottawa some months later, and was asked about Scott's presence. He certainly did not tell the Dakota that Scott had no authority to be on the reserve, or live in their school, or in any way interfere in their lives.

As at Birdtail, a distinct economic gradient was developing at Oak River. Two farmers had cultivated ninety-three acres each, and as Wadsworth put it, all but eight of the forty-two farmers had acreages in the double figures, with a average of twenty-five acres under cultivation. There is no record of incomes, since the Oak River people had done their own buying and selling during the previous winter, but there is nothing to suggest that incomes were distributed in any way different from that at Birdtail.

Thirty-four households had cattle, with a total herd of 163 head. Wadsworth correctly encouraged mixed farming. Amongst the settlers, the provincial Department of Agriculture and the farmers' societies were actively encouraging greater use of livestock in a farm strategy; the prevailing low grain prices made a good return on grain crops very difficult, except for the biggest farmers in the most favourable areas. As well, a market for Canadian beef had developed in England. Like any farmers, the Dakota would have known the prices and returns on the cattle, but the year before, just when the inspector was reporting that the Oak River people were handy with cattle, the department imposed the permit system on the sale of cattle and otherwise took over the management of that aspect of the enterprise. The Dakota promptly lost interest in the animals, except as a source of ready cash when they could wheedle a permit out of the agent.[25]

In terms of agricultural development, the Oak Lake Band was definitely trailing behind the other two. The small population of ten families, including forty-eight individuals, was engaged in farming. They had a total of 141 acres of crop in 1892, most of which was stunted wheat; their crop was a failure. Until this time, the Oak Lake Band had not been affected by the recent policies of the Indian department, had no resident official, and had only occasional visits from Markle. Unfortunately, the Oak Lake people had not had the opportunity to invest in technology before the policy crunch came and, by the next year, when the official eye was upon them, the chance to make a technological advance had passed. From this time on, the gap between the technologically advanced bands and the others widened rapidly.

In December 1892, Markle learned that the Dakota at Oak River were $4,000 in debt, and still had balances owing on purchases made in 1890. In his own words, Markle was "shocked" by this state of affairs, and he made a greater effort in controlling buying and spending of the Dakota.[26] The Indian defiance of the permit system made confrontation inevitable. The Dakota put in one more season under the rules of the Indian department before attempting to regain control of their own economic strategies.

In his report on the inspection of the Birtle agency for 1893, Wadsworth wrote that the previous two poor farming years had greatly discouraged the Birdtail people, "and they are not so enthusiastic in their farming operations."[27] This was a considerable understatement. Another four farmers had abandoned their enterprises that year, and twelve people had returned to the United States. The cultivated acreage was reduced from about 590 acres in 1892 to about 275 acres in 1893, and over the year the cattle herd went from 110 head to seventy-six. No doubt, the poor years did overwhelm some of the smaller farmers, but also to blame were the department's regulations, as an increasing number of Dakota decided that they were not going to live with such intolerable intervention in their affairs. For the first time in years, the band was compelled to ask for winter rations and received a thousand pounds of flour.

The Oak River Dakota reduced their croplands by a hundred acres in 1893 to about 964 acres in all, but the continuing drought had greatly reduced yields. Until this season, the Dakota had been cutting hay in common fields, stacking it where it was cut and then taking their supplies over the winter as needed. In 1893, each farmer began to cut his own hay and haul it close to his own barn. While Wadsworth saw this as a more efficient way of handling cattle feed, and it probably was, it can also be seen as another consequence of individuation. There were few other improvements on the reserve, but the department had built a new residence for Farmer Scott, who had been returned to his position on the reserve.

The Oak Lake Band did not suffer so much from the drought as either the Oak River or Birdtail Band did, and it took off a better crop. They had not increased acreage in 1893, but that summer they prepared considerably more land for seeding in 1894. The Oak Lake Band was the only one not to receive any food assistance over the year, as even the Oak River Dakota had taken fifteen sacks of flour.

The disagreement over policy came to a head in late October 1893 when three men of the Oak River Reserve, Harry Hotain, Kiyewakan and Mahpiyaska, travelled to Ottawa to lay their complaints before Deputy Superintendent General of Indian Affairs D.C. Scott. Their visit to Ottawa filled everyone with consternation as they made the journey on their own and without an interpreter. Almost all of the interview with Scott was in signs, but he understood them well enough to comprehend their complaints. First, they complained that the permit system was ruining their economy. As well, they said that the Oak River Reserve was too small to support three white representatives – Agent Markle, Farmer Scott and Anglican

Missionary Hartland, who had been at the reserve the previous two years teaching and preaching. The men stated that they approved of Hartland, but could do nicely without the other two. Scott ordered Assistant Indian Commissioner Forget to immediately launch an enquiry into the complaints, but at the same time it was made clear to the Dakota that they were never again to make such an unauthorized journey away from their reserve.[28]

As Inspector Wadsworth understood it, the Dakota had three complaints: first, they objected in general to having the permit system forced upon them; second, they suspected that Farmer Scott was retaining some of their earnings for his own use; and third, if they were obliged to accept some form of non-Indian management, they wished it to come from Rev. Hartland. Wadsworth dismissed the first complaint by saying that enforcing the permit system was part of the resident farmer's job. He again alleged that the Dakota had fallen into debt and been unable to pay for their purchases. Did Farmer Scott retain the Indians' money? Wadsworth concluded that as Scott made it a practice to retain some part of an individual Indian's earnings in order to pay for custom threshing, it was probable that the Dakota mistook this for embezzlement. Scott had receipts and records of transactions to show that he was doing nothing untoward. The practice was necessary, wrote Wadsworth, because the Dakota could not be trusted to meet their just debts. As for Missionary Hartland, Wadsworth dismissed him with the comment that he had performed his duties as teacher "imperfectly." Forget accepted Wadsworth's first and last observations, but felt that the charge of financial impropriety should receive further investigation, and he assigned the task to Agent Markle. At no time did the Indian department look into the wisdom of the permit system.[29]

Markle reported that he had found nothing amiss in Scott's books. While on the reserve, the agent inquired about who knew of the three Dakota's journey to Ottawa, and found that besides close friends and relatives of the men, nobody was aware of their plans. This suggests that by the early 1890s there were significant political divisions in the reserve population. Markle concluded that the "principal agitators" were those who wanted relief from the permit system.[30]

Markle forwarded to Ottawa the records of business transactions of thirty of the thirty-five Dakota farmers at Oak River Reserve. Ironically, this document makes it possible to examine the details of the band's use of credit since 1891. Twenty-five farmers never took goods on credit; of the remaining ten, only four had debts outstanding at the time of Markle's report, and these were the men the agent called "agitators and drunkards." In all cases, debts had been incurred only to make purchases of agricultural implements and supplies, or to hire special services such as blacksmithing and custom threshing. No food or clothing was purchased on credit, since the Dakota preferred to pay for these with cash earned off the reserve.

In 1886, one of those identified by Markle as an agitator, Harry Hotain, had a total of 6.25 acres of crop and by 1893 he had fifty-two acres; in addition he had a number of cattle and a full line of farm implements. Another, Mahpiyaska, had farmed off the reserve until the mid-1880s, but by 1886 had seventeen acres in crop at Oak River; by 1893 he had increased that to forty-seven acres. Charles Dowan started with three acres in 1886, and had increased that to fifty-one acres in 1893. Kiyewakan had not been on his own farm in 1886, but by 1893 he had over fifty acres in crop. Together, then, these four men had increased their holdings of cultivated land from 26.25 acres to two hundred acres. The average size of a farm on Oak River Reserve at that time was about thirty acres, while their settler neighbours were averaging about seventy acres in crop. For both, improved land was valued at $10.45 an acre, and unimproved at $5.40. In short, the "agitators" were amongst the most progressive farmers on the reserve. They were approaching the regional average farm size, and had increased the land value of their operations by about $873. The total investment associated with this increase was about $900, all but $200 of which was paid off. It is impossible to see from Markle's own figures any support for his conclusion that the Dakota were unable to manage their affairs. Some were in debt, but the debts were associated with investments in increased productivity and an increase in capital asset value.

In addition to his own assessment, Markle included a letter from James Johnston, agent at Griswold for the Massey Harris Company, that he thought would support his charges. Until that summer, Johnston had been selling implements and seed to the Dakota on credit, but he had not been paid when the crops failed. Johnston gave up selling to Indians without permits, and embraced the new order, "knowing the Company would be protected by the Instructor in charge." There is no doubt that the permit system, as applied to the Dakota, was working to the disadvantage of the Indians and to the advantage of the implement dealers, who were now always paid for authorized purchases. These same dealers had earlier been supportive of the Dakota in their resistance to the department's policies, but as the depression deepened on the prairies, the only debts they were sure would be paid promptly, if at all, were those incurred by the Indians under the permit system.

Finally, Markle spoke to the Reverend Hartland about his role in this. Markle said of the missionary: "He is in sympathy with the Indians in their grievance, and stated that the Indians are in a most discontented state of mind, and fears that I will have trouble unless various matters are altered or amended." Hartland's wife supported her husband in his conclusions, and Markle recommended that all effort be made to have them removed from the reserve. It was only a matter of time before this was accomplished.[31]

Wadsworth and Markle hoped that the issues had been settled and that the Dakota had learned a lesson, but the sale of grain without permits increased from the very day Markle left Oak River after his investigation. Within two weeks he was writing again to Ottawa, complaining that the Dakota were simply going to the storage sheds, taking their grain, and selling it. They would not talk to either Markle or Scott about how much grain they were selling, to whom, or at what prices. The grain buyers were openly taking grain from the Indians and Markle wanted Reed to crack down on the buyers, which the commissioner fully approved. Reed also wrote Forget a letter which was to be delivered to the Indians, warning them that "their Agent and Farming Instructor have dealt with their affairs judiciously and in their own best interests."[32]

Markle spent eighteen days in September trying to secure evidence that would convict the illegal buyers of Indian grain. It took much longer than he had anticipated because nobody would volunteer information. Mahpiyaska told the agent that he had indeed sold grain without a permit, but would say nothing about who bought it. At last, Markle caught two private buyers who were dealing with Indians, one of whom was convicted and fined $25 with costs.[33]

On January 11, the *Virden Chronicle* ran a full three-column article about the permit system. The newspaper saw the present treatment of Indian farmers as being such a source of potential conflict that another rebellion was feared. It may have been alarmist, but the paper accurately reflected the situation as seen by Indians and some settler farmers. It stated: "They farm their own land, work hard all summer, and through the obnoxious order are not allowed the full benefit of the fruit of their own labour. They are thus placed at a disadvantage in competition with their white and more highly civilized neighbours."[34] Reed was incensed with the newspaper article but, not wanting the grain dealers to retaliate by refusing to buy the Indians' most important cash crop, he was conciliatory.[35]

Early in 1894, Peter Hunter, a Dakota preacher at Oak Lake, complained that Markle was refusing to forward Indians' letters to the authorities in Ottawa. Hunter went with a number of Dakota from Oak River to visit T.M. Daly, minister of the interior and superintendent general of Indian affairs, when he was in Brandon. In November, a petition signed by forty-two of the men at Oak River was sent to Ottawa. The petition set out all of the old complaints and added some new ones. The agent had appointed Tukancikeyana chief, over the objections of the reserve's leading men. As well, Markle was refusing to forward any mail from the Indians to the Indian department, and had threatened to jail any person who protested his actions. Markle suspected that Hunter was behind this action, and he bent to the task of having the preacher removed from his position; he finally succeeded in having the Presbyterian Church revoke the appointment. As soon as this was done, Reed instructed Markle to hound Hunter, described as "one of the American Sioux," off the reserve. Settlers joined the Dakota in their protest and when letters in their support began to arrive on his desk, Reed instructed Wadsworth to investigate the complaints in full.[36]

A month later, the inspector's report was sent to Ottawa. This report is one of the more interesting documents in Dakota history, in that it includes a verbatim record of a meeting between a number of Dakota at Oak River and the inspector, all taken down in shorthand by Wadsworth.

Wadsworth began his investigation into the Dakota's complaints by seeking character references for Farmer Scott. This he did by going to Griswold on municipal election day and talking to the assembled settlers and townspeople. Wadsworth claimed that the references came from unbiased people who had no reason to dissemble. All of the testimonies were glowing. Included in the sample were settlers Hanna and Cairns, who had farms adjacent to the Oak River Reserve and who had, with Scott's approval, benefited by impounding stray cattle. Settlers Hall and Young had done custom threshing for the Dakota and had their fees guaranteed by Scott, who also gave them preferential access to the Dakota's business. Another was an implement dealer whose debts were protected by Scott. Another was the poundkeeper who seized the Dakota's cattle and turned them over to Hanna and Cairns, and yet another was a close personal friend of T.M. Daly, minister of the interior. Wadsworth summarized all this unbiased opinion and concluded that Scott was not only exonerated of all complaints by the Dakota, but deserving of a raise in salary, which he got.

A band meeting was held at Oak River on December 19 and 20, 1894, to enquire into the record of Farm Instructor Scott. The inspector, Agent Markle, Interpreter Antoine Flament and thirty-five Indians were in attendance. Farmer Scott was not present, but he and Markle were invited to read the transcript and prepare rebuttals to the Indians' charges. These comments were added to the written record, but the Dakota had no opportunity to examine these later comments or to answer the counter charges Markle and Scott made against the Indians. Inspector Wadsworth kept a verbatim record of the proceedings:

Harry Hotain: We are short of ploughs, wagons, etc., and that is why we are so much in debt, it takes all our crops to pay our debts. Since Scott came here, we are getting poorer every day; about the debts we owe, we couldn't do anything to pay them as our wheat was all wet, since then we never have a cent in our pockets. If we have money, we have to go to the village to pay our debts. If we have grain we take it to the market, we only see it weighed, we never see if we get anything for it or not. For that reason, these people don't care if they raise a big crop or not, and these Indians don't know which is their own land; a good many are good workers, a good many young fellows would like to have a section of land, but Scott says "You have no wife yet. You don't want land"; if they have no wife, they have no one to make a living for, then it is of no use having a wife at all.

Three years ago Scott got us to do fall ploughing before we got the thresher. Four of us got a machine at last. It came as far as the trail, and Scott wouldn't let us bring it any further. After that, we got another and Scott stopped that. He stopped three machines coming: then it commenced raining and rained every day. Then we got a machine and I had 600 bushels of wheat, all wet.

[Marginal note added later by Scott and Markle]: One [thresher] offered to come and thrash out four Indians' grain, but these Indians owed this party and he probably expected to get his claim settled. If this allowed, other creditors would get little or nothing and make it difficult then to get a thrasher to come and thrash the remnant as the four Indians referred to had the largest stacks in the best locality to do this work.

[Marginal note added later by Wadsworth]: It does not always rain to any serious extent in the autumn in this country, and the Farmer could not forecast the weather.

Hotain: A man who has his ploughing here, and the Agent always tells us to go fishing and hunting, he says it is a good place (the fishing lake) to make a living.[37]
   I don't like to go there. I would sooner live on this reserve. The Agent told John Noel about the fishing. We don't care about going there to fish. At this place we always have the river.
   That is why we want to know all about these things. That is why we went to Ottawa last year. We didn't speak much there. We only talked by signs. We heard after we went that we did wrong in going and we found out after there was no kind of law in Ottawa. We didn't know. We thought it was the right place, where the head men lived, to go. Then we heard we went for nothing. We got no law there.
   Scott is the second from the Agent to advise us. That is what delays us in our work. We all gather up to talk and he tells us the Agent is going to drive us away to the States.

[Marginal note added later by Scott and Markle]: When they complained about the permit system, refused to do as instructed and in accordance with the rules made to govern them, they were told by the Agent that the young men should not forget that they were "Sioux" that the Canadian government had taken pity on their forefathers and protected them when in trouble and those that did not feel disposed to be governed now by the rules of the Government had better return to their home in the United States.

Hotain: About a month ago we sent a letter to Ottawa. We didn't say much in it, only a few words. We sent this letter explaining what was going on on this reserve and to get a right answer what we are going to do. I am talking for us all. We don't want Scott any more here.

Wadsworth then asked Hotain what recent charges he had against Farmer Scott, and Hotain described a situation where the farmer refused to allow him to cut more hay on his own land than the farmer thought Hotain needed for his own purposes. Scott feared that the Dakota might take some of it away for sale, so a considerable amount of hay was left uncut and wasted. In the spring, Hotain was forced to buy straw to feed his cattle. Scott could not recall the circumstances of this particular event, but supported himself by saying that the Indians did not know how to manage their own hay supplies. In this case, though, Scott would seem to be the incompetent. Thus, Hotain, without an income from hay sales, was unable to pay a five-dollar threshing debt, and had still owed that amount. On the other hand, Scott gave permission to a settler friend to help himself to the Indians' haystacks when he ran low in the winter, and Hotain was threatened with jail if he complained. Scott excused this by saying that the settler who took the hay held a debt of Hotain's, and this was one way of paying it off. Hotain did manage to stop the sale of the hay after he learned that Scott had sold it to his friend for $3.50 a ton. Hotain knew that he owed the man a debt, and offered to sell it for $4 a ton, which the settler accepted. Hotain had then paid an additional $1 out of pocket and the debt was settled. Scott dismissed all of this as being of no account.

Hotain then complained that, when Scott was removing a steer from the reserve, he did not see to it that the rest of the herd did not follow, as cattle tend to do. Two animals left the field, tried to cross the Assiniboine on the ice, fell into the river and drowned. Scott wrote this off as an unfortunate accident, and replaced the dead cattle with a plough.

Hotain: All we ask at Ottawa is that anything we have to sell will be our own and do what we like with.

The men that got up against Scott. Scott has always a little trouble against the men here. We would rather have a stranger than Scott. We would like another man in place of Scott to look after us, and if we are doing anything wrong we will let this man know, so that he can write to the Commissioner: that is all. I want to tell you no lies.

Wadsworth: Did you sell any wheat last year without a permit?

Hotain: Yes, I sold grain (or rather my son sold it for me) without a permit. I gave him liberty to sell it.

Wadsworth: Did you know it was against the law and rules of the Department to do that?

Hotain: Yes, I knew that. Another thing, I took forty bags of wheat to Griswold, and Scott caught me there and I brought it all home again.

[Marginal note added later by Scott and Markle]: The Indians or "Hotain" and the agitators with him not only want the right to sell all their produce, but the cattle as well, and object to any restrictions being placed upon them as to the disposal of their money.

Hotain then told the inspector of a time when Scott refused to allow him to sell enough grain to feed his threshing crew, and the crop suffered in quality as a result. Scott replied in a marginal note that had Hotain been allowed to get more food, "there was a liability of waste."

A number of other men opposed to the department's rule also spoke on the matters that Hotain had raised. Mahpiyaska was so fed up that he was no longer reporting to anyone when he left the reserve; nor did he say where he was going or why. More than that, he was no longer improving or expanding his farm, having not bothered to break land in the previous year or more. He did not trust the hearing to air the Indian side of things and, with others, had resolved to send his own report to Ottawa. Mahpiyaska was dissatisfied with the permit system to such a degree that, if he could sell his grain only through the agent, he would not sell it at all, preferring to give it away as pig feed to anyone who wanted to come and cart it off.

Mazacaga: We have never been against the white men: don't think that. The white man who is here don't know his business and that is what we want to tell you today. We will just let you know how that man has not succeeded in his work as he should. We don't go against the Head Man's words, we want you to know that, but Scott is not doing right and we want you to fix it. So far as I can see, the work don't go. He don't tell us right how to do it.

Kiyewakan complained that the Dakota were treated in a rude manner by Scott, and that they did not even have the right to enter any of the buildings on the reserve: "Any Indian going into Scott's house should be given a chair to sit down and be talked to like a gentleman." Rather than that, Scott refused Kiyewakan a permit, because the Dakota had gone to the agent's home to ask for it. Scott agreed that he was at times short with the Indians, but as he was not being paid at the time (in fact, he had no right to be on the reserve), he did not see why he should put up with the aggravation. Kiyewakan, too, rejected the idea that they leave the reserve to fish, as the Assiniboine River was right there with fish in it. As Scott and Markle pointed out, however, the Dominion Fisheries agents had been at their fishing station near the Little Saskatchewan and ordered them off, saying they could no longer fish in the river, and had threatened to prosecute if they continued.

The only people to speak in favour of departmental policy were Chief Tukan-cikeyana and his brother, John, and they were willing to do whatever the department demanded of them. Others, however, spoke against the troubles that Hotain and his supporters had forced to the surface. In speaking to Hotain, Padokasni said, "You have a good face to meet a man and tell him all the lies you are telling today." In his turn, Hotain refused to use Tukancikeyana's Dakota name, referring to him throughout the meeting as "Chief Pat." The meeting drew to a close with both Hotain and Tukancikeyana promising to abide by whatever ruling the department devised, and Wadsworth wrote up his report.

Hotain and his people never did understand that the meeting was not called to look into government policy. At no time then or later did the department examine the rationale for their policy: the meeting was solely for the purpose of discovering whether the agent and farmer were scrupulous in applying the rules and regulations as they then stood. The Dakota were widely divided as to the necessity for the rules (or, at least, the necessity of their complying with them), a division of politics that has persisted for many decades. Without so much as a word about the wisdom of the department's edicts, Wadsworth found that Scott was doing as he was told and again recommended that he be given an increase in salary. In addition, he was to be given rations for "entertaining" Indians in his home (more of a ration than had been received by the band over the past decade), and his living quarters were to be renovated.[38]

Even Wadsworth's hearing did not settle matters. In the winter of 1894–95, Minister of the Interior Daly received two more complaints from settlers that the Indians were being unfairly treated by the man in charge of the local livestock pound. The Dakota were being assessed fees they had no ability to pay. Once again Markle was instructed to investigate, and once again he found that there was nothing wrong with the manner in which the impoundment of the band's cattle was being conducted. Even while the last such "investigation" was being carried out, Reed arrived at his final decision on the full spectrum of complaints that the Dakota had been pressing, and sent a letter, through Markle, expressing his wishes:

> The Department . . . is quite convinced that the real cause of the dissatisfaction with the farmer expressed by one faction is, when sifted to the bottom, because he does not allow them to dispose of stock or farm produce without a permit to do so. . . .
> The Farmer, in putting a stop to their selling produce without permission, was only doing his duty, and carrying out the provisions made by the Government in the best interests of the Indians themselves, and to prevent advantage being taken of them by white men.
> The Department may now add that what it then said about the Farmer stopping the sale of produce being by its instructions and in the best interests of the Indians themselves, applies also to the stock, to the purchase by them – especially on credit – of articles which they cannot afford and do not require also to the traffic in intoxicants.
> The Department is . . . compelled to express its strongest disapproval of the conduct of that section of the Band of whom Hotanin appears to be the representative, that is, in so far as concerns devoting themselves to trying to find faults in their instructor, refusing obedience to lawful instructions, and agitating generally.
> The Department hopes that in their own interests these malcontents will settle down to steady work under the Farmer's guidance, and in this respect emulate the example set by Chief Pat and his followers, whose conduct meets with the approval of the Department and will, if persisted in, end by making them independent and comfortable.[39]

As directed, Markle read the letter to the Dakota and reported that "Harry Hotanin made no comments at the time I read the letter, . . . but he afterwards told me that he had decided to give up the fight and see if work would bring better results, than agitation, and seemed pleased that this dispute was settled." It is likely that Markle misrepresents Hotain's reaction to Reed's decree, since he was a proven hard worker at the time of his "agitation," but he did retire from the issue, having been subject to character assassination, and threats of imprisonment or expulsion to the United States.[40]

It was not that the Dakota gave up their struggle; to the contrary, the Dakota continued to sell grain without a permit whenever possible, and continued to make purchases of farm implements and other goods, often on credit. They simply ceased to speak of these transactions or to complain about government regulations. The department did make a token objection to the continuation of these practices, but several events in the latter part of the decade cooled the situation. First, Farmer Scott left the reserve and was replaced by a man whose corruption was so obvious that even the Indian department found him unsatisfactory, and terminated him on very much the same grounds as those presented by the Dakota concerning Scott. As well, the Dakota continued to improve their farm operations, and the department called a truce in the pursuit of permit violaters when it became obvious that they would have to commence wholesale arrests of the band's very best and most productive farmers.

Markle turned his attention to other evils, especially the suppression of giveaways and dances, and lost his former fervour about agitators and credit buying. By this time, the department had altered its policy and decided that its primary function, among the Dakota at any rate, was to concentrate on aspects of cultural assimilation. Agents were instructed to seek the improvement of housing quality, and to encourage the cutting of long hair, attendance at school, the use of English, wearing better clothing, and so on. Since at this time the Dakota themselves began to place greater emphasis on formal education, attended the Anglican churches near the reserves, and wanted to purchase household consumer goods, little was to be gained by re-opening the earlier nightmarish issue about permits and credit. Even that problem was reduced in importance as each year the bands increased equity in their enterprises and reduced the load of debt. Debt remained a part of modern agriculture for Indians as well as whites, and it may be that the department decided so long as the debt load was under control, there was no point in raising dust.

Perhaps because economic prospects looked so poor in the mid-1890s, Markle paid less attention to the Dakota's material betterment and concentrated on cleaning up "immorality," which for him was embodied in the giveaway and dancing:

The Sioux are particularly fond of dancing and spend entirely too much of their time and earnings at "pow-wowing," which is the appellation given when conducted by Indians in their style. I have discouraged the continuation of this custom for the reason that Indians so engaged were wasting their time and earnings, and I failed to observe any benefits therefrom; also that the Indians who were most zealous to retain this custom were those strongly opposed to educational and Christian advancement, and I regret that the Indians under my charge receive so many invitations from the whites to attend celebrations, picnics and other gatherings to give such exhibitions, which, if accepted, usually take them off their reserves and away from their work for several continuous days, and encourage them to cling to customs that are neither elevating, refining nor profitable.[41]

At this time, the Farm Extension Services were developing in Manitoba, as were farmers' associations. The primary responsibility of each was to offer practical information to farmers. After the Riel Rebellion in 1885, the Department of Indian Affairs had established a regulation whereby Indians were not allowed to leave their reserves unless they had a permit to do so from the Indian agent. This was never applied to the Dakota of Manitoba until the mid-1890s, and when Markle began to forbid Indians to leave the reserve, he also separated them from sources of recent agricultural information. The very events that he condemns were usually attended by extension officers, and held in association with farm fairs and agricultural exhibitions, from which the Indians were excluded. In such a circumstance, the Indians were left to re-invent agricultural techniques already in use elsewhere in the province.

The season of 1894 was more or less what the Dakota farmers had come to expect as normal, with its dryness and low crop yields, but it was not necessary for any of them to receive rations. Many had made enough income, both on and off their farms, to make considerable improvements to their homesteads. Whenever new houses or other permanent structures were being built, the farmers tended to locate them on their own surveyed plots if they had not been located there before. Individuation of property was becoming more entrenched, and by the mid-1890s, there were no farm implements, except one horse-powered thresher at Oak River Reserve, that were jointly owned. Wherever possible, each farmer strove to own his own productive assets. As might be expected, there were considerable differences among farmers' equipment. Some were able to handle a few acres of cropland, while others were expanding to the maximum area to which they had subdivision title, though they had little prospect of further growth.

The cattle herds decreased in size at this time, for a number of reasons. The drought had reduced the extent of pasture suitable for cattle range, and even that land "looked like travelled roads" at the end of a season, according to Wadsworth. All of the Dakota bands were very much restricted by the amount of hay they were able to secure on their own reserve lands, and as the grain farmers expanded, more and more grassland was taken out of production. To counter the decrease in wild hay stands, they planted first small fields of brome, and later Timothy grass. In the first years of these experiments, dryness retarded the growth of the tame hay, or else it was battered into the ground by hail. As well, the Dakota had moved their opposition to departmental regulation underground in an effort to maintain some control over their own economic management: cattle were not easy to sell secretly because they were difficult to move to market, noisy, and easily counted and branded. Handling grain, however, was much easier, and it had a higher value than beef did. The cattle herds were so thoroughly controlled by the department that the Dakota lost interest in them.

During the poor years of the 1890s, the Dakota put considerable effort into improving domestic production of a subsistence base. The individuation of land and separation of buildings made it easier for each household so inclined to keep a milk cow near the house for easy, regular milking. Most households had chickens, many had turkeys and ducks, and a few had goats for milking and sheep for meat and wool. Women knit much of the wool into garments used in the household or sold in neighbouring towns, for which there was always a good demand. Since the early part of the decade, the Indians had been encouraged to alter their division of labour within the household so that men were responsible for heavy field and livestock work, and women were responsible for keeping small livestock and the gardens, and doing much of the production of handcrafts for market. It seems possible and even likely that during this time the women were producing more income than were the men, primarily because a small garden and small animals could be nurtured through drought years when large fields of grain and hay, or large herds of cattle, might fail.[42]

The soil of all the reserves was rapidly being depleted. The land shortage had forced all the farmers to put as many acres as possible into crop, with a minimum of summerfallowing and other restorative culture, and the dryness had reduced the return of organic material to the soil. Birdtail and Oak Lake reserves were the most seriously affected and, in the summer of 1896, a number of families from Oak Lake asked that they be allowed to relocate on better land. Waoke, chief of the Oak Lake Band, had been to Fort Qu'Appelle Industrial School to visit two of his sons and had taken the opportunity to look at other locations. The area he preferred was near Moose Mountain, in present-day southeastern Saskatchewan, where there was plenty of hay and wood, both of which were lacking on Oak Lake Reserve. Nothing came of this request.[43]

In 1896, the crops at Birdtail were completely wiped out by hail, and the band was forced to accept a few bags of flour over the next winter and seed in the spring. They pulled their economy together by tanning and selling hides, working for settlers, and selling firewood cut close to the towns. Their church was doing well, and the band had enough of a surplus to support the Church Mission Society, a chapter of the Ladies Aid, and weekly meetings of a branch of the YMCA. Mahpiyahdinape spent a part of the winter writing a history of the Dakota.[44] The herd of cattle was much reduced, as the band had been forced to eat a number of their animals after their crop losses. This was a problem for the other reserves as well. In times of shortage, it was no longer possible to fall back on hunting and trapping to supply the table even at Oak Lake, which was the closest to the ranges of wild game. The number of persons holding cattle at Birdtail was further reduced, from twenty-two in 1893 to fifteen in 1896. There were no joint herds, since most of the farmers had provided their own home pastures and stables. Over the summer, each farmer had raised piles of rocks, painted with his name and subdivision number, at the corners of his own fields. The process of individuation was all but complete at Birdtail Reserve and each family was conducting its own business, in conjunction, of course, with departmental officials.[45]

From 1886 until 1897, all but one year, 1887, were dry to the point of drought, and flooding often accompanied the spring melting. Over the same time, prices on agricultural products, especially wheat, were depressed. The province as a whole reflected these conditions; towns were not growing or failed altogether; immigration was reduced to a trickle; cash was scarce; small industries, especially those making agricultural products, went under; there was little demand and low wages for labour; and all credit was strained. By 1896, however, grain prices began to rise and continued to go steadily upward over the next decade and more, in response to the food demands of Europe's growing industrial population. The amount of gold backing the world's currency increased with its discovery in South Africa and the Yukon, making money available for farm and industrial credit. The price of rail and ocean transport dropped and it became cheaper to ship agricultural produce. The price of manufactured goods fell behind that of agricultural produce, and the purchasing power of western farmers increased. The year 1897 was the last of a long series of poor growing seasons, and 1901 produced one of the greatest bumper crops of all time. For the Dakota, like their settler neighbours, it was only necessary for them to hang on until the lean years were past, and this they managed to do.

The season of 1897 was one of recovery for the Dakota and their white neighbours. The weather was generally favourable for crops, although a little on the dry side. The Birdtail people, having been wiped out by hail the previous year, were not able to put in all the seed they should have, and their crops were light. In that summer, four families at Oak River Reserve built balloon frame houses which could be insulated, the first on any reserve in the Birtle Agency, and more families were planning to do the same when they had the capital. Three families moved from the Turtle Mountain Reserve to the Oak Lake Reserve, and that band, already short of farm land, was then truly over-crowded. The people at Oak Lake kept up what farming operations they could, but tended to increase garden crops and household herds and flocks. Most cash income came from the sale of labour.

By 1898, further growth in the Oak Lake farming operations was impossible without additional lands. Assistant Commissioner A.E. Forget wrote to Secretary J.D. McLean on behalf of the band:

My attention has been drawn to the fact that only about twenty tons of hay can be secured on the Oak Lake Reserve, practically precluding the possibility of the raising of cattle by the Indians of the Reserve, which is very discouraging to them.

The Indians of this Reserve being Sioux, formerly from the United States, are not entitled to the same assistance as those born on this side of the line, yet the country is interested since they are now permanent residents amongst us, to have them become self-supporting at as early a date as possible, and for this reason it might be found advisable to secure for them say a half section of hay land in the vicinity of their reserve for their exclusive use.[46]

In early October 1898, Pereira, assistant secretary of the Department of the Interior, wrote to McLean telling him that S1/2-34-8-26-W1M had been temporarily set aside for the use of the Indians at the Oak Lake Reserve.[47]

The decade of the 1890s saw a number of significant changes that were to affect the Dakota in Manitoba in far-reaching ways: individual ownership of lands and products, imposition of appointed leadership, suppression of credit, usurpation of economic management roles, depletion of game and wildlife stocks, opposition to the giveaways and wacipi, and restrictions on personal movement and access to information. All of these factors tended to nullify an earlier Dakota economic strategy that emphasized mutual access to community lands, sharing of labour and products, diversification of labour so as to take advantage of opportunities on behalf of the whole community, leadership based on consensus and guidance from the Elders, and sharing of economic benefits and responsibilities.

At the same time, the three Dakota bands in Manitoba improved the operation of their farms and homesteads. Experiments in growing alfalfa and clover were conducted, many began to routinely spread manure on their depleted grain fields (a practice Inspector of Agencies McGibbon referred to as unique for that part of the country), most increased their crops of garden stuff and production of handcrafts, and took opportunities to increase cash flow by labouring for the settlers. As the amount of cash available in the province increased, labouring became a more rewarding pursuit, and much of the earned money was spent on improved housing. New frame houses were common and many had indoor toilets. Considering all that the Dakota had been through in the previous decade, they had done very well.

Limited increase,
1900 to 1940

7

In 1901, Manitoba proved to be a significant agricultural zone in the world by producing one of the largest grain crops in history – over fifty million bushels of wheat. There were eager buyers for all the grain the province was capable of producing, and unprecedented amounts of capital were available for further agricultural expansion. Land prices remained very low, and the high prices for farm products, with the availability of loan capital, prompted a great flow of immigrant settlers. Often the newest settlers were experienced farmers who came fully equipped to establish their operations and go into immediate production. In 1902, the Canadian Northern Railway completed the second link from the West to shipping terminals at Port Arthur. The efficiency of the grain export system increased as prices for rail cargoes dropped, with a resulting rise in the value of farmers' products.

Further technological development, especially steam-powered ploughs and other tools for cultivation, greatly increased productivity, but also raised the minimum number of acres required for commercial agriculture. There were no longer free acres available for homesteading anywhere in the farming heartland of Manitoba, and the pressure to increase farm size drove the price of lands up until they could be purchased only by well-established and extensively capitalized operators. The use of credit reached absurd levels, with entire farms, including houses and even seedstocks, being purchased at the bank by prospective farmers who fully expected to discharge their debts with the crops of one or two seasons of work. There was a chronic shortage of all kinds of labour and the wages paid to those few who were able to resist the lure of farming were high, especially since in the midst of the farm boom many related industrial enterprises were also launched, including stockyards, abattoirs, packing houses, transportation systems, implement and container-manufacturing businesses, and mills of all kinds.

Between the turn of the century and 1940, however, the western economy plunged from brilliant highs to the depths of depression, and like all farmers in western Manitoba, the Dakota had to contend with these dramatic changes. Perhaps the most powerful indicator of the new order was that, by the first decade of the new century, Indian land had become a commodity with a market value. There were, however, limits on the exchange of these lands. The subdivision of the reserves had been attended by the assignment of surveyed, eighty-acre plots to families who were prepared to farm. In most instances, the Dakota had already selected and been farming on what were to become their subdivision plots before the actual surveys were conducted. These plots could be bequeathed or, in the case of families where there were no heirs prepared to farm, the lands could be assigned to another Indian of the same band. In no circumstances, however, could the land be alienated from the reserve, or transferred to a person not a member of the band. Thus, while the owner of a plot did not have the power to dispose of the title to the land, he or she could dispose of use rights, and it was this aspect of the lands that acquired market value.

This market responded to economic factors in much the same manner as did the market in settlers' lands held in fee simple; that is, as arable lands became scarce, it was necessary to acquire use rights by purchase, and the price of those rights rose in accordance with the land's ability to produce an income. The decade from 1900 to 1910 was a time of most favourable conditions for farming in the West – good weather, high prices for produce, and low prices for farming supplies – and the price of use rights rose as farming became an increasingly attractive occupation. As might be expected, the buyer's market was restricted to those with the incomes required to purchase land-use rights, and by the end of the decade, some of the more progressive farmers at Oak River were in possession of up to four eighty-acre plots, which was at that time a substantial farm. As well, there were some households that had access to only the minimal acreage, or even partial subdivisions, and were not able to farm commercially at all.

Accompanying the redistribution of land-use rights was a tendency among small operators to restrict agricultural production to that necessary for subsistence, and to turn to other, non-farm enterprises for sources of cash income. At the time of these developments, the Dakota communities had acquired characteristics similar to those of other agrarian "ethnic" communities in Manitoba, such as the Icelanders and Mennonites: the Dakota identified with discrete tracts of land, shared a common recent history and a degree of cultural homogeneity, and worked in an economy based upon agriculture in all aspects from subsistence to large-scale commercial farming, while simultaneously supporting a diversity of economic strategies unrelated to agriculture. The economic developments in the Dakota and ethnic communities were the result of similar forces, chiefly the scarcity of arable land. Ownership and use rights to land became concentrated in the hands of the most efficient farmers and those without the lands or capital required to farm took up other income-getting opportunities. The contemporary accounts make it clear that at this time, the three Dakota reserves developed marked economic gradients ranging from subsistence poverty to relative prosperity, with the greatest wealth being in the hands of the commercial farmers.

The changes in the economic order were not manifested in precisely the same ways among the three Dakota reserves. The people at Oak River adopted the most diversified economy, with about one-tenth of the households accounting for about one-half of the total agricultural product. The remaining households with land-use rights were subsistence growers and marginally viable commercial farmers. Other households based their economic strategies on the sale of farm labour both on the reserve and off; they provided special services such as blacksmithing, steam engineering, freighting, hide curing and tanning, manufacturing small agricultural implements and household furnishings, and construction. Other households established labouring roles off the reserve, on the railroads, for example, that persisted for many years and, indeed, through many generations. There were even households that depended upon extensive and carefully managed trapping, hunting and purveying of firewood and sawlogs, the economic strategy adopted by the Dakota when they first settled in Canada half a century earlier.

At Birdtail Reserve, there were a number of large-scale farmers, including a few enterprises equal to those of their settler neighbours, but the tendency was to remain at a small scale. The smaller farmers tended to specialize in the production of crops that required considerable management skills and labour but less land area and machinery, such as sweet corn and potatoes, which were sold widely in southwestern Manitoba. They also grew seed crops of corn, potatoes and forage, which were sold through seed dealers in Birtle, Brandon, and many other farm centres. Other households depended upon manufacturing and selling handcrafts, gathering wild foodstocks, and trapping.

Arable land was in shortest supply at Oak Lake Reserve where there was only a small number of commercial farmers. Many more households depended upon the sale of labour supplemented with subsistence agriculture, trapping, hunting and gathering marketable wild products, such as berries and seneca root. In 1901, newly appointed Indian Agent G.A. Wheatley was trying to decide whether the reserve should be further subdivided or the band relocated completely to the Birdtail Reserve.[1] David Laird consulted Markle, the former agent of many years who was then posted in Alberta, who argued that unless the band unanimously volunteered to move to Birdtail, "it would be a waste of time trying to induce them to do so." Hay was very short at Birdtail and could not sustain the small herd already there, much less the cattle at Oak Lake as well. Wheatley's proposal was discarded, but between the 1890s and the 1930s, government officials decided that since the band was doing so poorly at their present location, they should either be moved to a new reserve or be amalgamated with one of the other Dakota bands. For well over a generation, this threat was prominent in the minds of the Oak Lake people, and it can hardly be doubted that this stifled whatever interest the Dakota had in making long-term improvements to their farm operations.[2]

The rapid expansion of settlement and of the economy created other pressures upon the lands confirmed as Dakota reserves. In 1898, the municipalities of Woodworth and Whitehead negotiated with T.D. Green of the Dominion Land Survey, who represented himself as speaking for the Oak River Dakota, for the release of lands to construct a road across the reserve. The municipalities agreed to fence the roadway, but when they later refused to fulfill this obligation, Agent Markle offered to do the job using materials intended for the use of the Indians. The band refused to go along with this arrangement, and at the end of August, Markle was compelled to write that the matter was stalled.[3]

Markle had called a band meeting to obtain a surrender of the land, but since he was "of the opinion that a majority of the band will vote against giving a Right of Way," he did not actually bring the matter to a vote.[4] Instead, he and Sam Bray, the Indian department official in charge of Indian lands, advised that the Indian Act be changed so as to allow expropriation of lands whether the Indians approved or not.[5]

Markle eventually brought the band around to his thinking, but the method he used to accomplish this is not recorded. The Dakota did not refuse to yield land rights under any circumstances. To the contrary, when the the bands wished to admit non-Indians to their lands, for example allowing the construction of churches on the reserve, permission was unanimously given and properly documented.[6] Once the formula for imposing right-of-way surrenders upon the Dakota had been perfected, however, other concessions to municipalities followed.[7]

The Dakota had begun to diversify their economies well before the grand years of the first decade of the twentieth century, largely in reaction to their inability to make a living solely from farming. On the surface, the strategies adopted in the early 1900s would seem to be nothing more than what the Dakota had been doing for years, but there is an important difference. In the 1870s and early 1880s, the exploitation of natural resources was done largely for subsistence, the resources being sold as they were taken, and only to meet immediate needs. The modern resource workers, however, laboured according to the seasons of maximum productivity of wild foods or other crops, furs and firewood. They also sought out the best market for their produce, often travelling many miles to secure the highest prices. Products such as firewood, furs and storable roots were retained by the producer until the most favourable market conditions were achieved and then sold for the greatest return. The exploitation of natural resources was much more closely managed and planned than had been possible earlier. When the farm boom came, many families had already specialized in the exploitation and careful marketing of wild resource crops, and did not attempt to re-enter farm production. As well, since many of these families had not kept up with technological changes or expansion of their cultivated lands during the lean years of the previous two decades, they were in no position to leap back into the larger-scale farming methods of the early 1900s. Farming was largely left to those who had persisted in their operations, maintained their fields and herds, and kept abreast of changes in technology; they were the ones who were best able to maximize the opportunities that the farm boom represented.

Others began to develop and market new skills. Moses Bunn at Birdtail discovered in himself an aptitude and liking for stonemasonry, first by building the foundations for his own new house in 1900, and later by working for settlers and townspeople for many miles around the reserve. Bluecloud at Oak River trained himself as a blacksmith, invested in a complete smithing shop and became a metal-worker for the reserve and surrounding settlers. A small crew of workers of the same reserve acquired skills in building stud-frame houses, and built a number of houses off the reserve in surrounding towns, where skilled labour was in short supply. While this diversification may have been compelled by necessity, the boom years made enough money available to support skilled labour, and the shortage of labour assured the Dakota of good incomes outside the agricultural mainstream.

The year 1901 brought good fortune to the Dakota, as it did for their settler neighbours. In previous years, there had been only minimal expansion of the farms, but the bumper crop of that year so greatly increased the farmers' returns that all who were able immediately prepared more land for the next year and invested in the most advanced technology. At Oak River, Chaske Hanska bought and paid for a new threshing separator and steam engine, with which all the band's crops were threshed and when they were done, the owner and crew went into the settlers' fields and threshed for them under contract. This was a complete turn for the Dakota who had, only a year earlier, been hiring and paying skilled labour to secure their crops. Itoyetanka at Oak River built one of the first barns with a hayloft in the district, and used it to house a large flock of laying hens and a small herd of dairy cows, in addition to his eight head of heavy horses. That winter, he sold two hundred dozen eggs and 180 pounds of butter, all at good prices.

Simultaneously, the giveaway, the Christian churches, and the YMCA flourished.

For many years, the YMCA held large camp meetings on the Birdtail and Oak River reserves, and by the end of the decade, this organization was taking on much of the responsibility for looking after the needs of the bands' elder members – cutting their wood, feeding their livestock in the winter, and generally making sure that they were at ease. Most of the people at Birdtail were confirmed churchgoers by that time, having had a missionary amongst them since the 1870s, but at Oak River, the band was divided amongst the Christians and pagans, as the non-Christians were called, and both groups made it their business to look after the needs of their poorer members, the Christians through church collections and the pagans through the giveaway. There was little, if any, conflict between the two groups until later. The clear favouritism that Indian-department officials showed the Christians, as well as the scorn heaped on the pagans, added to the political divisions in the communities, but for the first few years of the decade, there was largely a live and let live attitude on the part of the different groups.[8]

The season of 1902 was better than that of 1901, as the farmer Indians had even more land in crop than they had the year before, and the demand for labour off the reserves was insatiable. A considerable amount of money had been made from the sale of ponies and cattle to the new settlers, and that year a number of Dakota purchased high-priced, heavy draft mares and stallions and began to breed draft animals for the eager market. Much of this breeding was done by the subsistence-scale farmers who were able to add considerable cash value to their otherwise modest agricultural enterprises. All bands took to the production of baskets, beaded articles and mats, all of which were readily sold in the towns, and the people at Oak River picked and sold over $2,000 worth of berries that summer. Extensive additions were made to lines of machinery, and even Birdtail Reserve boasted its own new, debt-free steam separator costing $1,500. That year, the owners hired a steam engineer, but as soon as possible were urging the department to be sure that those of their children who were enrolled in the industrial schools learned how to run the machines themselves. A syndicate of three of the largest farmers at Oak River invested in a larger steam separator and set about having one of their number trained as a steam engineer by working with a neighbouring settler at that season's crop. In 1902, over twenty new wells were put in, doing away with long trips to the creeks and sloughs for water, and greatly increasing the attention given to cattle. Even with all the added investment, a number of the band members went into Brandon and opened bank accounts, perhaps the first significant number of Indians to do so in western Canada.

At Oak Lake, the Dakota had settled into a more modest scale of agricultural development, in keeping with the limitations imposed by the size and productivity of their reserve. They added considerably to their line of machinery, but compared to the Oak River Reserve, they were about a generation behind in technological adaptation. On the other hand, their modest ambitions placed them on the best of terms with their storekeeper neighbours, as was reported by Inspector Marlatt: "In conversation with merchants at Pipestone, they said the Indians at Oak Lake and Oak River had paid their bills fully better than the white people, and they were always willing to trust the Indians for a reasonable amount, knowing that they were honest and would pay the last cent."[9]

By 1904, many Dakota had become commercial farmers. The successful farmers were those able to underwrite all costs associated with production, provide their households with income to meet subsistence requirements, and to meet social and ceremonial obligations – all with income generated from their farming operations. As well, a good many of the successful commercial farmers were making enough income either to save or to make extensive consumer and capital purchases.

At this time, there was no wholesale collapse of farms on the Dakota reserves; product prices and incomes were sufficiently high that debt loads were more a constant and inexorable grind on the security of marginal farmers than they were the author of sudden devastation. Slow attrition among the marginal farmers led to even greater concentration of farm lands in the hands of the successful, as those who were squeezed out parted with their land-use rights. Before 1912, the defunct farmer was not facing destitution when he was forced to give up agriculture; jobs were plentiful, and since the Dakota were skilled and trained workers in a number of fields, they commanded high wages, often earning more than the going rate for the labour in their localities. An indication of this circumstance is that the Indian department distributed no rations or assistance to the Dakota in the first decade of the century. This is not to say that there was no poverty in individual households. Rather, the communities were able to assist the aged, infirm and destitute on their own, and even to collect considerable funds for the YMCA and the churches for use in their general, off-reserve programs of aid.

By 1905, Inspector Marlatt was able to report that the Dakota "vie with their white brothers in their farming operations. They have settled down to agricultural pursuits in a manner that almost warrants success." The Dakota continued their practice of acquiring good information upon which to base their operations, whether in the form of subscriptions to newspapers and other publications that emphasized agricultural news, or by means of instruction from their youth recently graduated from the Birtle and Elkhorn industrial schools. Many of the graduates had been introduced to modern concepts and techniques of farm production and returned to the reserve ready to start farming in their own right. This, however, led to another, virtually insoluble problem: there was simply not enough land on any of the Dakota reserves to absorb an increased number of commercial farmers. The

Dakota commercial farmers were already using up to 150 acres of land each, more than was being farmed by the average settler. In early 1905, the Birdtail Band tried to make this clear to the Department when the agent was toying with the idea of dissolving the Oak Lake Reserve and moving the entire population to Birdtail. A letter was sent to the department and signed by twelve farmers who stated bluntly that there was not enough farm land even for those then active in farming, nor was there enough wood on the reserve to last the present population more than twenty years. They argued that if they were to admit the Oak Lake people, they would soon be the poorest of Indians.[10]

In 1904, the Oak Lake Band members were approached by the department to see if they would be willing to surrender that part of the reserve lying south of the Pipestone River. The land was difficult to reach without a bridge and the department could not see any value in the lands. Wheatley met with the majority of adult members of the band, and reported that "the Indians were not at all in favour of surrendering the land, and after two hours discussion amongst themselves, all refused to part with any of their reserve. The principal reason for not wanting to surrender was on account of the wood. The soil is also a heavy clay loam and they intend to break up and crop the cleared parts next season."[11] This decision was duly reported to the secretary of the Department of Indian Affairs. Over the following months, several settlers applied to purchase lands that were part of the reserve. The department continued to entertain these requests until talk of dissolving the reserve reached the Oak Lake Dakota, who sent in a letter of protest, and the scheme was shelved, at least temporarily.[12]

Compared to the Birdtail Reserve, the Oak River Reserve still had sufficient unused land to absorb a small number of additional people, and in 1906, five persons in two households moved from Portage la Prairie to Oak River, attracted by the reserve's agricultural possibilities. In this instance, it was not the ratio of persons on the reserve to the size of the reserve that was important; it was the diversification of income-getting strategies on the Oak River Reserve. There were more people per acre at Oak River than at Birdtail, but a good part of the Oak River population was not directly involved in agriculture and did not occupy the acreage required for farming. By the end of the decade, however, the reserve could not absorb more people. Severe conflicts over access to lands first materialized at Oak Lake where farms were smaller than at Oak River and where there was less first-quality land. By 1906, there were charges of "claim-jumping" on the reserve at Birdtail, especially infringements of haylands, since by that time, hay was very scarce and the band's cattle herd had been reduced to work animals and a few animals for home food production.[13] Nevertheless, in 1905 Inspector Marlatt described Dakota agriculture in glowing terms: "It is a real pleasure to visit the reserves. Here results are to be seen in the large, well-cultivated fields, comfortable dwellings and stables and the latest and best make of agricultural implements, well-bred horses, etc. This band (Oak River) has, I consider, passed the crucial point and their advancement is assured."[14]

Besides working the large area under crop, the bands considerably expanded their marketing of "traditional" materials such as fish, seneca root and handcrafts. The renewed flow of immigrant settlers created a high demand for virtually any kind of household goods and foodstuffs, but it does not appear that the Birdtail or Oak River people did much hunting during the wheat-boom years, either for sale or for home consumption. Hunting would have entailed journeys of some considerable length and few were willing to take themselves away from their reserves for long periods. The Dakota still fished in the Assiniboine near the mouths of the smaller rivers and creeks within a few hours' travel from the reserve, and enjoyed greater success at this than they did at hunting.

Several new houses were built on the Dakota reserves, "put up at a cost of over $300 for the lumber alone." This was at a time when the very best settlers' homes cost $500 for lumber, windows, chimney, doors and hardware, or about the same as the new Dakota houses. Those raising heavy draught horses were selling a few for up to $200 each, when the average price for a heavy horse in the West was about $150. Good crops were taken off in 1906 and 1907, and the bands were able to pay off all their past debts, as well as add considerably to their lines of machinery. In 1907, a severe grain blockade occurred when the railways were unable to move the huge prairie yield, and the Dakota were obliged to sell their grain in small lots, which spread cash flow over the year. Agent Wheatley reported that this slowed the Dakota's ability to make snap purchases of implements and other goods, and greatly reduced the modest accumulation of debt.[15]

In the spring of 1907, J. Hollies was assigned as sub-agent at the Oak River Reserve. Two years earlier, Oak River, Oak Lake and Turtle Mountain reserves had been reorganized into a single agency, called the Griswold Agency, under the direction of a sub-agent. The move was prompted largely by the bands' success, which in the past had served as a trigger for the Department of Indian Affairs to intervene more directly in their business. Inspector Marlatt objected to the appointment, saying that Hollies was "not acquainted with Manitoba agricultural work."[16]

The sub-agent had an ally in the Reverend John Thunder, the Presbyterian missionary at Oak Lake, who could see an incompatibility in the level of his people's economic progress and their level of moral and spiritual development. In particular, Thunder objected to the Dakota's dances, especially the giveaway. It appeared, though, that the giveaway had been restructured somewhat in the years just before Thunder's arrival: no longer were the Dakota divesting themselves of all material goods other than the shells of their homes. The massive investments that many had made over the years in their homes and farm operations were not being dissolved and distributed throughout the community. Property concepts had extended so far toward individuation that there was no room left for such grand acts. As well, the YMCA branches that had been organized on all of the reserves had assumed much of the responsibility for aiding those who could not provide for themselves, and they seem to have done a good job. Commissioner Laird approved Reverend Thunder's views. Revisions in the Indian Act of 1901 had made Indian dances and festivals illegal, and the commissioner told Thunder that the department had hired detectives to attend the Brandon Fair to "see that the law is obeyed and if violated, that the violators be punished."[17]

In the autumn of 1907, land disputes became rife, especially on the Birdtail and Oak River reserves. At all three reserves, haylands were held by the band in common, and each of the farmers was permitted to cut the hay he required. Each household had established a certain place in the haylands as particularly theirs, and over the years there had been little change in the extent and location of the cutting areas. There had, however, been considerable change in the size and distribution of the herds amongst the households. Some households that had acquired considerable hayland areas when they had large herds of cattle still cut hay, but they were selling it rather than using it for their own cattle and horses. For some of these families, cutting and selling hay, for which there was a good market, was a primary source of income, but Hollies consistently resolved disputes in favour of commercial farmers who had large herds.[18]

Describing himself as a "court of equity," Hollies assembled the farmers and haycutters in August 1907, and arrived at what he, at least, found to be a more suitable distribution of cutting rights. The result was that a number of smaller cattlemen at Oak River gave up their herds. This was, at best, a temporary solution to the problem. That same autumn, Assistant Indian Commissioner J.A. McKenna reported: "As there are about fifty-five Indians farming on this reserve, good arable land uncultivated is getting somewhat scarce, and quite a number are anxious to acquire more before it is all taken up, and this is the cause of many disputes and some hard feeling between the older men of the Pagan element who hold some good land with only a small portion cultivated and the younger generation who are more progressive and desire to acquire and develop it."[19]

Expropriation of lands and resources continued to undermine the Dakota economy. In mid-summer of 1907, Frank Pedley, then deputy superintendent general of Indian affairs, wrote to David Laird, then Indian commissioner, notifying him that the department had received a request for the sand and gravel located on the Oak River Reserve. He asked if the Indians would be willing to surrender the resource. Laird passed the request along to Sub-Agent Hollies who called a meeting with the band to discuss and vote on the matter.[20] Hollies reported "that the old men of the Band took the floor at once and set up a vigorous attack against any surrender, and monopolized the time with speeches. The young men listened, kept quiet and voted as directed by their Elders."[21] The vote unanimously opposed any surrender.

This decision was duly communicated within the Indian department. But Hollies, like Markle, did not let the matter rest. In the summer of 1908, he reported: "I allowed gravel from the reserve to be used by County Council for a portion of a road crossing this reserve, the Council doing the necessary work; for the removal of the gravel, I allowed the Indians 'Permits to Sell' gravel to the Council."[22] This may have been "for their own good," as the officers of the Indian department put it in those days, but it was totally contrary to the express wishes of the band, and possibly in violation of the Indian Act.[23]

Hollies's early winter project was to suppress interest at Oak River in the election of a band chief. Hollies reported that band members had been discussing the matter, and several "cliques" in the population had identified a person whom they thought would be suitable. As well, the band had arrived at a plan for the election and a guide for the conduct of the chief. Elections would be held at the end of each year, and the chief would be responsible for advising members of relevant laws, regulations, and policies, and to generally show a good example through his own behaviour. While Hollies was willing to humour the band in their political interests, he felt no real sympathy for the plan: "For myself, I have no use whatever for a chief! Yet, it seems a necessary step just now in the path of peace and progress, and to give the restless portion some ideas of self-government. I might add, I am not afraid of the Sioux thereby getting the top hand. The fight between us is over, and they lost! It is my turn! I do not mind giving a little rope."[24] Commissioner Laird shared Hollies's attitude. "I am not satisfied that the benefits that would accrue from such a provision would offset the disadvantages which experience shows frequently result from the system of chiefs. In the case of Treaty Indians, of course, there is some ground for their insisting upon the right, but these Sioux are in a different position, and nothing should be done that might interfere with their development along individual lines."[25]

In 1906 and 1907, the band had made considerable capital investment in farm implements, especially of the modern and more efficient kinds. There were three separators and steam engines on the reserve, including a new unit purchased by three Dakota farmers for a cost of $2,800. All three of the "syndicates" that owned the machines did a considerable amount of custom threshing for the settlers and were just barely able to keep up with their credit payments. Altogether, Hollies estimated a total debt load of $15,000 for the Oak River and Oak Lake bands, a figure that he was unable to substantiate. Hollies wanted more power to direct the course of the Dakota's economic strategies: "This vast sum, as a debt to be paid by the Indians solely out of their earnings, would on most reserves be appalling! but the untiring industry and activity of the Sioux are the most interesting, vital and encouraging views of Indians I have experienced, and if properly led and directed by me, every dollar that is a just debt will be paid!"[26]

Hollies planned to totally restrict the Dakota's access to credit, much of which had been incurred in the form of lien notes on machinery and other equipment. In order to do this, however, he wanted an interpreter so that his detailed instructions on farm business matters would be indisputably clear, and so that he could be "in constant touch with every man in word and in deed."

It is possible that the Dakota had overextended themselves in the use of credit in the early 1900s. The chief form of credit available to the Dakota was a lien note on purchased goods which permitted the seller to reclaim goods upon default, and to retain the amount already paid on the debt. The white settlers, however, had access to a much wider range of credit instruments and could borrow against their land. Settlers who had cleared their homestead and proved up their titles had about $1,000 in collateral against which they could borrow at favourable rates, while the Dakota owned no property that they could put up against a loan. Loans were available at rates between seven and eight percent, while most liens carried at least ten-percent rates of interest and were even as high as fifteen percent. The Dakota were paying these higher rates for most goods purchased on credit.

Departmental policy on Indian credit worked against Dakota interests and weakened their competitive position with the settlers. The terms of the lien notes to which Dakota credit was restricted offered no protection to the borrower. As Hollies himself makes plain, the Dakota were willing to work off their debts, but were unable to exactly meet their payment schedules due to unforseen circumstances. In 1907, for example, a number of the farmers at Oak River suffered frost damage in low-lying wheat fields, and lost their machinery through seizures. Many dealers profited nicely from lien defaults by seizing the machinery, keeping the amount already paid, and reselling the stock. Government agencies in Manitoba and further west were beginning to express alarm about the extent of credit assumption by farmers, and could see real problems developing should the crops fail or markets decline. In the case of the Dakota, it was not that they were accumulating exorbitant debt in order to increase production in a land-tight situation; it was that they were restricted to the most expensive and risky forms of debt.

During the winter of 1907–08, the rail system was overloaded by grain from the harvest, but the effects were not nearly as severe as they were earlier in the decade.

For those Indians and settlers who had payments to meet at set times, this was an additional hardship, but those who were able to meet outstanding bills avoided the temptation to take on new debt. Once the Dakota farmers had their permits to sell in hand, they were allowed to take their grain to market at any point they wished. Those with grain to sell spent most of their time on or near the reserve so as to be able to go to the best-priced market on a moment's notice. Other members of the Oak River and Oak Lake bands spent the winter trapping near the reserves, and still others hauled hay to sell to settlers.

In the quiet of winter, Hollies turned his attention to dancing and giveaways:

I sent for the Chief one evening to come and see me as I wanted to have a private talk. However, the Chief who is a Christian refused to come alone, but collected all of the Christians and Missionary at the Agency office, and what was to be a private talk, became a meeting. No good came out of it, except, when each man was asked to give what he considered the best method of ending the pagan feasting and dancing said he would leave it to the Agent to stop it as he (the Sioux) had no place.

The Chief, who was the complainant to the matter, resembled the rest in leaving it to the agent. So much for the Christians. Another evening within a week after, the Pagan leaders, who had heard of the other meeting, called on the Missionary and said he was wanted by the Agent, and with him, brought an interpreter to the office without the slightest notice to me. At once, with oily sweet words and savoury wishes, declared their intention on behalf of the Pagans, for the future, of going to church every Sunday, of making large subscriptions to the new stone church building in prospect. All the Pagans would combine in making the crooked straight, they would moreover build a boarding school for all the children so they could be fed and instructed! I was astounded! The Sioux millenium was at hand! And after a pause, the next speaker said the funds to be collected for all these things would be $50.00 each collection and was already arranged for and to be handed over and given to the Missionary for the church! It would be collected from the attendance at each Pagan feast and dance! I stopped further proceedings by reading Sec. #149 of the Indian Act! with the comment that the law is made for all and all had to keep it. The Agent. The Missionary. The Commissioner! Even the King was under the law! And so were they! All must keep the law!

It was their turn to be astonished! Who had made the law? was asked in great surprise! I said "The Government". It was the best I could do for a short answer! The law was read by the interpreter once more! Then I was asked to lend "The Indian Act" which I did for one day! They departed! and thus ended abruptly another Nicodemus meeting! Truly the Sioux are an extraordinarily busy and fertile-minded people! I report these meetings to show the workings of the Sioux mind.[27]

Only at this late date, some seven years after the passage of the Indian Act of 1901, did Hollies attempt to explain the legal basis for his opposition to Indian dances and rituals. However, he was not allowed to dwell on this matter too long, as other problems required Hollies's immediate attention.

Land shortages at Birdtail were causing severe problems and, in the late winter of 1908, George Bearbull requested that he be allowed to move to Waywayseecappo Ojibwa Reserve and set up farming. The chief and band there were only too willing to have an experienced farmer join them. Because of the land, hay, and timber shortages at the Dakota reserve, Bearbull thought his removal would ease the pressure at Birdtail. Laird, however, ordered Bearbull off the Ojibwa reserve, saying, "The fact of your being a Sioux Indian debars you from the privilege of joining a Band of Treaty Indians." At the same time, Hollies refused to admit a Dakota from Fort Totten, North Dakota, to the Oak Lake Reserve, on the grounds that there were no lands to spare on any of the Dakota reserves in Canada, and if there were, he would move the band from Turtle Mountain before he would admit American Indians. Hollies then went ahead and moved the first three families from the Turtle Mountain Reserve onto the already crowded Oak Lake Reserve in the autumn of 1908.[28]

Hollies records that the people at Oak Lake were pleased to have their relatives join them and did all they could to ease them into their new life. The newcomers themselves, however, were completely baffled by what was expected of them in their new home. Hollies wrote that the Turtle Mountain people were "where the present workers were twenty years ago. If their friends have the patience, they could not have chosen, or been received in a better place."[29] It should be noted that the Turtle Mountain people had not chosen to go to Oak Lake. They had not wished to be farmers beyond the most basic level of subsistence production. It is doubtful that they ever sold a bushel of grain or a ton of hay in all the years they were on their own reserve. They were hunters first, and were wood merchants, trappers and labourers a distant second. It is no wonder that they did not immediately appreciate the mode and scale of production of the Dakota at Oak Lake.

As for Oak Lake, the additional population, along with later arrivals from Turtle Mountain, caused increased pressure on the available land and tended to confirm a pattern of economic diversification that had been developing for several years before that. The additional numbers took up whatever available lands there were on the reserve, leaving very little for expansion by established farmers. Thus, it remained that there were three or four large-scale farmers, and another three or four who managed subsistence-plus enterprises; the remaining households, about ten in number, were gardeners involved in non-farm economic strategies. The lands available to the Oak Lake Band could no longer support agricultural expansion.

As the pressures on the Oak Lake Band's land and resource base mounted, the Dakota made a point of asking whether they still had rights to the hayland designated for their use in 1898. Hollies reported the problem to Indian Commissioner Laird.[30] Laird, however, could find no record of there being a hayland attached to the Oak Lake Reserve. He assumed that the Indians had been renting Crown lands for making hay, and if they wished to continue doing so, the agent was authorized to seek a permit on their behalf.[31]

Over the next two decades, from 1908 until 1926, this hayland faded in and out of the memory of the Indian department. In 1909, one-half of the land was lost when the Government of Manitoba issued a haying permit to a local farmer and later received the land in the right of the province by Order in Council. The section of land was further whittled down until, in 1926, the remaining quarter section, described as "useless for any purpose . . . all water and bullrushes," was confirmed as a part of the Oak Lake Reserve.[32]

At the time that Hollies and the department were discovering the Oak Lake people's haylands, the band brought it to the agent's attention that the Canadian Northern Railway's line cut across some twenty acres of their reserve. The department was "not aware that a railway passed through any part of the Oak Lake Reserve," a statement from which it may be assumed that no surrender was secured for the expropriated land. This problem was circumvented by Order in Council, which gave title to the railway in return for a pittance of compensation, and the productive base of the Oak Lake Dakota was further eroded.[33]

Land pressures were exacerbated by the increased use of the only available method of weed control in the West – summerfallowing. Weed infestations, especially sow thistles and wild oats, had been intensifying, and it was becoming common practice to leave a field fallow for a season, cultivating it as the weed seeds germinated. This, however, meant that a large acreage, representing a considerable value in operational and capital inputs, produced nothing for a season. Improved crop growth, a higher grade of marketable grain, and moisture conservation partially offset these losses, but for many farmers, the necessity of summerfallowing often implied increased capital investment, either to purchase new land or to increase technological efficiency in order to maintain previous levels of income. As the Dakota adopted these changes in agricultural technique, lands became even more scarce and land conflicts more acrimonious.

Another, more specific, land problem existed for the Dakota of the Oak Lake Band. John Hunter, a Dakota, was one of the few Indians in western Canada to receive a land grant for having served in the Boer War. Hunter had served with the Strathcona Horse, and at the end of the conflict had applied for 320 acres of Crown land near the reserve. There was some question as to whether an Indian could take advantage of such a grant, but Laird told Hunter to go ahead and apply for the grant, and if there were any objection the commissioner's office would take the matter up on his behalf. There was none, and Hunter received his land. Soon, however, the Oak Lake people were requesting that Hunter's lands on the reserve be returned to the band, because he had, with his soldiers' grant, over four hundred acres of land in his possession or under his control. The band believed that the reserve lands, being "public" lands, should be made available to others in the band who had no use rights at all. The department refused to dispossess Hunter of his on-reserve allotments, and he remained one of the largest farmers in the Oak Lake district.

Hunter understood the band's land problems and later acted as spokesman for a part of the band who objected to Hollies's plan to move even more of the Turtle Mountain people onto Oak Lake Reserve.[34]

The crops in the 1908 season were not as large as they had been in the previous few years, having been retarded by a slow spring and a wet autumn, and incomes on the reserves were much reduced.[35]

There were a number of developments on the Dakota reserves in the last year of the decade. Hollies was elevated to the status of agent and immediately commenced the prosecution of dances and giveaways and the suppression of liquor, though none of his efforts resulted in arrests or convictions. A telephone was installed at the Oak River Agency office, which had been renovated for Hollies at considerable cost to the department. The cattle herd at Birdtail was sold off, since there was no longer enough hay to support it. Up to ten families from Oak River Reserve were absent for most of the winter trapping, as there were enough fur animals selling at high prices to make a good income for that few. Others went hunting, for the sport, no doubt, but also to put food on the table. Hollies's vigorous efforts to collect debts had left the Dakota with virtually no cash to purchase food supplies, and they had little choice but to hunt, which involved a ten-day trip to the north. Immediate cash needs prompted the Oak River Band to further reduce their cattle herd and sell the hay they had cut at $6 a ton to surrounding farmers. Again, the Oak River people approached Hollies about electing a chief of their own choosing, but the agent refused to even discuss the matter. As soon as their crops were in, a number of Dakota at Oak River sold all their produce and departed to visit relatives in the United States so as to avoid Hollies's continual interference in their affairs. A few failed to return.

Hollies's attention was mostly occupied with "the land question" at the Oak River Reserve. The fact was that there was not enough acreage for all those who wanted to farm. A number of the smaller, poorer farmers had reduced their activities to a subsistence scale, leaving a large part of their eighty-acre plots unworked. Hollies proposed that these people give up their lots to younger men; this proposal was strongly protested by the lot holders, but over-ridden by Hollies. The Dakota then learned that they did not in fact control the lands on which they were living and working. The land which would be freed by Hollies's proposal, however, was still not enough for all the farmers' needs, and he then suggested that all the larger farmers should reduce their acreage, work the smaller area more intensively, and turn the surplus land over to the youth. He thought that forty acres would be enough land for most households, though many of the band's white neighbours were expanding to 360 and even 480 acres in this era. His plan was rejected by all the Dakota, both those without land and those with the large farms. Hollies managed to assemble enough land for those in need during 1909 and 1910, but he could see that from then on there would be an unending and, eventually, insoluble problem created by the insufficiency of land.[36]

The economic boom in Manitoba and the West reached its zenith in 1912, and soon began a rapid decline. Political unrest in Europe, Canada's biggest market for agricultural produce, pushed down the price for all products. The flow of investment money from England stopped. As prices for farm products dropped, all of the secondary industries that processed or handled agricultural produce also suffered, and for the first time, large numbers of unemployed people appeared in the streets of Manitoba's cities and villages.

By 1912 the Dakota bands had stabilized their community economies and were able to meet the newest depression in comparatively good shape. The debt load had been much reduced, in part as a result of Agent Hollies's suppression of credit purchases. More important, however, was the effect of severe shortages of reserve land. Most available land was being farmed by 1912, and those who were doing the farming were as well equipped as the size and nature of their operations warranted. There was no longer the need to acquire new technology to increase production. Capital investment had already declined on the reserves before the general depression made itself felt, and the Dakota escaped the rash of implement and cattle seizures that elsewhere attended the fall in farm prices. However, the inability to get further credit, and the lack of incentive represented by the low prices, eliminated any possibility that the smaller farmers would make more efficient use of their lands. There was further attrition in the numbers of commercial farmers and more households turned to alternative economic strategies, leaving farming to those best prepared for the task, that is, those with substantial lands and lines of equipment.

At Birdtail Reserve, the depressed economic conditions, in combination with declining soil fertility and a general shortage of arable lands, confirmed the band in their earlier tendency to develop small farms requiring intensive labour input to produce small but valuable crops. Wheat and other grains were still grown, but garden produce increased in importance, especially storable crops such as potatoes, roots and corn. For many years before, the people had been growing several varieties of corn for sale fresh and dried. In 1910, the band sold over 4,100 pounds of seed corn to the McKenzie Seed Company in Brandon, the most valuable single crop they had ever sold.[37]

At Oak River, the band withdrew completely from beef production; its reward was so poor that it did not warrant investment in fences, water development and commitment of lands to pasture and hay production. Instead, the Dakota cut hay crops for cash. Much of the hay harvest was secured by the subsistence farmers and by those who were not otherwise involved in agriculture. At Oak River and Oak Lake, an increasing number of households withdrew completely from farming. By 1910, there were fifty-three farmers at Oak River and twenty at Oak Lake, with another fifty on both reserves who earned their living solely from the sale of labour, trapping and fishing. Most of the trappers and fishermen were at Oak Lake. They made a comfortable living when fur animals were numerous and fur prices were high. The people at Oak Lake also reduced their cattle herds, and instead sold their hay crops to the white settlers.

The depression of 1912 to 1914 was immediately relieved by the onset of World War I. Grain prices rose sharply, encouraging greater production, but the shortage of labour that accompanied the war compelled farmers to invest in technology. Again, those who were able to maintain their operations through the depression were in the best position to take advantage of the strong market. At this time, there was further attrition in the number of farmers on the Dakota reserves, as the insatiable demand for labour attracted many of the marginal operators off the reserve and into wage employment. By 1916, the number of farmers at Oak Lake Reserve was reduced from twenty to thirteen. The reduction in the number of farmers at Oak River and Birdtail was not so dramatic, but many of the small operators tended to put in no more than a subsistence crop and then seek work off the reserve, leaving the bulk of their land unworked. Thus, both the numbers of farmers and the acreage being worked were reduced. This led to further conflict between those commercial farmers who needed more land and those households that had use rights to land, but were neither interested in working the land themselves, nor in turning over their land to others. It may well be that these landholders could see a future for themselves in farming, but by the end of the war, this was only a remote possibility. The cost of establishing a farm, starting with nothing more than a land base, was out of the reach of most Dakota.

By the end of World War I, the economic character of the Dakota communities in Manitoba had become entrenched. They suffered chronic land shortages, a growing population, soil depletion, limited access to capital, and technological underdevelopment for commercial scale agriculture. As early as 1923, the economy of the Oak Lake Band seemed to be failing. The inspector of Indian agencies recommended that the Indians should either be moved to another location or given improved farming equipment.[38] Duncan Scott responded that it would be preferable to move the Indians than to provide them with new farming equipment.[39]

All was settled except the matter of funding the relocation. Even this was no problem, as Graham reported that he did "not think there will be any additional expenditure of money, if there is it will be so trifling that it will be hardly noticeable."[40] Despite this enthusiasm for moving the Oak Lake people, the suggestion was dropped, only to be raised again in the next decade.

In 1921, it was discovered that the Province of Manitoba had in error built a road across a part of the Oak River Reserve lands, cutting off about forty acres of cultivated land. When this was first brought to the attention of the Indian department, moves were taken to have the Dakota compensated for the loss of land, but by 1928 it had been decided not to demand compensation, and the expropriated land was transferred to the province by Order in Council. No surrender was obtained from the band. Again in 1931, lands were turned over to the province for road improvement. In this instance, compensation was obtained, but a surrender was not. These expropriations further reduced the land base of the Oak River Dakota.

The depression immediately following the war limited Dakota economic recovery. While a number of farmers had previously been able to maintain a scale of operation comparable to that prevailing in the surrounding area, the gap in the size of farms maintained by the Dakota as compared to the neighbouring farmers widened. Since they were no longer able to generate incomes necessary to underwrite technological advance, most of the Dakota farmers were operating at a considerably smaller scale than their neighbours, and so their competitive position deteriorated. What technology they did acquire was generally considered by their white neighbours to be obsolete or inefficient.

Being located in the north of Manitoba's agricultural zone, the Birdtail Band was spared the devastation that occurred elsewhere in the 1930s, and was able to carry on with a strategy of small-scale, intensive growing, but even there an increasing number of households withdrew from commercial agricultural production.[41]

The drought of the 1930s was the last blow sustained at Oak Lake. By the time the drought had broken, most of the land was unfit for any use but small hay crops. Farming all but ceased at Oak Lake, and the Dakota there faced a generation of deprivation not experienced by other bands. The deputy superintendent general of Indian affairs attributed the failure of farming to both a lack of industry on the part of the Dakota and, to a lesser extent, the climate. One solution proposed for this problem was to move the band north to the forested zone, where they could hunt, fish and trap. This the deputy superintendent general rejected, on the one hand because the Indians knew little about hunting and trapping, and on the other because the cost of relocating them would be prohibitive. An alternative was to move them in with some other band where there was sufficient room and agricultural opportunity.[42]

After a delay of twenty months, the Indian agent at Griswold agreed that the band would benefit from a couple of generations in the forest where they could hunt and fish, but said he "would not be in favour of any forcible transfer." He had spoken of the matter to the Indians and they evinced no interest in moving. There the matter rested for another decade and a half.[43]

In 1949, a lawyer from Deloraine, G.H. North, wrote to the Department of Indian Affairs, stating that he had learned that the majority of Dakota at Oak Lake Reserve wished to give up their lands in exchange for a new reserve in the Turtle Mountains. He wanted to know the department's thoughts on such an idea. To this, D.J. Allen, superintendent of reserves and trusts, responded: "Generally, I do not think that the Department would be opposed to a move if the same would be in the best interests of the Indians. Before such a proposal could be seriously considered, more information was required. Again, the matter was dropped, this time, permanently.[44]

By the end of World War II, the primary economic features of Dakota life were established. Assuming contemporary standards for agriculture – large capital and little labour – the Dakota reserves of today could not support more than a dozen farming families. Many individual farmers in Manitoba manage lands greater than all of those possessed by the eleven hundred Dakota who live at Oak River, today called Sioux Valley Reserve. Those farms that do operate are small scale, and may be compared to surrounding farms of the 1950s. The Dakota farms range in size from forty to 320 acres, and the total cultivated acreage is about three thousand acres. These farmers demand a fair degree of cooperative labour and technology sharing, especially within kin lines, and are labour intensive. Households still rely to some degree upon domestic production of food, shelter and heat.

Today, greater numbers of Dakota have no connection with agriculture. These people work at a vast range of jobs, both on and off the reserves. Many have formal education in technical fields, and a good number hold university degrees. The history of the farming Dakota in Canada is similar to that of many settler communities. They arrived in the Northwest with nothing but their bodies and their knowledge; they developed a base in agriculture; the security which agriculture provided was a platform for expansion into economic diversity. A crucial difference, however, was the unprecedented influence of government on the fabric of Dakota life, an influence that had no parallel amongst their settler neighbours. At the time the Dakota were wrestling with the fluid nature of western Canadian agricultural economics, they were also compelled to deal with strenuous assaults on their political, religious and artistic expression. These assaults were not wholly successful; the effect of land shortages, declining productivity of the soil, and lack of development capital encouraged forms of production and distribution that were, at a general level, compatible with the essence of Dakota culture. As a result, the

Dakota language, family structure, personality and religion are all doing well, and the giveaway is still enjoyed as it always was.

The hunters of Turtle Mountain, 1877 to 1915

8

Only one of the Dakota bands which settled in Canada elected the ancient arts of hunting, fishing and trapping as the basis for an economic strategy. The band was headed by H'damani, who had crossed into Canada in late 1862 and taken up residence in the Turtle Mountains after having entered into an agreement with the Ojibwa that permitted him to take the lands for his own use. By 1911, the band and the reserve that it occupied had been obliterated by the Department of Indian Affairs and little was left to document its existence. The destruction of the band broke the continuity of tribal history, so that all that remains today in the living memory of the Dakota is a general awareness of ancestorship. The band was never large, and over the years relentless pressure from the Indian department forced one or two families at a time to abandon the Turtle Mountains. These families and their children were absorbed into the communities they joined, and detailed recollections by the Old Ones faded. But the story of their existence and eventual dissolution can be pieced together, particularly from records concerning the land in the Turtle Mountains.

When the Oak Lake Reserve was created in 1877, H'damani and his people were excluded and left without home lands of their own. With no other option available, they simply moved onto a part of the northwest slope of Turtle Mountain, and dug in. H'damani had acquired rights to the Turtle Mountains from the Ojibwa in the early 1860s. For the next few years, this band of Dakota escaped the attention of Indian department officials, but this was not to last.

In late 1882, Lawrence Herchmer, the agent at Birtle, wrote the commissioner of Indian affairs to discuss a conflict between the Dakota and a party of settlers concerning timber rights in the area of the Dakota camp:

These Indians are described by all the prominent Settlers including the Registrar and the Storekeepers,

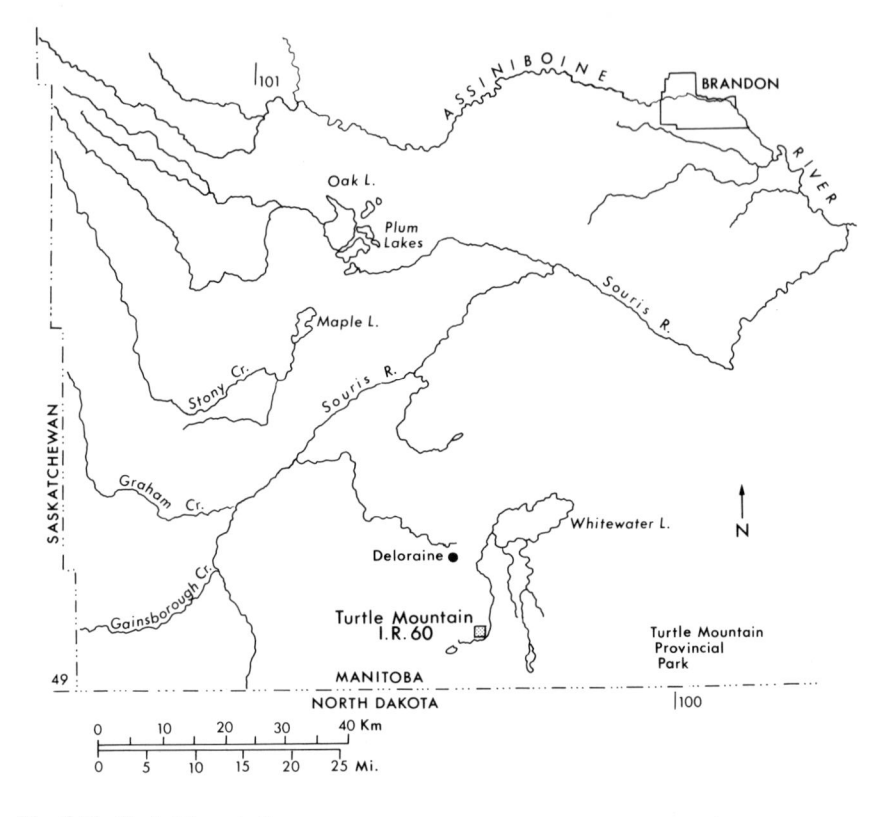

Map 5. The Turtle Mountain Reserve

as harmless law abiding people. . . . They have two gardens, one of good size, and a very neat house, and there is no doubt that they objected to the settlers cutting the wood on this section close to their gardens and as far as I can learn, the settlers were cutting the wood without license or permit. This section is very rough, broken with lakes and ponds and is useless for white settlers, but would make a very good location for Indians as it is close to a fishing lake. During the troubles on the American side lately between Indians and Halfbreeds on the one side and settlers on the other, these Sioux have kept strictly neutral, they receive no assistance from the government and have purchased their own plows, harrows, etc. I have the honour to suggest that during good behaviour they may be permitted to occupy Sec 31, T.1, R.22, W, and that I may be permitted to lend them a yoke of oxen.[1]

Officials in Ottawa made no objection to this proposal, and the minister of the interior concluded that "these Indians should not be disturbed, so long as they behave themselves in an orderly and law abiding manner."[2]

In July 1886, A.W. Ponton surveyed the section of land and it was recorded as Reserve No. 60. This, however, gave the Indians little security, for no Order in Council was issued to create the reserve. In early 1887, P.B. Douglas, assistant secretary of the Department of the Interior, wrote to the surveyor general, notifying him of the department's intentions "to constitute that section an Indian Reserve."[3] No other action, however, seems to have been taken.

The first Indian agent to attend the Dakota, Lawrence Herchmer, had not favoured the location in the Turtle Mountains, but his objections were based on the perception that the band was much too distant from other settlers for band members to become farmers themselves. The Turtle Mountain Dakota had small gardens worked with hand tools and enough heavier technology to grow and harvest hay, but they were mostly interested in exploiting the rich natural resources of their territory, and making whatever income they could from the sale of labour.[4]

The advance of settlement was a mixed blessing for them. Work was plentiful and there was a ready market at Deloraine for all the handcrafts, wood, berries, fish, meat and tanned hides that the band cared to produce. In late 1881, the band was reported to be self-sufficient. As soon as they received word that they would be allowed to retain the section of land they occupied, members began to expand their gardens and to build permanent houses and stables. By 1883, forty members of the band – about eight families – had broken three acres, most of which was planted as garden, had fenced three acres as a holding pen for their horses, and had cut and piled ten tons of hay to winter their animals.

The next summer, at Herchmer's request, the band received two oxen from the Department of Indian Affairs. Band members greatly expanded their crop area to thirty-five acres, planting six acres of wheat, which barely supplied enough grain for their own use. They expanded the fenced pasture to seventeen acres and increased the number of horses they kept, since horses were needed for hunting, hauling firewood and finding work.

By 1884, all families dwelling on the reserve had built their own houses. Even though their gardens and field crops suffered from the dry years of the mid-1880s, the Turtle Mountain Band received very little in the way of aid from the department. In 1884, the most difficult year, the band received about six dollars worth of flour and bacon from the agent, or about the amount that might have been given as "gifts" during the rare visits Herchmer made to the distant reserve. The agent reported that the band was "doing very well indeed, . . . are building excellent houses, and are very ambitious to get along." Mostly, the Dakota were hunting and fishing in the Turtle Mountains. The agent noted game resources to be prolific there, and he arranged to get the band another yoke of oxen.[5]

With the additional oxen, the band increased the acreage under cultivation, but there was no great increase in the acreage planted to wheat until the gardens were of such a size as to provide for the basic subsistence needs for the people living on the reserve. In 1886, the reserve was subdivided, and Agent Markle reported the people were "so few in number that each family will have a lot for themselves." Markle was expecting that the households would cultivate separately, as had happened when the other Dakota reserves were subdivided, but this never happened. The Turtle Mountain people had been breaking land almost wherever they wanted before the subdivision, as had the Birdtail Band, but unlike the latter band, there was no attempt by the Turtle Mountain people to square up fields in accord with the survey lines. Expansion took place adjacent to the lands broken earlier, or wherever else there was suitable soil.[6]

In 1887, Inspector of Indian Agencies Alexander McGibbon reported that the population of the reserve was reduced to thirty-two from the earlier number of over forty. By that year, the gardens were large enough to support the population, and the band turned more to the production of grain crops, especially oats, which were used as feed for the horses and oxen.[7] Early in 1888, Agent Markle visited the Turtle Mountain Band and reported that the band was doing well, selling in Deloraine all the firewood they could cut.[8]

Between 1886 and 1888, there was a significant change in the economic strategy of the Turtle Mountain people. In 1886 there were six households engaged in growing wheat, in addition to potatoes and garden stuff. By 1888, there were only two grain-growers, and between them they had as many acres in grain as had the larger number two years earlier. Many of those who had earlier grown grain gave up their cultivated plots and concentrated more on increasing their gardens and hay production. The men who remained with grain production were the elders of the band, while the younger households preferred to carry on with hunting and trapping in the appropriate seasons and labouring in the town of Deloraine and surrounding areas in the summer. Markle and McGibbon saw this to be regression rather than progress, even though the band had significantly increased its income through diversification. McGibbon suggested hiring a farmer close to the reserve to keep an eye on the Indians, but by that time, the department had decided that the best thing to do with the Turtle Mountain Band would be to have it amalgamate with one of the other Dakota bands.[9]

For the next year or two, one Mr. Renton, a local settler, did pay occasional visits to the Turtle Mountain Dakota and send a few lines of comment on his observations to Markle. Except for one attempt to track down liquor users, the agent rarely, if ever, visited the reserve himself. Management of most of the band's affairs fell to Renton, including such decisions as whether a person was ill enough to warrant a call to a physician, and whether a cow should be sold. The official reports sent to Ottawa by Markle from 1889 to 1891 mention only that the band was doing well fishing and hunting, and that their health was good.[10]

In the summer of 1890, Markle visited the reserve. He commented that game was getting scarce in the Turtle Mountains and that the drought had dried up some of the small lakes the band had been fishing. Markle's primary complaint was that the Turtle Mountain Reserve was too close to the international boundary and the band was constantly being visited by Dakota from the United States. H'damani and his people had many relatives in the United States, and many travelling Dakota spent a day or two with the band, but H'damani was selective and those who were unwelcome were not permitted to linger. Whenever possible, H'damani expelled unwelcome visitors himself, but he was aging and when he was unable to do it himself, he asked for the help of the constable at Deloraine, with whom he enjoyed amicable and even friendly relations.[11]

In 1891 a long and pathetic story began that culminated in the extinction of the Turtle Mountain Dakota as a separate band. It took the Government of Canada over eighteen years to accomplish this goal. The documentary record reveals no particular reason for this government action, but greed, personal ambition, religious zeal, judgmental morality and ignorance are all very clearly shown.

In 1891 A.J. Kerr, a neighbour of the Dakota, wrote to T.M. Daly, minister of the interior, pleading for assistance on their behalf: "We have 8 families of Indians on the reserve at Deloraine who I think with many more want to be looked after. They are a good lot to work but last year lost their crop and the agent refuses to give them anything here. He wants them to go to Moosomin. The old chief, who is a fine old fellow says with the rest he will stay here and die before he will leave."[12]

Rather than force them to leave, he suggested giving them seed and an instructor for the summer. Kerr also mentions that the Dakota had been prohibited from hunting moose and prairie chickens, apparently in an effort to force them away.

Daly seemed unaware of any attempts to move the band and passed the matter on to Hayter Reed.[13] Reed drafted a reply for Daly, saying:

The Indians referred to are, as you supposed, refugee Sioux, and consequently anything done for them is a matter of grace and not of right. None the less we want to do what is best in their own interests, and consequently desire to get them away from a place where we find they are subjected among other temptations, to that of drinking, and are too near their friends across the line.

Could we get them removed to Moose Mountain, as we have been trying to do, they would get regular supervision and be kept out of temptation.

Many others have spoken as Mr. Kerr reports the old Chief to do, and yet by patience been brought to do what was wanted after all.[14]

Reed then wrote the agent at Birtle, suggesting that if the Dakota needed potatoes, they should be given some. However, he said, "It is of course very desirable not to relax your efforts to induce them to go to Moose Mountain."[15] Far from relaxing his efforts, Markle reported to Reed that he was pursuing his objective with considerable zeal. Markle told H'damani that if he moved to Moose Mountain, he would receive Commissioner Reed's "liberal assistance." Since the chief refused to leave his reserve, the agent did not feel "justified in supplying their wants when they will not do what you desired them to do, and which no doubt would be to their best interests."[16]

Reed thought that the agent intended to starve the Dakota off the Turtle Mountain Reserve, and wrote Markle instructing him that while his intentions were correct, he must use no force to have them abandon their land. In the meantime, however, the agent was not to trouble having the farmers in the band take up subdivisions. This effectively denied the band access to farm assistance, since assistance was meant only for progressive farmers who had abandoned their communal work patterns and taken up individual lands.[17]

Markle reported again in detail some two years later. When he first knew H'damani, the chief "appeared to be honest and industrious." Since the railway had gone through, however, liquor was readily available and the Indians were drinking. The chief had done little to stop this and "occasionally join[ed] the others in this illegal practice." He reasoned that if the department gave H'damani and his people assistance, they would simply make more of their own money available for liquor. Therefore, they should get no assistance.[18] Indian Commissioner Reed agreed and accepted Markle's appraisal of the chief and his band. He wrote to H'damani, warning the chief that it had been hoped the band would agree to move to Moose Mountain or to the Birdtail Reserve. Reed said, "[I am] very loath to compel you to do so, but I do not see how it will be possible to leave you any choice in the matter."[19]

In 1898, Indian Agent Markle was able to report a triumph. Two families – one headed by an elderly man and the other by a widow – were willing to move to Oak Lake Reserve, if they were compensated for the loss of their homes and improvements at Turtle Mountain. Markle concluded that "it would be a blessing to the Indians if that reserve was broken up."[20]

Assistant Commissioner Forget immediately authorized the expense to build new houses on the Oak Lake Reserve in the hope that if two families were settled at Oak Lake, others might decide to follow. Secretary of the Department of Indian Affairs J.D. McLean also approved the move, but warned that formal consent must be secured from the Oak Lake Dakota approving the admission of the Turtle Mountain people to their band, and the Turtle Mountain Dakota must renounce all "title, claim, or interest" in their old lands.[21]

Three families moved to Oak Lake, those of Iyojanjan, Kibanahota, and Widow Kasto. They wanted two burial plots fenced and preserved, but were otherwise willing to relinquish their claim to the Turtle Mountain Reserve. There still remained H'damani, Bogaga, and Tatunkanompa, and the chief was trying to convince other Dakota to join him and the three families on the Turtle Mountain lands. When Markle learned of this, he wanted to immediately sell the lands where the three families who had moved to Oak Lake had lived, so that no other Indians could settle upon it.[22]

McLean told Markle that it would be impossible to sell any of the reserve lands so long as Indians were still occupying any part of it. However, as for H'damani's plea for others to join him, he suggested that "it should not be difficult to prevent this by causing their ejectment and if necessary, their arrest for trespass." He agreed that the request for the preservation of burial plots should be respected, but the plots were never surveyed, never fenced, and were eventually sold along with the rest of the reserve.[23]

McLean pointed out that it would not be possible to dissolve the reserve without the assent of the majority of male members of the band. He suggested that Markle not encourage further migration until those willing to leave had signed a surrender of the reserve. If only those who adamantly refused to give up their lands remained on the reserve, a surrender would be impossible. McLean also advised the agent to threaten H'damani with being deposed from his position as chief if he did not do as the department wished. Markle barely restrained himself from having blind Iyojanjan, Widow Kasto and elderly Kibanahota returned to the reserve just long enough to sign the surrender as required by law.[24]

Markle's plans began to go astray. He had promised funds to help three families rebuild at Oak Lake, but the Indian department had promised assistance only for two, and refused to increase the amount. As well, when Widow Kasto left Turtle Mountain, H'damani had her house torn down and her furniture spread about on the prairie. The department refused to compensate her for these losses. With this loss of credibility Markle also lost his earlier zeal, and the whole subject of dissolving the reserve was quietly dropped for some years.[25]

A solution awaited the arrival of John Hollies as acting Indian agent at Griswold.

As Agent of this reserve it is up to me to report its immoral situation even as if it were a pestilence.

A change in its present conditions is imperative. But how, and how to end them, caused as they are by the position of the reserve, situated as it is near the south boundary line of the Province and subject to the calls, and almost at times of invasions of a lot of lawless Indians from the south, ready for any devilment in defiance of the law, makes a very difficult and knotty problem to solve.

It would seem that a plan could be devised by which nearly all could be deported gradually to different Sioux reserves, that have spare lands, and assisted. Hadamani and wife with Bogaga and wife are very old and unable to work for a living, should, I think, be provided for as "Old and Destitute". As they belong to this agency they could be placed without lands on Oak River reserve, under the Agent's care.

Sunkanapi is the only remaining voter, that has a say in the "surrender" of the lands of the reserve. A careful presentation of the benefits he would reap on a large reserve compared with the confined and cramped position he now occupies, would, I think, make him willing to request to be transferred to such a reserve, more especially if assistance and direction were given to establish him there.

The others have no vote on the "surrender" but in my opinion should have a share in the funds realized from the sale, applied as yourself or the Department see fit, to establish them in their new home.

The present immoral menace of the reserve of one square mile, made so by its unique position, would justify even drastic measures to end it, but the above are mild, turn no short corners, and seem practicable. The funds from the sale of 640 acres would go far to readjust the Indians in a better home, with hopeful prospects, and enable that menacing reserve to be blotted out.[26]

McLean studied Hollies's plan, and asked him to explain his opinions about who was and who was not required to sign a surrender of the land.[27] Hollies had reported that there were thirteen families and in total forty-five persons living on the reserve. Of these, only nine people in three families were listed in the reserve census, the rest being "stragglers," some of whom had been living on the reserve for fifteen years.

They have never applied for admission to the band. The method of application and gaining admission into the band, as I take it, seems to have been unknown to them, for it was never followed, neither is there any authority to place their names on the band list, for of course, not being reported, nothing was known of them by the Department! They have been severely let alone!

My conclusions were based upon the reasonableness of not giving a vote to Indians who had hitherto never been formally into membership of the band, and appeared legally not entitled to any say as to surrender of the lands. But at the same time in equity having been residents, for they now have houses, stables, hay and some lands they call their own, which some cultivate. It is their home! It is certainly no fault of theirs they are there. It seems to me they should have some share, perhaps not a pro rata share, but a share sufficient to give them a start on a larger reserve and among their own people.[28]

Hollies's sly way around the problem of a surrender had some appeal in Ottawa, after W.A. Orde, in charge of the Lands and Timber Branch of the department, managed to rephrase the agent's more distasteful perceptions and still retain the same intention.[29]

Hollies tried to get the permission of other bands to allow the Turtle Mountain people to move in with them. By August 3, 1908, four families had been accepted by the Oak Lake Band, those headed by George Naiyowaza, Mahtoita, Hinhansanna and Sam Eagle. He reported that H'damani and Bogaga refused to leave, and the chief had asked what would become of the reserve; to which Hollies had replied, "Oh, it will not run away." Quite clearly, he had not told them that the department intended to sell the reserve. When he left Turtle Mountain Reserve for the last time, Hollies gave those who remained a little food and told them that if they needed more, he "would be found at Griswold Agency on the Oak River Reserve," a journey of over four days for H'damani, then aged seventy-nine, and Bogaga, a man of eighty.[30]

Hollies used another clever manoeuvre to admit even more people to the Oak Lake Reserve. He got those who were just admitted to sign the acceptance papers of those who arrived later. Thus, the consent for Mahtohkita was signed by Mahtoita, Naiyowaza and Sam Eagle, all admitted to the Oak Lake Band a month earlier. This approach was seen as somewhat odd by the Oak Lake people and the admission of Mahtohkita was protested in a letter written by John Thunder: "Half of the Indians, that is, the principal Indians on this reserve has asked me to write to you about Mahtohkita's application, not to accept it as we are having trouble among ourselves. We haven't any room for any more, but except our own on the Reserve. Mr. Hollies has sent all Indians from Turtle Mountains Reserve to become the band on this Reserve, left two old men on Turtle Mts. Res. Now we are having trouble, not enough land for all."[31] Written beneath this letter is a note saying, "Majority of band gave consent." The letter of the law had been served, and that ended discussion of the matter.

Total success was imminent and Hollies's enthusiasm grew. He received the approved surrender forms and reported his readiness "to bring about inclination to surrender and then submit the papers, which are ready and on hand, so the iron, so to speak, can be hammered while it is hot. I confess that I have been waiting for the change of inclination in the Turtle Mountain Sioux which is against surrender before submitting the matter to the approval of the Band."[32]

In the early spring of 1909, Hollies reported the latest developments in the matter:

Two members out of three owning the Reserve, that is Bogaga and Tatunkanompa, have declared their desire to surrender the Reserve lands; whilst the third, Hadamani wishes to hear direct from you, the Head, as to your wishes in the matter, as he says "Whatever the head wishes me to do, I will carry out."

His reason for this is, that the head represents the man who gave him the reserve; that the reserve was given to him only, for he went to Winnipeg seven times before he secured it; that Bogaga and Tatunkanompa have no say, no ownership no rights whatever; that the reserve is all his own.

I visited the reserve . . . and met three members of the Band, at the house of Hadamani. Each man is over 65 years, and incapable of farming any of the 640 acres, and all three are on the ration list. It was the question of how they were going to cultivate the lands this year, and the knowledge of their incapacity and feeling of helplessness, that brought the question of surrender of the reserve so strongly to their attention, and finally, after many hours, to their adoption. Excepting that Hadamani wishes to receive direct advice from the head, which he says he will follow.[33]

This last letter makes it plain what conditions Hollies was awaiting before "hammering while the iron was hot." His opponents were now very old, destitute, facing a season of hunger, endlessly harassed, and in Bogaga's case, quite blind. Indeed, they had been reduced to a sufficiently compliant state for the surrender. Laird urged Hollies to complete the surrender, and wrote the letter H'damani required, sending it registered in order to "impress its importance upon him." H'damani chose to ignore the commissioner's advice that he give up the reserve.[34]

Hollies quickly returned to Turtle Mountain, only to find the chief confirmed in his intention to remain upon his lands. He insisted that Bogaga and Tatunkanompa had no share in the reserve. At the time Hollies was there, Tatunkanompa was not on the reserve, and he suspected that the chief had arranged for this, so the surrender could not proceed. Hollies said that as soon as Tatunkanompa could be located the surrender would be completed. Meanwhile, however, he wanted a new set of surrender papers, "with the word 'Chief' expunged." H'damani was to be deposed, as planned earlier. Hollies was also able to report, with some satisfaction, that "Bogaga, who has long been a victim of painfully weak eyes is now blind and is living on the Oak Lake Reserve #58 where I can look after him. This suits Hadamani exactly. Apparently the Turtle Mountain Reserve is all his own. He chuckled when I remarked, 'You have all the Reserve to yourself now!'"[35]

By early summer, Hollies had located Tatunkanompa and was ready to complete the surrender. H'damani, however, remained of the same mind. Hollies asked permission to make a special trip to Turtle Mountain to take the surrender. Permission was, of course, granted, and the surrender forms were amended so that H'damani no longer appeared listed as "chief."[36] In August, Hollies was able to report that the surrender had been obtained.

Bogaga, Tatunka-Nopa and his son Charlie voted in favour of the surrender; three; while Hadamani, and his grandson Chaske, voted against it; two. Surrender passed three votes to two.

Those members of the band voting for the "surrender" have been held strongly to this desire by Hadamani's insistence, that he alone owns the reserve and the rest have no rights whatever.

The voters in favour have requested that the reserve be disposed of at an early date so that they may receive benefit from its sale.[37]

The rules had been changed. Neither H'damani's nor Tatunkanompa's grandsons appear on the list that Hollies submitted to the department and purporting to identify the eligible voters. If the descendants of these two were permitted to vote in the surrender, why not those of others who lived there? But the arbitrary rules constructed by the department prevailed, and only the details of paperwork remained. The rest of the process happened with blinding speed. Hollies reported the surrender as complete on August 12, 1909. By August 17, Frank Oliver, superintendent general of Indian affairs, had prepared a submission to the governor general in Council, recommending acceptance of the surrender, and the Order in Council was approved August 28, 1909. The Turtle Mountain Reserve thus no longer existed.[38]

Historic documentation pertaining to the Turtle Mountain Dakota is extremely sparse for the period from 1891 to 1910, other than those papers internal to the department dealing with the efforts to dissolve the reserve. Nowhere in the sessional papers, the annual reports of the department, or in any other public source is there a reference to the plans made for the demise of the band. None of the problems of morality that so outraged the officials of the Indian department are even mentioned, and the hordes of American Dakota that were the bane of Markle are described only once with the term *scalliwags*. The internal and public documents are so much at odds with each other that one is led to believe the department was aware that an injustice was being perpetrated. The effects of policy, however, could not be disguised on the Turtle Mountain Reserve.

A brief summary of the reserve's last decade will illustrate its problems: By 1895, the population of the Turtle Mountain Band was reduced to twenty-one, and the total area under cultivation fell to sixteen acres, with ten acres devoted to oats for horse and cattle feed, and the remainder in gardens. Many of the younger people of the band had departed for the United States, in particular for the Dakota reservation at Poplar, Montana. The Old Ones who remained carried on with their chosen strategy of hunting, fishing, picking and selling berries, and working for the settlers from time to time. By that year, the band had increased their herd of cattle to fifteen head, for which they cared with the greatest attention.[39]

By 1896, the band was no longer growing field crops, as the agent had sold all of the band's cattle during the previous winter. Though Markle described the band as impoverished, he said many of the houses were well-equipped with beds, chairs, stoves, tables and other purchased consumer goods. Two years later the population was reduced to eleven as three families moved to Oak Lake. There was no more farming and no more sale of labour. Those few who remained were too old for such exertions, and without a cash income, poverty undoubtedly became real. As well, with the labour force so reduced, houses, stables and other equipment were fast falling into disrepair. The department refused to give the band any implements or assistance whatsoever, for fear that in doing so the Dakota would be encouraged to stay on the reserve.[40]

From 1898 until the reserve was lost to the Dakota in 1909, there are only two mentions of the band in the official documents. In 1909, Agent Hollies reported that there were a total of forty-five persons living on the reserve. It is difficult to say if this represented an actual increase in the numbers of residents or if Hollies included both the "official" Dakota residents and the "vagrants." Since he elsewhere reports that some of the "vagrants" had been living at Turtle Mountain for fifteen years, they must have been included in his count for that year. With this increase in available labour, the band had ten acres in cultivation, mostly for growing horse feed. As well, members were again hauling wood for sale to the settlers, working in the towns and on neighbouring farms, and selling handcrafts in addition to hunting, fishing and trapping. By 1910, the band population was reduced to fifteen by the migration to the Oak Lake Reserve, and after the surrender, six left for the United States. A year later, H'damani was alone, and when he died, the Turtle Mountain Dakota Band died with him.[41]

Having obtained the surrender of the reserve lands, the Indian department then had to settle the issue of compensation. When Hollies submitted the surrender, he reported that improvements totaling $217 were on the reserve. Of this sum, H'damani had $155 worth of property, Bogaga $26, Tatunkanompa $18 and Hinhansanna $18. In addition there were funds to come from the sale of the reserve, which Hollies had evaluated at $18 per acre, for a total value of $11,520.

In time, the surrender of the reserve was registered, and arrangements were made to have the land auctioned.[42] Following Hollies's advice, William Orde, in charge of the Lands and Timber Branch of the department, fixed the upset price of the lands at $18 per acre; any final bid over that price would be accepted.[43]

The auction was a complete failure. The auctioneer's announcement of the upset price was "met by the cry of 'Too high, too high!'" Not a single bid had been made on the land.[44] The auctioneer's fee, totaling $20, was deducted from the amount due the Indians.

The department was embarrassed by the failure to sell the reserve. Part of the inducement to dissolve the band was the revenue to be received from the sale. Hollies, it seems, had inflated the expected sale price, knowing well that his superiors would be less enthusiastic about closing the reserve if they suspected that it would cost the government money to do so. McLean asked that the lands and improvements be appraised once again. In the meantime, H'damani would be allowed to remain in his home.[45]

The Indians had received nothing thus far, excepting some unaccounted money

Hollies had donated when they signed the surrender papers. The claimants began to ask about their money and finally McLean was forced to report that there was no fund from which payments could be authorized. Indeed, the secretary had just been told by the auctioneer that he could expect only a fraction of Hollies's estimated return when the sale was completed.[46]

In April 1910, H'damani's old friend, J.E. Hughes, wrote: "[The chief] is living there alone on the reserve now for some time and is unable to do much work. He is willing to sell his share of the reserve for $2,000, a very small amount for the number of years he has lived there. He has lived here for the past 47 years. It really seems too bad the way the old fellow has to go around begging for a living and I think something could easily be done for him."[47]

By mid-summer of 1910, a problem arose that would plague the department well into the 1950s, and even then not be resolved.[48] The departmental officials discovered that the Dakota who had first moved from Turtle Mountain to Oak Lake Reserve had not signed any document renouncing their claim to the lands, or at least that no such documents could be found. With some apprehension, McLean bundled up all of the relevant correspondence and sent it to Markle, asking for clarification.[49] Markle, then inspector of Indian agencies at Red Deer, Alberta, responded in revealing detail: "I cannot remember whether the renunciation of all claim, title or interest in the Turtle Mountain Reserve was taken or not; . . . the fact that nothing appears on the file . . . leads me to the conclusion that no written renunciation was taken. I do not remember whether the written consent of the Oak Lake Band was taken to admit these people into the Oak Lake Reserve or not."[50]

As the problem became ever more complex, a detailed report was requested from David Laird, which he submitted in September 1910. Laird discovered, at this late date, that the Turtle Mountain Reserve had never been confirmed by Order in Council. He correctly reiterated the incorrect but official history of the reserve's creation and concluded that H'damani and his followers were "simply squatters, so far as alien Indians can be such." In 1902, Surveyor Ponton had been assigned to subdivide the reserve and allocate individual land holdings, "which would, in a manner, confirm them in their possession." Laird, however, could find nothing in the files that authorized the subdivision, and nothing is to be found today.[51] In conclusion, Laird wrote: "The right of these Indians . . . whatever it was, has been yielded to the Crown by the surrender of Aug. 9, 1909. It only remains therefore to consider how the funds which will accrue from the sale of the lands can properly be disposed of."[52]

Laird was unaware that Hollies had determined that only five persons were entitled to a share of the sale proceeds, and when he examined the matter, the commissioner decided that eight others, in addition to Hollies's five, were also entitled.

While officials in Ottawa were considering Laird's report, they received the completed survey and valuation of the Turtle Mountain Reserve. H.W. Fairchild estimated the value of the reserve lands and improvements at $5,200. In May 1911, the lands were auctioned, netting $6,329, or slightly more than half the figure first put forward by Hollies in 1909. Of this amount, $155 was forwarded to Hollies to be given to H'damani for his improvements, which had lost $60 in value over the years, and the Agent was asked for advice about what to do with the remaining funds. Commissioner Laird noted that "the sale of the reserve having yielded so much less than was expected at the time of the surrender it is not worthwhile placing anything to their credit, on which they could draw interest."[53]

Over the next few months, there was a proliferation of obstacles to finally disposing of the Turtle Mountain Reserve and settling obligations to the Dakota. It was pointed out that the terms of the surrender stated that a part of the sale proceeds must be used for re-establishing the Turtle Mountain people in new homes, with the remaining capital invested and drawing interest. Therefore, it would not be possible to make individual payments, as Hollies had promised.[54]

McLean then became aware that there were more people with an interest in the Turtle Mountain reserve than he had been led to believe by Hollies. While trying to deal with the problem of dividing the sale proceeds, McLean received a letter from one Luke Bigtrack of Fort Totten, North Dakota. He was H'damani's son-in-law, and he wanted to know if his wife was entitled to a share, since she had been born on the Turtle Mountain Reserve. McLean confirmed H'damani's share in the sale money, but did not mention the possibility that Bigtrack's wife might also have a claim.[55]

In early August 1911, Hollies sent another report. Iyojanjan was dead, as was his wife. The rest of the beneficiaries were alive, but none were doing well. Tatunkanompa and his son Charley had moved to Montana and would return only to get their money. H'damani's son, Charley Eagle, had applied for membership in the Oak Lake Band, but the band wanted $500 to admit him and there was no money in the account for this. H'damani had just been at the agency office and refused either to recognize the sale of the reserve, or to accept payment owed for his improvements.

He relies considerably upon a letter, with green ribbon and sealing wax from Lieutenant Governor Morrison [sic] stating he, the Governor, would do his best to secure a reserve for the Sioux Indians on Turtle Mountain. This letter I read to him, and explained as I have often done, that the majority in favour of selling the reserve always rules. I asked him to make this Oak River reserve his home. He said I might sell the reserve. Yes, I said, if fifty one out of a hundred wanted to surrender it for that purpose it would be sold. He wished me good-bye as he would never see me again. I repeatedly asked him what should be done with the $155 allowed for his house, but he would make no statement as to that or of his future.[56]

In March 1912, Hollies wrote Mclean imploring that Bogaga be allowed to purchase a team of horses. Bogaga was to own the horses, but they would be cared for and rented by his son-in-law, Angus McKay. Bogaga needed the source of income and McKay needed the team. Finally, McLean acceded to Hollies's wish and a bay mare and a dark bay stallion were purchased.[57] This was the first of the money from the sale of the reserve to move out of the hands of the department and into those of the Indians.

McLean then wrote Hollies asking for yet another report on the beneficiaries. McLean, it is assumed, was stalling for time, since the department was having a very difficult time dislodging any payments from the purchasers of the reserve land, but it was too much for Hollies. He made two more futile efforts to have Ottawa clear up the question of who was entitled to get proceeds from the sale of reserve land. Before he could receive an answer, however, Hollies died.[58]

In mid-August 1912, and before any further progress was made, H'damani died at Oak Lake Reserve, never having seen any compensation from the loss of his land. If the departmental officials received any joy at the passing of this singular and difficult man, it was short-lived, for now they had to deal with his heirs, and they had learned well from the old chief how to attend to their own interests.

John Thunder wrote Hollies's replacement, Agent James McDonald, telling him that the cheque for H'damani's improvements at Turtle Mountain, amounting to $155, had been sent first to Fort Totten and then back to Ottawa. This money, he claimed, was actually due to Charlie Eagle, or Chaske, as it was he, H'damani's grandson, who had built the chief's house at the old reserve. He wanted this money. McDonald passed this letter on to McLean, along with the news that H'damani had a grandson at Oak Lake Reserve. Later, he ominously notified McLean that "there are other heirs."[59] As for making available some of the money owed, there was no money in the fund, and McLean was reduced to pleading with the debtors, saying, "The Indians are clamouring for the money due them, and for the Department to carry out the agreement, the purchasers must carry forth the money due."[60]

In December 1912, Agent McDonald had secured the required information about who and where H'damani's heirs were. He reports H'damani having had one daughter and four sons: Anna Bigtrack, or Mazadusawin, who herself had two daughters, both dead; one son, Charley Eagle, who was then at Oak Lake with his son Hayetuaduzahad and his two children, also dead; Hokenaske and his son, now dead; and Tamazawaste with one son, Alexis Mazawasicuna, who in turn had three daughters and one son, all living at Oak River Reserve.[61] With his grandson Chaske, this listing gave H'damani eleven living heirs.

Officials in the Indian Department spent another whole year trying to work out an appropriate way of dispersing the funds received from the sale of the reserve.

Having finally decided on who was entitled to a share and who were the descendants and heirs of those who died during the span of delays, a schedule of payments was drawn up. On March 11, 1913, three years and one day after the sale of the reserve, the appropriate cheques were mailed out.[62]

The department had not yet succeeded in getting all of the money due from the sale of the reserve lands, and this first cheque was only an installment. In 1917, the department determined to make a final payment to the heirs of H'damani and the surviving Turtle Mountain Dakota. In all, the Indians received $155 for H'damani's improvements, and $3,980 from the proceeds of the sale of the reserve. An additional $47.75 went to the department for managing the fund, leaving an unexpended balance of $2,066.25; it was proposed to give this balance to the Oak Lake Band as compensation for taking in the eight people from the old reserve. This conclusion was "considered reasonable to all concerned."[63]

In 1954, a rumour was circulating within the Dakota communities of Canada that there was still a substantial balance in the trust account established to hold the funds from the sale of the reserve. An inquiry made by Father Gontron Laviolette, who was serving as priest to Dakotas of the Catholic faith, revealed that a balance did indeed remain after the last distribution in 1917, and that the sum had grown to $18,625.25.[64] The money remains to this day on the books of the Indian department. The enquiry did, however, evoke an all-too-familiar response from the department: it requested a report. This was provided by A.E. St. Louis, archivist for the department.

The report, which St. Louis described as "this exhaustive official recital of events anent to the settlement of the Turtle Mountain Sioux Band of Indians on Reserve No. 60," is so laden with error as to render it virtually useless. It does, nevertheless, contain some remarkable conclusions on the part of the archivist. Possessing only a garbled knowledge of the matter, St. Louis was able to see quite clearly that the course of dispossessing the Indians, and afterwards of distributing the money from the sale of the reserve, was attended by blatant disregard for departmental policy and regulation and violation of statute. Markle, Hollies and Laird were seen to have been moralistic, self-righteous, and dictatorial in their treatment of the Dakota. He does not doubt that the reserve was wrongfully extinguished by the department, and he saw the concern as an opportunity. He said, "At long last, Canadian justice, as represented by this administration, [will be] extended to the descendants of the small group of American refugees who settled on Canadian soil at Turtle Mountain in 1863."[65] This opportunity was never taken up, and probably never will be.

Cattle and wages in the South:
Standing Buffalo's Band,
1876 to 1940

9

For many years, change west of Manitoba was neither as rapid nor as dramatic as it was in Manitoba itself. Lands were taken up even more slowly in the North-West Territories. Even after the Canadian Pacific Railway was completed in 1885, communications, transportation and services were underdeveloped until the end of the century. Much of the vast territory between Manitoba and the Rocky Mountains remained in the hands of the Indians, Métis and traders. When settlement and agriculture did begin to expand in what is now Saskatchewan, the arid environment dictated a course somewhat different from what had occurred in fertile Manitoba. The sparse population, small local markets, and a virtual lack of regional manufacturing greatly limited the demand for commodities, handcrafts and labour. The alternatives that the Dakota in the West could include in an economic strategy were considerably fewer or more constrained than had been the case for the Dakota in Manitoba.

The Dakota led by Tatankanaje and Wapahaska, that is, those who had moved directly from the United States to the western prairie beyond the Assiniboine River, were for many years able to carry on a nomadic, hunting lifestyle ranging over both sides of the international boundary. By the late 1870s, however, settlers were trickling into the valleys of the Qu'Appelle and Saskatchewan rivers, and the American army was attempting to halt the passage of Indians from Canada into the United States. The time had come for the Dakota in the far West to take up home lands.

Tatankanaje's people had been invited by Lieutenant Governor Morris to locate a place where they would settle. In the late spring of 1877, Interior Deputy Minister Meredith wrote in favour of the location and recommended that David Laird be authorized "to inform the band of Indians . . . that there is no objection to their beginning farming operations at the locality selected by them on the north side of

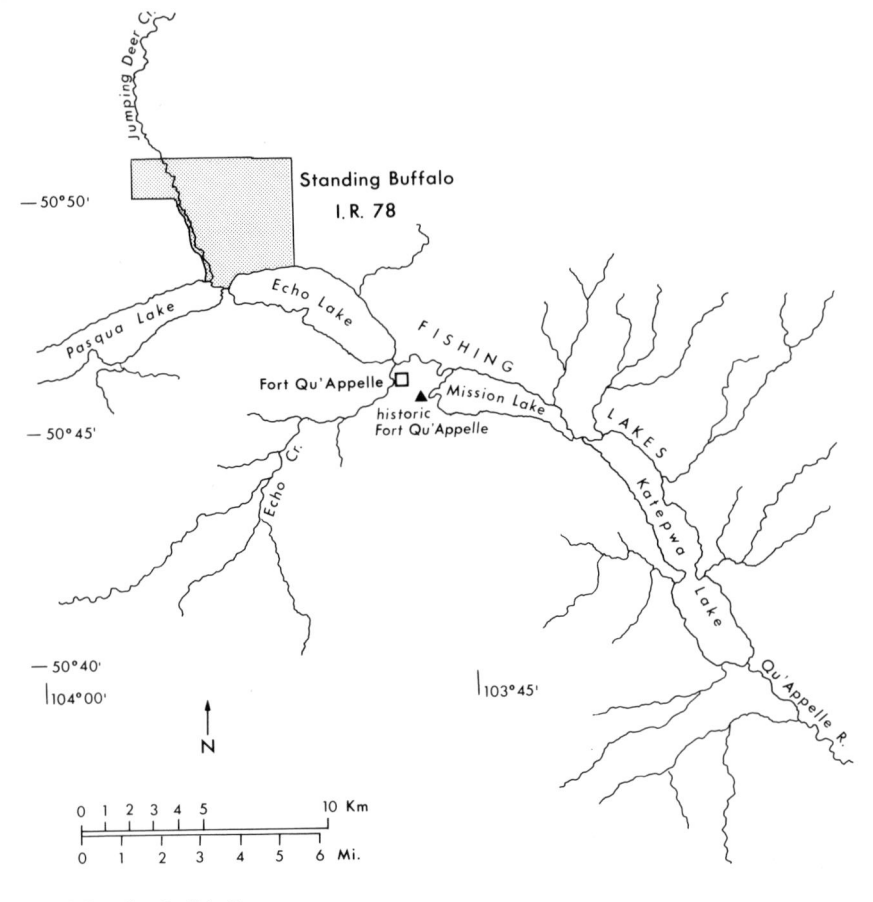

Map 6. Standing Buffalo Reserve

the Qu'Appelle Lakes as a desirable site for a reserve, but that the Government does not think it desirable at present to fix on that or any other locality as a reserve for these Indians."[1] This decision was transmitted to Laird in a letter the next day.[2]

Morris's earlier correspondence indicates that he and the Department of Indian Affairs were confused about the identity of Tatankanaje's and Wapahaska's bands. It had been assumed that they were one band with two chiefs, and the department had intended to assign only one piece of land to both. The two chiefs did make an attempt to settle together on the land selected by Tatankanaje, but were soon dissatisfied with this arrangement. In the summer of 1878, Laird wrote that he had been visited on separate occasions by both chiefs: "They are of the opinion that the locality they have selected for a reserve at Jumping Creek near Qu'Appelle is not well suited for a reserve owing to the scarcity of wood. These two Chiefs have had some dispute and will not settle together. Each of them . . . asked to be allowed to settle about half way between the telegraph line and Dumont's crossing on the South Saskatchewan, but to this I would not consent."[3]

Considering the fact that the two bands had maintained separate territories and band structures for most of the time they had been in Canada, it is quite possible that a dispute could have arisen. In the course of time, it was Wapahaska who moved to the South Saskatchewan River, while Tatankanaje remained at the Qu'Appelle Lakes. No special executive action was taken to assign and confirm lands for Tatankanaje; rather, authority for the assignment was drawn from the Order in Council of January 4, 1873, which approved in general the allocation of reserves for the Dakota in Canada.

In 1880, the government began to survey the allocated lands. Dominion Land Surveyor John Nelson visited Tatankanaje that summer, and completed the survey the following year. He reported: "This reservation has a remarkably beautiful situation. It has an area of seven and a half square miles – bounded on the west side by Jumping Creek and on the front by the Qu'Appelles. The soil is a clay loam of the first order and there is abundance of wood. Hay is scarce and consequently a small meadow was reserved for them at the extensive hay grounds further up the river."[4]

When lands were tentatively assigned to Tatankanaje's band in 1877, the Department of Indian Affairs agreed to give the Dakota some material assistance in setting up, in particular, agricultural implements and seedstock. The level of assistance was arbitrarily set at $4,000 for the needs of the entire band, then numbering over two hundred persons. That amount was the balance left unspent in the parliamentary appropriation for Indian matters in the Northwest. The money was used in 1878 to buy a dozen spades, six axes, sixty-four hoes, eight trace chains, two ploughs and one harrow, but no oxen. Needless to say, David Laird was compelled to report that, since they had no oxen, the band had done very little planting in that season.

The following spring, two oxen with harness were appropriated, so that the ploughs, harrow and trace chains might be of some use. With these, the Dakota planted about five acres of potatoes, two acres of corn and two acres of oats. Since there was a heavy rainfall in the last two years of the 1870s, this planting would hardly have made a dent in the food requirements of more than two hundred people.[5]

In 1881, the governor general of Canada toured the western territory and Tatankanaje had the opportunity to address him directly. He said:

All the men of my band are very poor. My men are all naked and when winter comes they will be cold. We have not enough tools to begin to farm. For five years we have had no ammunition to kill game. Now that I am living on English soil, I try to live the same as a white man. I shake hands with them all strongly, and I belong to the Great Mother.

When I shake hands with you I hope I may receive ammunition to kill game with, and when I see you again, I hope I shall not be poor anymore. . . . I have been very poor, but now that I see you I shall be poor no longer.[6]

The governor general responded by promising: "Help will be given you to build a school, and implements also will be given to the young men who work, and those who work well will receive food."[7]

The governor general's response to Tatankanaje's plea was generous, but by the late winter of 1882, nothing had been done to relieve the band. In early February of that year, Robert M. Smith, who had been the interpreter at the meeting in 1881, wrote to His Excellency on behalf of Tatankanaje, describing the band's situation, and asking that his promises be fulfilled: "The Sioux Chief says that seven years ago Governor Morris promised his people farm implements, teams, cows, etc. Up to the time of your Excellency's arrival not one thing of any account had been received of all that was promised by that authorized deputy of the Great Mother. He therefore wishes your Excellency that the matter might be seen to. The Sioux wish to be self sustaining and will work only if they get a good chance. They live on potatoes a good deal, and only two bushels for each head of family is allowed. They want more to plant in the spring."[8]

The governor general learned that the promises had indeed been made. His secretary sent Smith's letter to John A. Macdonald, along with His Excellency's confirmation of its contents. The Indian department, however, was not about to be rushed into action by the governor general, and Dewdney was asked to comment on the whole matter.[9]

Dewdney noted that what the governor general had actually said was that implements would be given to the young men who work, and he interpreted this to mean that the "promises made can be carried out by assisting those who satisfy the Agent that the possession of more agricultural implements will make them independent of government aid." Dewdney was then instructed to request the agent to determine what implements and livestock would be necessary to supply the band.[10] In the meantime, whatever food was immediately needed was to be provided.[11]

In May 1882, Agent Macdonald submitted a list of tools and implements required by the Dakota, including twelve oxen with complete harnessing, ploughs, harrows, a mowing machine and rake, and a variety of hand tools for gardening and woodwork. In June, a month later and well past the planting season, Assistant Indian Commissioner E.T. Galt, was instructed to make the necessary purchases, excepting the mower, as Dewdney thought scythes would do.[12]

While it seems likely that the Dakota would not have received the cattle and implements at all had Tatankanaje not spoken to the governor general, even the personal intervention of His Excellency was not spur enough to move the Department of Indian Affairs to more than the usual level of exertion. As it was, the band had only one yoke of oxen and a plough to use in the season of 1882, with which they managed to put in twenty acres of grain crops and break an additional forty acres of sod, about the maximum work to be expected of a single yoke. In 1883, with the late start in the spring, they broke another fifty acres, but little more was actually planted. As Wadsworth reported, the band had left the reserve to trap and did not return until mid-May, too late for the long growing season required by the grain seeds of that era.[13]

In 1884, the band had acquired most of the cattle and implements required for a start in agriculture, and over a hundred acres of land had been broken and prepared for cropping. The use of the lands was evenly divided between wheat and garden stuff, especially root crops that could be stored over winter for domestic use. As well, the band had fenced off a hundred acres for their horses and cattle, and had constructed twenty-six houses. Progress was being made so rapidly that Commissioner Dewdney requested even more oxen and equipment for the Dakota, to a total value of about $700. Considering the fact that the department estimated the population on the reserve to be 247, it is obvious that all of the farming gear supplied to the band would have been barely sufficient to provide a base suitable for subsistence production. Superintendent General Macdonald noted, however, that the Standing Buffalo's Band was requesting a very large part of the total appropriation made for the Dakota in Canada, which was only $2,000. Despite departmental misgivings about the large sum, the request was granted. At the same time, Dewdney advised that "the Indians . . . should be made clearly to understand that they will be expected in the future to provide those articles and animals for themselves."[14]

The band seems to have done fairly well over the winter of 1884–85, at least well enough that the agent was compelled to complain that the Dakota spent a good part of the winter dancing and holding giveaways, during which they disposed of much of their crops to the surrounding Cree. A considerable part of their income came from the sale of horses, which, being of good stock, were in considerable demand by the small flow of settlers that had arrived in the Qu'Appelle district. The agent stated that they would have sold many more of them had he not kept an eye on the band and prohibited some sales. Considering that the department had never given the Dakota horses, it is difficult to understand why he felt justified in this intervention.[15]

Unfortunately, the implements and cattle authorized by Dewdney the previous autumn had not been delivered when the Riel Rebellion occurred, and in the ensuing confusion, such matters were overlooked. It was not that Standing Buffalo's Band was in any way connected with the rebellion; to the contrary, Indian Agent Macdonald reported that the band had requested that they be allowed to camp temporarily near the North West Mounted Police barracks at Qu'Appelle, after they had heard that Indians who refused to join the rebellion would be attacked along with the whites. Macdonald, however, was not keen on the idea of having a large body of Dakota so close to the barracks, and they were told to remain on the reserve. That year, the band had 158 acres broken and in crop and had increased the size of their pasture to 240 acres, and had built an additional nineteen houses. Of the estimated forty-five families that made up the band, thirty-nine were engaged in some form of mixed agricultural production, but few of the Dakota had moved beyond subsistence-scale growing.[16]

The season of 1886 was very dry and much of the crop was not worth cutting, but again the acreage under cultivation was increased. Tatankanaje's people were the only ones in the Qu'Appelle district who managed to retrieve a potato crop from the drought, and they lived on that for the winter, supplemented by whatever game and fish they could take. The failure of the grain crops caused the department to propose greater attention be given to the raising of cattle and, in that spring, the Dakota were given eight bred cows and a bull. By fall, they had eight calves as well. In that year, the department reported only 148 persons to be living on the reserve, a reduction of a hundred individuals. There is no explanation of this dramatic decrease, but it is likely that most of those who were no longer at Standing Buffalo Reserve had returned to the United States.[17]

The very poor crops, both of grain and garden stuff, forced the Dakota to look elsewhere for their subsistence. They had been receiving no rations for some months, but occasionally were given a little ammunition when they went hunting. Agent Lash reported that small game was very scarce and required a lot of work and travel to yield a satisfactory return, so the Dakota asked that they be allowed to cut wood off the reserve for sale. The reserve had no surplus wood for such purposes, and the agent suggested that the appropriate permission to cut wood on government land be given. The Dakota did fairly well at selling wood and fish, but even they, in late winter, were driven to ask for rations, which they did not receive.[18]

Until the summer of 1887, the Indian Agent Lash had assigned Farmer Hockley to the Dakota reserve, but by then the band was willing and able to do all of its own work and planning, so the resident farmer's services were withdrawn. Lash reported that the people were somewhat discouraged by the crop failures of the previous years, and had decided to concentrate more on gardens and the production of root crops. As it turned out, this decision was a timely one – virtually all grain crops in the district were lost to gophers that year. The potato crop, however, was excellent and produced a heavy yield. The Dakota had no trouble selling their large surplus. Despite this success, the light soil that had been planted over the previous several years was becoming overrun with weeds, and a considerable area was in need of summerfallowing and deep ploughing.[19]

Settlement of the prairies west of Manitoba was very slow. In 1886, Canada began to export beef to Britain, and this encouraged potential ranchers to move into the dry lands of the West. In the late 1880s, construction was begun by the Qu'Appelle, Long Lake and Saskatchewan Railway Company on their line to Prince Albert. This modest expansion created an equally modest demand for casual labour, which the Dakota immediately moved to fill. By the autumn of 1887, the people had decided to leave the reserve and seek work where it was available. At first, this was approached as an experiment, but by December, Agent Lash was able to report that "Standing Buffalo's Band are making a good living and appear perfectly contented." By mid-winter, however, they experienced the plague of all casual labourers – seasonal unemployment. Their cash income, which they had been using to buy flour, disappeared, and with the poor seasons of the recent past, they had little to eat other than fish and potatoes. In truth, though, a good many of their neighbours, both Cree and white, were reduced to the same fare. By spring, this situation was turned around. Many of the young men left the reserve as early as the beginning of March to seek work with settlers, and were immediately successful. The older people who remained on the reserve set about improving their houses, using timbers taken from a woodlot recently assigned to the band. Over the winter, the Dakota had acquired "a more comfortable appearance than the other [Cree] Bands, notwithstanding they are entirely independent [sic] on their own resources, the sick only receiving a little assistance."[20]

In 1888, the band again decided to reduce their grain crops rather than risk losses to gophers and drought, and to increase production of root crops. This was a sound decision. The soils of the Standing Buffalo Reserve were too light and the location too susceptible to early and late frosts to risk dryland cereal farming. On the other hand, many of the incoming settlers, having gone into debt in order to establish themselves, elected to concentrate much of their time and resources on grain production, virtually the onl, cash crop then grown in the West, and purchased their basic winter food supplies, especially potatoes, turnips, carrots and other root crops that could easily be transported and stored. The Dakota cropping tactic required less dedication of resources and labour than did commercial-scale grain production, and made it possible for them to reap the benefits of wage labour as well as cash crops. The band possessed no more implements and cattle than could be used by about fifteen households, but there were between thirty and fifty households on the reserve at any one time. The younger, mobile families went to work away from the reserve, setting up their tipis wherever they found opportunities, while the older, less vigorous people remained to tend the larger gardens and to cut hay for the cattle. In 1888, about twenty acres of garden and root crops as well as thirty-two acres of barley and wheat were planted, which was much less than in previous years.

The band's cattle were mainly in the hands of those households that remained more or less permanently on the reserve. They had increased the herd from the original size of eight cows in 1886 to thirty-two in 1888, which suggests careful management and attention. Two hundred and fifty acres were fenced as pasture and that year a new, large corral was built for the cattle; as well,a hay yard holding a hundred tons of fodder was constructed.[21]

This pattern persisted over a number of years and, while it was similar to the economic strategies developed by the farmer bands of Manitoba, especially in the earlier years, there were some important differences. In Manitoba, the Oak River, Oak Lake and Birdtail bands developed their agricultural pursuits to the point that virtually all labour, capital and resources were dedicated to that form of production. Once that was accomplished, the young men were integrated as agricultural labour and ultimately as management on the reserve, and trained in that capacity. Often the people who left the reserves to labour elsewhere were the older men, already accomplished in the management of their own enterprises and therefore able to divert some time away from their home concerns. At Standing Buffalo Reserve, by contrast, the young men went to work off the reserve while the older people remained to tend the gardens, root crops and cattle. Then, as the documentary records suggest and the tribal historians confirm, as the young people matured, improved their personal assets, and had children ready to attend school at Fort Qu'Appelle, they too became the herdsmen and farmers. That a substantial amount of labour was diverted from agricultural production is evident in comparing the area of cultivated lands at Standing Buffalo and Oak River. The populations of the two bands were similar at various points in their contemporary history, but in 1888, the Oak River Dakota had three hundred acres in grain crop and the Standing Buffalo people had about thirty. This is a good comparison of the strategic approach of the Oak River Band, which resulted in long-term diversification of labour and production, and the "serial" diversification resulting from the tactical, short-term approach of the Standing Buffalo Dakota. Both enjoyed success.

The crops of 1888 were superb on the reserve, and there was a considerable surplus of roots – the prime market garden crop – which was sold throughout the district. All who sought labouring jobs found what they wanted and turned a good dollar. New houses were built, as Inspector McGibbon reported, "of a better class." As well, the stables were enlarged, better ventilated and warmer. As the harvest of the crop was in progress, people went to fish and hunt ducks and prairie chickens, which were preserved for winter use. As soon as possible, people who had jobs returned to them, and the reserve was reported as being "very thinly populated" for October and November. At that time, the Dakota were working as farm hands during the harvest and as railroad section hands.[22]

In these years, the primary employer of Dakota agricultural labour was Major W.R. Bell's farm. This corporation, known as the Qu'Appelle Valley Farming Company, was an interesting example of a large-scale farm. Bell invested $400,000 in fifty-two thousand acres of government and railroad land, 106 buildings, and all the accoutrements of progressive, vast-scale agriculture. The company was formed in 1882, and by 1883, seven thousand acres had been broken and two thousand seeded. Unfortunately it folded in 1889 as a result of bad crops and the ensuing restricted cash flow. But the enterprise attracted settlers, and created many more labouring opportunities. Much of the labour expended to construct the Bell operation was Dakota.

The settlers who were attracted into the Qu'Appelle district elected to establish along the railroad route, for reasons of easy access to transportation, and this same service took the Dakota labourers to the settlers, a mutually satisfactory arrangement. In those days, the demand for Dakota labour was insatiable, and top wages were asked and paid. Standing Buffalo's Band was by then completely independent of government aid, a position they were able to maintain for the better part of a generation.[23]

Wood was very scarce on the reserve, and in early 1888, the band applied to the department for an additional woodlot. After months of negotiation, the band was given permission to use three-quarters of a section of land lying to the west of the reserve that had not been settled. No Order in Council was approved at this time for adding the land to the reserve.[24]

The band lived very comfortably over the winter of 1888 and 1889, and went into the next spring with a surplus of food. No new land was broken that summer, and what land was available for cropping went into increased root and garden production. As Agent Lash reported, "They do better in this line, than with grain farming. They are off the Reserve so much working at different points and do not take the same interest in grain farming."[25] For the next several months, Agent Lash made only the most general and brief comments about the Dakota; they were not receiving assistance from the Indian department, were not influenced by the coercion of annuities, and were not overly interested in expanding agricultural enterprise. Thus in their economic success, the Standing Buffalo people escaped the bane of successful farmer bands in Manitoba – the resident agent, sub-agent, or farm instructor. Lash did send Farmer Hockley over from time to time, when he could leave his base at Pasquah's Reserve, but Lash recognized that he had little to tell the Dakota, and his visits were more social than business in nature.

Tribal historians say that the earlier economic tactic was continued for some time. By 1890, the Dakota were cutting a considerable amount of firewood and selling it at Qu'Appelle during the winter off-season, and a number of men were working year-round for one employer. This was at a time when labour was fairly plentiful in the North West, especially in winter, when settlers would be seeking winter jobs of their own. This speaks highly of the Dakota as labourers. At the same time, they were attending to their domestic production; many families would leave the reserve to seek work, and others would remain to work the gardens, which were somewhat reduced in size. All would return to the reserve for the haying in July and August, and immediately return to their off-reserve work when that was done. By September, there were only five families left on the reserve, looking after the cattle while the rest – about forty families – were working on settlers' farms. By mid-winter, those who did not have or desire full-time jobs were back on their reserve. In the immediate neighbourhood, of course, fish and game of all kinds were plentiful.[26]

In the spring of 1891, Inspector of Agencies Wadsworth paid his first visit in eight years to the Standing Buffalo Reserve. Wadsworth acknowledged that the Dakota were very much independent of the department, to the point that the band refused a census on the reserve, as a matter of "national objection." He estimated that there were forty households on the reserve and a total population of 175. Most investment made by band members was for improved transportation, such as buggies, wagons and sleds, or for improving their stock-handling facilities, such as fences, barns, stables, hay yards and corrals. There were thirteen families who farmed independently and fifteen others who planted a common field of potatoes and turnips. Almost all had gardens, but these were near the separate houses. Many of the men were selling firewood to the flour mills at Fort Qu'Appelle, receiving $2 a cord if they took their pay in trade, and $1.75 if in cash. Wadsworth reported that the Indians were regularly being shortchanged by the gristmills when they took their wheat in to be ground, but this was a common problem for all the growers in the North West. Fourteen households had possession of a total of forty-seven head of cattle, and over the winter had killed six head for band use.[27]

Until 1891, all of the Dakota had been living in the gullies that run from the prairie tableland into the abrupt valley of the Qu'Appelle, so as to get some protection from the winter winds and to be close to a source of water. In that year, a number of families moved up onto the tableland and built new houses there. This was seen as an advantage in that no extensive farming could be contemplated in the restricted gullies. On the tableland, however, each family could have its own square, surveyed plot of farm land. Thus began the pressure to establish individual farm plots, a situation incompatible with the tactics then being followed by the band. Wadsworth saw the relocation as real progress, and hoped that all of the Dakota would soon move out of the gullies.

In 1891, the band began to increase the area of land planted to grain crops. This was a reaction to a sudden and sharp decline in the demand for their labour. The drought years of the late 1880s and 1890s, combined with a steady drop in the prices for all farm produce, obliged the established settlers to spend less on hired labour. Immigration into the West fell off in the dry years. The government began to send trainloads of farm workers from Ontario to the West, not so much to fill a diminished demand for labour as to introduce the West to potential immigrants. The Dakota could not compete with these people, who had been guaranteed jobs if they went to the North West for a season; the openings for the Dakota closed.

The Dakota had increased their farm operations from the thirty acres cultivated in 1890 to over one hundred in 1892, with most of the additional land planted to wheat and oats. Again, Lash reported that the people had received no assistance from the department, having harvested enough grain to provide all their own needs, with a modest surplus for sale. Their gardens and an income from selling wood kept them "very comfortable." Still, many families were able to find work after they had put in their own crops, and were off the reserve until mid-November.[28]

By the turn of the century, Agent W.M. Graham, wrote that the situation was changing rapidly.

This Reserve is small, containing in all 7.6 square miles and is absolutely destitute of hay. In the past the hay supply for these Indians has been cut on Dominion lands, off the Reserve, on permits received each year from the Department of the Interior.

The country is now settling up, and it is questionable if this system of obtaining permits can be carried out with safety any longer. I would therefore strongly recommend that some arrangement be made with the Department by which these sections viz: 5, 7, 16, 18, 13, and 23, T.23, R14, W 2nd M be set aside permanently for the use of these Indians.

Unless this be done, I fear it will only be a very short time before these lands are taken up, and the Indians will have to give up cattle raising as a means of earning their livelihood.[29]

In response to this suggestion, Laird wrote that, "considering the small number of

Indians on the Standing Buffalo Reserve I fear that the Department would not grant this request, but if you will kindly select the three best sections and quote the numbers I will endeavor to have them reserved. It is thought that this area should meet all the requirements for the number of cattle owned by these Indians."[30]

The number of people on the reserve, of course, had nothing to do with the appetites of cattle, and the number of cattle kept by the Indians was necessarily limited by the amount of feed available for them. Graham bowed to his superior's assessment and agreed to make the limited selection in the spring when the snow was gone. He cautioned, however, that he feared "some other arrangement will have to be made if these people are to increase their herds."[31]

In April 1902, Mathew Wacihewaste of Standing Buffalo's Band wrote to Laird: "Now I want to let you know something. I am displeased with our reservation being not large enough. There is some pupil at School who will need the land when they come out to the reserve, so we want you to see about that. We want to hold fast to our land."[32]

Laird's response to this letter is penned in the margin: "No answer necessary." In 1903, however, Tatankanaje sent a letter to the governor general, asking "that we have more land as we have not enough for our own children." The petition was signed by sixty-seven male members of the band.[33] This letter must have by-passed the agent and the Indian commissioner, either of whom would have diverted it, to arrive directly in the hands of Lord Minto. He in turn passed it on to the departmental officials, and a report was requested.

Sam Bray, chief surveyor, provided the report, stating that there were 215 Dakota occupying 4,864 acres, or about 22.6 acres per person. He agreed that the reserve was small for the population.[34]

The matter was referred to Indian Commissioner Laird for his opinion. Laird reported that, as "American refugees," the band was not entitled to more land. If the reserve lands and the hayland assigned to the Dakota opposite Muscowpetung's Cree Reserve were not adequate for farming, then perhaps they should be relocated entirely to a more suitable location.[35] While Laird's recommendation that the band be relocated was not taken up by the department, his comments were used to reject the idea of giving them any other additional lands as well.[36]

Early in the new century, the territory west of the Province of Manitoba began to attract a steady flow of settlers, and available lands became scarce, in particular near the established settlements along the Qu'Appelle River. The Department of the Interior began to make enquiries about whether lands used under permit by Standing Buffalo's Band might be made available for settlers, and was even accepting applications for land. The issue was discussed at various levels of the bureaucracy, but most officials who had had experience with the western reserves were well aware that the Dakota were themselves short of land, and these approaches were fended off. Nevertheless, the Indian department did not apply for an Order in Council that would have secured the lands as a part of the reserve.[37]

In the following years, attempts were made to increase the extent of the reserve. In 1913, however, N.O. Cote, controller of the Department of the Interior, argued that the Dakota, being "a Band of Sioux and apparently not entitled under treaty," were in no position to ask for additional lands.[38] The Indian department continued to press for the lands being used by the Dakota to be added to the reserve and confirmed by Order in Council. Again, Cote responded that "the matter of making this addition to the reserve has been considered and it has been decided that it is advisable not to do so." No reason was given for refusing the request.[39]

In March 1918, Agent Christianson asked that a section of land adjoining the Standing Buffalo Reserve be acquired as pasture for one of the members of the band.[40] During the two months of delay that followed this request, the Department of the Interior offered the land for sale at auction. On May 27, 1918, the west half of the section was sold and lost to the Indians. The east half was still available, and in January 1919 all the paperwork required to transfer the land to the reserve had been completed. Rather than add the land to the reserve, however, the half section was simply held for the use of the band with the proviso that the "Department will agree to release the land should this Department decide at any time to offer it for sale by public auction." For this privilege, the Indian department was required to pay a rent of $7.50 each year. McLean agreed to these conditions, and insisted that the agent collect the rents from the Dakota.[41]

For a few years after World War I, Dakota lease lands came under considerable pressure as the government sought farmsteads for returning soldiers. The Indian department insisted that lease lands and lands held by temporary order be retained for the band, and the Department of the Interior reluctantly agreed, but nothing was done to add the land to the reserve, the only action that could be taken to assure the Dakota that they would have full and durable use of the land.[42]

At the time Standing Buffalo's Band was being subjected to erosion of their lands, they came under attack on another front. There was a serious attempt to suppress dancing, with results comparable to the Manitoba Dakota experience. Over the years from the time when Tatankanaje and his people settled in the Qu'Appelle Valley until the turn of the century, there are few mentions, let alone complaints, of any dancing or giveaways being practised by Standing Buffalo's Band. This is not to say that there were no dances; to the contrary, tribal historians make it clear that both grass dances or wacipi and the giveaway were fairly common. The extent to which these events were "noticed" depended on the views of those departmental officials most familiar with the reserve. For many years, the agent responsible for the Standing Buffalo Reserve was J.B. Lash, and he was no Markle or Hollies. His rare comments on the dances were not complimentary, but he observed that the band was self-sufficient and, if they wanted to dance it was their concern, especially since at that time there were no laws prohibiting the dances. The only aspect of dancing to which he objected was what he called the "torture" parts of the sun dance. When, by the end of the 1890s, fewer men were submitting to the sacrifice, his criticism ended. Lash was more concerned with the Cree sun dances, where the sacrifice was an integral part of the ritual. The Dakota attended the Cree sun dances when they were held, but only rarely assembled the great celebrations themselves. There were, and are today, considerable differences between the sun dance as practised by the Cree and by the Dakota, and the Standing Buffalo people made no attempt to remake the ceremony in a Dakota image. In their turn, the Dakota regularly invited Cree from far and wide to attend their wacipi and giveaways, notably less traumatic events for sensitive Indian department personnel. So long as the agent did not make an issue of the dances and giveaways, there was no pressure on the band to mend their ways.

This came to an end when the department introduced laws in the 1890s for the purpose of suppressing the sun dance, giveaways, and other dances and religious ceremonies. Active enforcement began in 1901, when the Indian Act was revised to include the new laws. The department hired a young man of the Dakota band, a recent graduate of the Qu'Appelle Industrial School for Indians, to assist the agent in identifying and prosecuting those who conducted the dances. Thirty men of the band sent a petition to the Indian commissioner, asking that the informer be sent away from the reserve, as his only function there was "to find the least little thing to put someone in jail."[43] The recently appointed Indian agent, J.A. Mitchell, sent the petition on to Laird, with his own comments:

With regard to [the petitioners'] statement that they have complied with the wish that they should work well and also send their children to the School, I must give them credit for having done very well indeed, especially when it is considered that they receive neither money nor supplies from the Department and it was with sincere regret that I found myself compelled to prosecute some of the best men in the Band recently for illegal practices.

If it is your intention to reply to their communication, may I say that it would afford an excellent opportunity for reiterating to them what you told them last Summer at Fort Qu'Appelle with regard to illegal dances and also make them clearly understand that the repressive measures which I have taken do not originate with myself, but are carried out under the instructions and in accordance with your wishes and policies.[44]

Clearly, this was not the kind of fervour sought by the department, and the next month Mitchell was fired by Order in Council. The way was open for the appointment of a firmer hand, filled by W.M. Graham, who was later to rise high in the ranks of the department. Graham immediately recommended that a resident farmer be assigned to keep a closer eye on the Dakota, and requested $1,200 to build the farmer a new house on the reserve. This sum represented more money than the department had spent on the Dakota in the previous fifteen years. Graham's request was granted, and he was assigned unusual authority over other employees of the department who were elsewhere responsible to the superintendent general of the Department of Indian Affairs.[45]

Soon after Graham's appointment, the Dakota began to send letters to Ottawa, complaining that the agent was interfering in their lives. Tatankanaje the Younger wrote to say that he had done all the things asked of him by the department and was working hard and doing well. Nevertheless, Graham came onto the reserve and immediately ordered a number of the men to tear down the band's dance house. As far as the chief was concerned, what was his was his; he had worked for his own benefit, and when there was a bad day for work, he "wanted to keep [his] amusement on this kind of days."[46] Wacihewaste wrote: "We do not need an instructor under Standing Buffalo's Reserve. You do not know how much you loose your expense. . . . The Crees have everything from the Indian Department and treaty, so they can have to do everything the Agent says so. We do not want the same thing. We can get on very well with ourselves. You try us."[47] Laird's only response was to scrawl across both letters his usual answer to unfavourable communications: "No answer necessary. File. No Action." Confrontation was inevitable, as it had been in Manitoba, and early in 1903 Tatankanaje went directly to the governor general in an appeal for land, and demanding less interference from the Indian department. The band had decided to ask for enfranchisement so that they could exercise control over their own affairs.[48] This was utterly rejected by Laird. In March he wrote: "These Indians although nearly self-sustaining for the past twelve years, follow to a large extent the Indian custom and habit in the summer of living and travelling from place to place during the summer and autumn. Their knowledge of the English language is very slight so that they have not yet arrived at such a state of intelligence and civilization as it would be prudent to grant their enfranchisement. I would therefore recommend that their request under this head be not entertained."[49]

Less than a month later, Tatankanaje wrote to complain that Agent Graham had commandeered the chief's broken land and planted it to oats, and had kept the crop for himself. Tatankanaje had intended to plant the land to wheat in the season of 1903, but again the agent had insisted upon oats. The chief wanted Graham to pay for the loss of the previous season's crops and to vacate the land. As usual the complaints were ignored, and early that winter a delegation of Dakota embarked for

Ottawa to lay their complaints before the government. The delegation, however, was taken from the train before they had left the territory, and forced to return to the reserve.[50]

The combined effects of religious and political suppression, tightened control by the Indian department, and mismanagement of lands tempered the economic tactics adopted by Standing Buffalo's Band. When the great flow of immigrants began after the turn of the century, the Dakota had considerably expanded their agricultural production to the point that all households were able to produce all of their own domestic food supply, livestock and animal feed. They had purchased all of their own implements, including seeders, ploughs, discs, horse harness and other gear. When their labour was again in demand, the band was well able to grow its own food supply, and the renewed cash income moved it towards greater prosperity. Their commitment to the production of their own foodstuffs was such that when the only gristmill at Fort Qu'Appelle burned in 1901, the band voluntarily donated funds so that it could be rebuilt. By 1901, the herd of cattle had increased to sixty-four head, a significant increase considering the fact that the herd provided a good part of the band's meat supply.

The next year, 1902, proved so favourable on the Standing Buffalo Reserve that forty-five band members returned after having spent a decade and a half in the United States. The total population residing on the reserve was 215. That was the last year the Dakota sold hay and wood, since they no longer had more than they needed. Rather, they began to sell surplus beef animals, and expanded their selling of root crops. They invested in extensive wire fencing for their cattle and dedicated more time to their livestock. They broke more land and bought two binders with their own funds. Until 1903 all field crops had been taken off with scythes and sickles. Also in 1903, Inspector Chisholm reported that many of the band members could read and write English, in direct contradiction to Laird, who stated that the Dakota were illiterate.

In 1904, the Dakota made even greater investments in their farm operations and completed the fencing of all pastures and haylands. With the Pasquah and Piapot Cree bands, the Dakota purchased a steam-powered grain separator valued at $1,900. The people were gradually bringing the scale of their farm production into line with that prevailing among the settlers of the district. Nevertheless, farming remained an adjunct to the wages that were earned from labour. Increased efficiency in the production of domestic food supplies released time for wage labour more regularly. Chisholm reported that this combination of income sources had put the Dakota in comfortable circumstances and made them completely independent of government aid.

By 1906, the Dakota had over 150 head of cattle in their herd and were making an important contribution to their general economy by selling beef in the developing towns. The next year, however, the band lost haying rights on government lands to the north of the reserve. The herd was reduced to a mere fraction of its earlier size, which destroyed cattle and beef sales as a source of income. Much of the earlier investment in cattle-handling facilities was lost and never recovered.

No longer able to look to their herds as a source of income, the band immediately turned to the maximum expansion of crop lands. By 1907, it was reported that all arable land on the reserve was under the plough, and all available hay was being harvested. Further expansion was impossible. In an attempt to increase productivity, the Dakota took to breeding and raising superior draught horses, for which there was a ready market among the settlers. But were it not for members' skills as farm labourers, the band would have been in severe financial difficulties by this time. As it was, they earned and saved enough that a number of new frame houses were built on the reserve.

In the early part of the second decade of the century, national economies again collapsed in the face of war, and opportunities for the Dakota to sell their labour disappeared. They had few options; all arable lands were being used, and since they were no longer able even to maintain their herd of cattle, small plots of grain and gardens were all that sustained the band. Indeed, the time before the Great War was the period of greatest economic trial for the Standing Buffalo people, a stagnation from which they were unable to recover. In recognition of their obligations to the Crown, a number of men enlisted to fight oversees, but after the war, the opportunities for labouring did not again appear, and the band was reduced to a subsistence economy of small-scale gardening, cattle raising and labouring.[51]

From the early 1920s, Standing Buffalo's Band was engaged in maintaining their weakened economy and in defending their access to lands and resources. By this time, land problems had become so serious that Tatankanaje and his son, Julius, took their concerns to Ottawa. In a meeting with Duncan Scott, the chief said that the farmers were no longer able to meet all their hay needs from the lands provided at Reserve 80B. As well, with a growing population, the band required more arable land. Scott told them that the Dakota "were liberally dealt with by the Canadian Government. No promise could be made as to granting more land, but that enquiry as to their needs would be made."[52] Agent Walls provided the necessary report, recommending that Standing Buffalo's Band have the use of all the land at Reserve 80B. Until this time, the Dakota had been sharing the hayland with the Cree at Muscowpetung Reserve.[53]

In early February 1921, McLean responded to Walls's suggestion. He approved turning most of Reserve 80B over to the Dakota, and cautioned Walls to make this known to both bands.[54] The agent said that he would apportion the land in the spring, but by the time haying season arrived, nothing had been done. Julius Standing Buffalo, then chief after his father's death in the spring, asked what was being done to provide the band with more land. He also re-opened the question of subdividing the reserve lands. McLean replied that the agent was attending to the matters, but nothing more was accomplished in that decade.[55]

Between 1921 and 1956, there were gains of land for the Standing Buffalo people. In 1925, following protracted negotiations, the department bought out a bankrupt farmer who complained about the Dakota living on the reserve adjacent to his land. This land was added to the reserve in 1956, and for more than a decade, the Indian department tolerated continual attempts by the Department of the Interior to take it back. The Dakota had been leasing this land, and had asked to have it added to the reserve, but the department refused to take the appropriate steps until 1930, when the province of Saskatchewan assumed administration of Crown lands. Orders in Council came too late to secure a part of what was needed; it had been classed as school lands in the name of the province. When the province took over the land, they insisted that if it were to be added to the reserve, alternate lands must be offered in exchange. Negotiating this condition took three years, until 1933, when the fractional section became a part of Standing Buffalo Reserve.[56]

These additions came too late to promote agriculture on the reserve. The Dakota economy, faltering since the war, had become primarily centred upon wage labour. Few people owned the technology of commercial farming in the 1930s and 1940s. Much of the soil on the reserve was depleted, and all pasture and haylands off the reserve were in other hands. Considerable capital had been lost with the collapse of cattle raising. Finally, there was little opportunity for those interested in large-scale agriculture to acquire sufficient land on the reserve. In 1921, then Indian Commissioner W.M. Graham had offered the casual suggestion, "Would it not be a good idea to have surveyors subdivide Standing Buffalo Reserve."[57] Subdivision was, of course, departmental policy of long standing, but earlier agents and commissioners had seen that there was nothing to be gained by forcing the survey of the reserve, and had never insisted on doing so. The idea was once again alive, but no action was taken for many years.

In 1929, Graham requested the division of the reserve into 160-acre lots, but by the time the surveyor arrived at the reserve in September, he had again changed his mind, and had the land divided into eighty-acre lots.[58]

By restricting the lots to only eighty acres, all possibility of at least some of the band members being able to expand their farm enterprises to truly commercial size disappeared. Indeed, the lands added to the reserve after the subdivision were quickly divided into small lots and taken up by individual households. The band was permanently locked into a subsistence scale of domestic production on the reserve, supplementing an income from whatever casual work was available. In other words, the economy of the Standing Buffalo Reserve was set back almost to where it had been in the mid-1880s. In recent years, men and women have been seeking work and education in Regina, and the small-scale, self-contained economy has given way to expanding ties with the provincial economy.

Cattle and wages in the North: White Cap's Band, 1878 to 1940

10

Wapahaska had made his home in Canada west of Fort Ellice, north of the Qu'Appelle, and east of the North Saskatchewan River since late in 1862, and it was within this area he selected his reserve lands. Wapahaska and his people had made their living labouring, hunting, trapping and freighting, but he, like Wambdiska of Oak River and Mahpiyahdinape of Birdtail, could see that these occupations did not have the potential to provide for all his people. When Wapahaska selected his reserve lands, the buffalo were gone in what is now Saskatchewan, and neither were there entrepreneurs or settlers enough to hire Indian labour. In attempting to find lands suitable for agriculture, Wapahaska had planted crops at a number of sites along the Saskatchewan River, and finally found a place he thought suitable. As it happened, he was in error about the quality of the soils; as soon as this became apparent, the band shifted to cattle production, and for many years had one of the largest herds of top-quality slaughter and breeding animals in their district.

While the switch was a good strategy, cattle farming was very difficult to sustain. Besides the agricultural potential, the attractions of the lands selected by Wapahaska included a mixed environment of sloughs, meadows, bushland and open prairie which provided a trapping ground, easy access to surface water and a shallow aquifer, a hayland, pastureage, firewood and building materials. The problem was that, while the lands proved satisfactory for cattle raising, they were not extensive. The reserve is located on a peninsula of aspen-grove environment, surrounded on three sides by the grassland proper. As time passed and settlers moved into the North West Territories, the Dakota had to compete with grain farmers for lands. The economics of agriculture demanded an ever-increasing scale of operation to maintain viability; in a cattle operation, this condition implies an increased access to hay and pasture lands. Wapahaska's people had no capital to

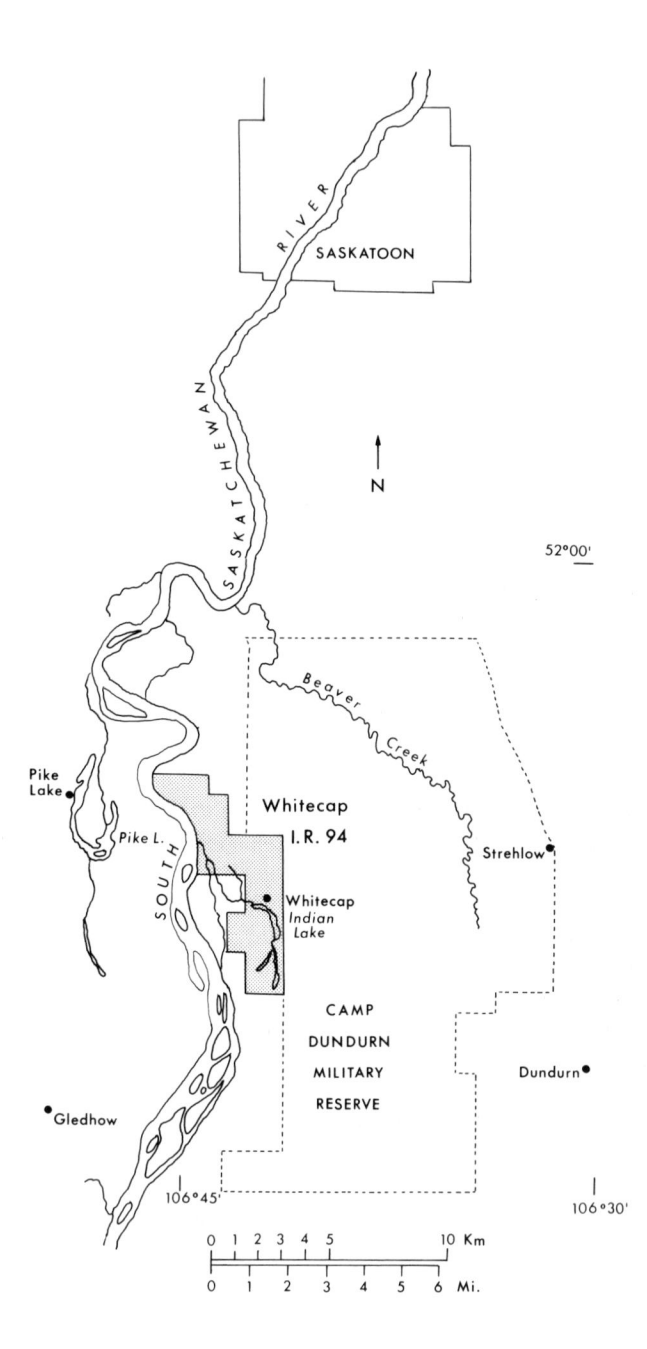

Map 7. White Cap Reserve

increase their land holdings, and were forced to rely completely upon the Department of Indian Affairs to protect their land interests, a reliance that largely went without reward.

After a brief and unsuccessful attempt to settle together on common lands, Tatankanaje and Wapahaska parted ways. Tatankanaje remained at Jumping Creek, while Wapahaska looked further to the north, along the South Saskatchewan River. In mid-summer of 1878, David Laird reported to the Minister of the Interior that Wapahaska had identified lands upon which he was willing to settle:

White Cap has agreed to have his reserve near the elbow of the south branch on both sides of the small stream marked on the map as "The river that turns." There are no settlers there, nor is there any likelihood of any settling at that place for years to come. I see no objection to the Sioux settling there, but I cannot recommend that the reserve be surveyed until it is seen that they will remain permanently.

I told White Cap I would likely be able to give him a definite answer by the first of November as to whether or not they could have their reserve at the place indicated.[1]

It would seem that Wapahaska had made a selection of land that complied with at least some of the department's requirements – far removed from whites and on soil unattractive to settlers – and designating the reserve should have been completed in short order. But this was not so, and in January 1879, Laird had to write asking what, if any, decision had been reached. Still no response was forthcoming, and in March, Laird wrote again, urging some form of action, "as White Cap is awaiting an answer, and he seems a very well disposed Indian, and his people are industrious it would be well that the matter should be settled before spring." In April, Vankoughnet wrote to the surveyor general asking if there was any objection to the Dakota settling the lands selected. Lindsay Russell raised no objection.[2]

This decision was wired to M.G. Dickison, acting Indian superintendent at Battleford, and followed up with a letter, but these communications seem to have gone astray.[3] The delays had worked to Wapahaska's advantage. That spring, he had taken the opportunity to plant test plots of crops, and had found the soil inadequate. Toward the end of July, Dickison reported that he had been visited by Wapahaska "in reference to his reserve. He said that the land in the vicinity of 'The river that turns' was principally sand hills and unfit for farming. He had consequently chosen a location half way between 'The river that turns' and the telegraph crossing. He has begun a farm there, and planted all the seed he received in the spring and is breaking up more land. If there is no objection to his remaining there, and I know of none, it might be well to have the quantity of land he is to receive decided on and the limits of the reserve defined."[4]

The surveyor general had no objection to the new location, and at the end of August 1879, W.L. Orde, the agent at Battleford, and Surveyor Simpson were instructed to proceed with the survey.[5] After much delay, the survey was completed on June 17, 1881. The reserve encompassed two sections of land.[6]

During the years that Wapahaska sought to acquire his reserve lands, the band endured very difficult times. In the spring of 1879, Laird had instructed that the band be given some implements, and like Tatankanaje, Wapahaska received small hand tools, a plough and a harrow, along with twenty-five bushels of potatoes, about enough for a two- or three-acre crop. Unlike Tatankanaje, Wapahaska had at least one yoke of oxen and set to work breaking land at the site where he had planted his test crops. For most of that summer and autumn, however, the band went to Prince Albert to seek work, and were successful enough that they had no need to call on the government for assistance.[7]

In 1866, the Reverend James Nisbet had established a Presbyterian mission at the present site of Prince Albert, and by 1880, the settlement had become the frontier of northwestern agriculture, complete with farmers, a gristmill and a Dominion lands office. As well, the settlement was the centre for a developing forest-products industry, and a major station for steamboat traffic on the Saskatchewan River. The resident population was limited to those people engaged in some aspect of agriculture, forestry or transportation. The Dakota moved into the area as a mobile, casual labour force, a role that they adopted over the next few years until they had established themselves on the reserve. In the spring of 1880, Wapahaska lost his yoke of cattle and asked the Indian department for another, both to work his land and to draw firewood into Prince Albert. Laird approved the request, and over the winter, James Walker of the North West Mounted Police reported that the band had been kept busy hauling fuel for the grist and lumber mills and for the steamboats.[8]

Early in 1881, Hayter Reed reported to Vankoughnet that he had hired George Weldon, a settler near the reserve, as farm instructor for White Cap's Band. This, however, he did on his own authority, and Sir John A. Macdonald enquired about how this had occurred without any reference to the Indian department. Reed explained that the omission was an oversight, but that the appointment was necessary for the welfare of the band. To this, Macdonald replied that Weldon had best be told that policy of assigning resident farmers to the Dakota was still being studied by the department. In a further report, Indian Commissioner Dewdney described the Dakota as deserving the assistance of the department. If they were expected to make any progress in the next few years, they would have to have good farming advice and a complete set of tools.[9]

Even though there was evidence that the Dakota were not at all dependent upon the government, Vankoughnet recommended that the farm instructor be confirmed in his appointment. He had looked over the recent history of the Manitoba Dakota bands, and had found that "the progress made by these bands in agriculture has been very satisfactory; far from being nomadic in their habits, they have become quite settled, living in houses and cultivating the soil with much assiduity for Indians." During the period of indecision, however, Weldon resigned from his temporary position and even though Assistant Indian Commissioner Galt was instructed to find another suitable man, it was several years before the band was assigned an instructor.[10]

By the end of the summer of 1881, the band had broken and planted thirty acres of crop, over sixteen acres of which were in wheat, oats and barley, with the remainder in root crops and gardens. As well, they had built eight houses and fenced another thirty acres for their cattle. At that time, there were reported to be between seventy and eighty people living on the reserve, and the cultivated area was divided into ten or twelve fenced fields, or probably one for each household. Over the previous three years, forty of the Dakota had died of an unknown illness and a good number of those who remained were old. Expansion was slow for the band, but in 1883, the Dakota had control of six yoke of oxen. They increased their cultivated lands to thirty-eight acres in 1884, and fifty-five acres in 1885.[11]

In 1883, the Temperance Colonization Company acquired two hundred thousand acres of land immediately to the north of White Cap Reserve and on both sides of the South Saskatchewan River. Settlers began to come into the area, especially to the vicinity of Saskatoon, which had been designated the capital of the venture, and the Dakota stopped travelling all the way to Prince Albert in search of work. They were able to spend more time close to the reserve, but still progress was slow. In late 1884, J.W. Powers, a justice of the peace at Saskatoon, forwarded notes from an interview that he had had with Little Crow and Long Nose of White Cap's Band.

What is the average strength of your reserve, Little Crow?

In the summertime there are about one hundred of us. Now we have twenty two "bucks" and sixty three squaws and papooses.

Where are the other seventy eight "bucks"?

Up the river between this and the elbow hunting and trapping. They look for the red fox, badger, skunk, mink, rabbit, etc. We remain at home cutting wood, hauling logs, etc.

Are not deer plentiful in the vicinity of your reserve?

Yes, we have lots of deer in the Sand Hills. Since the heavy snow set in, we have shot sixteen.

How are you employed in summer?

Chiefly in agriculture. We have got five ploughs, five harrows, and three yoke of oxen got by White Cap at Carlton some five or six years ago.

What do you grow chiefly?

Wheat, barley, potatoes, turnips, carrots and onions.

How about seed?

Some years we were able to save seed for the next season, and some years we are not. Last spring we got seed at Carlton and of course owing to the almost total failure of crops this year we must get seed somewhere next spring.

What have you got in the shape of food at your reserve just now?
A very small quantity of potatoes and a few turnips. I believe we have three sacks of flour.
Then you look for hard times this winter?
We do not wish to tell "The Big White Chief" (the Lieutenant Governor) of our poor condition.[12]

The band received seedstocks from the department the spring of 1885, as did many of the settlers in the area, but before the crops could be taken in, Wapahaska and his people were swept up in the tempest of rebellion, and there was no harvest beyond a few bushels of potatoes.[13]

On May 15, 1885, Louis Riel and his forces surrendered to Major-General Middleton at Batoche. Before the final battle at Batoche, Wapahaska had declared his people to be neutral, and on more than one occasion the chief had refused to throw in with the Métis on the grounds that to do so would be to violate the historic relationship of alliance between the Dakota and British. The band had kept and displayed two King George III medals, dating from the War of 1812. In April, a large band of Cree surrounded Wapahaska and his people and forced them to join the insurgents or be presumed by them to be a part of the British-Canadian following. Under this pressure. Wapahaska reluctantly joined Big Bear. At the first opportunity, after the skirmish at Fish Creek, a number of the band slipped away under cover of darkness and slowly moved south to Tatankanaje's reserve. Some had been wounded. This created considerable alarm among both the Dakota of the Qu'Appelle Valley and the whites of the region. Tatankanaje feared that he and his people would be implicated by the presence of those who had participated in the rebellion, and the settlers feared an extension of the war.

It soon became apparent, however, that the remnants of the band were no threat to either Tatankanaje's people or to the whites. When they fled the scene of battle, they left everything behind them, including food, tents, horses and even footwear. They were starving and suffering from exposure. Agent Lash agreed to feed the band, but objected to giving provisions to the rebels while the loyal Dakota at Standing Buffalo Reserve received nothing. He recommended that the wounded be treated by the military physician at Fort Qu'Appelle and then, if necessary, given transportation back to their own reserve. Dewdney, on the other hand, favoured the immediate expulsion to the United States of all Dakota who participated in the rebellion. Sir John A. Macdonald wired the Indian commissioner, saying that he was to act as he thought best, but that the Dakota were not to be allowed to starve. Cooler heads prevailed, and it was decided to give Tatankanaje a supply of rations with which to feed the intruding Dakota until Wapahaska, who had been charged with treason, was tried. In June, a court decided that Wapahaska had been forced against his will to participate in the hostilities to protect his people's lives. He was released to go home.[14]

In the wake of the rebellion, Indian Commissioner Dewdney and his assistant, Hayter Reed, drafted a policy giving the Indian department greater control in Indian matters. Dewdney did not favour reprisals, but he wanted the tribal political system abolished so that departmental officials could give direct orders to individuals, rather than having to consult with chiefs and councils. He also wanted the power to direct the spending of annuities and band funds. The commissioner recommended that Indians be required to bear passes when leaving the reserve. He wanted Indian rifles to be confiscated and the Dakota limited to the possession of shotguns. Dewdney and Reed wanted other changes, mostly pertaining to treaty Indians and treaty rights, but all changes affected the Dakota as well, even those who were exemplary in their loyalty to the Crown. Many of these suggestions were implemented as policy after 1885, but a strong recommendation that the leading Dakota who participated in the rebellion be hanged, and their bands expelled to the United States, was abandoned after Wapahaska's trial.[15]

Wapahaska's exoneration by the courts did not insulate his people from harassment by various government officials. In August 1885, Wapahaska was reported to be off his reserve visiting Tatankanaje. The police were ordered to find and arrest the chief and all people with him, even though the agent, Charles Adams, believed that this measure was unnecessary and likely to cause more excitement than what already prevailed.[16]

As the tensions of the rebellion died, Wapahaska called all of his band members back to the reserve. A number of families were at Prince Albert and Fort Qu'Appelle, but at their chief's bidding, they came back to help in rebuilding the band's economy. Crops were small in 1886, but were adequate for their summer needs. There were ninety-one people on the reserve, more than had been there in the years just previous, and as an example of the new control exerted by the Indian Department, Inspector J.C. Biggin of the North West Mounted Police was able to draw up a census of the band's population, even though the listing was later disputed by Wapahaska as being inaccurate.[17]

In the winter of 1886, Dewdney instructed Dakota interpreter E.A. LeQuesne to visit the Dakota and report on their condition. LeQuesne took down a letter dictated to him by Wapahaska:

I have the honour to state that myself and band are grateful to you for sending the white interpreter to see us. I thought we would all starve or freeze to death this winter, but when I saw the interpreter and found out that you sent him, our hearts were good as we know that the Queen will not let us die of starvation or cold after giving us land.

We have no clothing at all and all we have to eat is cherries and June berries or Saskatoons. We planted turnip seed, but the season was too dry and they all failed. We planted potatoes, some grew and some did not, so we have nothing at all. I would like all my men to remain on reserve and do their fencing, etc., this winter, in place of being on railroad working for provisions, but if they remain there they have nothing to eat. The last wheat and barley seed we got was very old, no good so we could raise nothing. I would like you to send us some clothing and provisions – viz. hats, coats, pants, boots, shirts, socks, blankets, tea, flour, bacon and tobacco.

I would like you to give us an Agent, and we would all like the white interpreter to be the Agent as we have known him for years, and know he only tells the truth. We would like to have a school so that our children could be educated and made white men of. We would like to see a railroad close so that flour, tea, sugar and tobacco would not cost so much and we would like you to have our seed sent early so that we can get them sown as snow goes in spring and then put in a good crop. We would like to have the following seeds wheat, barley, oats, potatoes, turnips, carrots and onions. We would like you to give us another team or two of cattle as with one team we cannot do as much as we would like to. When we came back here after the trouble was all over, we found to our surprise everything gone, even the box of tools, saws, axes, scythes, hayforks and plows. Riel and Dumont with a party of Halfbreeds came here to try to persuade me and my men to take part in the trouble. I am sorry to say that one or two took the advice of the Half Breeds and glad that they met their reward – I mean got shot or wounded while here.

The breeds killed four of the fattest of my oxen and took the other two away with them, and I forgot to say when we came back and missed everything we found six of our buildings burned to the ground and also found that six lodges of Crees had been camped here during our absence. We have nothing now to make doors, windows, floors or anything with and the two old plows we have are no good. One is very old and shaky and the other one which I received from Saskatoon this spring has no sod cutter on it.

We would like you to send us some powder, shot and caps as there is a little hunting here. There are a few blacktail deer and antelope, also a few foxes and wolves, but the rabbits and chickens have been killed by prairie fires.

I would like to go down and see you but have no clothes and am satisfied that this interpreter will tell you all I say and if you let him stop with us I am sure you will hear only good reports as he has only one tongue.

We would like the Queen to send us some clothing and supplies before it gets very cold. We would like to have a cow or a few cows so that we could raise some stock. We have hay and there is good grazing all around here.

There are 35 of us able to work but we can't work without food or clothes. We would like to have another wagon. Some of my men would like to have a hay cutter. I would like the Queen to give us a store. I would also like to have my reserve staked off through the bottom on the south west side now while there is no water, as it will be hard to do it in the spring when the water is high and we do not know exactly where the line runs.[18]

In his covering letter, LeQuesne agreed with all that Wapahaska had bid him write, and confirmed that the Dakota were in a bad way. Women and children were sleeping under oat bags stitched into thin blankets. They had rebuilt their houses, but had nothing to cover the doors and windows, and no source of heat except open fireplaces on dirt floors. The storekeepers in Saskatoon were charging the Dakota $6 for a sack of flour, or double the going rate. Over the summer, the Dakota had worked their one yoke of oxen until the animals were footsore, and had broken over sixty acres of land and put up forty tons of hay.[19] In other words, the White Cap's Band had been sent back to where they had been in 1878, though, even then, they had not been facing imminent starvation.

In December, LeQuesne again wrote to report on the band's condition and reported that game and fur animals were steadily becoming more plentiful. Because the Dakota had been deprived of their rifles after the rebellion, the interpreter loaned his gun to two hunters, who returned with the hides and meat of nine deer. Rabbits, wolves and coyotes were numerous; these provided both cash and food. The people possessed only a few traps and were so impoverished that they requested thread to sew moccasins, thread being about the least expensive article sold anywhere. LeQuesne concluded his report: "The Indians are very badly off for clothing and also provisions but as far as that report goes about one having starved to death on reserve, ''tis false.' He died a short distance east of the reserve with a badly swelled knee. He wanted bread and tea before he died and for 3 or 4 days previous, but they had nothing more than dried berries and badger and skunk meat."[20]

LeQuesne's report indicated a fine distinction between starvation on and off the reserve. Hayter Reed ordered provisions to be sent to the reserve and was sympathetic to the chief's requests. By April, somewhat late for the season, Reed had ordered implements and supplies and other "strictly necessary articles" for the band. The list of goods is almost a duplicate of that written up in 1877, when Wapahaska first asked for assistance to get a start in farming.[21]

Economic recovery was swift and steady for Wapahaska and his people, and by the second decade of the next century, the band was one of the most prosperous in the West. They managed a cattle herd of over three hundred head in addition to many ponies and blooded draught horses, other livestock, cultivated fields, large gardens and a dairy herd. As well, they were widely reputed as a well-trained and reliable labour force, and as skilled craftsworkers; they were literate in English (they subscribed to newspapers); and they were totally confident in their business dealings with Saskatoon's merchants and tradesmen who sought their custom. But this did not come easily.

In mid-summer of 1887, Commissioner of Indian Affairs Dewdney advised that more lands were "absolutely essential to the welfare of the Indians." It was his opinion that the original survey of the reserve had cut lands from the southwestern boundary of the reserve that "might very naturally have been included." When this comment was received in Ottawa, it was turned over to the surveyor general. There it was recommended that the reserve's boundary be redrawn to conform to the southern and eastern lines of Township 34, Range 6. This adjustment would take in a strip of land about one and a half miles long and sixty feet wide, which was, as A.M. Burgess put it, "of no use to us." The land was then withdrawn from pre-emption by settlers.[22]

In the late spring of the next year, Surveyor John Nelson reported to Dewdney that some of the Dakota were working land and building houses to the north and south of the reserve boundaries, on Crown land. They wanted the boundaries changed so as to take in these lands and improvements. Nelson refused to change the southern boundary, telling the Dakota that there was plenty of land in that part of the reserve. He did, however, add 424 acres to the north of the reserve to take in the people there. In exchange, he trimmed 240 acres off the northeast corner of the reserve, mostly land unfit for farming. The department was surprised by this unauthorized initiative, and wrote Nelson telling him to make no more reserve boundary changes without first consulting the Indian department and the Department of the Interior. Dewdney approved the changes, though, and went to L. Pereira, assistant secretary to the Department of the Interior, for his approval, which was granted. No surrender was taken for the exchange lands.[23]

In 1889, Inspector Wadsworth submitted to the department a report on White Cap's Band and the reserve. He said that Crown lands outside the reserve had been used by the Dakota for years as a pasture and hayland. He suggested that they be retained on permit from the Department of the Interior for the use of the Dakota. Wadsworth made an error in citing the land description, and during the resulting delays, a half section of the land went to a settler.[24]

Hayter Reed agreed that the band's haylands were insufficient and sent Surveyor Ponton with Tucker to locate suitable lands.[25] The land chosen, however, was part of the Temperance Colonization Company's grant. Nevertheless, Reed wrote to the commissioner of Dominion lands in Winnipeg, asking that other lands be substituted in the grant, and the sections identified held for the Dakota.[26] Nothing was done for the next nine months, and Reed finally wrote to ask if the lands had been secured: "The Department will no doubt remember that much importance is attached to the possession of those haylands, because owing to the want of success attending efforts to cultivate grain, the Indians must necessarily depend principally upon stock raising."[27]

The Temperance Colonization Company had objected to turning the land over to the Dakota. Some of the lands had been hayed on permit by settlers and to give it to the Indians would cause shortages for others. Furthermore, the minister of the interior had vetoed any move to add lands to the reserve. The plan was abandoned.[28]

Early in the winter of 1890, Inspector Alexander McGibbon visited White Cap Reserve and reported that the cattle herd was increasing rapidly. Very soon, an additional two sections of hayland would be necessary. McGibbon knew of the earlier attempts to secure lands for the Dakota, and wondered if anything had come of them. The inspector's report, with a request for reconsideration, was passed on to the Department of the Interior.[29] Another month had passed when the agent at

Moose Woods Reserve (as White Cap Reserve was sometimes called) wrote a letter that is unique in the records of the Department of Indian Affairs. In a passionate rage, directed at the policies of the department, Agent Tucker made a plea for more land.

I received your letter . . . intimating that these Indians are not to receive any more government help.

How do you expect that they are to live? From what income are they to derive the necessaries of life? Let us look back over their history for the last four and a half years (the time that I have been here). When I came here, I found an indolent, debauched, degraded, dying people filled with superstition, vice and bestiality, living in dirty hovels without floors or windows, clothed in rags, dirt and vermin, whose time was chiefly occupied in gambling, feasting and dancing, the weird cadences of the heathen chant and tomtom heard on the reserve seven nights in the week. Their children blearyeyed and delicate without clothes to cover their bodies.

Now what do we find today. A thrifty and God-fearing people living mostly in good houses, most of them furnished with floor, windows, chairs, tables, bedsteads and stoves. Their children attending school every day well clothed, healthy, intelligent and industrious, busying themselves after school hours in looking after cattle, every family on the reserve having from two to four cows. Most of the families make butter. They milked 25 cows regularly last summer. The men are willing to work at whatever they can get to do. They are good law abiding citizen as you can find.

It is a known fact that this reserve is utterly worthless except for pasture. The Indians have cropped it I understand for the last 14 years and got only one crop in that time. The fact was explained to you and you promised to enlarge the reserve by giving them some hayland south of here so as to enable them to make a living by raising cattle, but last fall I got a letter from you saying you had decided not to enlarge the reserve. *What do you mean?* Do you intend to drive the Indians away from here? What is to become of them? Are they to be driven back to the towns, where they will be debauched, their daughters prostituted, their children die from starvation, for they cannot live here if they have no protection from pestering whitemen.

I left a good home to come to this country to help the Indians and I don't think that I have spent five of the best years of my life in vain. Therefore I say that the Indians will get that hayland, and if you won't give it to them, I will write to the Minister of the Interior about it and if he refers me to you as I expect he will, I shall then carry it to headquarters, to the ratepayers of Canada. "Agitation," John Bright says, "is but the marshalling of a nation's conscience to right her laws," and I shall agitate this question together with some others.[30]

Five years previous, when Tucker arrived at the reserve, Wapahaska's people had survived the North West Rebellion, but had lost every material thing they owned. The agent's perception of their condition, and his reasoning about why things were the way they were, are at complete variance with all other observations made at that time. Still, the contents of this report resulted in some action in Ottawa. The first response was a letter from the Indian commissioner to Tucker:

Another letter in the tone of that now acknowledged, could hardly fail to result in the severance of your connection with this Department.

You may be very sure the Commissioner is at least as much interested in the welfare of the Indians as you can possibly be, and in the way of responsibility has a good deal more at stake, but he has a duty to perform for the Department with regard to public funds, and that is to see that none is expended on purchasing for Indians, even within our own Treaties, as the Moose Woods Sioux are not, anything they can be made to provide themselves.[31]

In February 1893, Hayter Reed directed his assistant, A.E. Forget, to report on the number of cattle on the reserve, and on the availability of hay. Forget replied that the Dakota could expect a shortfall of about 150 to 175 tons of hay. This convinced the Indian department to send a homestead inspector to assess the reserve and surrounding lands. Also, a permit was issued, allowing the Dakota to cut hay on government lands.[32] Tucker was told of these actions the day after he received his letter of reprimand. He was assured that the inspection was being done "in order that a full investigation may be made into what the circumstances of the Indians really require and what can reasonably be done in the matter without interfering with the interests of white settlers."[33] Nothing more happened for two months.

In May 1893, Tucker wrote again. He argued that permits would not secure the haylands for the Dakota, as there was nothing to keep settlers from pasturing their cattle on the hay the Indians intended to cut. He also reported that the Temperance Colonization Company withdrew its objections to giving the Dakota more hayland. Tucker said that the Dakota were anxious and wrote: "[They] are asking me every little while when they are going to get the land you promised them. They think it must take a long while to settle it as it is two years since you promised them it."[34]

Reed responded that he "never made any further promise in the matter than I do now, namely to do my best in their interests." After another two months and another investigation of the Dakota's circumstances, Surveyor Ponton wrote to Reed. He said he wished to "draw attention to the immediate necessity of securing haylands for this band, otherwise they must dispose of their fine herd of cattle and wander to the towns to seek work." He concluded that "owing to the nature of their lands by which the Reserve is surrounded, no settlement is likely to approach the immediate neighbourhood, there will be no danger of interfering with the interests of future settlement, through granting the application of hay lands." Finally, in October 1893, 19-, 30-, and 31-33-5-W3M were added to the reserve by Order in Council. However, it was not until early 1894 that the Indians were notified of the addition, and over that winter, settlers had allowed their cattle to consume the Dakota's haystacks.[35]

With the increase in haylands, the band's cattle herd continued to increase and improve in quality. In 1898, Agent Tucker reported that a settler was applying for a quarter section of land that the Dakota had been using for hay cutting. He appealed to the department to have the lands secured for the Dakota; otherwise, they "would likely another year have to reduce the number of cattle we have." Only a few weeks later, Pereira approved the application, and E1/2-25-33-6-W3M was added to the reserve on November 24, 1898.[36]

Over the years since 1886 until 1898, the size of Wapahaska's reserve increased by 5,344 acres to a total of 6,944 acres. As well, in this time of sparse settler occupation, the band was able to herd its cattle over a considerable area of unoccupied Crown land, thus preserving reserve grasslands for hay, rather than summer pasture. With each addition of land, the productivity and well-being of the people increased. At the time the Dakota were transforming their economy to one based almost solely upon cattle husbandry, there were also transformations in other aspects of their culture. In particular, there was a general abandonment of Dakota religious and ceremonial functions, such as the medicine dances, wacipi, and giveaway, and an embracing of Christianity. Household units of production replaced early structures of joint production and distribution. This was the only Dakota band in Canada to request the division of the reserve into separate lots. The Dakota greatly limited their interaction with other Dakota bands and their Cree neighbours. Many of the overt trappings of "Dakotaness" were dropped in favour of "whiteness"; indeed, clothing and hair styles, housing and household goods, sports and entertainment practices all came to resemble those of the band's white neighbours.

In 1888, the Methodist Church of Canada sent the Reverend Alfred Andrews to White Cap Reserve, where he was welcomed with considerable interest. Within weeks of the missionary's arrival at the reserve, White Cap and all of the adults of his band submitted a petition to the department, asking that a school be built on the reserve. Andrews carried the petition to Hayter Reed. Vankoughnet assured Reed that money would be available in September, and Andrews returned to the reserve with this promise.

Andrews made his return journey to Wapahaska's people in the company of A.W. Taylor, who was quite familiar with the Dakota in Manitoba and the Qu'Appelle Valley, and who was fluent in the Dakota language. Taylor reported that the band had been divided into three separate "villages," each conducting its affairs independently. The "villages" were under the leadership of Wapahaska, Mahtomani and Little Crow. In all, there were eighteen houses and eight stables on the reserve, all well built and kept in very good condition. Ninety-five acres were in crop, including sixty acres in grains and thirty-five acres of gardens and root crops. More land was being prepared for crop, but much of their heavier equipment was in poor condition. Breaking of the prairie sod could only be done with a tremendous amount of effort. A number of band members had been working at Moose Jaw and other places, and Taylor suggested that as soon as possible, the system of off-reserve passes be applied to the band. This was done that same year, with no complaint from the band. Taylor wrote: "These Indians are most intelligent and energetic, and very anxious to better their condition." He requested a breaking plough and wagon, fish hooks and lines, and a few cows. Dewdney approved the fishing gear, since the items were cheap, and authorized the dispatch of a few cows to the reserve.[37]

For the time being, the band had sufficient hay, even enough for considerable sales to the North West Mounted Police at Saskatoon. The Dakota were, however, beginning to run short of other resources. Prior to 1889, the band had been cutting saw logs on public lands, but after that year, there was a shortage of good construction materials in the vicinity of the reserve, and what remained was jealously guarded by the government. From this time on, the band was obliged to adopt frame or pole structures rather than log-wall houses and stables. This caused a significant increase in the cost of housing, since all sawed lumber was imported and expensive.[38]

In June 1889, Surveyor Ponton subdivided the reserve into forty-acre lots, as requested by the band. Later that same summer, Inspector Wadsworth toured the reserve and reported that each of the households had its own house, stable, fields and garden. All houses were well equipped with standard furnishings and the people were indistinguishable from their white neighbours in terms of clothing and appearances. The year before, the band had received ten cows from the department, and the Dakota were subsisting for the summer on milk, potatoes, goldeye and sturgeon, taken from the South Saskatchewan River. Since the Dakota were milking the cows, the calves were raised by hand; because of this close attention all the cattle were very domestic and quiet. Eighteen households had planted wheat, oats, potatoes and turnips, in all, 137 acres. The largest fields were twelve and a half acres; the smallest was a large, one-acre garden, maintained by Wapahaska's wife. At the time of Wadsworth's visit, the chief was ill with consumption and died later that year. The grain crops suffered from the drought, but the root crops were in fine shape. The band had kept enough wheat to plant the next year's crop, which shows considerable foresight, since in 1890 seed grain was very difficult to obtain on the prairies.[39]

Two years later, the farming members of the band determined that the reserve was not suited for growing grain crops, so that aspect of agriculture was all but abandoned. The low-lying lands were subject to early and late frosts, and the higher lands were too light except in years of plentiful rainfall. The Dakota decided to concentrate on raising cattle, and in a two-year period increased their herd of ten cows to twenty-nine, some from natural increase and some from the private purchase of stock. That season, only twenty-nine acres of crop were planted, down from 137 acres in 1889, indicating the extent to which field crops were replaced by cattle husbandry. Root crops were reduced in acreage, but the yield was sufficient to allow a surplus for sale. All families had milk cows and had begun to make butter. One woman had three of her own cows and sold surplus milk and butter to settlers. After calving season, the Dakota had fifty head of cattle and had put up enough hay to winter the herd. In earlier years, the Dakota had been building their stables by digging caves into the banks of hills, but were beginning to construct improved surface shelters, which were better lighted and ventilated and generally healthier for the livestock. Things looked so good at the reserve that Tucker had invited families to come from Tatankanaje's reserve and settle on Wapahaska's lands, where they would have more room. One family accepted the offer.[40]

By 1893, the cattle herd had increased to eighty-six head, and it was expected that there would be an increase of thirty calves. The Dakota were no longer able to get enough hay from the reserve or from the Crown lands they were cutting by permit. The Crown lands were being taken up by settlers moving away from areas infected by blackleg, a highly contagious and fatal disease of cattle. The cattle the settlers brought with them were consuming the Dakota's hay supply as well as endangering their herd's health. Nevertheless, the band's calf crop was somewhat larger than expected and the Dakota had 120 cattle and fifty horses to feed that winter. R.S. Cook, Dominion lands agent at Saskatoon, supported the band's plea for additional hayland, saying, "[I have] known these Indians since 1880 and am surprised and more than pleased to see the rapid strides they are making towards civilization and self-support and I feel they are deserving of every encouragement so long as it does not unjustly interfere with the interests of other settlers."[41] The band was at the limit of its ability to expand, and the reports by Tucker and Cook eventually moved the department to secure more land for the reserve.

Until the advent of the global depression that preceded World War I, Canadian cattle raisers enjoyed a very strong market for beef animals in the United Kingdom. But, in 1892, the market for unfinished cattle began to weaken. England placed a ban on importing cattle from North America because of contagious diseases. By the summer of 1894, Tucker was complaining that, while the Dakota had a large and strong herd of cattle, they had few of the kinds most desired by buyers. The overseas ban left eastern producers with an oversupply of young stock, so they began to send their calves west for finishing. While this introduced a supply of cheap cattle to the West, it also depressed the price of locally grown stock. This situation persisted for three years, until those young cattle were market-ready and sent back to eastern consumers.

In the meantime, Wapahaska's people did what they could to earn an income, including bone picking. Many people, among them the Dakota, supplemented their incomes by searching the prairie for the last reminder of the great herds of buffalo – their bones – which were shipped east to be manufactured into lampblack, charcoal and fertilizer. In 1894, the demand for bones fell suddenly as the investment in agriculture declined, and along with it, the demand for fertilizer. In that year, Tucker reported that the price of bones fell from $120 to $60 for a rail-carload, if it was possible to sell them at all. In order to get at least some cash for the winter, the band wanted to sell the beef animals they had intended for their own use and try, instead, to subsist on game meat. They had no difficulty selling their bulls, which were widely known as quality breeding stock.[42]

By 1895, the Dakota had all but ceased to grow crops of any kind, other than household gardens; in a drought year, the land was incapable of returning a yield larger than the amount of seed put in the ground. The cattle numbered 171 head, and 650 tons of hay had been stacked for winter use. The cattle were held severally by eleven households, and many had dairy cows, hogs and poultry. Joe Hanke had three stables, including a new one, in which he kept his twenty-four cattle, the result of having acquired one heifer six years earlier, along with his horses, purebred hogs, many chickens and a few turkeys. New houses and stables had been completed, and a number of families had purchased complete household furnishings. Households received newspapers from Saskatoon and from the Santee Agency in Nebraska, where a Dakota language press was operated by the Presbyterian Church.

Wild game was plentiful; there were deer, rabbits, ducks and prairie chickens. Inspector McGibbon estimated that the band had made about $320 in "private earnings," mainly from the sale of handcrafts to the few settlers in the area. Because of the crop failures, the band was receiving a considerable quantity of food staples from the department, but some households were providing all of their own food. McGibbon was able to report that the Dakota were "an industrious and hard working lot of Indians and deserving of every encouragement."[43]

In 1896, there were 231 head in the cattle herd, held by ten households. A large corral had been built that summer, greatly improving handling operations. Since 1894, the band had sold thirty-four beef animals for $1,086, and had killed ten for domestic use. Inspector McGibbon was impressed by the band's efforts, and wrote, "[This] gives an idea what can be done by careful management, good winter feed and stabling." At the same time, greater emphasis was put on the domestic production of food. Gardens were large and diverse, containing all the vegetables then being grown in the vicinity of the reserve. The women worked in Saskatoon at a variety of jobs, while the men managed the on-reserve operations. Considerable investment had been made in haying equipment, and a small house had been built at the haylands so as to be more comfortable in haying season. Seneca root, berries and bones were collected and sold for cash.[44]

By the end of the decade, lands were again insufficient to carry the band's growing herd of cattle, and the Dakota applied for and received an addition. Since it was then clear that the band would never control enough land for substantial increases in herd size, the Dakota took to improving the management of their stock so as to produce better-quality and more-valuable sale animals. In 1898, Inspector Chisholm reported that the band received $37 to $42 for three-year-old steers, which was the highest price being offered for cattle in the district.[45]

This approach to cattle raising was able to show a good return as long as the prices for slaughter and replacement stock remained high enough to underwrite production costs. By the turn of the century, this was becoming more difficult. Settlers were pouring into the North West, and the haylands so long used by the Dakota were being taken up. Increased settlement and the increased production of grain crops put a burden on the railways. The policy of the railways and of government was to give shipping precedence to grain, and since both cattle and grain were sold at the same time of the year, cattle producers either had to pay a premium or wait until after the grain flow. Often this meant that cattle were being sold after they had reached peak condition, for lower prices. Buyers came to prefer only the very best slaughter animals, and while the Dakota were able to supply this market, the steady decline in prices demanded that they increase production in order to maintain income – the classic agricultural dilemma.

The band did not approach the Department of Indian Affairs for lands again until 1911, and from 1898 until that time, there was some considerable diversification in income sources. As settlers came into the vicinity of the reserve, the Dakota began to market wood and hay taken from recently acquired lands, but only in quantities that were clearly surplus to their own needs. As well, they started what must have been one of the first commercial feedlots near Saskatoon. They took cattle on consignment to winter over for settlers who did not have their own haylands, and finished slaughter animals for meat buyers and packers. From the late 1880s until the end of the first decade of the new century, the band numbered about fifty, but between 1905 and 1907 tuberculosis killed seven of the band's young men, leaving them with a much diminished labour force. Those who remained had difficulty maintaining a large, closely managed cattle herd. Inspector Chisholm reported that in 1905 there were only six men working the ranch, feedlot and haylands, and some of them were old.

In 1904, prices as high as $42 per head were being paid for cattle, but the next year, the price fell to $35 and remained low for the next while. The beef markets continued to decline over the long term, however, and the band again tried growing grain. In 1909, the Dakota had planted an experimental plot of twenty acres in grains, but it was apparent that yields would be poor. Farmer Tucker had retired that year, and Charles Eagle, a band member, took over direction of the reserve. Eagle maintained his role as overseer for many years; he was one of the first Indians in the West to be recognized in that position by the Indian department.

The band also took up breeding and selling draught horses. The Dakota were selling their horses for over $200 each at a time when the average price for a good work horse was about $150. Still, cattle remained the mainstay of the band economy, and in 1910 Chisholm reported, "Their cattle industry yields a larger rate of profit than any other band within my knowledge."[46]

In order to maintain their economic position during the uneven performance of the Canadian economy after 1912, the band was again compelled to apply for additional lands, but much of the land had been taken up by settlers. For the next two decades, the band was involved in a tedious and unending effort to secure more land. After numerous letters, memoranda, reports and attempts at inter-departmental negotiations, the Dakota finally acquired an additional 160 acres of grazing land in 1921, another quarter section in 1926, and a final partial section in 1933.[47]

In 1917, however, the Dakota had begun to fight a losing battle that saw them stripped of all the lands they had been using for years by permit. Agent Schmidt, who replaced Tucker, wrote in 1918, "Unless something is done in the near future to relieve the situation the cattle industry on this reserve which is flourishing, will come to a standstill." He wanted the three and a half sections of lease land turned over to the Indians permanently. The Dakota had fenced all the land and had been maintaining it as a free pasture. Volumes of correspondence deal with these lands, since title to them shifted through two levels of government, four departments and the University of Saskatchewan, the latter as a part of a land grant. By the early 1930s, the lands were completely lost to the Dakota, and as Agent Schmidt foresaw, the cattle enterprise came to a standstill. Unable to compete in an expanding cattle industry, the herd was reduced and finally eliminated.[48]

At the start of World War I, a number of men from White Cap Reserve enlisted, drawing off vitally needed labour. With the decline in the herds, and a final failure in field cropping, a number of men and women sought skilled and semi-skilled jobs in Saskatoon. After World War II, many households were sustained solely through the sale of labour, a pattern that has persisted to the present. The population of the band grew slowly, but the unrelenting demand for increased production eventually led to competition for land, with results similar to those experienced by the farming bands of Manitoba. Band members hotly debated the boundaries of subdivision lots, assignment of lots, and proportional shares in such common resources as haylands and wood. The few relatively prosperous cattle raisers were able to appropriate much of the land for themselves while others became labourers.[49]

The practice of concentrating use ownership in the hands of fewer band members breathed a little life back into cattle production for those households still engaged in agriculture. However, the inevitable squeeze associated with the need to expand, as well as the ever-declining prices for farm products, slowly forced even well-established cattle producers out of business. In 1932, Agent C.P. Schmidt wrote to say that the cattle enterprise on the reserve was at the point of failure: "I beg to say that while these Indians are making a fair and comfortable living, they are unable to buy land for themselves, and being near the City of Saskatoon, many strangers pass through the reserve, and it would be too bad if it were noticed or known that their herd of cattle was decreasing and they did not show they were leading a happy and contented home life and were self-supporting."[50]

Within months, of course, there were few people there who would be overly critical of their neighbour's appearances. The depression of the 1930s all but destroyed White Cap's Band as an agricultural entity, although there was some modest recovery just before World War II. As for many people in the world, the war came with its dubious blessing of increased demands for foodstuffs and labour. The Dakota moved to fill both. The few farmers who were able to survive the Dirty Thirties re-established themselves, while the others went to work in Saskatoon and at the military camp at Dundurn, which was constructed in this period, with the help of Dakota labour. After the war, Saskatoon and the surrounding district continued to expand and maintain a steady demand for skilled and unskilled labour. White Cap Reserve is within easy reach of this market, and since there are few economic possibilities on the reserve, increasing numbers of Dakota have gone to the city to work. Labouring in the cities of Saskatchewan has become a tradition of Wapahaska's people for almost three generations.

The southern labourers:
The Portage la Prairie bands,
1886 to 1973

11

Immediately after struggling into Canada in the winter of 1862–63, and for some time thereafter, many Dakota families lived in the vicinity of Portage la Prairie. Later, as the first reserves were designated, they moved west to take up their lands. By the mid-1880s, the majority of the Dakota in Manitoba had taken up more or less permanent residence on their reserves. One small group, numbering twenty-three families in 1886, remained in the vicinity of the old stopping place near Portage la Prairie, largely unnoticed by the officials of the Department of Indian Affairs. These Dakota quietly established an independent lifestyle, at first based upon fishing and trapping around the south end of Lake Manitoba and, later, upon the sale of their labour in the town of Portage la Prairie and on surrounding farms. In the spring, during the spawning run, they camped close to their fishing stations, in the summer they moved to the farms where they worked, and in the late autumn, they moved to the southeast end of Portage la Prairie, where their winter jobs were close at hand.

So matters remained until 1886, when it was noticed by the Reverend James Robertson, superintendent of the Presbyterian missions, that "nothing of any account has been done to Christianize them . . . nor has anything been done to teach the children and their people have no reserve there; . . . if the Indian population are to cease to be a menace to the peace and progress of the country, they must be Christianized and educated." There is nothing to suggest that the Dakota would have welcomed such attention, but now that officials had been apprised of their existence, change was unavoidable. Deputy Superintendent Vankoughnet ordered E. McColl, inspector of Indian agencies at Winnipeg, to investigate the matter and report. McColl, in turn, instructed Agent Frances Ogletree to report to him.[1]

Ogletree wrote that the Dakota had no reserve at Portage la Prairie and were in

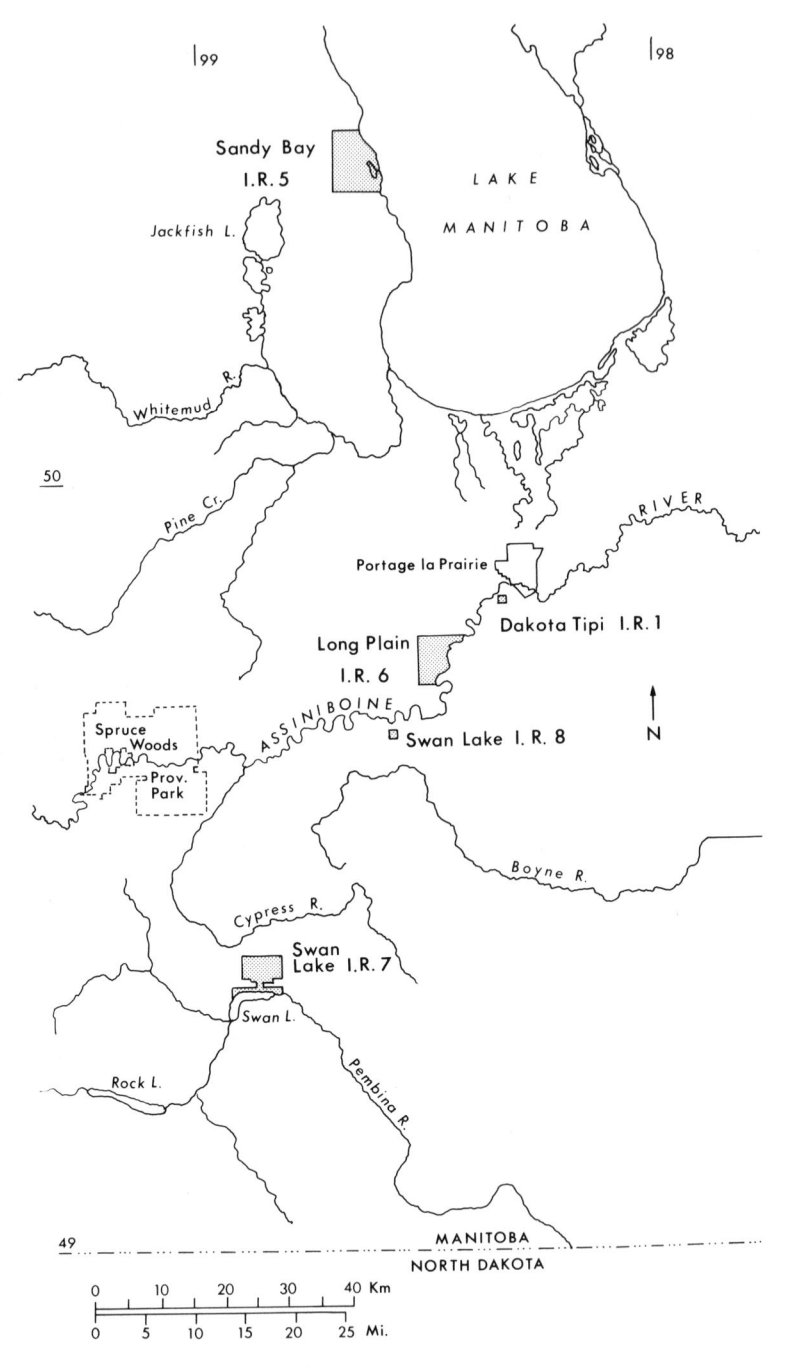

Map 8. The Portage la Prairie bands

fact members of Wambdiska's band at the Oak River Reserve. He reported that the Portage families were unwilling to move, having established a life for themselves without government aid.[2] This report was passed from office to office and finally Indian Commissioner Dewdney rendered a policy judgement:

These Indians belong to Oak River and Oak Lake Reserves and if they are desirous of having a school established for their benefit on the reserve, I would recommend that aid be given them, but I would not advise the granting of assistance under the circumstances to a school off the Reserve.

If the Department established a precedent we should have applications from all over the country for similar assistance, possibly resulting in its being used as an instrument to encourage Indians to leave their reserve.[3]

As was common in Dakota history, the people at Portage la Prairie had been wrongly identified. As Molyneaux St. John had reported on October 8, 1874, the bands then encamped at Poplar Point and Portage la Prairie had made it clear that they did not agree with Wambdiska's acceptance of the reserve on the Assiniboine and would not move there. To make their point, St. John reported that Taninyah-dinazin had been assaulted by the Poplar Point people. They had not traditionally been a part of the bands that later settled at Oak River and Oak Lake. Some time between 1875, when the reserves were taken up, and 1886, the Poplar Point people moved to join those Dakota at Portage la Prairie. Given this history, it would have been futile for government officials to hope that that the Portage la Prairie people would consent to reside with Wambdiska and Taninyahdinazin, just twelve years after their falling out with the two chiefs. Nevertheless, that was the position adopted by the government, for the reason put forward by Dewdney and amplified by Sir John A. Macdonald: "The Department is anxious to discourage Indians from locating themselves in the vicinity of towns or white centres where reserves do not exist, as serious evils inevitably attend their doing so. There is . . . no excuse for the Indians leaving their reserves and camping in the neighbourhood of town and white centres and such a course is attended with the demoralization of themselves and Indians so situated are a nuisance to the white settlers."[4]

These Indians, of course, had not left a reserve, since they had never lived on one. Neither were they a nuisance to the white people; their labour was much sought after and was high-priced for the time. The Dakota refused to leave Portage la Prairie merely for a school, and the department refused to provide a school anywhere but on a reserve. The Dakota did not suffer any inconvenience from this rigidity, because the Presbyterian Church had established a school of sorts for them the previous summer, and it operated for many years.

Nevertheless, it was now necessary for the Dakota to acquire their own land. Before 1891, the people had begun to collect small sums of money with which they intended to purchase land. This money was placed in trust with A.D. Mackay of the Manitoba and Northwestern Railway Company, a man well known to the Dakota. By 1892, the fund amounted to $120 and the band enquired of the government about available lands. Agent Ogletree reported to the department that twenty-two families were involved. The land where they were camped, and which they wanted to buy, however, belonged to private parties or to the University of Manitoba. The department assumed that the Dakota were requesting a reserve, and while volumes of paper (reports largely critical of the idea) passed from office to office, the Dakota went ahead in November 1893 and arranged the purchase of River Lot 99, in the Parish of Portage la Prairie, for $174.50. Title was in the favour of Samuel Marlatt, Daniel Mackay and William Miller, all of Portage la Prairie. Marlatt was inspector of Indian agencies, and Miller a local businessman. The title was held in trust for twenty-one Dakota men and women who had saved the money for the purchase.[5]

River Lot 99 was about twenty-five acres in area, enough to satisfy the Dakota's land needs for the next five years. In the spring of 1898, they requested additional lands to accommodate their expanding gardens. Pereira of the Department of the Interior reported that the land the Dakota wanted, that is, River Lot 100, was not available, but that other small parcels were. By October, River Lot 14, which had been described by Inspector Marlatt as "of little value to any but the Indians," was reserved by Order in Council for the use of the Portage la Prairie Dakota.[6] River Lot 14 was rarely used, however. It was some miles distant from both River Lot 99, where the Dakota had their homes, and the town, where they had their jobs. It would have been necessary for them to divide their population to occupy both sites, and instead, they chose to leave the lands fallow. In 1910, D.C. Scott, in charge of the department's finances, argued that either the department should build a school on River Lot 14 or they sell it to another party. Indian Agent Logan reported that the north end of the lot was good crop land, valued at $3 an acre, but that the south end was suitable only for sheep pasture.[7]

But in March 1911, trouble visited the Dakota: The secretary-treasurer of the City of Portage la Prairie wrote to Agent Logan to complain of the "immorality and drunkenness at the Indian Village."[8] As late as 1905, Inspector S.R. Marlatt had described the Dakota as "industrious and thrifty."[9] . . ."Too much praise cannot be accorded them: they have raised themselves from one of the most degraded of peoples to one of the most enlightened and progressing bands in this inspectorate. . . . Naturally, these Indians are good workers."[10] "They are a hard working industrious people, and their labour is of considerable benefit to this town; both men and women find constant employment. The only trouble we have with them is from liquor, a few of them are addicted to its use."[11]

Some Dakota may have used liquor, but to such a limited extent that Marlatt referred to the group as being "far ahead of the others in this agency."[12] The descriptions of the band began to change with the appointment of Agent R. Logan. Soon after he arrived at Portage la Prairie in 1907, Logan wrote: "While above the average Indian in morality and temperance, these Indians also squander a lot of money in purchasing liquor and paying fines."[13] A year later, he was suggesting that if "instead of being fined, they were imprisoned with hard labour, the punishment would probably have a more salutary effect."[14] Logan applauded the city's resolution, and advised that the band be moved far away from Portage la Prairie.[15]

Departmental machinery was put into motion and plans were laid to move the Portage la Prairie Dakota either to one or several of the established Dakota reserves, or to the nearby Long Plain Ojibwa Reserve.[16]

The Dakota at Portage la Prairie were not farmers. Rather, they were labourers who at times sold their labour to farmers. Moving the people to other Dakota reserves would have done neither themselves nor their hosts much good; the department was then trying to close down the Oak Lake and Turtle Mountain Reserves, claiming that they were overcrowded and non-productive. Finally, the Portage la Prairie people were already independent. Since they did not live on a reserve, they received no help from the Indian department.[17]

In 1913, Agent Logan was still at work on the problem:

I had a meeting with the Sioux at the Sioux Village, when there were 30 of them present over twenty one years of age.

I explained the matter to them, of moving to some other part, where they could have more land. Their answer was, they would not go away back from civilization, as they were all born here, and that they could get good wages with the farmers in the Portage district, could also get musk rats, and sell some wood in winter. I asked them if they would go to Griswold where a number of their relatives are, they said all good land taken up, no rats, no wood, and wages better around Portage than Griswold.

I went into the matter of Lot 14 which was given to them by the Department some years ago, and they stated that they wanted this land for a number who do not own land in the Sioux Village, and there were seven who wanted to go on this land. I informed them they would have to make a start between now and the 1st of July next, or the Department might dispose of the land, this they agreed to do.

They were all very anxious for the Department to purchase two or three sections off the Long Plain Reserve for the use of their children who are attending the Portage la Prairie Boarding School, and for some who have already graduated.

The Long Plains Band are not disposed to take them into their Band on any terms, but would be satisfied to surrender to the Department two or three sections for the use of the Sioux.[18]

Logan had reported in late 1911 that the Dakota were willing to give up Lot 14, a statement which is contradicted in his 1913 letter.[19] The report of 1911, however, was the one acted upon by the department, which recommended to the governor general that the Order in Council of October 6, 1898, be rescinded. On November 17, 1913, a new Order in Council was issued and River Lot 14 was thus lost to the Dakota.[20] At no time did anyone suggest that a surrender might be in order.

Soon after they had purchased their own land in 1892, the Portage la Prairie Dakota transformed their lifestyle. Their economy continued to combine the sale of labour, trapping, fishing and wood cutting, but the sale of labour clearly dominated economic activities from this time on. Excursions for fish, fur and wood became of much shorter duration and more closely timed to coincide with maximum yields and so as not to interfere with employment opportunities. As well, having acquired their own lands, the Dakota began to establish permanent, substantial housing and stables, as well as sheds, furnishings and all the other paraphernalia of living that tends to anchor a people in one place. By 1898, when the Dakota had been on their lands for less than six years, Inspector Marlatt reported that the band was "living and prospering as a village community. They have good houses and gardens and have surrounded themselves with many of the comforts and conveniences of life."[21]

In 1898, many of the houses built by the Dakota were still of the pole-and-sod-roof variety, with low walls and dirt floors. By 1901, Marlatt reported considerable change:

Their village is a model of its kind, straight street, good houses with shingled roofs, nicely whitewashed, clean and comfortably furnished, some with flower gardens in front, and all with splendid gardens of vegetables. They vie with each other as to whose home is the most attractive; the consequence is that each is almost perfect in its own way and comparison cannot be drawn.

Situated in the center of the village is a nice frame church, which is well-attended.

Naturally these Indians are good workers; the men take what they can get to do in town or country, and the women can always find work of a domestic kind in town. There are quite a number of aged people among them, who are faithfully provided for by those who are able to work."[22]

The school that had been established when the Dakota bought their land had trained a number of young women in the homemaking skills of the white townspeople, and they were earning good incomes as domestics. The demand for labour was intense throughout the district visited by the Dakota, and none lacked for work. From the turn of the century until the Great Depression of the 1930s, the Dakota received nothing from the Department of Indian Affairs, and preferred it that way.

In the spring of 1902, the band was dealt a serious setback: the Assiniboine flooded the village, carrying away much property, including several fine houses. As soon as the water receded, the people began to rebuild and clean up. By the following summer, the gardens were re-established and their houses rebuilt. But in 1905 the Assiniboine flooded again, just as the band had recovered from the disaster of 1902. They immediately set about cleaning up, but, ironically, there was a particularly strong demand for their labour that summer, and little was done on their own property. By 1906, however, the village was back in its prosperous and well-kept condition, and the Dakota finished the decade quite comfortably. Their twenty-six acres, occupied by more than 125 people, was becoming crowded with houses, stables, gardens and other structures.[23]

Within a few years, the department began an assault on River Lot 99, the land privately purchased by the Dakota. In late 1918, McLean wrote Agent Ogletree at Portage la Prairie, asking him to enquire about whether or not the Indians would favour transferring their land to the Crown. This could be accomplished by having Marlatt, the surviving trustee, convey the title to the Crown. Otherwise, a court order could be obtained authorizing the transfer, in which case the consent of the band members would not be necessary.[24] This suggestion was not carried forward in the next seven years, but at least the idea had been seeded.

Early in the spring of 1924, Agent Ogletree argued, "These Indians are only an expense here," and again proposed that the Dakota be relocated. The agent suggested that they be sent to a reserve where they could hunt and fish.[25] Ogletree could make a much stronger argument for moving the Dakota in 1924 than could have been made in 1911 by Agent Logan. Western Canada was in the grip of post-war depression. Prices paid for agricultural products fell to all-time lows, wages in 1924 were less than half the 1920 level, and there were few jobs. As a source of reliable labour the Dakota were welcome in and around the city, but as unemployed street vagrants they were not. But then, of course, neither was any person in similar straits.

Ogletree found that Marlatt would be willing to transfer the title to Lot 99 to the department for $2,000, and the agent recommended that the price be paid.[26] However, nothing more happened in the following three years.[27]

From 1910 to the mid-1920s, the population of the Portage la Prairie Dakota declined sharply, from about 125 persons to about sixty. In some instances, individual families moved to the farmer reserves in Manitoba, in particular to Oak River. These families were the ones interested in farming and who had kin ties to that band. One of the families to move was that of Tasinawakanhdi, the man who had been the Portage band's representative in the purchase of River Lot 99. Some of those who remained at Portage la Prairie were engaged in very specialized agricultural production of seed, especially corn seed, which was harvested, cured and sold to MacKenzie Seed Company in Brandon, as had been done by the Birdtail Band for many years.[28]

In late 1927, there was another ineffectual attempt to have the Dakota moved from their homes, and a year later, Inspector Graham applied new zeal to the task. He proposed that the Dakota be moved onto lands that had been just previously surrendered by the Long Plain Ojibwa Band. Two months later, he reported on his efforts. The younger people were willing to move, but the older ones were still hesitant. Graham, however, felt sure that they could be brought around if provided housing and food assistance. The young men wanted log houses and farming machinery as well, and Graham approved, giving them a few work horses and a plough, neither of which were appropriate for that era. He estimated that the expense of relocating the Dakota would be about $8,000 above the cost of the land. If the Dakota and the government agreed to his proposal, Graham insisted that the Indians be compelled to turn the trust to their private lands over to the Crown, so that they could be evicted if they returned to their village near the city. That Graham found it necessary to prepare this means of coercion well in advance suggested that the level of opposition to the move may have been greater than Ottawa was led to understand.[29]

The Lands and Timber Branch of the Department of the Interior checked the list of surrendered lands that Graham had suggested as appropriate for the relocation of the Dakota. It found that two quarter-sections had been sold. However, not all the conditions of the sale had been met by the purchasers, and the department felt that the sale could reasonably be cancelled. Meanwhile, Graham went ahead with his plans. By mid-April he had logs shipped from Fisher River, over one hundred miles to the north of the proposed site, to be used for housing the Dakota. This was before the Dakota had agreed to the move, before they had transferred title to their old lands, and before the Long Plain Band had accepted them into membership. Only after he had gone this far was Graham asked to meet with the purchasers of the site, to enquire about their intentions. The remainder of the lands were still available, and Secretary McLean assured Graham, "There should be no further difficulty in connection with the suggested removal."[30]

This, however, was not satisfactory to Graham. He pointed out that one of the disputed quarters provided the only access to the river, which would be necessary for watering stock. Graham deemed it "almost imperative that we have the quarter." He urged that the sale of the land be immediately cancelled, so that the Dakota could get onto the land for the spring season. Before these matters were settled, however, the move went ahead, and by autumn of 1929, a number of families were building on the site.[31]

Soon, neighbours were complaining that the presence of the Dakota in their district would depress land values. Graham did not think that this "should be reason for the Indians being deprived of the lands." He reported that thirteen families had each been given eighty acres, and another seven were awaiting the availability of their surveyed lots. The agent was instructed to carry on with the allotment of lands.[32] Between 1929 and 1931, more families made the move to the distant Long Plain Reserve. In 1930, Agent Waite wrote that, while construction and farming were progressing well, the Dakota were having difficulty getting jobs as farm labourers. A number of families, mostly those of the elderly and of three men who held full-time jobs in the city, were still at Lot 99. The department had not completed securing all the land promised the Dakota, and there was no place to accommodate them. The department had tried to compel farmers who had purchased parts of the surrendered Long Plain Reserve lands to either honour their commitments or relinquish their title. The buyers, however, had soon discovered that the lands were unfit for farming, and had abandoned them without communicating their intentions to the Indian department. This greatly slowed the task of reclaiming these non-arable lands for the prospective Dakota farmers of Portage la Prairie.[33]

The families at Long Plain worked quickly to establish themselves as farmers. By the late autumn of 1929, they had built six houses and barns and had broken 150 acres of land, ready for the crop next spring. The women had abandoned their jobs in the town, and according to a newspaper of the time, Edward Pashee "stated that when the move took place to the new land, the women would cooperate with the men in making farming successful, and would devote their time to poultry, selling eggs and raising good fowl. They would also attend to the gardens."[34] That winter, three families remained on the new lands, while three others returned to the old village, since the men had made arrangements to work for a city icehouse that winter. In the spring of 1930, the small community planted ninety-five acres of oats, 140 acres of barley, and one acre of corn and potatoes. Each household planted five acres of tame hay for their horses. The crops, however, did not do well, due particularly to the weed infestations that had accumulated over the preceding decade when the land had been unworked. The men had been obliged to seek labouring jobs in order to subsist, and this took them away from their fields and the task of weed control. In 1930–31, the Indian department issued the first rations ever given to the Dakota at Portage la Prairie.

By 1933, the emigration from the old village to the reserve was almost complete. Nine families were on the new reserve but, of those, two still lived at the old village during the winter in order to maintain their jobs in the city. Many of the twenty-eight people at the village were elderly and had neither horses nor equipment to begin farming at the reserve. By 1945, the department had settled their obligations to the Long Plain Band for the surrendered land that was taken over by the Dakota. An Order in Council was passed setting the land aside as the "Long Plain Sioux Reserve 6A."[35]

The people who continued to live in Portage la Prairie faced another serious problem: the Assiniboine River was slowly eroding River Lot 99. It was this, and not any particular action by the department, that eventually forced the abandonment of the first Dakota lands in the Portage la Prairie district. More than ten years passed after the designation of the Long Plain Sioux Reserve before the matter of relocating the Dakota still at Lot 99 was again brought up. In 1955, Superintendent J.H. Staunton met with the band and found all but one family willing to move, providing that suitable lands were found. Even the majority that was willing to move would do so reluctantly, however, since many of the women who worked in the city could see that they would not be able to keep their jobs if they were moved far away. Parish Lot 25 was identified as "an ideal location" for gardens, with fifteen acres cultivated and ten acres in bush that could be used to gather fuel. The site was three miles from the nearest school and transportation would have to be arranged for students.[36]

After a year's delay, the plan was implemented. By autumn of 1956, the village site on the new land was laid out, houses were nearing completion and plans were being made for electrical power and water connections. Superintendent Staunton recommended that when the people moved into their new homes, the department would "create a Police Constable and create as nearly as possible a model community."[37]

With the relocation well in hand, it was time for the department to attend to a particularly difficult problem, that is, what should be done with River Lot 99, the private property of the Dakota, which was being eroded into the Assiniboine. In late January 1957, D.A.H. Nield, the Indian agent at Portage la Prairie, went to discuss the matter with the villagers. He reported: "All of the older Indians who are direct descendants of the original lot owners wish to obtain authority to sell their lots and the Band members presently living at the new village are most desirous to obtain authority to sell the remaining lots and request that monies received be put into a trust account and used for the construction of a community hall."[38]

Nield had been overly quick in raising the issue at this time. The new village site on Parish Lot 25 had not yet been declared a reserve, and would not be declared one until the department was sure that the relocation was working as desired. As well, there was discussion of adding more land to the new village site to allow the Dakota a cemetery. The old village at River Lot 99 had not been completely abandoned, and there was some discussion within the department about dividing the band into two. W.C. Bethune, Ottawa's director of Indian affairs, favoured neither adding land to the village nor dividing the band.[39]

Toward the end of 1957, the idea of dividing the Portage la Prairie Dakota into two bands was again put forward, this time by the Dakota themselves. Since the community had physically divided itself in the previous decade, significant differences had developed between the two segments (between the urban labourers and rural small farmers), and each needed appropriate services at the band community level. Ottawa approved the division in general, and Agent Nield was directed to examine the matter in detail and report. He found that the Long Plain segment would not approve the division of band funds and assets on a per-capita basis. Most of the band fund came from the lease of Long Plain lands, and the rural people felt the villagers had no claim upon the money. At this, Ottawa withdrew approval of the plan. It was considered that all the Dakota had equal rights to resources, and each had the right to select either community for their home following any division of the band.[40] This disagreement stalled matters for fourteen years.

In 1971, Ernie Smoke, headman of the Long Plain Dakota people, raised the issue with the Department of Indian Affairs. He asked that the Long Plain people be recognized as a band with the authority to elect a chief and band councillors, and that their lands be given reserve status. J.R. Bell, district supervisor at Brandon, discovered that it would not be possible to designate a band and reserve without including the village Dakota. He suggested instead that the two groups come to an agreement for the selection of a single headman, or that they request the creation of two separate bands and reserves. Five months later, it was decided by the Dakota to lobby for separate bands, with each retaining the lands they then occupied and band funds being divided on a per-capita basis. The department and the Manitoba Indian Brotherhood supported the concept, and Ernie Smoke, headman at Long Plain, along with George Chaske, representative of the villagers, were sent detailed instructions for the conduct of a referendum to approve the plan.[41]

The referendum was held on April 24, 1972. Of the fifty-two persons who voted, forty-two were in favour of the division and eight were opposed. The department recommended that the Dakota's wishes be respected. Officials in the band-management division of the department discovered in Ottawa, however, that the referendum had not been conducted in strict accordance with the department's regulations. As well, if the proposed plan was carried forward, the majority of the people (who lived at the village near the city) would receive the smaller proportion of the land, while the minority (those at Long Plain) would have much more. Both Chaske and Smoke argued that most of the Dakota were not interested in farming, preferring to remain near the city and their employment. Fewer than six households made their living from farming and a large area of the Long Plains land was being leased to neighbouring farmers, since it was surplus to the needs of the Dakota. The Dakota had been trying for over eighty years to explain the basis of their economy to the Indian department, and in 1972, they still had not succeeded.[42]

The Dakota urged the Department of Indian Affairs to accept the people's wishes. On July 18, 1972, a final meeting was held by the members of the Dakota communities and local, district, regional and national representatives of the department. At this meeting, H.H. Chapman, chief of the department's membership division, was convinced to take the matter to the minister of Indian affairs, who approved the Dakota's plan on August 24, 1972. In February 1973, the Dakota Tipi Band, as the village group was named, requested reserve status for their lands. This was approved by Order in Council on June 26, 1973. The division of the Portage la Prairie Dakota was complete.[43]

By 1957, the original Dakota lands at River Lot 99 had been abandoned. Most of it was gone, eroded away by the spring floods of the Assiniboine. The department then took on the task of formally extinguishing Dakota title to the lot. The deaths of the original purchasers and trustees created many complex legal problems, and by 1960 a variety of legal approaches were being considered, all of which involved a great amount of paperwork, and none of which appeared to be satisfactory.[44]

Then, in the late spring of 1961, the Prairie Farm Rehabilitation Agency of the federal government asked for permission to construct water-control dykes across the land. If permission had not been forthcoming soon thereafter, a gap would have been left in the dyke, which would have to have been completed later, a costly alternative. The Indian department spent considerable time and effort trying to find a way to transfer the old Dakota lands to the Crown. Finally, the Government of Manitoba was approached and asked to pass a special bill in the legislature that would extinguish the trustee title to the land and transfer it to the Crown in the right of Canada. This manoeuvre was completed on May 4, 1963. The first Dakota lands in Portage la Prairie and one of the first privately owned Indian communities in western Canada thus no longer existed.[45]

While these actions were in progress, the Prairie Farm Rehabilitation Agency went ahead with their dyke, with or without permission. The Dakota band worked out an arrangement of compensation for the occupied land, and offered the remaining few acres for sale by public tender. In all, the band received a little less than $2,000.[46]

In 1957, the department had considered purchasing additional lands for the Dakota living near the city. The farmer who owned the land adjacent to the village site had offered his land for sale, but in the course of a few months, he had raised his asking price from $2,000 to $6,000. The department felt that the owner was "taking advantage of an opportunity to sell his property as it is adjacent to the reserve," and refused the offer. A short while later, the asking price had dropped to $3,500, but by then, the decision had been made not to add to the village lands. In 1960, the owner renewed his offer to sell at the lower asking price. He had the help of G.C. Fairchild, member of parliament, who wrote in support of the offer. Fairchild wrote that the owner was subject to "invasions of his property by the warlike Sioux," and wished to leave the neighbourhood of the village. The department offered $1,000, which was declined. By 1964, the Dakota were getting crowded on their small piece of land, so when their neighbour again offered his land, this time at a price of $3,000, there was considerably more interest. The department offered $2,000, which was accepted. In the spring of 1965, the village lands were increased by 5.4 acres.[47]

The other part of the Dakota community too had faced hard times in the decades after its move to Long Plains in 1929. They soon discovered that the lands were scarcely fit for farming, especially in the 1930s. Many of the men and women attempted to re-establish themselves as labourers, but had already found out that they were not able to compete with the Ojibwa for local employment. The Ojibwa had been farm labourers in the area for many years, while the Dakota were newcomers, and were not particularly well trained for agricultural tasks. When agriculture failed during the Dirty Thirties, many families drifted back to the city, but jobs were non-existent.

   Improved growing conditions and increased demand for farm products at the time of World War II encouraged an expansion of farming at the Long Plain Dakota Reserve, but the band never did come close to bringing all of their lands into production. Rather, during the war, band members took labouring positions, and much of their land was leased by the Department of Indian Affairs to neighbouring white farmers. The leasing of farm lands was continued after the war, and by the 1950s most Dakota in the vicinity of the City of Portage la Prairie – those at the village and those at Long Plain – had once again become general labourers. The difference is that today they are not restricted to semi-skilled tasks. Dakota people work at a great range of tasks in the professions and arts, as well as in traditional skilled and unskilled jobs. The few farmers at Long Plain have experienced the same pressures as did other farmers in Manitoba who do not have enough land or capital to keep up with the demands for ever-increasing scales of production. What agricultural development there has been recently has favoured enterprises that make considerable use of labour and relatively sophisticated technology rather than a great area of land – greenhouse operations, bee-keeping and seed production. The Dakota Tipi Reserve, adjacent to Portage la Prairie, looks much like a suburb of the city, except that there is a magnificent dance bower overlooking the Assiniboine River. The Dakota at Portage la Prairie are self-supporting, as they have been, with a brief exception in the 1930s, for over 120 years.

The northern labourers:
The Prince Albert bands,
1876 to 1963

12

Since the early 1870s, most of the major divisions of the Dakota nation have visited and dwelt in the Prince Albert district. From the late 1870s until the 1910s, a few of the Tetonwon who had fled from the United States after the Battle of the Little Bighorn lived in and near the city, but by 1920, they had left for the Wood Mountain Reserve in southwestern Saskatchewan, or for reservations in the United States. The Sissetonwon who resided there were members of Wapahaska's band, and eventually most of them returned to his reserve near Saskatoon. The Ihanktonwon were travellers, moving among the Dakota settlements in Manitoba and Saskatchewan, and eventually settling in the Moose Mountain district of southeastern Saskatchewan. This chapter, however, relates the history of the Wahpetonwon, M'dewakontonwon and Sissetonwon who have lived near Prince Albert over the years and remain there today.

According to Tribal Historian Robert Goodvoice, the Wahpetonwon and M'dewakontonwon ancestors of a part of the present Dakota population at Prince Albert did not cross into Canada with the main body of Dakota who left the United States in late 1862 and early 1863. When they first fled Minnesota after the Sioux Uprising of 1862, they followed the trails to the north, but rather than heading for the Red River settlements or the Qu'Appelle, they remained near the international boundary, on the American side. Being no more than one or two days' travel from Canada, and often crossing the line into British territory, they ranged through the woodlands of northern Minnesota and North Dakota until 1877. Following Custer's inglorious defeat at the Little Bighorn in 1876, the cry for Sioux blood again rose on the western frontier. The band quietly crossed the line for the last time and headed for Portage la Prairie.

The presence of these Dakota seems to have gone completely unnoticed by

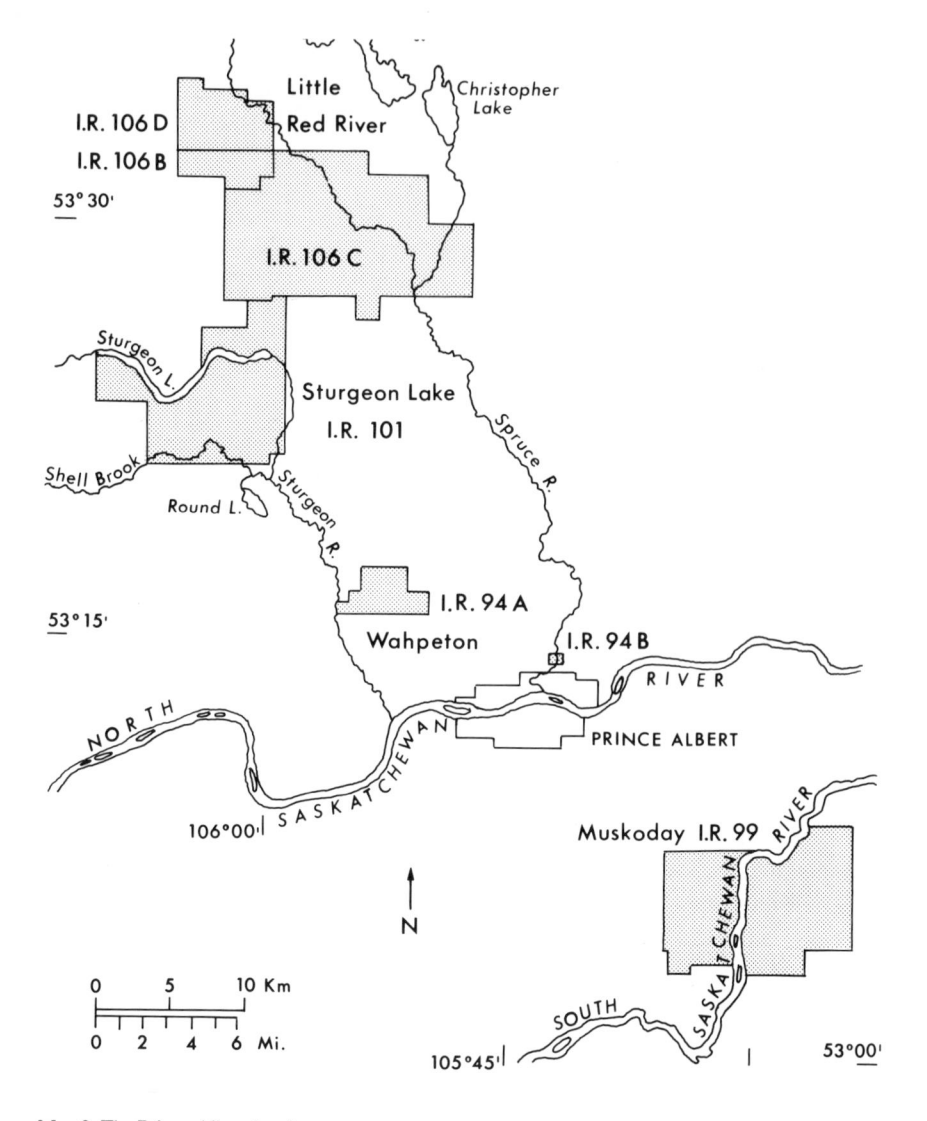

Map 9. The Prince Albert bands

government agents which was not unusual since few officials had any way of distinguishing the various Dakota bands. Upon the advice of James McKay, whom Goodvoice describes as having been the band's trader while they were in the northern states, the band of about twenty lodges moved to Prince Albert in the summer of 1878. McKay had extensive ties with the Hudson's Bay Company, spoke Dakota, and had had much to do with the Dakota bands in Manitoba. The Hudson's Bay Company needed skilled workers for a new lumber mill at Prince Albert, and immediately upon arriving in the settlement, the Dakota went to work cutting and hauling saw logs.

The following summer, a camp of seventy lodges of Sitting Bull's Tetonwon followers arrived at Prince Albert, throwing the settlement into near panic. Indian Commissioner David Laird complained that the starving Indians were killing cattle for food, and that the local settlers were planning to raise a militia to expel all the Dakota from the neighbourhood and even from the country. Laird knew that this would be quite impossible, and begged the minister of the interior to send police. When confronted, the Tetonwon apologized for the thefts, and offered to pay for any animals the young men had killed. This offer was accepted, but Laird continued to call for assistance.[1]

The government was unable to reinforce the settlement with either regulars or police, and so had little choice but to tolerate the presence of the Dakota. This, however, was not an end to the objections. Over the winter, the Dakota had been cutting wood for a number of lumber producers, and Indian Agent Clarke reported that they "have done an immense amount of work. They have cut about 3,500 cords of long wood besides several thousand fence rails, etc., etc." The problem with this was that the Dakota were taking the jobs previously filled by settlers, and Clarke estimated, "They cannot have cost the settlement less than fifteen thousand dollars during the past winter."[2] In the spring of 1879, Clarke reported that the Dakota were planning to leave the settlement. The Tetonwon intended to go to the Cyprus Hills and Qu'Appelle, the Ihanktonwon to Wapahaska's reserve, and a few Sissetonwon to Oak River. Clarke encouraged these plans, since he "could not throw the burden of their support another winter on the people, as I have done." To keep the Dakota from taking all the settlers' jobs, Clarke had given out a little food. Vankoughnet warned the agent that if the Dakota remained near Prince Albert, nothing more must be given them, as "the Sioux are not properly Canadian Indians."[3]

The Dakota did not leave Prince Albert permanently, and returned later to cut wood and work for the settlers. The department gave them minimal rations from time to time, but in general the Dakota were able to make their own living. There they remained, beyond official notice until the events of 1885 brought all Indians in the Northwest to the close attention of the authorities. It was the Tetonwon, however, who attracted the most attention, and at one point, Hayter Reed suggested disarming them as a precaution against settlers who might take fright and shoot them on sight. This idea was abandoned when it became clear that there was not a police force of sufficient strength to carry out the measure.[4] The Dakota did not intend to take part in the troubles, as they had agreed to abide by the Queen's laws. Since they received no annuities or other assistance from the government, and provided their own subsistence, they were ignored by the department.

Early in 1890, one group of Dakota made a request for a reserve, some farm implements and a school. Their supporter, R.I. Pritchard of Prince Albert, viewed the Dakota as "hard working Indians and know how to work and they want a start and I am satisfied they will make good farmers, much better I am sure than the Crees."[5] He enclosed a letter in which the leading men of the band laid out their wants.

We did not want to go with White Cap on the reserve the Government gave him, because we did not like him and would never acknowledge him as our chief. If we had gone with him he would have led us into the rebellion as he did the Indians who went with him. It is now thirteen years since we have come to the NWT and have since that time been loyal subjects of our Great Mother. We now want to know if the Government can do something for us. We would like to get a reserve somewhere north of Prince Albert and would like to get some agricultural implements and animals to work them.

But the main thing we want is a school where we can get our children taught. We find out now that we cannot live unless we live like our white brother. We all know how to work and if our white mother helps we will do our best to get along and will always be good loyal children to her as we have always been. There is now in our band forty-one men, fifty-four women, twenty-five boys and twenty-eight girls. These children have all been born in Prince Albert.

We have a chief of our own, who is a real chief, a descendant of the great Chief Flying Thunder who saved the life of a Government officer when he was shot and wounded by a Yankee officer. For which he was rewarded by the Govt. with a medal which our present Chief now has.[6]

The leading men who composed this letter say that they had been in Canada thirteen years, that is, since 1877, which is the year Goodvoice says his people crossed into the Northwest. Furthermore, the chief who led Goodvoice's parents into Canada and to Prince Albert was Hupa Yakta, a descendant of Flying Thunder. This clearly identifies the petitioners as those who eventually took up Wahpeton Reserve or, as it was known in these early years, Round Plain. Once again references to obligations incurred in the War of 1812, expressions of loyalty to the Crown, and the display of medals make it certain that the Dakota believed they had a right to the things they requested.[7]

Pritchard had written to D.P. Macdowell, member of parliament, and he turned the correspondence over to the Indian department. Dewdney and Vankoughnet wanted to know if some of the lands at White Cap Reserve had not been intended for the Dakota at Prince Albert. Sam Bray of the Technical Branch reported that lands at White Cap Reserve were meant only for those already living there. Bray concluded that "it therefore would appear that these Indians have never been provided with a reserve."[8]

Vankoughnet communicated the essentials of the matter to Hayter Reed, with the advice that the government approve setting aside a reserve for these Dakota, "the extent of which would probably be calculated at (80) eighty acres for every five souls, as was done with regards to White Cap's Band." Assistant Commissioner Forget reported the band to number 149 individuals.[9]

In August, two representatives of the Presbyterian Church wrote separate letters to the Indian department requesting financial aid for a school that had been set up in a tent near the Dakota camp. Assistant Indian Commissioner Hayter Reed expressed considerable enthusiasm and went so far as to promise funds for the next school year.[10] However, he changed his mind after Dewdney recommended that no funds be given to these Indians who were "not only non-Treaty, but American Indians." He wanted the band moved to White Cap Reserve.[11] Vankoughnet instructed Reed to determine "to what reserve these Indians belong and why they do not stop on their reserve, which is the proper place for them."[12]

Reed remodelled his opinions in a reply to a renewed request for assistance from the Reverend A.B. Baird of the Presbyterian Church's Foreign Missions Committee. Baird agreed that it was probably not good policy to construct Indian schools off reserves, and that in the best of circumstances, the Dakota should be moved away from the town. However, he said, "The people of Prince Albert are not anxious to have them go because it is found to be a convenience to have these people at hand for work in the town – the women especially do a considerable amount of the rougher kind of work."[13] Like the Dakota at Portage la Prairie, the band that had followed Hupa Yakta to Prince Albert had proven themselves as workers and had become indispensable in the local economy. Gone was the panic and fear that had accompanied their first appearance in the district.

Finally, in early 1891, Reed went to Prince Albert to discuss the matter of a reserve with the Dakota themselves. He reported:

These Sioux strongly object to leaving the neighbourhood of the town, and they advance such excellent arguments in favour of being allowed to remain close to the settlement. Here they get constant work in the houses and fields of the settlers, and where the aged and infirm receive assistance, that I really felt unable to justify myself in any attempt to insist upon their removal to a distance.

I could not learn that their removal is desired by any but Messers. Moore and Macdowall who object to their presence on their land, but they are willing to give it up to them, provided they receive an equivalent elsewhere. The land, although not much good to them, is well adapted for the cultivation of such little gardens as will produce all that these Indians aspire to or probably can be induced to raise.[14]

The Dakota were indeed living upon lands near the mouth of the Little Red River to which Moore and Macdowall, Ltd., held title. They had not been disturbed for the previous thirteen years because they had been cutting wood for that company. In more recent years, the business had been suffering, Dakota labour was no longer needed, and Macdowall wanted them off the land. He also alleged that the Dakota had damaged the property by cutting wood on it. Reed responded by stating that the department was no more responsible for the actions of the Dakota than it was for those of the white settlers.[15]

While he was in Prince Albert, Reed met with the Wahpetonwon and Sisseton-won Dakota. The first group were those requesting the school and reserve, while the latter were members of Wapahaska's band, who were in Prince Albert seeking employment. Reed concluded that all of the people were "more nearly related to White Cap's Band than to any other." Having arrived at this erroneous conclusion, he was reluctant to speak more about a reserve, but did approve a departmental contribution in support of the school. Vankoughnet agreed, and the department paid the teacher's salary for the rest of the fiscal year. In the spring, the department again approached Macdowall to acquire his lands, if he was willing to take other Crown lands for the site occupied by the Dakota. Macdowall responded that he would rather sell the land to the department, with payment made partly in cash and part-ly as credits for timber royalties. Later that summer, Macdowall made a definite offer to sell the lands. He wanted $50 an acre for five hundred acres of land, a price he felt compared well with that paid for another parcel of land "situated within a rifle shot of the 500 acres in question." If the department would not pay the asking price, he wanted the Indians removed from the land at once. Inspector of Indian Agencies Wadsworth was sent to investigate.[16] He reported on June 25, 1891:

They have chosen and occupy a table of land or plateau containing about one hundred acres formed by an elbow of the Little Red River near its confluence with the Saskatchewan. . . . Within this they have built their houses. From the Little Red River, they obtain water, and they are surrounded with plenty of dry wood. As a residence, camping ground and winter quarters for Indians, it cannot be surpassed, but it is of no use whatever for agriculture, the soil being too light, and the Indians have not, in the slightest degree, attempted it. They have twenty nine houses and a number of stables, and as nearly as I can un-derstand them, they claim to number thirty three men, forty three women and forty two children or all told one hundred and eighteen (118) souls.[17]

Wadsworth felt that at least some of the people he visited were from Wapahas-ka and Tatankanaje's bands, and this may have been so since visitors from the southern reserves were common. He disputed Macdowall's valuation of the lands the Dakota were occupying, saying that a very high calibre rifle must have been used to measure the distance to the site. He also found that Macdowall was com-paring the land with a small parcel located within the limits of the town and not in the wilderness on the other side of the river. As for the Dakota having damaged the land, he found that the trees had been cut by white people in the employ of the

Hudson's Bay Company. He said that this band had never been woodsworkers, not even cutting trees for firewood, preferring to use the dry tops of fallen trees. He concluded that the lands were of no commercial value, "and it would be impossible for anyone to fix a price upon that basis." Finally, he added, "These Indians hold a very high place in the estimation of the people of Prince Albert, as a peaceful, law abiding, hardworking people, and they are looked upon as a very necessary part of the community. On all sides, good words are heard regarding them."[18] As a postscript, he noted that the Dakota had been occupying the site before it was purchased from the government by Macdowall and Moore.

Wadsworth was in error when he stated that this band had never been woodsworkers; both the documentary and tribal history make it clear that woodswork was a primary source of cash income. Reed had been told that the band was interested in gardening, if not farming, but "if it were intended to make farmers of them, the lands under consideration could not be recommended at all." Early in July 1891, Vankoughnet instructed Reed to examine the Macdowall property and to discuss with Macdowall other lands he might be willing to take in exchange.[19]

Reed sent Surveyor Ponton to Prince Albert on this task, and the surveyor identified a site, about three miles southwest of the town and away from the river, which he felt was much better suited for the Dakota. Ponton was instructed to visit the Dakota and discuss the possibility of their moving to these lands. This he did, and learned that the Dakota feared having to abandon their houses just as winter was approaching. Ponton suggested that they be left where they were until spring when arrangements for housing could be made. Negotiations dragged out over the winter of 1891–92, without any conclusion.[20]

In the summer of 1891, the Anglican Church had made known its interest in the Dakota. Archdeacon J.A. Mackay wrote to Hayter Reed saying, "Some of the Sioux Indians now living in or in the neighbourhood of Prince Albert are anxious to move onto a reserve if one could be allotted to them somewhere on the north of the Saskatchewan or near the Shell River." Reed was not yet aware that there were three bands of Dakota at Prince Albert, and his response could only be based upon what he already knew: it had been decided not to move the Dakota away from the town where they were able to make a good living. He also, delicately, suggested to Mackay that the Dakota were already the concern of the Presbyterian Church. At this, Mackay replied that he was not referring to "the band that wishes to remain in the vicinity and among whom the Presbyterians have commenced a school." Reed, however, was "yet in the dark with regard to the Sioux at Prince Albert," and asked Mackay to detail the numbers, origin, length of residence in Canada, and general character of the people to whom he referred.[21]

Reports from Inspector Wadsworth and Archdeacon Mackay arrived in Ottawa one day apart. Mackay wrote: "The Sioux who wish to settle in the Shell River section of the country number 14 tents. The first comer reached here thirteen years ago, I think, from the neighbourhood of Ellice. The chief came 12 years ago. His name is 'Ayanki.' They call themselves Wapayto, but so far as I can find out, they are Dacotahs like most of the others in Prince Albert. They are certainly not Teton. They bear a good character for industry and general conduct."[22]

This band settled in the Prince Albert district shortly after Goodvoice's ancestors under Hupa Yakta, and were perhaps drawn there by the success of the earlier arrivals. The two bands were distinct, and in certain respects their economies differed. Hupa Yakta's people were independent resource workers, primarily woodsworkers, although they also sold fish, fur and meat. Iyanki's people were labourers in the town and the growing farm settlement. There was some overlap in production activities, but it does not seem that there was competition between them. To the contrary, relations were cordial, and Goodvoice relates that families from one village moved in with the other for considerable lengths of time. Wadsworth's report added more information.

One party of about fifteen tents, say seventy souls, live a nomadic life and generally camp – when in town – in the West End in the vicinity of the English Church Mission; they are related to the White Cap Sioux of Moose Woods, one of the leading men being the son of the late Chief White Cap, but he stated they have never lived there, having been about Prince Albert for the past twelve years.

As these Indians cannot be said to be squatting or trespassing anywhere, for they usually spend the summer near some farmer's house for whom they work, and in winter they return to the west end of the town, they may for the present be dropped for they do not require immediate attention.[23]

Nevertheless, the band renewed their application for a reserve, and once again Reed went to Prince Albert to talk to the Dakota.

These Indians are distinct from the Sioux of Moose Woods, and from those Indians in the neighbourhood of Prince Albert, to provide land for whom negotiations were carried on with Messers. Moore and Macdowall.

They belong to the Santee division of the Sisseton Tribe, and have always refused as they still do, to have any connections with the other Sioux just referred to.

They claim to have been in this country for the last thirty years and have been in the vicinity of Prince Albert for some twelve years. During their sojourn at Prince Albert they have maintained themselves by working for the settlers and have earned a character for diligence, orderly conduct and morality. They number some eleven heads of families and between 50 and 60 souls all told.

Despite their good character, as settlement is closing in the lands about Prince Albert, the presence of these Indians is becoming a source of annoyance to the settlers, who desire to have them removed.

As already said, these Indians express a desire if not given a reserve to be allowed to homestead and from the experience gained by them in working for the settlers, and their industrious habits, one is tempted to regret that the law does not allow of their becoming homesteaders; however, as the matter stands I beg to recommend that they be granted a Reserve of an area calculated at the rate of 80 acres to 5 souls, or say 800 acres altogether.

From what is known of these Indians it is felt that were the land given them together with a couple of yoke of oxen, a plow or two, and so forth, there is every prospect of their maintaining themselves without in any way interfering with the settlers or being a burden on the Government.[24]

Reed made it clear that these self-sufficient, hardworking and moral people were a problem for the townspeople because they were taking jobs from the growing number of whites in the vicinity. It is, however, unclear about why the Dakota were refused homesteader status. The government consistently refused the Dakota access to lands, schools and money by arguing that they were not Canadian Indians; they were immigrants. Back in 1872, William Spragge, then deputy superintendent of Indian affairs, had noted the parallel between white immigrants and the Dakota. Still, it was taken for granted that the Dakota, like all other Indians, had no homesteading rights.

Nothing more was done to set aside reserve lands until late in 1893, when Reed's assistant, A.E. Forget, was asked to report on the circumstances of the Dakota at Prince Albert. The request was passed on to Agent Mackenzie at Duck Lake, who was instructed to find enough land to allow eighty acres for five persons, but if this area were not available, "then a smaller one might be made to suffice."[25] It would appear that Reed did not take seriously the Dakota's interest in farming.

Mackenzie visited Hupa Yakta's band, as he was instructed, and talked to the heads of the nine families in the group. He suggested that the government would give them forty acres for each family, but the Dakota protested that this was not enough to farm. The agent then promised that if they worked the forty acres satisfactorily, they would each be given an additional forty acres. This was accepted by the Dakota, provided each family was given "a document showing that the land was their own so that they might improve it and put up good buildings." The Dakota had located a site some seven miles north of Prince Albert, and Mackenzie found that the location was available for settlement. Reed accepted Mackenzie's recommendation that the Dakota be given the lands they requested: "Since the lands are on the north side of the river, and little, if any settlement has been made there, it is not thought that the proposed reservation can cause any inconvenience to any legitimate interest." The Department of the Interior approved the arrangements, and in early 1894 an Order in Council was passed setting aside 35- and 36-49-27-W2M for the Dakota reserve. Agent Mackenzie was given the task of arranging for the survey and issuing location tickets for each family.[26]

In early 1894, just as the department was congratulating itself for having efficiently and economically settled the land needs of the Dakota, the Presbyterian Church in Prince Albert forwarded another request for a Dakota reserve. Mr.J.E. Young described these Indians as long-time residents of the city, self-supporting, dwelling in their own houses, and experienced as labourers who "give satisfaction for their employers." The church favoured moving the Dakota away from the evil influences of the town, and even though only a few "progressive" young men agreed with this plan, Young felt that if a few were settled on a reserve and equipped for farming, the rest would follow. Once again, the Indian department was confused. It had been felt that the newly allotted reserve north of the town had met the needs of the Dakota with whom the Presbyterian Church was involved. Hayter Reed was aware of another band of Dakota at Prince Albert, those near the city, but whom the department had decided were not in immediate need of lands, since they lived in the town over the winter and near their employers' farm homes in the summer. Indeed, he had promised those who were to settle on the new reserve that they would not be obliged to live with the other Dakota.[27]

The Dakota to whom Young referred were the members of a third band. Band One was located at this time on the Moore and Macdowall land along the Little Red River. The people of this band were Wahpetonwon and M'dewakontonwon, whose chief had been Hupa Yakta. Band Two and Band Three lived together much of the time, but clearly saw themselves as separate economic and political entities. The people of Band Two were mainly Sissetonwon under the leadership of B'do, although he was not a chief as reckoned by the Dakota. This was the band for whom the reserve north of Prince Albert was secured. Band Three, then being championed by Young, were the Wahpetonwon who had arrived from Fort Ellice under Iyanki. It had taken a personal visit to Prince Albert for Reed to understand that there were two bands of Dakota at Prince Albert, and it is doubtful that during his tenure he ever did realize that there were three bands near the town. Reed called for a more detailed report.[28]

Young responded that eight families, or thirty individuals, were ready to move to the reserve. Six other families, or twenty individuals, would follow as soon as land was available. He did not know if the remaining families would also go to the new reserve, as they were "very reticent when spoken to about the matter." Young wanted the department to move the Presbyterian school from the Little Red River village to the new reserve. A good, substantial school under the control of the church would, he felt, attract all of the Dakota to the reserve, even though his own letter shows that he realized the Dakota bands had no intention of taking up lands together, and would not even discuss such a proposition.[29]

Reed rejected Young's suggestions on the grounds that, as he had learned in 1891, the "Sioux Indians in the neighbourhood of the town . . . are so strongly adverse to any connection with those who have been camping for some years back across the river . . . that it is very doubtful whether they would remain on their own lands if the others were to join them." Reed advised that after that, Young communicate on Indian matters with Agent Mackenzie, "who understands the whole situation, and can readily explain what is wanted to the department, and so save, possibly, a good deal of correspondence." This unmistakable brush-off had the desired effect. Young sent one last letter, setting out a bit more detail, but from this point on, Band Three, Iyanki and his people, disappear from the documentary record.[30]

Shortly after Young had written to Reed, Hilton Keith, agent at Fort Carlton and within whose jurisdiction the new reserve lay, reported that he had met with the Dakota on the new reserve. At that time, there were thirty-five people in seven families camped on the land, with two more families yet to move. When he arrived at the reserve, the agent and the Dakota agreed that the lands were "altogether unfit for farming purposes, being bush and swampland." Keith made the decision to allow the Dakota to plant their gardens in natural clearings on two adjacent sections of land, and asked, if it were possible, to have the sections added to the reserve. This problem had developed as a result of the department's attempt to identify the lands the Dakota wanted solely from a description that passed through an inadequate translator. When the Dakota arrived with Keith at the surveyed land, they found that the wrong place had been identified and set aside by Order in Council.[31]

Reed responded with some alarm to Agent Keith's report. He cautioned that the separate bands were to be kept separate, and if the Dakota who were camped near the town wanted a reserve, "then some arrangement [would] be made about land for them." He was irritated to hear, after having expended the effort to have a reserve set aside by Order in Council, that the wrong lands had been secured. He wanted "something more definite to go upon, before making any further applications in the matter." Chief Inspector Wadsworth was sent to investigate, and in early June 1894, he sent in his report.[32]

As far as I can learn there is a misapprehension regarding this particular lot of (9 families) Indians being separate and distinct from those trespassing upon the Moore and Macdowall property.

Not long ago the old Chief Wi-za-ta-ca or Bear lived on the Moore property too, and was the one among them most favourable to the building of the school house and establishing a school and he left there because the other Indians objected to him encouraging the school and other things tending to civilization: but it is thought that if those now settling meet with success, many of those now on the Moore property will also join this settlement in which case it will be as well that several sections of land should be set apart while it is still vacant.[33]

Wadsworth recommended that four sections of land be added to the original two, which would provide enough lands for all the Dakota in and near Prince Albert.

The inspector's report did little to clear up the confusion about the identities of the Dakota bands. The chief, Wi-za-ta-ca, cannot be identified from either tribal or documentary sources, but Goodvoice feels that this is a poor transcription of the name *Waditaka,* or *Brave,* who did camp at Little Red River. Reed asked Forget to determine if indeed the various bands were yet willing to live together, in which case more land could be secured but, "considering the nature of their agricultural pursuits, lightness of soil is not regarded as any objection, provided there is enough of hay land."[34]

In the autumn and early winter of 1894, Reed and other officials in the Indian department struggled to determine the needs of the Dakota, and to have the required lands set aside as a reserve. In his most recent report, Inspector Wadsworth had disparaged the Dakota's farming abilities, and had considered irrelevant the quality of the land they were to be given, as long as there was enough for them to establish self-sufficient, small-scale household economies. He reached this conclusion when he was selecting the reserve and had the larger group of Dakota at the Little Red River in mind. These people had no interest in farming, being quite satisfied with their roles as resource workers and the sale of labour. The Sissetonwon, however, who were then on the reserve, had intended to be farmers and had asked for agricultural lands. Their requirements had been forgotten. This misdirected decision locked all of the Dakota at Prince Albert into an essentially non-agricultural future. Finally, in late 1894, the Order in Council creating the Dakota Reserve at Prince Albert was approved. As surveyor Ponton reported, the land was suitable for an Indian camping ground, a place for gardens and pasture, a woodlot, and the establishment of a "berry picking industry," but little else.[35]

Soon after the reserve had been set aside, plans were formulated for the Dakota to make use of the lands. In April 1894, Agent Hilton Keith was sent to meet with the Dakota and determine their immediate needs. The agent reported that the Indians would not be able to stay on the reserve unless they received considerable assistance from the department. Since leaving the vicinity of the town, they no longer had access to employment and so could not support themselves as they had been doing. As for the long term, however, the Dakota stated that they were labourers, not farmers, and did not require the services of a resident instructor or farmer. They assured Keith that "they would not burden the Department with the expense of keeping a man that would not be of service to them." As for equipment, they requested garden seed, small tools, field implements, haying gear and cattle, valued at $900 to $1,000.[36]

Forget found that there was no money in the Sioux Vote for these purchases, but suggested that Reed buy what was immediately needed and charge the cost to the Current General Destitute Vote. He forbade the purchase of a mower and rake, as it was policy that the Dakota be obliged to use scythes to take in hay and grain crops. The Dakota were also to get two yoke of oxen, but no other cattle. Duncan Scott cautioned that nothing should be done to have the Dakota think they could rely upon the department for their support.[37]

By mid-May, the Dakota were on their reserve and starting to get themselves established. They had no small tools whatsoever, and Agent Keith sent in a request for axes, augers, glass and putty. He also requested three cows. A month later, the band had one acre planted to potatoes and a rootcrop and had broken five more acres. As it was late in the season, no grain crops were planted. Even soon after taking up the land, Wadsworth could see that the soil was too light to sustain agriculture for long. He distributed some supplies to the Dakota, and warned them not to expect such treatment in the future. He added that, until they were operating farmers, he would allow them to leave the reserve and seek work. This position ignored the fact that some of the older people were unable to travel the longer distance to the few jobs in town. The reserve had been surveyed into forty-acre lots, with each family assigned a lot of its own where it was expected to settle and break land.[38]

Later in the month, Keith visited the band. He found that the Dakota had broken twenty acres of land and had planted and fenced their crops of roots and potatoes. The department had not yet decided how the band was to be distributed on the land, so the agent told the Dakota to stop breaking until the department's wishes were known. Keith could see that the band was going to have to make its living through the sale of labour, so he recommended that the Dakota be allowed to live together in a village and to work their land in common. He wanted them to receive haying equipment, as they had plenty of hay and there was a good market for animal feed in the town.[39]

Keith had learned that the Dakota were preparing for a sun dance, "but upon my telling them that this was distinctly not allowed by the Government, that if they persisted, they would, no doubt, lose the help the Government were inclined to give them, they pulled down the tent and promised to abandon the idea." Threats of being dispossessed of their lands and of being viewed by the Queen as an enemy were effective with this band of Dakota as they had been for the others; no one was willing to risk expulsion to the United States.

Wadsworth agreed that there was nothing to be gained by insisting that the people live and work separately, but he was unwilling to fly in the face of clear departmental policy. He suggested as a compromise that the Dakota locate in a central place on the reserve where they they could have a school, gardens and stables; as each family took up farming, he said, they could move to their own lot. He even drew up a utopian sketch embodying his ideas. Reed agreed with this approach as a last resort, but insisted that first all effort must be made to "get them to fall in with the Department's view" that they should live and farm separately. Reed refused to issue a mower and rake, holding to policy that the Indians must use scythes.[40]

After the reserve was established the three distinctive groups of Dakota at Prince Albert began to change and blend membership. Individuals and families began to move into the location where they felt they could best conduct their preferred life-styles. The political boundaries between the groups, such as they were, diminished in importance, as Sissetonwon, Wahepetonwon and M'dewakontonwon mingled. By the mid-1890s, several families had gone to Wapahaska's reserve on the South Saskatchewan River near Saskatoon, when the old chief attempted to re-consolidate after the Riel Rebellion of 1885. Some Dakota still occupied the Moore and Macdowall property on the Little Red River, but many who had supported the Presbyterian school had gone to the reserve, and those who remained were hostile to the church. Others had gone to reserves in southern Canada, and a few to reservations in the United States where they had relatives.

The Presbyterian Church wanted the reserve expanded. They intended to move their school to the reserve, and felt that additional lands would be needed to accommodate those who would follow the church. The reserve was made up of one quarter section less land than had been intended, but the department rejected this plea in 1896. The church again applied for an enlargement of the reserve in 1898 and 1899, on the grounds that the expansion would allow other Dakota who still lived and worked in the "unsuitable location" outside Prince Albert, to move. Sam Bray, in charge of reserve lands, replied that "both men and women find ample employment in and near the Town, and are self-sustaining in every particular. They are a highly moral and temperate people, and have not been injured by their residence among the whites for the past 20 years." Bray concluded that additional lands at the reserve were not necessary, since only forty-five persons in nine families were then resident on the reserve. Instead, he suggested that lands be made available near the town for those who worked there. This in no way deterred the Presbyterian Church, and the Reverend Baird renewed his appeals to Ottawa.[41]

Another departmental review began. Inspector Chisholm wrote that there were then only twenty-five people in five families at the reserve, and that an additional twenty-one families numbering eighty-seven individuals lived near the town. The latter he reported as being well-dressed and earning "a rather good livelihood." They were "perfectly satisfied with their present condition, and could not easily be induced to remove to a reserve. The prospect of assistance in the way of implements and cattle has little weight with them. They like the prompt cash return which at present they realize from their labour, as compared with the slower returns from farming and stock-raising. There is no immediate prospect of any of these Indians removing voluntarily to the reserve."[42]

Sam Bray suggested that the department temporarily set aside the two sections to the north of Round Plain for the use of the Dakota. If enough of the Indians near the town moved to the reserve, the land could then be permanently added. Secretary McLean accepted this recommendation.[43]

It would seem that the departmental admonition against house construction and extensive cultivation was effective for a number of years after 1894. By 1895, there were only seven stables and one house built. Most of the Dakota lived year-round under canvas. Only potatoes had been planted, but using their primitive department-issue tools, the people had harvested over 110 tons of hay and transported it to town for sale. Almost all able-bodied men and women had returned to working in the town. At this time, the workers were making a sixteen mile trip to and from town, most of them travelling on foot.

No policy decision had been made by 1896, so the Dakota acted on their own. By the summer of that year, six houses had been built, and their four acres of rootcrops had increased to thirty-five acres of gardens and grain crops. All fields were fenced and well tended. Most income came from the sale of hay and wood in town, and from pay for their labour, while those Dakota living near the town relied solely upon the sale of labour. Agent Keith reported that the Dakota at the reserve were doing their field work in common, with each household having a share of the produce. This was totally unacceptable to Indian Commissioner Reed, and he insisted that the Dakota be compelled to work their fields and plant their gardens as individual farmers.[44]

The resident farmer at the Sturgeon Lake Cree Reserve had been ordered to visit the Dakota every two weeks, but he had not done so for more than two years. He found the distance between the reserves to be too great for a one-day trip. Agent Keith was ordered to see that the Dakota got the instruction they needed. As an incentive for greater effort, Keith stopped giving the Dakota the rations they had been assured when they moved away from town. This forced the people to seek more work in town in order to subsist. Such a pattern caused the department to complain about the slow progress in agriculture on the reserve.[45]

Even though the department considered making technology, instruction and information available to the Dakota, nothing actually materialized. A year after Keith had been ordered to see that the Sturgeon Lake instructor visited the reserve, the man had not been on the Dakota lands for more than ten minutes. The Dakota so lacked implements and information that they neither owned nor knew how to use a flail to thresh the small grain crops they had planted. They were cutting their grains with scythes and feeding it to their livestock in the stook. As it was, those Dakota living near and working in the town were much better off. As time passed and the difference between those living at the reserve and those at Little Red River became increasingly obvious, Agent Keith met increasing resistance to any suggestion that all the Dakota move to the reserve. Still, the department continued to press the idea over the years.[46]

Unknown to the Dakota, since it was never discussed with them, the department entered into a protracted struggle to retain the two sections of land to the north that were temporarily reserved for the Dakota. For the three years that the temporary reserve was to last, the land went unused and unoccupied; neither the Dakota nor their agent had been notified that they could use the land. A squatter moved onto the land to cut hay for sale. Later, the Indian agent at Carlton stated that the land was too poor for the Dakota to farm, and then applied for homestead rights to the land himself. David Laird insisted that the land be retained for the Dakota, but then the Department of the Interior insisted that the Department of Indian Affairs purchase the lands from the Crown, a totally new concept in the management of Indian lands that was only applied to the Dakota. The Indian department, however, had abandoned the promise that the two groups of Dakota would not be obliged to live together, and had come to accept the idea that the Dakota would have to leave the vicinity of the town "in the public interest." Reluctantly, the Department of the Interior extended the temporary reserve.[47]

In 1905, the nineteen Dakota families living at the Little Red River attempted to purchase their own land through the Dominion Lands Office. Chisholm reported that they wanted eighty acres of land, which was evaluated at less than $1 an acre. However, the land they wanted was adjacent to lands set aside for a city park, and this made the Dakota's selection "so objectionable as to be almost out of the question." Chisholm concluded, "It does not appear to be in the interest either of themselves or of the white community that they should continue to live in such a degraded condition in such proximity to the city." Chisholm meant that while the Dakota made a good living for themselves, they had little furniture or other trappings of civilization. He recommended most strongly that the Dakota not be encouraged to remain near the town. Rather, they should be relocated on the reserve, as three families had done the year previous.[48]

The department tried several tactics to induce the Dakota to leave the town. David Laird suggested that they be offered all the material help they needed to start farming on the reserve. The department considered moving the people to White Cap Reserve near Saskatoon and offered to keep the two groups separate if the town Dakota took up the two sections held as a temporary reserve. All of this was to no avail; the Dakota firmly refused to leave the town and their jobs.[49]

In the summer of 1905, the Indian department finally concluded that the Dakota could not be forced away from the town, and a new effort was put into buying the Macdowall lands they occupied. These negotiations were not discussed with the

Dakota. The department strongly preferred to have the Dakota move to the reserve, and to suggest that the government might buy the lands they wanted would only encourage them to stay where they were. A tremendous amount of effort and paper was dedicated to this task. At last, just as it seemed that the purchase would go through, Inspector Chisholm told the Dakota of the department's plans. He said that while the government was going to buy the land, the Dakota should not get the idea that the lands would be theirs. They would not be disturbed in the occupation of it, but it was not a reserve. Chisholm reported: "They seem grateful for the action of the Government in buying the land in order that they may have the privilege of living upon it; but this does not entirely satisfy them. They want to own the land themselves, either as a band or as individuals, and to hold the title in their own name."[50]

The Dakota had been involved because the cost for the land had been approved in the budget of 1905–06 but, due to bureaucratic delays, the appropriation was lost.[51]

Given the poor quality of their land, the total lack of capital, implements and seedstock, and the inadequacies of instruction and information, the Dakota had little choice but to again restructure their economy on the reserve. By 1903, the people had begun to reduce their acreage in grain crops and instead increased the exploitation and sale of firewood and berries, along with whatever hay they could spare. In 1902, the department had given the band a few cows, and in 1903, they had twenty-two head, many of which were draught oxen. This turn to the sale of commodities greatly improved the economic circumstances of the band. Fuel, hay and foodstuffs were all in strong demand in the growing city. The agent reported that the Dakota were "industrious and steadily advancing."

By 1907, the band was no longer growing any kind of field crops, and relied solely upon the sale of commodities. Housing, clothing and furniture were all improving rapidly, and the band was independent of government aid. The cattle herd had increased to forty head, along with seventeen good horses the Dakota had purchased themselves. By 1908, the band was referred to as "the most industrious for their number of any reserve of this agency and are making good progress." Those Dakota still at the Little Red River continued to be totally independent of government aid and virtually refused to have anything whatever to do with the department's officials, preferring to make their own way through their own labour.[52]

In 1911, Archdeacon J.A. Mackay of the Diocese of Prince Albert wrote to the Department of the Interior saying that the Macdowall lands had been sold, and that the new owner wanted to know if the Dakota had some right to live there. Inspector Chisholm reported that most of the younger men were prepared to move to the reserve, but the older people preferred to remain where they were and to own their lands outright. The Dakota had applied for a homestead, but "that was plainly out of the question."[53] Chisholm concluded that if "these people were likely to become a nuisance living in the vicinity of the city, it might be advisable to compel them to occupy the reserves already set aside for the band." However, the Dakota were known to "lead moral lives and seldom use liquor, and they are all able to provide themselves with an ample supply of food and clothing here, which several of them could not do if living on the reserve." He recommended, instead, that lands be purchased for the Dakota near the town, and a new reserve be created.[54]

While the department went about the protracted business of buying marginal land near the town, the Dakota tried to impress upon the government that they did not want a reserve. However, they had dismantled their houses on the Macdowall land and were ready to move, just as winter was coming on. The Dakota finally gave up arguing the matter and moved, without permission, onto lands the department was negotiating to purchase. This was regarded as a "somewhat extraordinary" action which the department did not learn about for over six months.[55]

There were sixty people and thirty ponies on the newly acquired land, and they were using the site in much the same way as they had used the Macdowall property. They lived there during the coldest part of winter, but otherwise went where their jobs took them. Chisholm found that most of the Dakota would accept the site as a reserve, but the older men still refused the idea. Willie Gunn, the principal man, told the Inspector that "the rest of the band might do as they chose but his part, as he had paid nothing for the land, he would not ask and did not wish to have any interest in it." Gunn and several others had purchased a few acres from a farmer about ten miles northeast of the city. Even this demonstration of their wishes failed to convince the department; at Chisholm's insistence, McLean applied to have the site confirmed as a reserve.[56]

Late in 1916, Agent S.A. Miller reported on the latest of a number of attempts to take a census of the Dakota at the new site. The band refused to allow this. Miller told the Dakota that they would have no school if they did not submit to a census; the Indians replied that they did not want a school anyway. He then told them that the land would not be declared a reserve without a census; the Dakota then offered to buy the land from the department. They would get no rations if they did not provide a census; the Dakota declared that they had never received rations and did not intend to receive any. Finally, Miller gave up and decided that the Dakota were "gradually dying off, and it will only be a few years until the remaining ones could be moved back (to the other reserve), and the land disposed of."[57]

Some months later in 1917, Inspector Crombie reported that very few Indians were living on the older reserve. Tribal Historian Goodvoice says that at this time, the Dakota left the reserve and moved to the site near the city to escape the tuberculosis and influenza that had taken the lives of many. The Dakota refused to return to the reserve, so on November 14, 1917, the department went ahead with an Order in Council confirming the town site as a reserve. This did not impress the Dakota, and over the next few years, the band made further attempts to purchase their own lands, attempts that were actively discouraged by the department.[58]

By 1913, the demand for commodities sold by the Dakota had fallen off as the depression settled over the land. The band's herds had increased considerably and the Dakota were getting a significant part of their income from the sale of cattle and horses. The band had again increased grain production, and this gradually expanded in the years before World War I. During the war, the demand for labour increased, and the populations on the reserve and near the town were able to make a good living through the sale of labour, in addition to grain production and the sale of commodities. After the war, the demand for labour dropped off and the department again stepped up their attempts to have the Dakota move away from the city and onto the reserve. Goodvoice states that in the years following the war, it became increasingly difficult for the Dakota to get jobs in the city, and one by one they moved to the reserve. The population on the reserve increased to the point that lands even marginally suitable for gardens and haycrops were scarce. Agent John Weir asked that the two sections to the north of the reserve still held as a temporary reserve be permanently added to the Dakota's lands. The department struggled with this problem for over thirty years until the band approached Saskatchewan Premier T.C. Douglas and Prime Minister John Diefenbaker to request their personal intervention. The influence of these two men resulted in the lands being confirmed as a part of the Wahpeton Reserve in 1963.[59]

Over the years, the Wahpeton Band made several attempts at farming, and in the late 1970s approached a commercial scale of beef and grain production, as had the people at Portage la Prairie. Like the latter, however, these attempts were short-lived and without any notable success. These more recent attempts in the 1970s suffered from all of the disadvantages that had plagued the Dakota for the previous century and more, that is, insufficient land to provide a resource for more than a few farmers, insufficient capital to establish a competitive scale of operation, and insufficient experience with farming skills. By 1977, few individual Dakota of the Wahpeton Band could claim expertise in farming, although many were skilled at a variety of farm-related tasks. Most Dakota had, since their arrival at Prince Albert in the late 1870s, remained as sellers of labour and commodities. Many worked in the city or for farmers in the neighbourhood, and some had travelled far afield in search of jobs. For several years, a number of men went to Churchill, Manitoba, to work in the grain-handling facilities there.

In this day of rapid transportation and communication, it is no longer necessary for the Dakota to be near the city of Prince Albert in order to find work. They can hold jobs in the town and live on the reserve where they are able to maintain the lifestyle that they prefer, free from the threats of dispossession and relocation that had plagued them since their arrival in the area.

Conclusions

13

Dakota culture has been considerably transformed since the original migrants arrived in Canada as an impoverished and landless people. They did not, however, come to Canada without possessions; they brought their own labour, their knowledge and their customary way of doing things. They adapted these skills to the social and natural environment of the Canadian Northwest and went from there.

The Dakota arrived in Canada in the nineteenth century, when social and environmental change was rapidly accelerating. The natural environment, which had sustained generations of Indians and Métis, was being inexorably depleted of resources crucial to hunters, fishers, trappers and gatherers. Canadian and American nationalism was quickly imposing a new political and legal order on the northern and western plains, displacing older institutions that had allowed the aboriginal peoples to flourish. Between 1860 and 1940, there were few periods of extended stability and tranquility; all was flux.

In the winter of 1863–64, the Dakota probably formed the largest assembly of people in the entire Northwest. Experience in the previous eighteen months had taught them the dire consequences of violence and coercion, and social controls within Dakota culture restrained their impulse to seize whatever they needed. Instead, the Dakota people called upon their experience in hunting, fishing and gathering to wring a subsistence from land they had no acknowledged right to occupy. Simultaneously, they drew upon diplomatic skills and protocol to settle the question of basic rights, and established treaties with the Indians, peace with the Métis, and trust with the whites.

Gradually, as the bands established themselves in different areas each adopted innovative strategies suitable to prevailing local conditions. In general, the extent and direction of their adaptive measures depended upon whether economic strategies elaborated relationships with the natural environment or with the social environment. A continuum of strategies can be seen to range from H'damani's people, who lived closest to a customary lifestyle with only modest concessions to local labour and commodity markets, to the bands at Portage la Prairie and Prince Albert, whose members sold their labour with enthusiasm and took what little they could from nature. Between are the farmer bands that developed strategies based upon the soil and an increasing experience in commercial agriculture and individual skills useful in the local labour markets. This continuum also had implications for the changes which occurred in other parts of Dakota life.

The farmer bands at Oak River and Birdtail, and at Oak Lake, Standing Buffalo, and White Cap reserves embody features of both the hunting and the labouring peoples. With progress in their involvement in agriculture, these bands experienced increasing division of labour into task specialties. Later, the organization of labour was transformed so that individual productive effort replaced communal effort. A primary factor in this transition was the federal government's decision to impose division of what had been joint productive technology, labour and resources, shifting economic responsibility from the group as the unit of production to the household. This transformation was never complete; even today Dakota farmers rely extensively upon the donated, and sometimes hired, labour of other band members, especially kin.

True, the competitive nature of commercial agriculture would have encouraged what the Indian department imposed upon the Dakota. Still, some other communal peoples in western Canada at that time – notably the Hutterite and Mennonite neighbours of the Dakota – were able to maintain their economic structures in the face of similar pressures. In distinction, however, the farming Dakota accepted elements of the prevailing society's ideology, which their neighbours did not. The farmer bands were the first of the Dakota to embrace Euro-Canadian education, religion, language and associations. Even Wapahaska and Tatankanaje, upon taking up their reserves, requested schools, teachers and missionaries. All of these institutions were geared for Euro-Canadian models.

The Turtle Mountain and Wahpeton reserves were surveyed for subdivision, but the system was never effectively implemented. The Government of Canada could not justify the cost and effort, since these bands were not farming, and primarily used their reserves as seasonal homes. At Portage la Prairie, the reserve land held by the band was so small that subdivision was impossible. Individuation also prevailed in these bands largely because of the economic strategy they assumed. As hired workers, they placed their labour in the hands of others. Their employers decided the task, how, when and by whom it would be done, and the disposal of production. To some extent the Dakota were able to influence the level of compensation for their labour, but this compensation, in the form of cash, went into the hands of individuals who supported households at the site of employment.

The bands that were the most individuated with an extensive division of labour by task, soon became, and are today, the most stratified. As in most Canadian households, the family's standard of living varies according to the value of the skill its members have to sell. For many years, the Dakota formed the backbone of a dependable urban and rural labour force in their localities. However, the quality and content of knowledge available to the Dakota had been controlled by the Department of Indian Affairs – agents, farm instructors, missionaries, teachers, medical personnel and advisors – and these institutions lagged far behind the changes in the larger community. Moreover, the Dakota were not allowed to leave their reserves, nor was anyone but a band member allowed in. The Dakota were virtually excluded from a rapidly changing labour force. In the long run, demand for Dakota labour declined and unemployment became endemic. Since the late 1970s, responsibility for education has been returned to Indian control and already a new generation of trained Dakota youth has entered the labour market.

These problems, of course, mostly affected the Dakota who relied upon wage incomes. For many years, the farmers fared best, even though they faced their own economic perils. However, lands were limited, which in turn limited the accumulation of capital and the ability to increase production through investment. The scale of Dakota agriculture declined, and the incomes of Dakota farmers declined with it. Since the early 1980s, a variety of government programs has made capital available to Dakota farmers. They are using this capital in enterprises that require little land, considerable technology, and even more labour.

Inevitably, with historical changes in economic circumstances among the Dakota, political differences arose. Although political interests never wholly coincided even at the band level, divisions grew wider as economic strategies diverged. Competition for lands and commodities intensified on the farm reserves. Expropriation of lands and bureaucratic error made matters worse. Customary political organization and leadership was all but suppressed by the Indian department. Political expression took the form of greater or lesser degrees of alliance with the agents of external power, who gradually developed an overwhelming ability to force compliance from individuals, factions and entire bands of whom they disapproved. This process was not complete. Try as they would, no agent or succession of agents succeeded in extinguishing key elements in Dakota culture: language, family structure, ceremony, art, gambling, good-natured debate and argument, generosity, dancing and singing, and an often irreverent sense of humour are still largely intact, or are being revived from well-tended embers.

Perhaps the Dakota could have improved their economic lot by dispersing into the general population as so many other people did in western Canada. Race, of course, would have kept the Dakota distinctive in a society that, unfortunately, takes considerable notice of race. Nevertheless, the historic record indicates that the Dakota drew a line at sacrificing the last of their distinctive Dakota ways, and accepted that their economic strategies would leave them poorer, but wiser. This acceptance, as well as the versatility of Dakota economic culture, has served them well and has even allowed them to resist powerful and often brutal assaults from the national society of which they are a part.

However, new forces are at play, and it will require all of the Dakota's resourcefulness to deal with them. When the Dakota recently asked the Government of Canada about the status of their rights, they were told that since they had no history in Canada, they had no aboriginal interest in this country.[1] This is clearly in error. A firm, documented case can be made for their assertion of aboriginal and diplomatic rights.

It has been asserted and demonstrated in this book that the Dakota still thrive in Canada, although their way of life has changed considerably since 1862. As long as the Dakota were able to guide their own pace and direction of change, they were able to defend their culture and maintain their band and household economies. Recent thought and debate on matters of aboriginal rights has been distilled into the rubric of "Indian self-government," by which is generally meant a people's right to manage and nurture their own lands, resources and people in ways that are culturally comfortable. The history of the Dakota is virtually a demonstration of the validity of this concept. No doubt, not every aspect of Dakota survival strategies was a success, but only when the Dakota were independent to act within the general framework of Canadian law were they able to flourish economically and culturally. When constrained by law, they faltered. Nothing in the historical record suggests that the Dakota would fail either themselves or Canadian society through the exercise of their rights.

Notes

ABBREVIATIONS

PRO Public Record Office, London, England
PAC Public Archives of Canada, Ottawa
HBCA Hudson's Bay Company Archives, Winnipeg, Manitoba
PAM Public Archives of Manitoba, Winnipeg, Manitoba
SAB Saskatchewan Archives Board, Regina, Saskatchewan
PRSHC Papers Relating to the Sioux, House of Commons, London, England
DIAND Department of Indian Affairs and Northern Development

CHAPTER 1

1 Louis Hennepin *A New Discovery of a Vast Country in America* (Toronto 1974) 241-275
2 George A. Lothson *Burial Mounds of the Mille Lacs Area* masters thesis, University of Minnesota, 1972; E. Johnson "The Arvilla Complex" Minnesota *Prehistoric Archaeology* no 9 (1973); D. Arthurs "Sandy Lake Ware in Northwestern Ontario: a Distributional Study" *Archaefacts* 5 nos 2-3 (1978); R.S. MacNeish *An Introduction to the Archaeology of Southeastern Manitoba* (Ottawa 1958); S. Saylor "The 1977 Season at Wanipigow Lake (EGKX-1)" *Archaefacts* 5 nos 2-3 (1978)
3 M.G.M. Rajnovich and C.S. Reid "Selkirk and Clearwater Lake Ceramics on Lake of the Woods: An Overview" *Archaefacts* 5 nos 2-3 (1978)
4 J. Warkentin and R.I. Ruggles *Historical Atlas of Manitoba* (Winnipeg 1970)
5 A.J. Ray *Indians in the Fur Trade: Their Role as Hunters, Trappers and Middlemen in the Lands Southwest of Hudson Bay* (Toronto 1974) 14-15
6 M. Cook and S. Mirasty, personal communication (1977)
7 C. Ballantyne, personal communication (1978)
8 C.A. Bishop and E.M. Smith "Early Historic Populations in Northwestern Ontario: Archaeological and Ethnological Interpretations" *American Antiquity* 40, no 1 (1975) 54-63
9 J. Carver *Travels Through the Interior Part of North America in the Years 1766, 1767 and 1768* (Toronto 1974) 81-113
10 R.W. Meyer *History of the Santee Sioux: United States Policy on Trial* (Lincoln 1967) 86
11 Dickson Papers PAM
12 Hull to Eustis 08/04/1812 PRO CO42 147

13 Brock to Prevost 12/03/1811 PRO CO42 146; Prevost to Liverpool 01/13/1812 ibid; Prevost to Liverpool 01/22/1812 ibid; Prevost to Liverpool 05/16/1812 ibid
14 Bathurst to Prevost 08/17/1812 PRO CO42 197
15 Ibid
16 Prevost to Bathurst 08/17/1812 ibid; Prevost to Bathurst 09/22/1812 ibid; Prevost to Bathurst 09/24/1812 ibid
17 Prevost to Warner 10/05/1812 PRO CO42 147; Bathurst to Prevost 10/11/1812 ibid; Prevost to Bathurst 10/05/1812 ibid
18 Bathurst to Prevost 12/09/1812 PRO CO43 23
19 Dickson Papers PAM
20 Bathurst to Prevost 05/15/1813 PRO CO43 23; Prevost to Bathurst 03/19/1813 PRO CO42 150
21 Prevost to Bathurst 09/22/1812 PRO CO42 151
22 E.A. Cruikshank *Documents Relating to the Invasion of Canada, and the Surrender of Detroit, 1812* (New York 1912) 153
23 Prevost to Bathurst 09/22/1812 PRO CO42 151
24 Committee of Trade at Montreal to Nathan Acheson 10/22/1813 PRO CO43 155
25 Bathurst to Prevost 12/15/1813 PRO CO43 23; Inglis and Bainbridge to Bathurst 01/31/1814 PRO CO42 159; Prevost to Bathurst 02/08/1814 PRO CO42 156; Prevost to Bathurst 07/10/1814 PRO CO42 157
26 Prevost to Bathurst 07/10/1814 PRO CO42 157
27 Ibid
28 Prevost to Bathurst 07/10/1814 PRO CO42 157
29 McDouall to Prevost 07/20/1814 ibid
30 McDouall to Drummond 07/16/1814 ibid
31 McDouall to Prevost 08/14/1814 ibid
32 McDouall to Drummond 10/11/1814 ibid
33 Prevost to Bathurst 11/05/1814 ibid
34 Bulger to McDouall 11/14/1814 PAC MG19 E5
35 Bulger to McDouall 03/10/1815 ibid
36 McDouall to Bulger 02/26/1815 ibid
37 McDouall to Bulger 02/26/1815 ibid; Bulger to McDouall 04/15/1815 ibid
38 McDouall to Bulger 03/19/1815(a) PAC MG19 E5
39 McDouall to Bulger 03/19/1815(b) ibid
40 Ibid
41 Bulger to Renville 04/08/1815 PRO CO42 162
42 Bulger to McDouall 04/15/1815 PAC MG 19 E5; Clarke to Bulger 04/16/1815 ibid; McDouall to Bulger 04/25/1815 ibid
43 McDouall to Bulger 05/01/1815 PRO CO42 162
44 McDouall to Bulger 05/05/1815 ibid; Bulger to McDouall 05/07/1815 PRO CO42 162; Bulger to Clarke 05/23/1815 ibid
45 D. Robinson *A History of the Dakota or Sioux Indians* (Minneapolis 1974) 100
46 D. Robinson *History of the Dakota*; S.R. Riggs *Mary and I; Forty Years with the Sioux* (Williamstown 1971); Meyer *History of the Santee Sioux*; S.R. Riggs *Tahkoo Wakan* (New York 1972); *Annuity Lists of the Lower Sioux* United States Bureau of Indian Affairs (1859)
47 L.F. Hubbard and R.J. Holcombe *Minnesota in Three Centuries* (St Paul 1908); E. Van Dyke Robinson *Economic History of Agriculture in Minnesota* (Minneapolis 1917)

CHAPTER 2

1 W.B. Cheadle *Cheadle's Journal of a Trip Across Canada, 1862-1863* (Edmonton 1971) 54
2 Anon. 02/28/1863 PAM MG19 A28
3 Lyons to Seward 06/03/1863 PRO CO42 649; Lyons to Russell 06/03/1863 ibid; Hammond to Monck 07/06/1863 ibid; Newcastle to Monck 07/10/1863 ibid
4 Dallas to Fraser 12/11/1863 PRSHC 4
5 Dallas to Fraser 12/18/1863 PRSHC 4-5
6 Mactavish to Fraser 12/25/1863 PRSHC 5
7 Lyons to Rogers 01/09/1864 PRO CO42 645; Pope to Kelton 01/12/1864 ibid
8 Pope to Kelton ibid
9 Seward to Lyons 01/21/1864 ibid
10 Dallas to Fraser 01/15/1864 PRSHC 6
11 Seward to Lyons 01/21/1864 PRO CO42 645
12 Head to Rogers 02/05/1864 PRSHC 2; Hammond to Rogers 02/09/1864 PRO CO42 645
13 Dallas to Fraser 02/24/1864 PRSHC 13
14 Fraser to Dallas 02/26/1864 PRSHC 6
15 Canadian News 03/03/1864 PRSHC 6
16 Dallas to Hatch 04/07/1864 PRSHC 14
17 Dallas to Rogers 03/12/1864 PRSHC 15
18 Dallas to Rogers 03/16/1864 PRSHC 16
19 Dallas to Head 03/24/1864 PRSHC 17
20 Elliot to Head 03/24/1864 PRSHC 9; Head to Fortesque 04/11/1864 ibid; *Montreal Telegraph and Daily Commercial Advertiser* 04/13/1864 PRSHC 15; Hansard's Parliamentary Debates, Commons Victoria 27 1864 174
21 In 1980, during a wacipe at Fort Totten, North Dakota, an elderly woman from Rosebud Reservation lamented that it was impossible for her to meet Dakota people from Canada. As she understood it, it was illegal for Dakota of either country to cross the international boundary, and it was especially dangerous for the Canadian Dakota, who were still being sought for the crimes of 1862.
22 Ross Papers 08/19/64 PAM MG2 C14; 06/11/1864 ibid
23 Hill to Cameron 01/26/1874 PAC RG10 3607 2988
24 Fort Ellice Journal, 1868-1869 HBCA B63 a/10
25 Fort Ellice Journal, 1871-1872 HBCA B63 a/11

CHAPTER 3

1 Archibald to Howe 01/25/1872 PAC RG10 3604 2174
2 Spragge to Howe 02/06/1872 ibid
3 Ibid
4 Ibid
5 Ibid
6 Ibid
7 Spragge to Anon. 06/15/1872 PAC RG10 3577 422; McKay to Archibald 06/24/1872 PAC RG10 3596 1303
8 Simpson to Spragge 07/02/1872 PAC RG10 3596 1303; Spragge to Anon. 01/06/1873 PAC RG10 3577 422
9 Morris to Howe 12/16/1872 PAC RG10 3577 422
10 Simpson to Howe 12/15/1872 ibid
11 Spragge to Anon. 06/15/1872 ibid

12 Spragge to Anon. 12/31/1872 PAC RG10 3583 1128
13 Order in Council 01/04/1873 ibid; Spragge to Anon. 01/06/1873 PAC RG10 3577 422
14 Howe to Morris 01/08/1873 Morris Papers PAM 49; Simpson to Howe 02/17/1873 PAC RG10 3577 422; St. John to Howe 03/01/1873 ibid
15 Order in Council 1723 PAC RG10 2 25
16 Morris to Howe 06/07/1873 PAC RG10 3603 2118
17 St. John to Spragge 05/04/1873 PAC RG10 3577 422; St. John to Spragge 05/05/1873 ibid; Morris to Macdonald 06/06/1873 Morris Papers PAM 253; Morris to Dawson 06/07/1873 Morris Papers 254; Dawson to Morris 06/07/1873 Morris Papers 257; Morris to Provencher 06/19/1873 Morris Papers PAM 282; Morris to Laird 07/04/1873 1873 PAC RG10 3605 2905; Campbell to Morris 08/05/1873 ibid; Order in Council 08/13/1873 PAC RG10 3577 422
18 Provencher to Campbell 08/27/1873 PAC RG10 3603 2118
19 Cameron to Morris 11/24/1873 Morris Papers PAM 563
20 Morris to Minister of the Interior 01/02/1874 PAC RG10 3603 2118
21 Morris to Minister of the Interior 02/10/1874 ibid; Meredith to Morris 01/14/1874 ibid
22 Hill to Cameron 01/26/1874 PAC RG10 3607 2988
23 Ibid
24 Hill to Ward 04/15/1874 Morris Papers 715 PAM; Cameron to Morris 04/13/1874 ibid
25 Cameron to Morris 04/29/1874 Morris Papers 718 PAM
26 Hill to Cameron 05/18/1874 Morris Papers 751 PAM; Cameron to Morris 05/30/1874 ibid
27 Council of the Northwest Minutes 03/16/1874 1873 PAC RG15 134 33; Dennis to Anon. 04/21/1874 1873 PAC RG10 3609 3289; Morris to Meredith 04/25/1874 ibid; Order in Council 04/27/1874 ibid; Meredith to Morris 04/29/1874 ibid
28 White Eagle and Antoine to Morris 04/30/1874 Morris Papers 721 PAM
29 Ibid; Morris to Laird 05/01/1874 1873 PAC RG10 3609 3289
30 When Morris writes of all the Dakota, or more probably all their chiefs, having signed the agreement, he was referring only to those with whom he was personally acquainted, since no mention is made of Mahpiyahdinape, Wapahaska, Weeokeah or Chaote
31 Morris to Minister of the Interior 07/07/1874 PAC RG10 3609 3289
32 Laird to Morris 07/09/1874 ibid
33 St. John to Morris 07/16/1874 PAC RG10 3611 3679
34 Ibid
35 Morris to Secretary of State 10/03/1874 PAM Morris Papers 852
36 Ibid
37 This pipe is now in the Royal Ontario Museum, Toronto
38 Morris to Laird 09/21/1874 PAC RG10 3609 3289
39 Wagner to Laird 10/03/1874 Morris Papers 352 PAM
40 St. John to Laird 10/08/1874 PAC RG10 3609 3289
41 Ibid
42 Ibid
43 Morris to Laird 10/21/1874 PAC RG10 3613 4048
44 Dennis to Laird 11/04/1874 ibid
45 Minister of the interior to the Privy Council 11/10/1874 PAC RG10 3609 3289; Order in Council 11/12/1874 ibid; Dennis to Laird 11/04/1874 PAC RG10 3613 4048
46 Provencher to Laird 06/03/1875 PAC RG10 3609 3289
47 Morris to Laird 06/14/1875 ibid
48 Ibid
49 Ibid
50 Provencher to Laird 06/26/1875 ibid; Meredith to Provencher 07/13/1875 ibid; David Laird reported in

the sessional papers that a formal surrender had been taken for the reserve at the Little Saskatchewan, but he was mistaken. Sessional Papers 39 Victoria no 9a 1876 11
51 Christie to Laird 10/07/1875 PAC RG10 3625 5489; Morris to White Cap and Standing Buffalo 10/11/1875 PAC RG10 3625 5494
52 Laird to Morris 11/25/1875 SAB AL114
53 Inhabitants of Manitoba to Morris 06/13/1873 PAC RG10 3577 422
54 03/08/1875 William Taylor Papers MG8 B68 PAM
55 Fort Ellice Journal 1874-1875 HBCA B63/a/13 PAM

CHAPTER 4

1 Wagner to Mills 07/15/1875 Archives, Federation of Saskatchewan Indians, Regina
2 Morris to Laird 01/07/1875 PAC RG10 3623 5068
3 McKenzie to Morris 07/26/1875 ibid
4 Ibid
5 Morris to Laird 08/10/1875 ibid
6 Morris to Laird 10/11/1875 PAC RG10 3625 5494; Laird to Morris 02/03/1876 Morris Papers 1203 PAM; Meredith to Morris 10/22/1875 PAC RG10 3625 5494
7 Laird to Morris 04/25/1876 PAC RG10 3623 5068; Scott to Laird 04/24/1876 ibid; Meredith to Morris 05/31/1876 ibid; Meredith to Morris 05/31/1876 ibid; Morris to Meredith 06/02/1876 ibid
8 Morris to Laird 06/24/1876 ibid; Morris to Laird 06/29/1876 ibid
9 McKenzie to Morris 07/26/1876 Morris Papers 1293 PAM. There are two versions of this report, the one cited here and another, which appears to be a copy prepared in Morris's office for transmission to Ottawa. The latter differs in some small details. (McKenzie to Morris 07/29/1876 PAC RG10 3623 5068)
10 McKenzie mistakenly identifies Wambdiska as being at the mouth of the Little Saskatchewan River, an error which was corrected in the version sent to Ottawa
11 Sinclair to Meredith 02/21/1877 PAC RG10 3642 7684; Morris to Laird 03/13/1877 ibid
12 Ibid. David Mills reported in the Sessional Papers that after the Dakota refused to aid the Tetonwon against the Americans, "they received the thanks of the Queen, who was pleased to direct that they should be officially informed of her gratification at this evidence of their loyalty and attachment." There is no documentary evidence that this message was ever communicated to the Dakota, nor do Tribal Historians recall such a message. (Sessional Papers 40 Victoria A1877 no 11 14)
13 Morris to Laird 05/21/1877 PAC RG10 3643 7684
14 Morris to Laird 11/02/1876 PAC RG10 3655 8933. The "Sioux Minister" to whom Morris refers was Solomon Tookanshaecheye, a close relative of Mahpiyahdinape. Solomon first arrived at Fort Ellice in June, 1875, and returned the next year at Mahpiyahdinape's written invitation. The missionary was supported by the American and Canadian Presbyterian churches. He remained in Canada until 1880, when he returned to the Sisseton Agency, South Dakota. Riggs *Tahkoo Wakan* (1972) 339
15 McKenzie to Morris 11/07/1877 PAC RG10 3655 8965
16 Morris to Laird 12/15/1877 ibid
17 McKenzie to Meredith 12/17/1877 PAC RG10 3655 8933; Meredith to McKenzie 01/04/1878 ibid; Mahpiyahdinape to Cauchon 01/19/1878 ibid; Laird to Graham 03/08/1878 ibid
18 Robertson and Bryce to Mills 05/23/1878 PAC RG10 3655 8933; Mills to Robertson and Bryce 05/28/1878 ibid
19 Robertson to Nixon 05/30/1878 ibid
20 Nixon to Meredith 05/30/1878 ibid; Meredith to Morris 06/26/1878 ibid; Morris to Meredith 07/02/1878 ibid
21 Graham to Mills 07/20/1878 PAC RG10 3655 8933; Vankoughnet to Mills 07/22/1878 ibid

22 These varieties of corn are still grown at Birdtail and Oak River
23 Herchmer to Vankoughnet 09/24/1878 PAC RG10 3668 10506; Vankoughnet to Macdonald 10/22/1878 ibid
24 Herchmer to Vankoughnet 12/16/1878 ibid
25 Vankoughnet to Herchmer 12/30/1878 PAC RG10 3668 10506; Herchmer to Vankoughnet 01/06/1879 ibid; Vankoughnet to Herchmer 01/13/1879 ibid; Vankoughnet to Nixon 01/13/1879 ibid
26 Herchmer to Vankoughnet 01/22/1879 PAC RG10 3668 10506; Vankoughnet to Herchmer 02/04/1879 ibid; Herchmer to Vankoughnet 02/10/1879 ibid
27 Cameron to Morris 02/03/1875 Morris Papers 922 PAM
28 Mills to Morris 03/12/1877 Morris Papers 1427 PAM; Morris to Mills 02/26/1877 PAC RG10 3644 7785-1; Meredith to Anon. 03/09/1877 ibid
29 Morris to Mills 03/24/1877 PAC RG10 3644 7785-1; Mills to Provencher 03/12/1877 ibid; Provencher to Mills 05/04/1877 ibid
30 Vankoughnet to Mills 06/05/1877 PAC RG10 3644 7785-1
31 Morris to Mills 06/20/1877 ibid; Mills to Morris 06/20/1877 ibid; Mills to Provencher 06/23/1877 ibid
32 Morris to Mills 06/23/1877 PAC RG10 3644 7785-1; Morris to Laird 06/26/1877 ibid
33 Morris to Meredith 10/01/1877 PAC RG10 3644 7785-1; Morris to Meredith 10/02/1877 ibid; Meredith to Anon. 08/29/1877 ibid; Morris to Mills 10/25/1877 ibid; Dennis to Meredith 10/23/1877 ibid; Meredith to Mills 11/02/1877 ibid; Order in Council 10/09/1877 ibid; Mills to Morris 11/13/1877; Mills to Provencher 10/13/1877 PAC RG10 3644 7785-1; Vankoughnet to Wagner 10/14/1877 ibid; Dennis to Vankoughnet 07/03/1878 ibid; Vankoughnet to Graham 07/24/1878 ibid; Graham to Vankoughnet 08/08/1878 ibid; Vankoughnet to Dennis 08/23/1878 ibid
34 R.E. Ankli "Farm-making Costs in the 1850s" *Agricultural History* 48 no 4 (1974) 51-74; R.M. Finley "A Budgetting Approach to the Question of Homestead Size on the Great Plains" *Agricultural History* 42 no 2 (1968) 109-114

CHAPTER 5

1 Young Chief to lieutenant governor of Manitoba nd PAC RG10 3753 30576
2 Graham to Macdonald 11/02/1881 Archives, Federation of Saskatchewan Indians, Regina; Macdonald to Graham 11/15/1881 PAC RG10 3770 33400; Macdonald to Graham 11/21/1881 ibid; Herchmer to Graham 11/27/1881 Archives, Federation of Saskatchewan Indians, Regina; Herchmer to Graham 01/05/1882 PAC RG10 3770 33800; Spiers to McTavish 06/19/1882 PAC RG10 3608 3030
3 Markle to Dewdney 09/04/1885 PAC RG10 3720 23368
4 Herchmer to Macdonald 09/27/1881 Sessional Papers 45 Victoria no 6 A1882 68
5 Sessional Papers 47 Victoria no 4 A1884; Sessional Papers 48 Victoria no 3 A1885 200
6 *Birtle Observer* 02/06/1885
7 Herchmer to Vankoughnet 02/07/1885 PAC RG10 3706 18470; Vankoughnet to Herchmer 02/26/1885 ibid
8 Peterson to Macdonald 08/09/1885 PAC RG10 3719 22817
9 Herchmer to Vankoughnet 11/29/1885 ibid
10 *Toronto Globe* 12/05/1885
11 Vankoughnet to Dewdney 12/05/1885 PAC RG10 3719 22817; Dewdney to Macdonald 12/10/1885 ibid; Vankoughnet to Dewdney 12/31/1885 ibid
12 Taylor to Reed 02/25/1887 PAC RG10 3719 22817
13 McGibbon to Reed 07/02/1887 PAC RG10 3782 40468-2
14 Markle to Reed 07/02/1887 PAC RG10 3783 40470; Markle to Reed 10/30/1887 ibid; Markle to Reed 12/09/1887 ibid; Markle to Reed 12/31/1887 ibid; Markle to Reed 02/14/1888 ibid; Markle to Reed 03/01/1888 ibid

15 McGibbon to Reed 07/18/1888 PAC RG10 3803 50774-1
16 Markle to Reed 07/18/1888 PAC RG10 3783 40470; Hodges to Markle 09/??/1888 PAC RG10 3598 1361; Burman to Markle 09/22/1888 ibid; Markle to Reed 10/01/1888 ibid; Reed to Markle 10/09/1888 ibid
17 Markle to Reed 01/02/1889 PAC RG10 3783 40420; Markle to Reed 02/02/1889 ibid; Markle to Reed 03/04/1889 ibid
18 Markle to Reed 11/02/1889 PAC RG10 3783 40420
19 Markle to Reed 12/03/1889 ibid

CHAPTER 6

1 Markle to Reed 01/15/1890 PAC RG10 3783 40470; Markle to Reed 02/03/1890 ibid
2 Markle to Reed 03/04/1890 PAC RG10 3783 40470
3 Markle to Reed 04/01/1890 ibid
4 Markle to Reed 04/03/1890 PAC RG10 3783 40470; Markle to Reed 05/06/1890 ibid; Markle to Reed 05/31/1890 ibid; Markle to Reed 07/02/1890 ibid
5 Markle to Reed 09/02/1890 PAC RG10 3783 40470; Markle to Reed 10/01/1890 ibid; Markle to Reed 11/01/1890 ibid; Wadsworth to Reed 09/07/1890 PAC RG10 3844 73406-2
6 Ibid
7 Markle to Reed 12/02/1890 PAC RG10 3783 40470; Markle to Reed 01/03/1891 ibid
8 Wadsworth to Reed 09/07/1891 PAC RG10 3859 82250-2
9 Ibid
10 Ibid
11 Ibid
12 Markle to Reed 02/01/1891 PAC RG10 3869 88145
13 Markle to Forget 11/25/1893 PAC RG10 3908 107243; *Virden Chronicle* nd ibid
14 Markle to Forget 11/25/1893 PAC RG10 3908 107243
15 Markle to Reed 04/02/1892 PAC RG10 3869 88145
16 Markle to Reed 06/01/1892 ibid
17 Ibid
18 Reed to McLean 10/08/1892 ibid
19 Markle to Reed 07/06/1892 ibid; Markle to Reed 07/30/1892 ibid; Markle to Reed 10/20/1892 ibid
20 Wadsworth to Reed 10/20/1892 PAC RG10 3895 97456
21 Pereira to Vankoughnet 04/20/1889 PAC RG10 7765 27106-2; Wheatley to McLean 07/1 /1909 ibid; Keyes to McLean 09/29/1909 ibid
22 Manitoba Crop Bulletin 34 07/01/1892
23 Wadsworth to Reed 10/20/1892 PAC RG10 3895 97456
24 Ibid
25 Forget to Reed 10/02/1893 PAC RG10 3908 107243
26 Markle to Reed 12/05/1892 PAC RG10 3869 88145
27 Wadsworth to Reed 10/23/1893 PAC RG10 3895 97456
28 Scott to Forget 10/28/1893 PAC RG10 3908 107243; Reed to Markle 10/30/1893 ibid
29 Wadsworth to Forget 11/02/1893 PAC RG10 3908 107243; Forget to Scott 11/02/1893 ibid
30 Hartland to Markle 11/11/1893 PAC RG10 3908 107243; Markle to Reed 11/11/1893 ibid
31 Markle to Reed 11/25/1893 PAC RG10 3908 107243; Hartland to Reed 11/27/1893 ibid
32 Markle to Reed 12/08/1893 PAC RG10 3908 107243; Reed to Forget 12/12/1893 ibid
33 Markle to Forget 12/13/1893 PAC RG10 3908 107243; Reed to Forget 12/18/1893 ibid; Markle to Reed 12/18/1893 ibid; Markle to Reed 12/19/1893 ibid; Markle to Reed 12/21/1893 ibid; Markle to Reed 12/23/1893 ibid; Markle to Forget 12/22/1893 ibid; Markle to Reed 12/27/1893 ibid; Markle to

Forget 12/29/1893 ibid; Thompson to Reed 01/02/1894 ibid; Forget to Scott 01/04/1894 ibid; Chambers to Thompson 01/04/1894 ibid
34 *Virden Chronicle* 01/14/1894
35 Reed to Thompson 01/12/1894 PAC RG10 3908 107243; Thompson to Reed 01/14/1894 ibid; Reed to Forget 01/24/1894 ibid; Thompson to Reed 01/15/1894 ibid; Chambers to Thompson 01/20/1894 ibid; Thompson to Reed 01/25/1894 ibid
36 Markle to Daly 09/20/1894 PAC RG10 3937 120445; Hunter to Reed 11/07/1894 ibid; Reed to Markle 11/14/1894 ibid; Reed to Forget 11/28/1894 ibid
37 Wadsworth to Reed 12/26/1894 PAC RG10 3908 107243; a small lake had been set aside for the band to discourage fishing in the Assiniboine River. Markle to Forget 09/04/1894 PAC RG10 7765 27106-2; Pereira to Reed 10/03/1894 ibid; Order in Council 10/30/1894 PAC RG2 618
38 Wadsworth to Reed 12/26/1894 PAC RG10 3908 107243
39 Reed to Markle 02/28/1895 ibid
40 Reed to Markle 02/28/1895 ibid; Stevenson to Daly 12/29/1894 ibid; Markle to Daly 12/12/1894 ibid; Reed to Forget 12/14/1894 ibid; Markle to Reed 01/04/1895 ibid; Reed to Stevenson 01/28/1895 ibid; Reed to Daly 01/28/1895 ibid; Daly to Parr 01/28/1895 ibid; Daly to Stevenson 01/28/1895 ibid; Reed to Forget 02/28/1895 ibid; Parr to Daly 05/03/1895 ibid; Reed to Daly 05/16/1895 ibid
41 Sessional Papers 58 Victoria no 12 A1895 pt 1 59-60
42 McGibbon to Reed 12/14/1896 PAC RG10 3895 97456
43 McLeod to Reed 06/09/1896 PAC RG10 3598 1361
44 Unfortunately, none of Mahpiyahdinape's manuscript has been found
45 McGibbon to Reed 01/21/1897 PAC RG10 3895 97456
46 Forget to McLean 08/08/1897 Archives, Federation of Saskatchewan Indians, Regina
47 Mclean to Forget 08/16/1898 ibid; Pereira to McLean 10/08/1898 ibid

CHAPTER 7

1 Wheatley to McLean 02/04/1901 PAC RG10 3811 55152-7
2 McLean to Wheatley 02/26/1901 ibid; McLean to Laird 02/26/1901 ibid; Orde to McLean 03/14/1901 Archives, Federation of Saskatchewan Indians, Regina
3 Vankoughnet to the governor general 02/16/1898 PAC RG10 7778 2133.3.2; Markle to McLean 06/09/1900 ibid
4 Markle to McLean 08/22/1900 PAC RG10 7740 23133-3
5 Bray to McLean 08/29/1900 ibid
6 Macdonald to Forget 07/12/1898 PAC RG10 3985 173735; Forget to McLean 07/23/1898 ibid; McLean to Forget 07/27/1898 ibid
7 Letter of agreement 05/25/1901 PAC RG10 3985 173735
8 Sessional Papers 3-4 Edward VII no 27 A1904 207
9 Sessional Papers 64 Victoria no 27 A1901 131; Sessional Papers 2-3 Edward VII no 27 A1903 121
10 Sessional Papers 4-5 Edward VII no 27 A1905; Hanska to Indian Department 02/23/1905 Archives, Federation of Saskatchewan Indians, Regina
11 Wheatley to Laird 02/26/1904 Archives, Federation of Saskatchewan Indians, Regina
12 McKenna to McLean 03/08/1904 ibid; Roe to McLean 02/10/1905 ibid; McLean to Flannery 03/15/1905 ibid
13 Waste to Laird 08/09/1906 PAC RG10 3569 95-2; Laird to Wheatley 08/14/1906 ibid; Wheatley to Laird 08/14/1906 ibid
14 Sessional Papers 5-6 Edward VII no 27 A1906 94
15 Sessional Papers 6-7 Edward VII no 27 A1907 78-79; Sessional Papers 7-8 Edward VII no 27 A1908 94-95; Yeomans to Wheatley 09/01/1906 PAC RG10 3569 95-2

16 Marlatt to Laird 05/13/1907 PAC RG10 3569 95-2
17 Thunder to Laird 07/16/1907 ibid; Laird to Thunder 07/18/1907 ibid
18 Hollies to Laird 07/01/1907 PAC RG10 23
19 Hollies to Laird 07/13/1907 PAC RG10 3569 95-2; Hollies to Laird 09/03/1907 ibid; Hollies to Laird 10/01/1907 ibid; Ben to Laird 09/17/1907 ibid; Laird to Wheatley 09/19/1907 ibid; Wheatley to Laird 10/18/1907 ibid; Hollies to Laird 11/01/1907 ibid; Hollies to Laird 12/02/1907 ibid
20 Pedley to Laird 08/27/1907 PAC RG10 3569 95-2; Laird to Hollies 09/03/1907 ibid
21 Hollies to Laird 09/07/1907 PAC RG10 3569 95-2
22 Hollies to Laird 07/02/1908 ibid
23 Ibid
24 Hollies to Laird 12/21/1907 ibid. The "fight" to which Hollies refers was the effort he put into depriving the Turtle Mountain Band of their reserve. At the time of his letter, he was sure he had won that battle and could feel magnanimous
25 Laird to Hollies 12/27/1907 ibid
26 Hollies to Laird 12/27/1907 ibid; Hollies to Laird 04/24/1908 ibid
27 Hollies to Laird 02/04/1908 PAC RG10 3569 95-2
28 Bearbull to Laird 03/10/1908 PAC RG10 3569 95-2; Laird to Bearbull 03/13/1908 ibid
29 Hollies to Laird 10/01/1908 PAC RG10 3569 95-2A
30 Hollies to Laird 08/16/1908 ibid
31 Laird to Hollies 08/18/1908 ibid
32 McLean to Pereira 05/04/1909 PAC RG10 3644 7785-1; Hollies to McLean 09/01/1909 ibid; Hollies to McLean 09/08/1909 ibid; McLean to Howe 09/18/1909 ibid; McLean to Hollies 09/20/1909 ibid; Hollies to McLean 09/20/1909 ibid; Howe to McLean 09/21/1909 ibid; McLean to Keyes 09/29/1909 ibid; Keyes to McLean 09/29/1909 ibid; Stewart to Hollies 10/19/1909 ibid; Pereira to Eyre 01/23/1911 ibid; White to Scott 09/18/1917 ibid; McLean to MacDonald 09/20/1917 ibid; MacDonald to McLean 12/10/1917 ibid; McLean to Peters 12/14/1926 ibid; Murison to Graham 12/21/1929 ibid
33 Hollies to McLean 09/21/1908 PAC RG10 3569 95-2; Stewart to Hollies 10/12/1908 PAC RG10 8046 501; Hollies to McLean 10/20/1908 ibid; secretary, railways and canals, to McLean 03/13/1909 PAC RG10 8046; Oliver to Privy Council 03/20/1909 ibid
34 Hollies to Laird 08/15/1908 PAC RG10 3569 95-2; Laird to Hollies 08/18/1908 ibid; petition from Oak Lake Band to Laird 03/01/1908 ibid; Laird to Ciuska 03/08/1909 ibid; Hunter to Laird 09/21/1908 ibid
35 Hollies to Laird 11/02/1908 PAC RG10 3569 95-2; Hollies to Laird 12/01/1908 ibid; Sessional Papers 8-9 Edward VII no 27 1909 79; Swinford to Laird 12/12/1908 PAC RG10 3569 95-2A
36 Hollies to Laird 03/01/1909 PAC RG10 3569 95-2A
37 Sessional Papers 1 George V no 27 A1911 80
38 Christianson to Graham 07/27/1923 Archives, Federation of Saskatchewan Indians, Regina; Graham to Pedley 08/09/1923 ibid
39 Scott to Graham 10/01/1923 Archives, Federation of Saskatchewan Indians, Regina
40 Graham to Scott 10/09/1923 ibid
41 McLean to MacDonald 12/21/1901 PAC RG10 7740 23133-3; Robertson to Anon. 01/09/1922 ibid; McLean to Manitoba highways commissioner 01/09/1922 ibid; McLean to Manitoba highways commissioner 02/27/1922 ibid; McLean to surveyor 10/20/1925 ibid; Manitoba highways commissioner to McLean 12/26/1925 ibid; McLean to Clarke 11/10/1926 ibid; McLean to Manitoba highways commissioner 12/30/1926 ibid; Clarke to MacKenzie 10/10/1930 ibid; Manitoba highways commissioner to MacKenzie 11/24/1930 ibid; MacKenzie to Manitoba highways commissioner 12/10/1930 ibid; Order in Council 03/11/1931 PAC RG2 1
42 Deputy superintendent general of Indian affairs to Anon. 11/15/1933 PAC RG2 1
43 Gordon to MacKenzie 07/08/1935 ibid
44 North to Department of Indian Affairs 08/19/1949 ibid; Allan to North 08/29/1949 ibid

CHAPTER 8

1 Herchmer to Laird 09/02/1882 PAC RG10 3608 3030
2 Vankoughnet to Russell 09/26/1882 ibid; Russell to Vankoughnet 10/10/1882 ibid; Burgess to Vankoughnet 11/24/1882 ibid; Vankoughnet to Dewdney 12/06/1882 ibid
3 Douglas to Surveyor General 03/24/1887 PAC RG88 299 0500-2
4 Sessional Papers 44 Victoria no 14 A1881 77
5 Sessional Papers 45 Victoria no 6 A1882 68; Sessional Papers 47 Victoria no 4 1884; Sessional Papers 48 Victoria no 3 A1885 202; McGirr to Macdonald 10/14/1885 PAC RG10 3085 12932-3
6 Sessional Papers 49 Victoria no 6 A1886 309; Surveyor General of Canada Field Book 26
7 McGibbon to Anon. 06/04/1888 PAC RG10 3803 50774-1
8 Markle to Reed 02/14/1888 PAC RG10 3783 40470
9 McGibbon to Reed 05/18/1888 PAC RG10 3803 50774-1; Anon. to Anon. nd PAC RG10 3782 40468-2
10 Markle to Reed 03/04/1889 PAC RG10 3782 40468-2; Markle to Reed 03/04/1890 ibid; Markle to Reed 04/03/1890 ibid
11 Markle to Reed 07/02/1890 PAC RG10 3782 40468-2; Cunning to McGibbon 05/02/1891 PAC RG10 3602 1840; Markle to Reed 04/03/1890 PAC RG10 3783 40470
12 Kerr to Daly 04/12/1891 PAC RG10 3602 1840
13 Daly to Reed 04/17/1891 ibid
14 Reed to Daly 04/21/1891 ibid
15 Reed to Markle 04/22/1891 ibid
16 Markle to Reed 04/25/1891 ibid
17 Reed to Markle 05/06/1891 ibid; Reed to Markle 05/09/1891 ibid
18 Markle to Reed 04/05/1891 PAC RG10 3602 1840
19 Reed to Hadamani 05/30/1893 ibid
20 Markle to Forget 03/08/1898 PAC RG10 3644 7785-1
21 Forget to McLean 03/11/1898 ibid; McLean to Forget 03/22/1898 ibid
22 Forget to Markle 03/28/1898 PAC RG10 3644 7785-1; Markle to Forget 05/03/1898 ibid
23 McLean to Markle 06/08/1898 PAC RG10 3644 7785-1
24 Markle to McLean 06/10/1898 ibid; McLean to Markle 06/23/1898 ibid; Thunder to Forget 05/23/1898 ibid; McLean to Thunder 06/29/1898 ibid; Pereira to McLean 06/18/1898 ibid; McLean to Pereira 09/13/1898 ibid
25 Markle to McLean 06/10/1898 PAC RG10 3644 7785-1; McLean to Markle 06/22/1898 ibid; Markle to McLean 08/09/1898 ibid; McLean to Markle 09/13/1898 ibid; Markle to Laird 09/01/1898 ibid; McLean to Laird 10/13/1898 ibid
26 Hollies to Laird 03/24/1908 PAC RG10 3569 95-2
27 McLean to Hollies 02/21/1908 PAC RG10 3644 7785-1
28 Hollies to McLean 03/07/1908 ibid
29 Orde to McLean 03/20/1908 ibid
30 Hollies to McLean 08/11/1908 PAC RG10 3569 95-2; Hollies to Laird 08/12/1908 ibid; Laird to McLean 08/18/1908 ibid; McLean to Laird 08/27/1908 ibid
31 Hunter to Laird 09/21/1908 PAC RG10 3569 95-2
32 Hollies to McLean 11/20/1908 PAC RG10 3644 7785-1
33 Hollies to Laird 03/15/1909 PAC RG10 3569 95-2A
34 Laird to Hadamani 03/17/1909 ibid
35 Hollies to Laird 04/28/1909 PAC RG10 3644 7785-1

36 Hollies to McLean 06/09/1909 ibid; Pedley to Hollies 06/16/1909 ibid; Hollies to McLean 03/23/1909 ibid
37 Hollies to McLean 08/12/1909 ibid
38 Oliver to Privy Council 08/17/1909 ibid; Order in Council 08/28/1909 ibid
39 Annual Report of the Department of Indian Affairs (Ottawa 1895) 143
40 Annual Report of the Department of Indian Affairs (Ottawa 1896) 145; Annual Report of the Department of Indian Affairs (Ottawa 1898) 119
41 Annual Report of the Department of Indian Affairs (Ottawa 1909) 110-111; Annual Report of the Department of Indian Affairs (Ottawa 1910) 112-113; Annual Report of the Department of Indian Affairs (Ottawa 1911) 107-108
42 Stewart to under secretary of state 09/09/1909 PAC RG10 3644 7785-1; Pelltier to Stewart 09/10/1909 ibid; Pelltier to Stewart 10/11/1909 ibid; Hollies to Stewart 10/19/1909 ibid
43 Orde to Anon. 10/28/1909 PAC RG10 3644 7785-1; Pedley to Hollies 12/04/1909 ibid
44 Hollies to McLean 12/18/1909 PAC RG10 3644 7785-1; Morrison to McLean 12/02/1909 ibid
45 Morrison to Indian Affairs 01/08/1910 PAC RG10 3644 7785-1; McLean to Pedley 01/15/1910 ibid
46 Hollies to Mclean 01/17/1910 PAC RG10 3644 7785-1; McLean to Hollies 02/04/1910 ibid; Morrison to McLean 03/30/1910 ibid
47 Hughes to McLean 04/01/1910 PAC RG10 3644 7785-1; McLean to Hughes 04/30/1910 ibid
48 Hollies to McLean 07/14/1910 PAC RG10 3644 7785-1
49 McLean to Wheatley 07/21/1910 ibid; McLean to Markle 08/06/1910 ibid
50 Markle to McLean 08/22/1910 PAC RG10 3644 7785-1; According to Arthur Wambdi, grandson of Bogaga and now of Sioux Valley Reserve, no waiver of rights was either requested or signed.
51 Arthur Wambdi has in his possession a sketch map of the reserve, with subdivisions drawn in. The map appears to be in Markle's hand.
52 Laird to McLean 09/23/1910 PAC RG10 3644 7785-1
53 Reid to McLean 11/24/1910 ibid; Orr to McLean 02/15/1911 ibid; Hollies to McLean 05/05/1911 ibid; McLean to Hollies 05/12/1911 ibid; Laird to accountant 06/19/1911 ibid
54 Paget to Scott 06/23/1911 PAC RG10 3644 7785-1
55 Bigtrack to McLean 07/07/1911 ibid; McLean to Bigtrack 08/15/1911 ibid; Stewart to Bigtrack 10/25/1911 ibid; Bigtrack to McLean 02/13/1912 ibid; McLean to Bigtrack 02/29/1912 ibid; Bigtrack to McLean 03/16/1912 ibid
56 Hollies to McLean 08/17/1911 ibid
57 Hollies to McLean 03/25/1912 ibid
58 McLean to Hollies 05/14/1912 ibid; Hollies to McLean 05/27/1912 ibid
59 Thunder to McDonald 08/26/1912 PAC RG10 3644 7785-1; McDonald to McLean 09/03/1912 ibid; McDonald to McLean 10/25/1912 ibid
60 McLean to Barr 11/22/1912 PAC RG10 3644 7785-1
61 McDonald to McLean 12/05/1912 ibid
62 McLean to McDonald 12/17/1912 ibid; McDonald to McLean 01/21/1913 ibid; Laird to Scott 01/22/1913 ibid; Bigtrack to McLean 01/22/1913 ibid; McLean to McDonald 02/08/1913 ibid; McLean to Zeibach 02/08/1913 ibid; McDonald to McLean 02/27/1913 ibid; McLean to Zeibach 03/11/1913 ibid; McLean to superintendent at Fort Peck 03/11/1913 ibid; McLean to McDonald 03/11/1913 ibid
63 Tonkawastena to McLean 01/19/1914 PAC RG10 3644 7785-1; McLean to Tonkawastena 01/28/1914 ibid; Phelps to McDonald 03/10/1914 ibid; McDonald to McLean 05/09/1914 ibid; Williams to Scott 05/13/1914 ibid; McLean to Zeibach 05/15/1914 ibid; McLean to Allen 05/15/1914 ibid; Ziebach to McLean 05/20/1914 ibid; Miller to McLean 05/27/1914 ibid; McLean to Miller 06/10/1914 ibid; Miller to McLean 06/19/1914 ibid; Miller to McLean 11/10/1914 ibid; McLean to McDonald 11/28/1914 ibid; McLean to Lohmiller 12/28/1914 ibid; McLean to Ziebach 12/28/1914 ibid; McLean to Miller 11/28/1914 ibid; Anon. to Anon. 01/03/1917 ibid

64 Laviolette to Indian Affairs, nd, Archives, Federation of Saskatchewan Indians, Regina
65 St. Louis to Anon., nd, Archives, Federation of Saskatchewan Indians, Regina

CHAPTER 9

1 Meredith to Anon. 03/26/1877 PAC RG10 7769 27114-5
2 Macdonald to Laird 03/27/1877 ibid
3 Laird to Macdonald 08/01/1878 PAC RG10 3673 11325
4 Nelson to Dewdney 01/10/1882 PAC RG10 3573 154-2
5 Meredith to Laird 03/25/1877 PAC RG10 7769 27114-5; Macdonald to Laird 03/27/1877 ibid; Sessional Papers 42 Victoria no 7 A1879 57; Sessional Papers 43 Victoria no 4 A1880 97
6 Laird to Macdonald 12/16/1881 PAC RG10 3768 33642
7 Dewdney to Macdonald 11/16/1881 PAC RG10 3768 33642
8 Smith to Governor General 02/09/1882 PAC RG10 3581 815
9 de Winton to Macdonald 02/20/1882 ibid; Macdonald to Dewdney 03/17/1882 ibid
10 Dewdney to Macdonald 03/18/1882 PAC RG10 3581 815; Macdonald to Dewdney 04/01/1882 ibid
11 Macdonald to de Winton 04/01/1882 PAC RG10 3581 815
12 Macdonald to Dewdney 05/15/1882 ibid; Macdonald to Galt 06/12/1883 ibid
13 Wadsworth to Macdonald 05/30/1883 PAC RG10 3694 14603; Sessional Papers 45 Victoria no 6 A1882 125; Sessional Papers 46 Victoria no 5 A1883 126
14 Scott to Meredith 07/31/1884 PAC RG10 3694 14603; Macdonald to Dewdney 08/04/1884 ibid; Dewdney to Macdonald 08/11/1884 ibid; Scott to Benson 08/22/1884 ibid; Macdonald to Dewdney 09/03/1884 ibid
15 Hockley to Dewdney 02/01/1885 PAC RG10 3706 18532
16 Macdonald to Dewdney 08/01/1885 PAC RG10 3710 19550-3
17 Lash to Reed 08/09/1886 PAC RG10 3761 32248; Lash to Reed 10/09/1886 ibid; Wadsworth to Reed 10/30/1886 PAC RG10 3760 32025-9; Lash to Reed 11/06/1886 PAC RG10 3761 32248
18 Lash to Reed 01/10/1887 PAC RG10 3761 32248; Lash to Reed 02/05/1887 ibid; Lash to Reed 03/07/1887 ibid; Lash to Reed 04/09/1887 ibid
19 Lash to Reed 08/09/1887 ibid; Wadsworth to Reed 08/26/1887 PAC RG10 3783 40468-7
20 Lash to Reed 11/08/1887 PAC RG10 3761 32248; Lash to Reed 12/07/1887 ibid; Lash to Reed 01/03/1888 ibid; Lash to Reed 03/06/1888 ibid
21 Lash to Reed 05/09/1888 PAC RG10 3761 32248; Lash to Reed 07/01/1888 ibid; Annual Report of the Department of Indian Affairs (1888) 181
22 McGibbon to Forget 10/31/1888 PAC RG10 3804 50774-8; Lash to Forget 11/07/1888 PAC RG10 3761 32248
23 Lash to Forget 12/06/1888 PAC RG10 3761 32248; Lash to Forget 01/09/1889 ibid
24 Reed to Macdonald 02/13/1888 PAC RG10 7769 27114-5; Lash to Dewdney 02/18/1888 ibid; Vankoughnet to Burgess 02/25/1888; Burgess to Vankoughnet 04/07/1888 ibid; Burgess to Vankough-net 05/05/1888 ibid; Douglas to Vankoughnet 05/14/1888 ibid; Vankoughnet to Lash 05/17/1888 ibid; Vankoughnet to Forget 05/25/1888 ibid; Forget to Vankoughnet 02/07/1889 ibid; Vankoughnet to For-get 02/16/1889 ibid
25 Lash to Forget 05/09/1889 PAC RG10 7769 27114-5; Lash to Forget 02/07/1889 ibid; Lash to Forget 05/09/1889 ibid; Lash to Forget 03/05/1889 ibid; Lash to Forget 04/09/1889 ibid
26 Lash to Forget 06/07/1889 PAC RG10 7769 27114-5; Lash to Forget 07/08/1889 ibid; Lash to For-get 08/09/1889 ibid; Lash to Forget 09/09/1889 ibid; Lash to Forget 10/05/1889 ibid; Lash to Forget 11/11/1889 ibid; Lash to Forget 12/11/1889 ibid; Lash to Forget 01/09/1890 ibid; Lash to Forget 02/06/1890 ibid; Lash to Forget 03/10/1890 ibid; Lash to Forget 04/10/1890 ibid; Lash to Forget 05/16/1890 ibid; Lash to Forget 07/09/1890 ibid; Lash to Forget 08/13/1890 ibid; Lash to Forget

09/08/1890 ibid; Lash to Forget 10/07/1890 ibid; Lash to Forget 11/11/1890 ibid; Lash to Forget 12/09/1890 ibid; Lash to Forget 12/30/1890 ibid
27 Wadsworth to Forget 04/08/1890 PAC RG10 3845 73466-9
28 Lash to Reed 02/11/1892 PAC RG10 3869 88192; Lash to Reed 03/10/1892 ibid; Lash to Reed 04/07/1892 ibid; Lash to Reed 05/09/1892 ibid; Lash to Reed 06/13/1892 ibid; Lash to Reed 07/16/1892 ibid; Lash to Reed 08/10/1892 ibid; Lash to Reed 10/07/1892 ibid; Lash to Reed 11/15/1892 ibid; Lash to Reed 12/07/1892 ibid; Lash to Reed 01/11/1893 ibid; Lash to Reed 02/14/1893 PAC RG10 3949 126345
29 Graham to Laird 12/24/1901 PAC RG10 3570 102-7
30 Laird to Graham 01/21/1902 ibid
31 Graham to Laird 01/27/1902 ibid
32 Wacihewaste to Laird 04/11/1902 PAC RG10 3569 95-7
33 Standing Buffalo's Band to Lord Minto 03/05/1903 PAC RG10 3917 116590-1
34 Bray to Anon. 02/22/1903 PAC RG10 7769 27114-5
35 Laird to McLean 03/18/1903 ibid
36 McLean to Standing Buffalo 03/25/1903 PAC RG10 3917 116590-1
37 Keyes to McLean 05/28/1903 PAC RG10 7769 27114-5; Bray to Pedley 05/02/1903 ibid; Pedley to Keyes 06/04/1903 ibid; Keyes to McLean 07/21/1903 ibid; Gordon to McLean 12/11/1907 ibid; McLean to Gordon 12/19/1907 ibid
38 Cote to McLean 10/13/1913 PAC RG10 7769 27114-5; Stewart to Cote 10/24/1913 ibid; Cote to Stewart 12/17/1913 ibid; McLean to Cote 12/22/1913 ibid
39 Cote to McLean 11/03/1914 PAC RG10 7769 27114-5; Christianson to McLean 03/19/1918 ibid; McLean to Christianson 04/06/1918 ibid; McLean to Cote 04/06/1918 ibid
40 Christianson to McLean 04/09/1918 PAC RG10 7769 27114-5; McLean to Christianson 04/20/1918 ibid; McLean to Cote 04/29/1918 ibid
41 McLean to Cote 05/23/1918 PAC RG10 7769 27114-5; Nelson to McLean 06/13/1918 ibid; McLean to Cote 07/12/1918 ibid; Nelson to McLean 07/20/1918 ibid; McLean to Christianson 07/25/1918 ibid; Christianson to McLean 12/18/1918 ibid; McLean to Nelson 12/02/1918 ibid; McLean to Christianson 01/23/1919 ibid; Nelson to McLean 02/14/1919 ibid; McLean to Christianson 02/24/1919 ibid; Walls to McLean 05/10/1919 ibid
42 Speers to McLean 08/28/1919 PAC RG10 7769 27119-5; Orr to Speers 09/05/1919 ibid; Cory to Scott 08/19/1919 ibid; Scott to Cory 08/21/1919 ibid
43 Men of Standing Buffalo Band to Laird 01/05/1901 PAC RG10 3569 95-7
44 Mitchell to Laird 01/16/1901 ibid
45 Sifton to the governor general 02/04/1901 PAC RG10 3878 91839-7; Graham to Laird 02/04/1901 ibid; McLean to Laird 03/02/1901 ibid
46 Standing Buffalo to Laird 04/23/1901 PAC RG10 3569 95-7
47 Wacihewaste to Laird 04/11/1901 ibid
48 McLean to Laird 03/05/1903 PAC RG10 3917 116590-1
49 Laird to McLean 03/18/1903 PAC RG10 3569 95-7
50 Standing Buffalo to Laird 04/07/1903 PAC RG10 7769 27114-5; Pedley to Laird 12/15/1903 PAC RG10 3569 95-7
51 Sessional Papers 64 Victoria no 27 A1901 173-174; Sessional Papers 2-3 Edward VII no 27 A1903 165-166; Sessional Papers 3-4 Edward VII no 27 A1904 184-185; Sessional Papers 4-5 Edward VII no 27 A1905 175-176; Sessional Papers 5-6 Edward VII no 27 1906 147-148; Sessional Papers 6-7 Edward VII no 27 A1907 144; Sessional Papers 8-9 Edward VII no 27 A 1909 151; Sessional Papers 9-10 Edward VII no 17 A1910 157-158; Sessional Papers 1 George V no 19 A1911 148; Sessional Papers 2 George V no 20 A1912 158; Sessional Papers 5 George V no 23 A1915 48; Sessional Papers 7 George V no 27 A1917 54

52 Memorandum 01/10/1921 PAC RG10 7769 271 14-5; McLean to Walls 01/12/1921 ibid
53 Walls to McLean 01/27/1921 PAC RG10 7769 27114-5
54 McLean to Walls 02/04/1921 ibid
55 Walls to McLean 03/09/1921 ibid; Standing Buffalo to McLean 07/05/1921 ibid; McLean to Standing Buffalo 07/15/1921 ibid; McLean to Walls 07/15/1921 ibid
56 Cory to Scott 11/10/1922 PAC RG10 7769 27114-5; Scott to Cory 11/15/1922 ibid; McLean to Dodd 11/15/1922 ibid; Dodd to McLean 02/02/1923 ibid; Gardiner to Scott 02/24/1923 ibid; McLean to Graham 03/20/1923 ibid; Graham to McLean 03/28/1923 ibid; Uhren to Cory 04/07/1923 ibid; McLean to Gibbon 04/14/1923 ibid; Uhren to Gibbon 05/07/1923 ibid; Graham to McLean 08/09/1923 ibid; MacKenzie to Graham 08/14/1923 ibid; MacKenzie to Graham 08/25/1923 ibid; Featherstone to Scott 11/21/1923 ibid; Scott to Featherstone 11/22/1923 ibid; Scott to Graham 11/23/1923 ibid; Scott to Gardiner 02/15/1924 ibid; Scott to Stewart 03/08/1924 ibid; Graham to Scott 06/26/1924 ibid; Graham to Stewart 11/15/1924 ibid; Scott to Cross 12/19/1924 ibid; Cross to McLean 12/30/1924 ibid; McLean to Cross 01/15/1925 ibid; Graham to McLean 04/08/1925 ibid; Scott to Graham 04/17/1925 ibid; Cross to Graham 07/25/1925 ibid; Graham to McLean 08/13/1925 ibid; McLean to Graham 08/19/1925 ibid; Cross to Graham 09/10/1925 ibid; Graham to McLean 09/23/1925 ibid; Lands and Timber Branch to Scott 10/21/1925 ibid; Uhren to Cory 10/16/1925 ibid; Cory to Scott 10/20/1925 ibid; Scott to Uhren 10/21/1925 ibid; Graham to Scott 11/23/1925 ibid; Graham to McLean 11/26/1925 ibid; McLean to Chisholm 11/12/1925 ibid; Chisholm to McLean 12/13/1925 ibid; Roberts to McLean 06/29/1926 ibid; McLean to Dodd 07/15/1926 ibid; Dodd to McLean 09/27/1927 ibid; McLean to Dodd 10/25/1926 ibid; Roberts to McLean 10/18/1926 ibid; McLean to Roberts 10/27/1926 ibid; Roberts to McLean 11/13/1926 ibid; Dodd to McLean 10/12/1926 ibid; McLean to Cory 10/22/1926 ibid; Roberts to McLean 10/29/1926 ibid; McLean to Dodd 11/05/1926 ibid; Dodd to McLean 03/19/1927 ibid; Rose to McLean 10/17/1927 ibid; McLean to Rose 11/16/1927 ibid; Martens to McLean 03/01/1929 ibid; MacKenzie to Dodd 03/06/1929 ibid; Davis to MacKenzie 03/21/1929 ibid; MacKenzie to Davis 04/04/1929 ibid; Davis to MacKenzie 04/18/1929 ibid
57 Graham to McLean 10/26/1921 PAC RG10 7769 27114-5
58 McLean to Graham 06/21/1922 ibid; Graham to McLean 05/29/1922 ibid; McLean to Graham 07/11/1922 ibid; Graham to McLean 05/22/1924 ibid; McLean to Graham 05/28/1924 ibid; Graham to McLean 06/04/1924 ibid; McLean to Graham 06/19/1924 ibid; Goodwill to Scott 04/12/1928 ibid; MacKenzie to Goodwill 04/17/1928 ibid; Goodwill to Scott 06/28/1928 ibid; Davis to McLean 06/29/1928 ibid; MacKenzie to Davis 07/06/1928 ibid; MacKenzie to Graham 03/12/1929 ibid; Graham to MacKenzie 03/16/1929 ibid; MacKenzie to Fairchild 07/15/1929 ibid; MacKenzie to Fairchild 07/29/1929 ibid; Fairchaild to McLean 08/29/1929 ibid; McLean to Fairchild 08/29/1929 ibid; Fairchild to McLean 09/16/1929 ibid; MacKenzie to Fairchild 09/23/1929 ibid; Fairchild to McLean 09/28/1929 ibid; McLean to Fairchild 09/28/1929 ibid

CHAPTER 10

1 Laird to Mills 08/01/1878 PAC RG10 3673 11325
2 Laird to Mills 01/01/1879 ibid; Laird to Mills 03/14/1879 ibid; Vankoughnet to Russell 04/17/1879 ibid
3 Vankoughnet to Dickison 04/23/1879 PAC RG10 3673 11325; Vankoughnet to Dickison 04/25/1879 ibid
4 Dickison to Vankoughnet 07/23/1879 PAC RG10 3673 11325
5 Vankoughnet to Russell 08/22/1879 ibid; Vankoughnet to Dennis 08/27/1879 ibid; Vankoughnet to Orde 08/30/1879 ibid
6 Simpson to Vankoughnet 12/01/1880 PAC RG10 3673 11325; Simpson to Orde 12/07/1880 ibid; Orde to Dewdney 12/08/1880 ibid; Vankoughnet to Simpson 01/05/1881 ibid; Office of the Surveyor General Field Book 1682

7 Sessional Papers 42 Victoria no 7 A1879 57-58
8 Sessional Papers 44 Victoria no 3 A1881 98
9 Dewdney to Macdonald 07/26/1881 PAC RG10 3747 29792
10 Vankoughnet to Macdonald 09/30/1881 ibid; Reed to Dewdney 05/01/1881 ibid; Vankoughnet to Galt 06/14/1881 ibid; Galt to Macdonald 06/23/1881 ibid; Macdonald to Dewdney 07/05/1881 ibid; Galt to Macdonald 10/18/1881 ibid; Galt to Macdonald 05/16/1882 ibid
11 Sessional Papers 45 Victoria no 6 A1882 46-47; Sessional Papers 46 Victoria no 5 A1883 262-263; Sessional Papers 47 Victoria no 4 A1884; Sessional Papers 48 Victoria no 3 A1885 202
12 Powers to Dewdney 12/30/1884 PAC RG10 3703 17589
13 Sessional Papers 49 Victoria no 4 A1886
14 Macdonald to Dewdney 06/03/1885 PAC RG10 3585 1130-B; Lash to Dewdney 06/03/1885 ibid; Dewdney to Macdonald 06/08/1885 ibid; Dewdney to Macdonald 06/09/1885 ibid; Macdonald to Dewdney 06/10/1885 ibid; McGirr to Dewdney 06/11/1885 ibid; Vankoughnet to Dewdney 06/15/1885 ibid; Dewdney to Macdonald 06/26/1885 PAC RG10 3710 19550-3
15 Dewdney to Macdonald 08/01/1885 PAC RG10 3710 19550-3
16 Molson to Dewdney 08/05/1885 PAC RG10 3583 1130-B; North West Mounted Police to Dewdney 08/07/1885 ibid; Reed to Macdonald 01/04/1886 PAC RG10 3773 3059; Adams to Dewdney 06/31/1886 PAC RG10 3752 30408
17 Biggin to Dewdney 06/09/1886 PAC RG10 3753 30628
18 White Cap to Dewdney 11/08/1886 PAC RG10 3773 36059
19 LeQuesne to Dewdney 12/09/1886 ibid
20 Ibid
21 Reed to Macdonald 01/07/1886 ibid; Reed to Macdonald 04/23/1887 ibid
22 Dewdney to Macdonald 08/08/1887 PAC RG10 3785 41713; Burgess to Vankoughnet 08/27/1887 ibid; Austin to deputy minister of Indian affairs 09/03/1887 ibid; Vankoughnet to Dewdney 09/08/1887 ibid; Reed to Macdonald 10/04/1887 ibid; deputy minister of Indian affairs to Burgess 10/14/1887 ibid
23 Nelson to Dewdney 06/18/1888 PAC RG10 3785 41713; Dewdney to Macdonald 06/29/1888 PAC RG10 3800 48536; Dewdney to Macdonald 07/07/1888 PAC RG10 3728 25705; Vankoughnet to Burgess 07/07/1888 ibid; Pereira to Vankoughnet 07/24/1888 ibid; Vankoughnet to Dewdney 07/27/1888 ibid
24 Wadsworth to Anon. 07/12/1889 PAC RG10 7768 27109-10; Forget to Vankoughnet 08/23/1889 ibid; Reed to Vankoughnet 12/16/1889 ibid
25 Vankoughnet to Reed 12/28/1889 PAC RG10 7768 27109-10; Reed to Vankoughnet 01/15/1890 ibid
26 Reed to Vankoughnet 07/29/1891 PAC RG10 7768 27109-10; Vankoughnet to Reed 08/05/1891 ibid; Vankoughnet to Hall 08/05/1891 ibid
27 Reed to Vankoughnet 04/26/1892 PAC RG10 7768 27109-10
28 Vankoughnet to Reed 05/03/1892 PAC RG10 7768 27109-10; Vankoughnet to acting deputy minister of the interior 05/03/1892 ibid; Pereira to Sinclair 08/30/1892 ibid; Vankoughnet to Reed 09/05/1892 ibid
29 McGibbon to Vankoughnet 11/28/1892 PAC RG10 7768 27109-10; Vankoughnet to Pereira 12/16/1892 ibid
30 Tucker to Reed 01/23/1893 PAC RG10 3598 1420-D
31 Reed to Tucker 03/08/1893 ibid
32 Reed to Forget 02/18/1893 ibid; Forget to Reed 02/20/1893 ibid; Reed to Burgess 02/24/1893 ibid; Hall to Dominion lands agent 02/28/1893 ibid
33 Reed to Tucker 03/09/1893 PAC RG10 3598 1420-0
34 Tucker to Reed 06/10/1893 ibid
35 Tucker to Reed 06/18/1893 ibid; Reed to lands agent 05/19/1893 ibid; Baggart to Reed 05/22/1893 ibid; Reed to Baggart 06/13/1893 ibid; Cook to Smith 07/08/1893 PAC RG10 7768 27109-10; Ponton to

Reed 07/13/1893 PAC RG10 3598 1420-D; Reed to Dominion lands agent 07/13/1893 ibid; Reed to commissioner of Dominion lands 07/13/1893 ibid; Reed to Vankoughnet 07/13/1893 ibid; Vankoughnet to Reed 07/18/1893 ibid; Vankoughnet to Hall 07/18/1893 PAC RG10 7768 27109-10; Order in Council P.C. 2809 ibid; Pereira to Vankoughnet 11/11/1893 ibid; Forget to Vankoughnet 01/27/1894 ibid; Vankoughnet to Forget 02/02/1894 PAC RG10 3598 1420-D

36 Burgess to Reed 10/14/1896 PAC RG10 7768 27109-10; Reed to Burgess 10/17/1896 ibid; Tucker to McLean 10/15/1898 ibid; McLean to Pereira 10/24/1898 ibid; Pereira to McLean 11/17/1898 ibid; Order in Council P.C.2668 ibid; Pereira to McLean 12/13/1898 ibid; McLean to Pereira 04/27/1899 ibid; Hall to McLean 05/05/1899 ibid; Stewart to Pereira 05/12/1899 ibid; Hall to Stewart 05/23/1899 ibid; Stewart to MacKenzie 06/05/1899 ibid; Stewart to Laird 06/05/1899 ibid

37 Members of White Cap's Band to Dewdney 01/21/1888 PAC RG10 7768 27109-10; Andrews to Scott 05/16/1888 ibid; Dewdney to Macdonald 05/25/1888 ibid; Scott to McNiell 05/30/1888 ibid; Vankoughnet to Reed 06/06/1888 ibid; Andrews to Dewdney 06/07/1888 ibid; Taylor to Dewdney 06/07/1888 ibid

38 Hall to Vankoughnet 05/07/1889 PAC RG10 3800 48536; Vankoughnet to Burgess 05/16/1889 ibid; Vankoughnet to Reed 05/16/1889 ibid; Reed to Macdonald 05/21/1889 ibid; Vankoughnet to Burgess 06/01/1889 ibid; Reed to Dewdney 06/05/1889 ibid; Pereira to Crown Timber agent 06/07/1889 ibid; Reed to Vankoughnet 07/06/1889 ibid; Macdonald to Burgess 07/12/1889 ibid

39 Wadsworth to Dewdney 07/12/1889 PAC RG10 7768 27109-10

40 Reed to Vankoughnet 07/29/1891 ibid; McGibbon to Reed 08/07/1891 PAC RG10 3860 82319-1

41 Cook to Smith 07/08/1893 PAC RG10 7768 27109-10; Tucker to Reed 05/10/1893 PAC RG10 3598 1420-D

42 Tucker to Forget 06/16/1894 PAC RG10 3920 116729

43 Annual Report of the Department of Indian Affairs (1895) 230-232

44 Ibid (1896)

45 Ibid (1898)

46 Sessional Papers 63 Victoria no 14 A1900; Sessional Papers 2-3 Edward VII no 27 A1903 184; Sessional Papers 4-5 Edward VII no 27 A1905 192-193; Sessional Papers 6-7 Edward VII no 27 A1907 150-151; Sessional Papers 8-9 Edward VII no 27 A1909 161-162

47 Chisholm to McLean 12/20/1911 PAC RG10 7768 27109-10; McLean to Chisholm 01/05/1912 ibid; McLean to Keyes 01/08/1912 ibid; Cote to McLean 05/06/1913 ibid; Cote to McLean 08/09/1913 ibid; McLean to Cote 08/25/1913 ibid; Chisholm to McLean 11/05/1913 ibid; McLean to Chisholm 01/02/1914 ibid; Chisholm to McLean 02/06/1914 ibid; McLean to Cote 02/12/1914 ibid; Cote to McLean 02/17/1914 ibid; Chisholm to McLean 04/14/1914 ibid; McLean to Cote 04/27/1914 ibid; McLean to Cote 05/29/1914 ibid; Cote to McLean 06/19/1914 ibid; McLean to Cote 06/29/1914 ibid; McLean to Chisholm 06/29/1914 ibid; Chisholm to McLean 10/24/1914 ibid; McLean to Cote 11/05/1914 ibid; McLean to Cote 02/11/1915 ibid; McLean to Cote 05/26/1915 ibid; Cote to McLean 05/23/1915 ibid; McLean to Cote 02/04/1916 ibid; Cote to McLean 02/25/1915 ibid; McLean to Cote 10/19/1916 ibid; Cory to Scott 08/01/1919 ibid; McLean to Cory 08/11/1919 ibid; McLean to Cory 10/06/1919 ibid; Schmidt to McLean 02/04/1920 ibid; MacKenzie to Cote 02/19/1920 ibid; Cote to McLean 04/25/1921 ibid; Nelson to McLean 05/06/1921 ibid; McLean to Schmidt 05/16/1921 ibid; Schmidt to McLean 05/26/1921 ibid; McLean to Cote 06/01/1921 ibid; Cote to McLean 07/12/1921 ibid; Order in Council 07/14/1921 P.C. 2442 ibid; Schmidt to McLean 03/27/1926 ibid; McLean to Cote 04/03/1926 ibid; Graham to McLean 09/15/1928 ibid; Page to Scott 09/26/1928 ibid; McLean to Graham 09/28/1928 ibid; McLean to Chisholm 09/28/1928 ibid; McLean to commissioner of Dominion lands 11/28/1928 ibid; Chisholm to McLean 10/04/1928 ibid; McLean to Chisholm 10/04/1928 ibid; Chisholm to McLean 10/09/1928 ibid; Chisholm to McLean 10/29/1928 ibid; Chisholm to McLean 10/16/1928 ibid; McLean to Graham 10/17/1928 ibid; McLean to Chisholm 10/17/1928 ibid; Chisholm to McLean 11/19/1928 ibid; Martin to McLean 12/12/1928 ibid; Finlayson to McLean 08/01/1930 ibid;

MacKenzie to McLean 10/24/1930 ibid; Barnett to MacKenzie 11/01/1930 ibid; MacKenzie to Barnett 03/03/1931 ibid; Barnett to MacKenzie 04/04/1931 ibid; Barnett to MacKenzie 12/19/1931 ibid; Mac-Kenzie to Barnett 05/20/1932 ibid; Barnett to MacKenzie 06/07/1932 ibid; Eastman to Anon. 01/26/1933 SAB S410649; Paterson to MacKenzie 04/07/1932 PAC RG10 7768 27109-10; Paterson to MacKenzie 04/07/1932 ibid; MacKenzie to LaFleche 08/10/1933 ibid; LaFleche to MacKenzie 08/15/1933 ibid

48 Anon. to Schmidt 08/21/1933 PAC RG10 7768 27109-10; Schmidt to MacKenzie 03/29/1934 ibid; Mac-Kenzie to Schmidt 04/13/1934 ibid

49 Chisholm to McLean 12/15/1913 PAC RG10 7768 27109-10

50 Schmidt to MacKenzie 02/05/1932 ibid

CHAPTER 11

1 Robertson to Vankoughnet 03/19/1886 PAC RG10 6029 127-4-1; Vankoughnet to McColl 03/31/1886 ibid

2 Ogletree to McColl 04/17/1886 PAC RG10 6029 127-4-1; McColl to Macdonald 04/19/1886 ibid; Macdonald to Dewdney 04/30/1886 ibid

3 Dewdney to Macdonald 06/29/1886 PAC RG10 6029 127-4-1

4 Macdonald to Watson 07/12/1886 ibid

5 Ogletree to McColl 04/30/1892 DIAND file 90274; Ogletree to McColl 06/01/1892 DIAND file 94074; McColl to Vankoughnet 06/03/1892 PAM EE32

6 Pereira to McLean 06/14/1898 PAC RG10 7774 27127-4; Order in Council 10/06/1898 P.C. 2338 ibid; Pereira to McLean 12/29/1898 ibid; Marlatt to McKenna 12/08/1897 ibid

7 Logan to McLean 10/07/1910 DIAND file 373068

8 Clayton to Logan 03/22/1911 PAC RG10 7774 27124-2

9 Sessional Papers 4-5 Edward VII no 27 A1905 105

10 Sessional Papers 64 Victoria no 27 A1901 107

11 Sessional Papers 3-4 Edward VII no 27 A1904 97

12 Sessional Papers 2-3 Edward VII no 27 A1903 300

13 Sessional Papers 6-7 Edward VII no 27 A1907 93

14 Sessional Papers 7-8 Edward VII no 27 A1908 102-103

15 Logan to McLean 03/25/1911 PAC RG10 7774 27124-2

16 McLean to Logan 04/11/1911 PAC RG10 7774 27124-4; Laird memorandum 04/19/1911 ibid

17 Logan to McLean 12/08/1911 PAC RG10 7774 27124-4; Logan to McLean 12/27/1911 ibid; Bray to deputy minister 01/04/1912 ibid; Meighan to Cory 01/21/1913 ibid

18 Logan to McLean 02/12/1913 PAC RG10 7774 27124-4

19 Ibid 12/27/1911

20 Order in Council P.C. 2866 11/17/1913 PAC RG10 7774 27127-4

21 Marlatt to McKenna 06/06/1898 PAC RG10 7774 27127-4

22 Sessional Papers 64 Victoria no 27 A1901 106-107

23 Sessional Papers 2-3 Edward VII no 27 A1903 300; Sessional Papers 3-4 Edward VII no 27 A1904 97; Sessional Papers 4-5 Edward VII no 27 A1905 93; Sessional Papers 6-7 Edward VII no 27 A1907 93; Sessional Papers 7-8 Edward VII no 27 A1908 98-99; Sessional Papers 8-9 Edward VII no 27 A1909 102-103; Sessional Papers 9-10 Edward VII no 27 A1910 106-107

24 McLean to Ogletree 10/07/1918 PAC RG10 7774 27127-4

25 Ogletree to McLean 03/29/1924 ibid

26 Ogletree to McLean 07/17/1924 ibid

27 Graham to Scott 04/19/1924 ibid

28 McLean to Graham 08/12/1924 ibid; Graham to McLean 08/19/1924 ibid

29 McPherson to Stewart 12/29/1927 PAC RG10 7774 27127-4; Scott to McPherson 12/27/1927 ibid; Graham to Scott 11/06/1928 ibid; Graham to Scott 01/31/1928 ibid

30 Caldwell to Scott 02/21/1929 PAC RG10 7774 27127-4; Graham to Scott 04/16/1929 ibid; McLean to Graham 04/30/1929 ibid

31 Graham to McLean 05/17/1929 PAC RG10 7774 27127-4

32 McPherson to Scott 10/21/1929 ibid; Graham to Scott 10/31/1929 ibid

33 Waite to MacKenzie 07/21/1930 PAC RG10 7774 27127-4; Bradley to Caldwell 04/15/1931 ibid; MacKenzie to Graham 06/30/1931 ibid; Graham to MacKenzie 07/14/1931 ibid; MacKenzie to Waite 06/07/1932 ibid; Williams to Scott 08/04/1932 ibid; Johnson to Caldwell 01/07/1933 ibid

34 *Portage La Prairie Daily Herald* 12/14/1929

35 Order in Council P.C. 3648

36 Wier to Jones 06/25/1955 DIAND file 127/30-4; Jones to Wier 06/03/1955 DIAND file 50130366A; Jones to Davis 06/16/1955 ibid; Staunton to Davis 07/05/1955 DIAND file 127/84; Davis to Anon. 07/07/1955 DIAND file 50130366A; Bethune to Davis 08/23/1955 ibid

37 Staunton to Davis 08/29/1955 DIAND file 127/8-4; Bethune to Ostrander and Davey 09/15/1955 DIAND file 127/30-4; Bethune to Staunton 12/29/1955 ibid; Staunton to Ragan 12/14/1955 DIAND file 127/8-4; Bethune to deputy minister 01/06/1956 DIAND file 127/30-4; Bethune to Ragan 01/09/1956 DIAND file 501-30-36-6A; Bethune to legal advisor 01/30/1956 DIAND file 127/30-4; Henderson to Wier 02/07/1956 DIAND file 501-30-36-6A; Ragan to Staunton 02/20/1956 DIAND file 127/8-4; Staunton to Anon. 02/23/1956 ibid; Jones to Wier 02/29/1956 DIAND file 127/30-4; Ragan to Jones 03/02/1956 ibid; Bethune to Staunton 03/05/1956 ibid; Bethune to legal advisor 03/07/1956 ibid; Porter to Pickersgill 03/17/1956 ibid; Ostrander to deputy minister 03/27/1956 ibid; Pickersgill to Porter 03/27/1956 ibid; Bethune to legal advisor 04/18/1956 ibid; Staunton to Meshoe 04/19/1956 ibid; Rogers to Bethune 04/19/1956 ibid; Pickersgill to Bethune 04/28/1956 ibid; Pickersgill to Porter 04/24/1956 ibid; Ragan to Ostrander 04/11/1956 ibid; Ragan to Ostrander 05/24/1956 ibid; Ragan to Bethune 10/09/1956 ibid

38 Nield to Ragan 01/31/1957 DIAND file 127/30-4

39 Bethune to Anon. 05/24/1957 ibid; Bethune to Anon. 06/06/1957 ibid

40 Ragan to Nield 12/29/1957 DIAND file 127/30-4; Nield to Ragan 12/23/1957 ibid; Ragan to Bethune 01/12/1958 ibid

41 Smoke to Safarin 07/12/1971 PAC RG10 7774 27127-4; Bell to Prince 07/20/1971 DIAND file 5.77.3-5-22; Bell to regional director 08/31/1971 ibid; Gran to regional director 09/03/1971 DIAND file 577/3-8; Chapman to regional director 09/03/1971 ibid; Chaske and Smoke to Bell 02/18/1972 DIAND file 577/3-5-22; minutes of meeting 03/06/1972 DIAND file 577/3-1-36; band council resolution 03/06/1972 ibid; Bell to district supervisor 03/08/1972 DIAND file 577/3-5-22; Courchene to Connelly 03/13/1972 DIAND file 577/3-1; Serafin to Smoke and Chaske 03/15/1972 ibid; Serafin to Jackson 04/01/1972 DIAND file 577/3-5-22

42 Tucker to Anon. 04/12/1972 DIAND file 501/3-5-36; Tucker to Daggitt 04/14/1972 DIAND file 517/3-8; Daggitt to chief, Band Management Division 05/02/1972 DIAND file 501/3-8-36; Chapman to Daggitt 05/29/1972 DIAND file 501/1-1; Daggitt to Tucker 05/31/1972 DIAND file 501/3-1-36; Tucker to Daggitt 06/30/1972 ibid

43 Daggitt to Chapman 07/07/1972 DIAND file 501/3-1-36; Chapman to Daggitt 07/14/1972 ibid; minutes of meeting 07/18/1972 ibid; Daggitt to Chapman 07/25/1972 DIAND file 501/1-1; Chapman to Daggitt 08/29/1972 ibid

44 Band Council Resolution 02/26/1973 DIAND file 501/30-1-36; Order in Council P.C. 1973-1784; Bethune to legal advisor 01/24/1958 DIAND file 127/30-4; Nield to Ragan 01/31/1958 ibid; Christie to Bethune 02/05/1957 ibid; Bethune to Nield 02/11/1958 ibid; Bethune to legal advisor 02/28/1958 ibid; Ragan to Bethune 06/25/1958 ibid; Christie to Clerk, Surrogate Court 06/26/1958 ibid; RCMP to Anon. 01/29/1959 ibid; RCMP to Anon. 02/11/1959 ibid; Goldsmith to Anon. 02/19/1959 ibid; RCMP

to Anon. 04/02/1959 ibid; Spalding to Anon., nd, ibid; McKinnon to Anon. 04/15/1959 ibid; Bethune to legal advisor 04/10/1959 ibid; Bethune to Leslie 01/19/1960 ibid; Chalmers to Bethune 10/17/1960 ibid; Bethune to Chalmers 11/02/1960 ibid; Chalmers to Bethune 01/16/1961 ibid; Bethune to Pauley 01/16/1961 ibid

45 Bethune to Riesen 06/14/1961 DIAND file 127/30-4; Riesen to Bethune 06/22/1961 ibid; Bethune to Williams 11/15/1961 ibid; Williams to Bethune 11/21/1961 ibid; Hodges to Williams 01/08/1961 ibid; Williams to Chapman 01/19/1961 ibid; Chapman to registrar 01/25/1962 ibid; Williams to Rutherford 04/02/1962 ibid; Vogt to Nield 06/06/1962 ibid; Tallin to Williams 02/05/1963 ibid; D'Astous to Williams 02/21/1963 ibid; D'Astous to Riesen 01/13/1964 ibid; Riesen to D'Astous 10/19/1964 ibid; Conn to Riesen 10/26/1964 ibid; Conn to Thistlethwaite 10/26/1964 ibid; Conn to Bethune 10/26/1964 ibid; Nield to Anon. 10/28/1964 ibid; Lamont to Pawley 07/09/1965 ibid; McIntyre to Nield 07/26/1965 ibid; Nield to McIntyre 07/30/1965 ibid; McIntyre to Johnston 08/16/1965 ibid; McIntyre to Thistlethwaite 08/16/1965 ibid; Long Plain Sioux Band to Anon. 10/22/1965 ibid

46 Nield to Anon. 10/22/1965 DIAND file 127/30-4; Battle to Anon. 11/3/1965 ibid; McIntyre to Saddlemeyer 11/09/1965 ibid; McIntyre to Anon. 01/11/1966 ibid; Nield to Anon. 05/25/1966 ibid; Anon. to Anon. 06/26/1966 ibid; McKay to Nield 06/30/1966 ibid; D'Astous to Anon. 07/11/1966 ibid; Battle to Minister 07/18/1966 ibid; Poupore to McKay 12/29/1966 ibid; Battle to Maxwell 04/06/1966 ibid; Land to the governor general 05/23/1967 ibid; Battle to Anon. 06/14/1967 ibid; Order in Council P.C. 1967-1419; Pressey to Vergette 09/08/1967 ibid

47 MacDonald to Anon. 06/01/1960 DIAND file 127/30-9; Bethune to Nield 08/29/1960 ibid; Fairfield to Moodie 01/27/1961 ibid; Bethune to Pawley 01/29/1961 ibid; Bethune to Nield 04/21/1961 ibid; Bethune to Nield 05/17/1961 ibid; Leslie to Nield 05/24/1961; Nield to Leslie 03/12/1964 ibid; Leslie to D'Astous 03/18/1964 ibid; D'Astous to Leslie 05/08/1964 ibid; McIntyre to Nield 06/14/1965 ibid; Nield to Connelly 06/17/1965; Lamont to Nield 09/08/1965 ibid; McIntyre to Connelly 09/24/1965 ibid; Nield to Connelly 10/05/1965 ibid; Connelly to McIntyre 10/06/1965 ibid; D'Astous to Battle 12/14/1965 ibid; McIntyre to legal advisor 04/15/1965 ibid

CHAPTER 12

1 Laird to minister of the interior 11/08/1879 PAM 91/190 and PAM MG26A 362
2 Clarke to Vankoughnet 04/10/1880 PAC RG10 3712 20500
3 Vankoughnet to Clarke 05/11/1880 ibid; Vankoughnet to Dewdney 05/14/1880 ibid
4 Rae to Laird 12/31/1880 PAC RG10 3739 28410; Dewdney to Macdonald 02/11/1886 PAC MG26A 213
5 Pritchard to Macdowall 01/27/1890 PAC RG10 3602 65933
6 Ibid
7 The medal to which this letter refers now reposes in the Prince Albert Historical Society Museum.
8 Bray to Vankoughnet 03/18/1890 ibid; Pritchard to Macdowall 03/31/1890 PAC RG10 7767 27107-10-1; Macdowall to Dewdney 04/12/1890 ibid
9 Vankoughnet to Reed 04/18/1890 PAC RG10 7767 27107-10-1; Forget to Finlayson 04/26/1890 PAC RG10 3602 1774; Finlayson to Reed 05/07/1890 ibid; Finlayson to Reed 05/12/1890 ibid
10 Macdonald to Dewdney 08/26/1890 PAC RG10 3929 117090; Mustard to Reed 09/02/1890 ibid; Reed to Mustard 09/03/1890 ibid; Reed to Dewdney 09/03/1890 ibid
11 Dewdney to Macdonald 09/05/1890 PAC RG10 3929 117090
12 Vankoughnet to Reed 09/22/1890 ibid
13 Baird to Reed 09/16/1890 ibid; Baird to Reed 10/09/1890 ibid
14 Reed to Dewdney 01/22/1891 PAC RG10 3602 1774
15 Reed to Dewdney 02/25/1891 PAC RG10 7767 27107-10-1; Reed to Macdowall 03/07/1891
16 Reed to Vankoughnet 03/02/1891 PAC RG10 3929 117090; Vankoughnet to Reed 03/11/1891 ibid; For-

get to Moore and Macdowall 05/01/1891 PAC RG10 3602 1774; Reed to Macdowall 05/06/1891 ibid; Macdowall to Reed 05/08/1891 ibid; Macdowall to Reed 05/22/1891 PAC RG10 7767 27107-10-1; Reed to Wadsworth 06/02/1891; Macdowall to Reed, nd, ibid; Dewdney to Reed 06/02/1891 PAC RG10 7767 27107-10-1; Reed to Dewdney 06/18/1891 PAC RG10 3602 1774; McGirr to Macdowall 06/19/1891 ibid; Macdowall to McGirr 06/21/1891 ibid

17 Wadsworth to Reed 06/25/1891 PAC RG 10 3602 1774

18 Ibid

19 Reed to Vankoughnet 07/06/1891 PAC RG10 7767 27107-10-1; Vankoughnet to Reed 07/06/1891 ibid; Vankoughnet to Reed 07/23/1891 PAC RG10 3602 1774; Reed to McGirr 07/27/1891 ibid

20 Ponton to Reed 08/19/1891 PAC RG10 7767 27107-10-1; Reed to Ponton 08/27/1891 ibid; Reed to Macdowall 09/04/1891 ibid; Macdowall to Reed 09/07/1891 ibid; Ponton to Reed 09/11/1891 ibid; Ponton to Reed 09/12/1891 ibid; Ponton to Reed 09/15/1891 ibid; Forget to Ponton 09/21/1891 ibid; Forget to Reed 09/21/1891 ibid; McGirr to Macdowall 10/09/1891 PAC RG10 7767 27107-10-1; Reed to Ponton 10/19/1891 PAC RG10 3602 1774; Forget to Ponton 10/23/1891 ibid; Reed to Macdowall 12/18/1891 ibid; Reed to Dewdney 12/23/1891 ibid; Dewdney to Reed 12/23/1891 ibid; Dewdney to Reed 12/28/1891 ibid; Reed to Macdowall 01/14/1892 ibid;Baker to Reed 01/12/1892 PAC RG10 3929 117090; Reed to Baker 02/06/1892 ibid; Macdowall to Dewdney 01/21/1892 PAC RG10 7767 27107-10-1; Dewdney to Vankoughnet 03/02/1892 PAC RG10 7767 27107-10-1; Vankoughnet to Burgess 04/08/1892 ibid; Pereira to Vankoughnet 04/12/1892 ibid; Vankoughnet to Reed 04/16/1892 ibid; Dewdney to Vankoughnet 04/16/1892 PAC RG10 3602 1774; Vankoughhnet to Dewdney 04/19/1892 ibid; Reed to Vankoughnet 04/25/1892 ibid; Reed to Mackenzie 07/21/1892 ibid; Reed to Forget 07/19/1892 ibid; Forget to Ponton 07/23/1892 ibid; Reed to Macdowall 08/02/1892 ibid; McGirr Memorandum 08/06/1892 ibid

21 Mackay to Reed 05/13/1891 PAC RG10 7767 27107-10-1; Reed to Mackay 05/20/1891 ibid; Mackay to Reed 05/27/1891 ibid; Reed to Mackay 06/18/1891 PAC RG10 7767 27107-10-1

22 Mackay to Reed 06/24/1891 PAC RG 10 3602 1774

23 Wadsworth to Reed 06/25/1891 ibid

24 Reed to Vankoughnet 02/14/1893 ibid

25 Reed to Forget 11/18/1893 PAC RG10 7767 27107-10-1; Forget to Reed 11/25/1893 ibid; Reed to Mackenzie 12/09/1893 ibid

26 Mackenzie to Vankoughnet 02/02/1894 PAC RG10 7767 27107-10-1; Reed to Burgess 02/10/1894 ibid; Pereira to Reed 02/10/1894 ibid; Hall to Reed 03/08/1894 ibid; Scott to Forget 03/10/1894 PAC RG10 3602 1774; Forget to Scott 03/14/1894 PAC RG10 7767 27107-10-1; Reed to Forget 03/19/1894 PAC RG10 3602 1774; Forget to Reed 03/24/1894 PAC RG10 7767 27107-10-1; Reed to Forget 03/29/1894 ibid; Forget to Mackenzie 04/03/1894 PAC RG10 3602 1774; Forget to Mackenzie 04/12/1894 ibid; Mackenzie to Forget 04/12/1894 ibid

27 Young to Reed 04/13/1894 PAC RG10 7767 27107-10-1

28 Reed to Young 04/26/1894 ibid

29 Young to Reed 05/11/1894 ibid

30 Reed to Young 05/21/1894 ibid; Young to Reed 06/05/1894 ibid

31 Keith to Forget 05/12/1894 PAC RG10 3602 1774; Forget to Keith 05/18/1894 ibid

32 Reed to Forget 05/26/1894 PAC RG10 7767 27107-10-1

33 Wadsworth to Forget 06/03/1894 PAC RG10 7767 27107-10-1

34 Reed to Forget 06/14/1894 PAC RG10 7767 27107-10-1

35 Wadsworth to Reed 06/28/1894 ibid; Forget to Reed 07/16/1894 ibid; Forget to Ponton 07/16/1894 PAC RG10 3602 1774; Reed to Burgess 07/17/1894 PAC RG19 7767 27107-10-1; Reed to Burgess 07/24/1894 ibid; Ponton to Forget 07/28/1894 PAC RG10 3602 1774; Forget to Reed 07/31/1894 ibid; Ponton to Forget 08/01/1894 PAC RG10 7767 27107-10-1; Burgess to Reed 08/01/1894 ibid; Reed to Forget 08/02/1894 ibid; Forget to Ponton 08/02/1894 PAC RG10 3602 1774; Reed to Forget 08/03/1894

PAC RG10 7767 27107-10-1; Reed to Burgess 08/03/1894 ibid; Forget to Ponton 08/03/1894 PAC RG10 3602 1774; Forget to Ponton 08/04/1894 ibid; Reed to Forget 08/06/1894 PAC RG10 7767 27107-10-1; Reed to Burgess 08/06/1894 ibid; Reed to Forget 08/06/1894 ibid; Reed to Forget 08/06/1894 PAC RG10 3602 1774; Ponton to Forget 08/08/1894 ibid; Reed to Forget 08/18/1894 PAC RG10 7767 27107-10-1; Ponton to Forget 08/27/1894 ibid; Reed to Forget 09/14/1894 ibid; Pereira to Reed 10/25/1894 ibid; Reed to Forget 11/05/1894 ibid; Pereira to Reed 12/06/1894 ibid; Reed to Burgess 12/10/1894 ibid; Forget to Reed 12/21/1894 ibid; Order in Council 3563 ibid

36 Keith to Forget 04/13/1894 PAC RG10 3602 1774

37 Forget to Scott 04/19/1894 PAC RG10 7767 27107-10-1; Reed to Forget 04/23/1894 PAC RG10 3602 1774; Forget to Keith 04/24/1894 ibid; Scott to Forget 04/26/1894 ibid

38 Wadsworth to Reed 06/03/1894 PAC RG10 3602 1774

39 Keith to Reed 06/18/1894 ibid

40 Wadsworth to Scott 06/28/1894 PAC RG10 7767 27107-10-1; Forget to Keith 06/26/1894 PAC RG10 3602; Reed to Forget 07/04/1894 PAC RG10 7767 27107-10-1

41 Young to Forget 05/07/1895 PAC RG10 3929 117090; Forget to Reed 05/20/1895 PAC RG10 8549-2; Reed to Young 06/02/1896 PAC RG10 7767 27107-10-1; Hart to Forget 09/10/1898 ibid; Forget to Chisholm 09/16/1898 ibid; Forget to Hart 09/16/1898 ibid; Smart to McLean 11/29/1898 ibid; Bray to McLean 11/30/1898 ibid; Smart to Hart 12/07/1898 ibid; Baird to Smart 12/16/1898 ibid; McLean to Laird 12/20/1898 ibid; Laird to Chisholm 12/28/1898 ibid

42 Chisholm to Laird 12/28/1898 PAC RG10 7767 27107-10-1

43 Gree to McLean 03/23/1899 ibid; Laird to McLean 05/20/1899 ibid; Ponton to McLean 06/20/1899 ibid; Bray to McLean 06/20/1899 ibid; McLean to Pereira 07/04/1899 ibid; Pereira to McLean 09/01/1899 ibid; McLean to Baird 09/14/1899 ibid; McLean to Laird 09/14/1899 ibid; Laird to Keith 09/27/1899 ibid

44 Annual Report of the Department of Indian Affairs (1895) 174; Annual Report of the Department of Indian Affairs (1896) 243-244; Ponton to Forget 01/11/1896 PAC RG10 7767 27107-10-1; Keith to Forget 03/31/1896 Archives, Federation of Saskatchewan Indians, Regina; Keith to Forget 06/30/1896 ibid

45 Forget to Keith 02/04/1897 PAC RG10 3602 1774; Keith to Reed 02/10/1897 ibid; Keith to Reed 04/12/1897 ibid; Annual Report of the Department of Indian Affairs (1897) 141

46 Keith to Reed 01/26/1898 PAC RG10 7767 27107-10-2; Chisholm to Reed 12/28/1898 ibid; Annual Report of the Department of Indian Affairs (1898) 132; Annual Report of the Department of Indian Affairs (1899) 137-138

47 Keyes to McLean 05/31/1900 PAC RG10 7767 27107-10-2; McLean to Keyes 06/04/1900 ibid; agent to Laird 04/09/1902 ibid; Keyes to McLean 03/16/1904 ibid; McLean to Laird 03/24/1904 ibid; Laird to McLean 03/28/1904 ibid; Laird to Clifford 03/28/1904 ibid; Clifford to McLean 04/30/1904 ibid; Laird to McLean 05/26/1904 ibid; McLean to Keyes 06/02/1904 ibid; Keyes to McLean 07/06/1904 ibid; McLean to Laird 07/22/1904 ibid; McKenna to McLean 07/26/1904 ibid; McLean to Keyes 08/23/1904 ibid; McLean to Laird 09/15/1904 ibid; McKenna to McLean 09/21/1904; McLean to Keyes 09/27/1904 ibid; Keyes to McLean 10/07/1904 ibid; McLean to Laird 11/04/1904 ibid

48 Cook to Laird 02/03/1905 PAC RG10 7767 27107-10-2; Laird to Cook 02/22/1905; Chisholm to Laird 03/07/1905 ibid

49 Laird to McLean 03/14/1905 PAC RG10 7767 27107-10-2; Bray to Smart 03/20/1905 ibid; McLean to Laird 03/30/1905 ibid; Campbell memorandum 04/15/1905 ibid; Scott to Pedley 05/10/1905 ibid; Fisher to McLean 05/13/1905 ibid; McLean to Fisher 06/02/1905 ibid

50 McLean to Justice 07/15/1905 PAC RG10 7767 27107-10-2; Macdowall to Pedley 08/04/1905 ibid; McLean to Macdowall 08/10/1905 ibid; Macdowall to Pedley 08/16/1905 ibid; Tyrgeon to Justice 08/12/1905 ibid; Power to McLean 08/17/1905 ibid; Power to McLean 08/21/1905 ibid; McLean to Ritchie 08/22/1905 ibid; Ritchie to McLean 08/23/1905 ibid; McLean to Power 08/25/1905 ibid; McLean to Chisholm 09/27/1905 ibid; Chisholm to McLean 09/27/1905 ibid; Carroll to Pedley 12/12/1905

ibid; McLean to Ritchie 12/21/1905 ibid; Ritchie to McLean 01/13/1906 ibid; McLean to Carroll 01/17/1906 ibid; Chisholm to McLean 01/30/1906 ibid; Borthwick to McLean 05/01/1908 ibid; Mc-Lean to Borthwick 05/16/1908 ibid

51 McLean to Ritchie 03/15/1906 PAC RG10 7767 27107-10-2; Pedley to Bray 03/19/1906 ibid; Bray to Pedley 03/22/1906 ibid; Pedley to Scott 06/06/1906 ibid; McLean to Ritchie 06/06/1906 ibid; Ritchie to Pedley 06/23/1906 ibid

52 Arthur to Laird 04/01/1902 PAC RG10 7767 27107-10-2; Chisholm to Laird 04/07/1902 ibid; Chisholm to Laird 04/21/1902 ibid; Sessional Papers 2-3 Edward VII no 27 A1903 135; Sessional Papers 4-5 Edward VII no 27 A1904 135; Sessional Papers 6-7 Edward VII no 27 A1907 123-124; Sessional Papers 7-8 Edward VII no 27 A1908 118-119; Sessional Papers 8-9 Edward VII no 27 A1909 128

53 McKay to Pereira 11/25/1911 PAC RG10 7767 27107-10-1; Pereira to McKay 12/26/1911 ibid; Mc-Lean to Chisholm 01/04/1912 ibid; McLean to McKay 01/04/1912 ibid; Chisholm to McLean 01/10/1912 ibid

54 Chisholm to McLean 01/10/1912 PAC RG10 7767 27107-10-1

55 McLean to Keyes 01/17/1912 ibid; McLean to Chisholm 01/18/1912 ibid; Scott to Pedley 03/13/1912 ibid; Pedley to Scott 03/15/1912 ibid; Keyes to McLean 07/12/1912 ibid; McLean to Keyes 07/19/1912 ibid; Keyes to Pedley 08/07/1912 ibid; McLean to Keyes 08/08/1912 ibid; Nelson to McLean 08/16/1912 ibid; McKay to McLean 08/24/1912 ibid; McLean to McKay 08/24/1912 ibid; McLean to McKay 09/16/1912 ibid; McLean to Keyes 09/16/1912 ibid; Pereira to McLean 10/08/1912 ibid; Pereira to McLean 10/19/1912 ibid; McLean to Pereira 11/04/1912 ibid; McLean to Keyes 11/06/1912 ibid; Cote to Cory 11/24/1912 ibid; McLean to Keyes 01/15/1913 ibid; McLean to Keyes 02/01/1913 ibid; Pedley to Scott 02/07/1913 ibid; Cory to Pedley 02/20/1913 ibid; Pedley to Cory 02/24/1913 ibid; Mc-Lean to Keyes 03/26/1913 ibid; Cote to McLean 03/31/1913 ibid; McLean to Chisholm 04/07/1913 ibid; Chisholm to McLean 04/08/1913 ibid; Chisholm to McLean 04/09/1913 ibid; McLean to Chisholm 04/18/1913 ibid; Scott to Pedley 04/09/1913 ibid; Pedley to Northrup 04/09/1913 ibid; Macdowall to Pedley 04/23/1913 ibid; Williams to Scott 04/28/1913 ibid; McLean to Ritchie 04/29/1913 ibid; Ritchie to McLean 05/19/1913 ibid; McLean to Ritchie 05/22/1913 ibid; Ritchie to McLean 05/23/1913 ibid; McLean to Cote 02/27/1915 ibid; Bray to Scott 02/27/1915 ibid; McLean to Chisholm 03/02/1915 ibid

56 Chisholm to McLean 03/02/1915 PAC RG10 7767 27107-10-1; Chisholm to McLean 05/07/1915 ibid; McLean to Cote 06/08/1915 ibid; Cote to McLean 06/12/1915 ibid

57 Miller to McLean 11/18/1916 PAC RG10 7767 27107-10-1; Crombie to McLean 02/20/1917 ibid

58 Crombie to Scott 07/23/1917 PAC RG10 7767 27107-10-1; Scott to Crombie 08/02/1917 ibid; McLean to Cote 09/07/1917 ibid; McLean to Cote 10/30/1917 ibid; minister of the interior to the governor general 11/06/1917 SAB 1799125; Order in Council 11/14/1917 PAC RG10 7767 27107-10-2; Cote to McLean 11/17/1917 ibid; Cote to McLean 12/20/1917 ibid; Pineo to Cory 05/08/1919 ibid; Cory to Scott 05/23/1919 ibid; Bray to Scott 06/17/1919 ibid; McLean to Graham 06/21/1919 ibid; Graham to Mc-Lean 04/27/1920 ibid; Orr to Graham 05/06/1920 ibid; Glidden to Cory 12/17/1920 ibid; Cory to Scott 12/20/1920 ibid; Scott to Cory 12/30/1920 ibid; Taylor to Anon. 01/14/1921 SAB 5416049; Glidden to Cory 02/17/1921 ibid; Cory to Scott 02/22/1921 PAC RG10 7767 27107-10-2; Scott to Cory 03/01/1921 ibid; Cote to Scott 03/10/1921 ibid; Sessional Papers 9-10 Edward VII no 27 A1910 134-135; Sessional Papers 1 George V no 27 A1911 124-125; Sessional Papers 2 George V no 17 A1912 134-135; Sessional Papers 3 George V no 20 A1913 127-128

59 Martin to Mackenzie 06/23/1930 PAC RG10 7767 27107-10-1; MacKenzie to Martin 06/23/1930 ibid; Order in Council P.C. 1872 ibid; MacKenzie to Martin 10/21/1930 ibid; Martin to MacKenzie 10/08/1930 ibid; MacKenzie to Graham 10/24/1930 ibid; Anon. memorandum 07/29/1931 SAB 4029206; Hume to MacKenzie 08/15/1931 PAC RG10 7767 27107-10-2; MacKenzie to deputy minister 08/20/1931 ibid; Weir to MacKenzie 08/31/1931 ibid; Weir to MacKenzie 09/08/1931 ibid; Painchaud to MacKenzie 12/29/1931 ibid; MacKenzie to Barnett 06/22/1932 ibid; Barnett to Mac-Kenzie 07/05/1932 ibid; MacKenzie to Barnett 12/19/1932 ibid; Barnett to MacKenzie 12/23/1932 ibid;

MacKenzie to Barnett 01/11/1933 ibid; MacKenzie to Barnett 01/29/1935 ibid; Amos to Turner 02/13/1935 ibid; Turner to Amos 02/28/1935 ibid; Turner to MacKenzie 02/28/1935 ibid; MacKenzie to Amos 06/08/1935 ibid; Paterson to Robertson 01/05/1937 ibid; MacInnes to Robertson 01/14/1937 ibid

CHAPTER 13

1 In 1978, with the approval of Dakota elders and leaders, Chief Cyrus Standing of the Wahpeton Band wrote to Minister of Indian Affairs Hugh Faulkner asking that his band be admitted to Treaty Six by way of adhesion. Essentially, this was a ploy to determine current government policy on the Dakota. Faulkner replied: "It is clear from the historical record that the numbered treaties such as Treaty #6 were prompted and entered into by the Canadian Government in an attempt to insure the peaceful development and settlement of Western Canada, with the Indians giving up their right or interest in the land covered by treaty, whatever the precise legal nature of that right or interest might be. At the time of Treaty #6 signing in 1876, the Sioux had been living in Canada only a short while, and not regarded as having any aboriginal interest in Canadian territory. Indeed, the Government of the day acknowledged them as seperate and distinct from the resident 'British Indians.'" (Files of the Dakota Association of Canada.)

Index